PARENTS & TEENAGERS

PARENTS & TEENAGERS

THE OPEN UNIVERSITY
IN ASSOCIATION WITH THE HEALTH EDUCATION COUNCIL
AND THE SCOTTISH HEALTH EDUCATION GROUP

Harper & Row, Publishers
London

Cambridge
Hagerstown
Philadelphia
New York

San Francisco
Mexico City
Sao Paulo
Sydney

© The Open University 1982

Designed, edited and produced by First Editions
All rights reserved
First published 1982
Harper & Row Ltd
28 Tavistock Street
London WC2E 7PN

For First Editions
Design/Art Direction: Richard Dewing and Nigel Soper
Editor: Sarie Wood
Picture Research: Marian Drescher

For the Open University
Course Team: Lorna Bailey, Simon Baines, Angie
Ballard, Frances Berrigan, Joan Carty, Monica
Darlington, Hilary Edwards, Mick Jones and Jane
Wolfson

Secretarial Support: Val Gregitis and Sybil Meacham

Consultants: Mary Bailey, Peter Barnes, Pat Bath,
Sarah Berry, Jean Cochrane, Ken David, Rex Gibson,
Marianne Hogbin, Eileen Hornsey, Moses Laufer, Bill
Law, Jenny Lewis, Marian Lever, Ruth Miller, Anton
Obholzer, Justin Price, Rosemary Randall, Hazel
Slavin, Christopher Watkins and Barbara Webb

External Assessor: Alan Beattie

Readers: Samuel Eggleston, Suzie Hayman,
Neil Mercer, Anton Obholzer, Phillip Priestley, Jill
Rakusen, Royal Shuttleworth and Anthony Watts

Group Developmental Testing Organisers: Marion
Jack, Joan Kidd and Helen Munroe

Academic co-ordinator for Community Education:
Nick Farnes

British Library Cataloguing in Publication Data
Parents and teenagers.
    1. Adolescence   2. Parent and child
    I. Open University
    649′.125   HQ796

ISBN 0-06-318-243-2

Phototypeset by Oliver Burridge & Co Ltd, Crawley
Printed and bound by New Interlitho S.P.A., Milan

Contents

Introduction

Who's this book for? And what's it about?

A book for parents . . .

This book is written for parents. It's about being the parent of a teenager today. It's for parents to share with their teenager – if that's what they both want to do.

Today, many parents are worried about adolescence, even before it begins. "Will my teenager turn out alright?" "Will she be happy?" "Will he ever grow out of . . .?" are questions which trouble nearly all parents at times.

This book doesn't provide *simple* answers to these questions: there aren't any. Nor does it just give the facts of growing up. Facts, on their own, aren't enough. It does offer knowledge parents can use and helps them build up skills they can apply – in everyday living with a teenager. Most importantly, it asks parents to use their hearts and their heads to look at what's happening in their families, and to decide with their teenager, what's best for everyone.

The book stands on its own; but it's also part of an Open University course (see page 11 for details). In planning the book, we – a course team from the Open University – asked parents about their concerns, their fears and their experiences. We also drew together the views of a wide range of experts and professionals in many different fields. We are particularly grateful to the Health Education Council and the Scottish Health Education Group for their support for the whole course.

. . . with the help of parents

As the book began to take shape, we invited panels of parents to read and comment on drafts. Over 400 parents, from a wide range of backgrounds, helped us as individuals and in groups. Almost the only thing they had in common was at least one teenager in the 11–16 age range. Many of these teenagers helped too.

Between them, our 'parent testers' read all the draft manuscript for this book. Their varied reactions, perceptive comments and vivid examples helped us to write the final version. Where their experiences seem helpful to quote, we have done so, sometimes at length. To all the parents who helped – a big thank you.

. . . about being a parent

Being a parent involves constantly being faced with choices, for yourself and for your teenager. The choices you make and the decisions you take will influence your relationship with your teenager, how easy for him or her the teenage years are, and what kind of an adult he/she becomes.

This book asks you to identify, and review, your choices. What alternatives are there? How do your feelings and concerns affect your decisions? How does your teenager respond? You may be satisfied – in which case, fine. Or you may want to change what you do – in which case, this book may help you to decide how, and what, you want to change.

This doesn't mean that parents need to – or should – spend these years watching closely over their teenagers. Teenagers need plenty of time on their own and with their friends. They need to have 'private' areas of life into which their parents should not pry. So a part of being a 'good enough parent' – and that's all you need to be – is to stand back, be around if you are needed and trust your teenager. Because teenagers have to sort out 'who they are' and shape their identities for themselves there can be long periods when parents wonder if what they do has any effect at all. It's hard, but necessary, to take a long-term view of being a parent.

In most families, a 'good enough' relationship does exist. Often, it's more a question of parents having confidence in their own opinions and skills – including the skill to change and grow themselves. Much of parenting is learned as you go along, from and with your teenager. So this book is based on activities, or exercises, which help you to review together what you are doing and learning.

Such a review can be quite challenging. So too can the everyday pressures on parents. Parents need support – people to talk things over with – from everyday and professional sources. Parts of this book look at the times when support is needed – and who you may get it from.

Inevitably, perhaps, this book concentrates on the problems and concerns parents may have. After all, there is little that needs to be said about the pleasures and the joys of parenthood.

. . . but for others to use

If you are a teenager – you may have a mixture of feelings if you find your parents reading this book. We do emphasise that parents should not pry into their teenagers' private thoughts and lives. However many of the activities in this course suggest that teenager and parent should examine their ideas and experiences of teenager-parent relationships, *together*. It's up to you to decide whether you want to do this. You can only join in these activities in a constructive way if you are willing to participate as an equal. Talk about what is involved in the activity – and why it's worth doing – before you commit yourself to do it.

You may decide to read this book to help you understand what you are involved in during adolescence. This book challenges both parents and teenagers to go beyond reading about the theory of adolescence. Its aim is to provide a working knowledge – *theory that can be used* – to help with the issues and concerns of everyday life. To put it to work you have to examine your own experiences, ideas, and opportunities for change.

If you work with teenagers – you may wish to read this book just to improve your working knowledge of adolescence. Does your work with teenagers involve discussing with them their relationships with their parents? If so, the 'activities' we suggest to help parents think about parenting skills, and their own feelings, should give you ideas for helping teenagers to communicate and empathise with their parents. You may like to use parts of this book directly in your work with teenagers.

If you work with parents of teenagers – this book will help you to help them examine their choices, reach their own decisions and start to implement changes. If you like to work in a very directive way you may see this as doing you out of a job. The whole approach of this book values the autonomy of both parents and teenagers. However we hope it will prove to be a useful tool in your work. It may stimulate you to think more deeply about the way you work with parents. You may even wish to recommend this book to the parents with whom you work to help them explore their relationships.

How to use this book

The first thing to do is to find your way around it. *Chapter 1* offers an overview of what it's like to be a teenager – and what it's like being the parent of a teenager today. *Chapters 2–8* then each deal with a particular 'task' of growing up for the teenager or with a particular setting, like school, in which he/she does that growing. *Chapter 9* takes a more general look at the routes to adult independence and identity. It ends with a look at a 'new life' for parents as teenagers finally leave their everyday care. The final section, "What next?" lists books and organisations which should help you find extra information, skills or support you may· need. Consult the separate index on page 208.

Choosing what to do

It will probably be most helpful if you read Chapter 1 first so that you get an overall view of what the book covers. It will also help you understand the importance of doing the various quizzes and activities, which help you analyse your own experience and ideas in the light of the information given.

The rest of the book does not have to be read in any particular order. You are unlikely to want to read the whole book straight through. Your teenager may be too young or too old for some issues – or you or he/she may not be interested. You may already know a good deal about some of the areas – or already be aware of certain areas about which you know very little. Or perhaps you feel worried about particular aspects of growing up – such as peer-group activities, sexual relationships or the apparent attack on your dearly-held values?

In a sense, the book is 'action packed' with things you might think about and do, but clearly it's up to you to choose the parts that interest and concern you. The contents list at the front and the index at the back will help you to locate topics of particular interest to you. Each chapter is divided into between six and ten topics – short articles each dealing with a particular issue. The topics are separate, but linked (essential cross-references are made) so that you can read them through in any order. The Study Guide, from the course, gives further advice.

Activities for you – and your teenager

This isn't simply a book about the theory of understanding teenagers. Above all it's a book about being the parent of a teenager. At certain points in each topic 'activities' which you may choose to do are signalled. These will help you to personalise what you have read for you and your family. They help you turn facts and theories into working knowledge – of use in your everyday life. Being a parent involves understanding yourself as well as understanding your teenager. So a good half of the activities are about you, the parent.

Very often, your child's adolescence has an uncomfortable way of raising 'unfinished business' from your own teenage years. It may also coincide with your own 'mid-life review' about what's important to you. Without you realising it, your own feelings about past or current concerns can stand in the way of you understanding or helping your teenager. To help you many of the activities ask you to reflect on your own feelings and concerns, and the impact these may be having on your teenager.

Other activities ask you to look in more detail at your own behaviour – what you actually say and do. For example, who decides what your teenager eats? How often this week did you praise him or her? Often, just noting things down objectively can be enough to trigger you into taking a new look at what you do, and perhaps deciding to do something differently with your teenager. A variety of quizzes and questionnaires also help you to examine your beliefs and values; and to consider how these affect your teenager.

Other activities in this book involve your teenager more directly. They take a very varied form. Some pose questions to discuss with your teenager. Others suggest problems or situations to look at together. Others still are basically designed for the teenager to complete on his or her own, and simply to discuss his/her reactions and conclusions with you.

Of course, you could read this book without talking to your teenager, or simply answering for him/her. But that in itself may be a reflection on your relationship, and you will truly get more from this book by sharing it with your teenager. The course pack includes a special guide to the book for teenagers.

Working together

Getting your teenager involved may not be as much of a problem as you might think. Teenagers are intensely interested in themselves, and in finding out more about who they are and what makes them tick, so a lot of this book may naturally be of interest to them. As with you and parenting, they will find out more about 'being a teenager' by taking part in the activities rather than just reading the book.

Of course, teenagers vary. Yours may be suspicious and think you're trying to 'psychologise' him/her. Or he/she may be in a moody, withdrawn period when he/she doesn't want to find out more, or look at life in a new way. Our parent testers suggested the following guidelines for using this book, and particularly the activities, successfully together:

○ *do* choose your time to talk – when there's a topic that interests you both, and you have time to listen to each other

○ *do* make it clear to your teenager that you're prepared to rethink your ideas and take on board his/her point of view

○ *do* remember that we assume that you and your teenager will treat each other as equals when you are discussing matters together

○ *do* be prepared to ask your teenager for his or her help, quite directly if you need it: "Can you give me a hand with my OU work?"

○ *don't* be offended if your teenager declines your invitation to be involved, or your request for help. It's his/her right as an individual to choose whether or not to become involved

○ *don't* make it sound like you're setting a test, or homework. Teenagers, like anyone else, dislike the idea of being judged in any way, by their parents

○ *don't* think you must do everything exactly as the book suggests. Some activities will work better for you and your teenager if you bring the point of them up casually in conversation rather than sitting with pencil poised and finger on the page.

You might get them interested by showing them The Teenager's Guide.

Other skills

Talking together isn't always easy. You may think there's surprisingly little in this book about communications between parents and teenagers, or negotiation. That's because these topics are impossible to deal with effectively in print alone. You need to be able to hear people speak, and see how they are relating together. In the rest of the course, of which this book is a part, are two audio-tapes with related booklets. These deal with communication, negotiation and decision-making skills. Like this book, they are activity based and help you build up your skills. There are also notes which go with the four TV programmes of the course.

Key symbols

A This symbol indicates some 'activity' you may want to do. There may be a chart to complete, or things to talk over with your partner or teenager. Or it may be a set of guidelines to follow, or simply questions to think over yourself. All these 'activities' mean you need to stop reading and start working in a different way.

These activities are usually followed by some comments on what you may have thought, or said. In many the answers and comments of our parent testers have been included. In any case take time to do the activity for yourself. It's assumed you will be honest with yourself.

D This symbol indicates that you may want to make a note of something. For example, you might want to record your own, or your teenager's view or behaviour. The activity will explain the purpose of your notes.

For students on the OU course, the course pack contains two special booklets. There is a *Personal Diary* for recording your own feelings and private thoughts. And there is an *Activity Pad* of pre-printed copies of many of the charts in this book.

If you have simply bought this book, you should find it helps to keep your own diary and draw up your own charts. By doing this you will make it easier for yourself to get involved in doing the activities. Just reading this book won't help you very much. Doing the activities *will* help you be able to make use, in your own life, of what you read.

This book and the Open University

This book forms part of an Open University short home-study course for parents. This course is not part of the undergraduate course programme. Instead, it is one of a range of Community Education courses open to anyone over the age of 16 – all of which deal with the interests and concerns of everyday life.

Part of a course

The full Open University *Parents and Teenagers* course includes:

○ **Television Notes** to accompany the **four TV programmes** for the course. These look at how parents deal with four typical incidents in adolescence: not wanting to go out, choosing subjects at school, an attempt at shoplifting – and a lover's quarrel. These TV programmes will be broadcast two or three times a year for several years. You may write and ask for a Broadcast Calendar if you are not a student on the course. Check in the Radio Times
○ A **skills package** of two audiotapes, Talking to each other, and two booklets, Communication Skills and Decision making and Negotiation
○ **A Personal Diary** and an **Activity Pad** to help you to complete your work on the activities in this book
○ **A Study Guide** to help you plan your own programme of study. This also tells you how you can get together with other students in self-help groups – and suggests some topics for discussion with other parents
○ A **teenager's guide to the course**, with activities and course references specially devised for your teenager
○ **Four optional computer-marked assignments,** which if completed satisfactorily lead to a Letter of Course Completion. This certifies you have taken a full part in the course.

You can sign on directly for this course in which case you will be sent a copy of this book with all the other materials direct to your home. If you already have the book you can simply sign on, at a reduced fee, for the rest of the course, i.e. the course related materials and the opportunity to obtain a Letter of Course completion.

You are free to study what, when and where you like. As a rough guide, if you do the full course over eight weeks it takes about five or six hours' study a week. But in fact you can pace yourself to take more or less time. You can sign on at any point in the year, and have the following 12 months in which to do your assignments.

Part of a series

Parents and Teenagers is the last course in a series for parents which stretches from pre-pregnancy, through pregnancy and childbirth, to the first years of life, the pre-school child and childhood five to ten. Some of the core course books are available separately, or you can sign on for a full course. If you have younger children in the family, this series may be of particular interest.

The parenthood series is just part of a wide range of Community Education courses which deal with the practical concerns of everyday life. All courses come in attractive, easy-to-follow packs which help you get to the root of matters that concern you, and decide what's best for you and your family. Currently there are courses on consumer issues, health, and planning retirement. New courses are added each year.

Each course is designed primarily for a specific target group: parents, consumers, or people who are retiring themselves. However many professionals use them in their own field of community or educational work. The Community Education Office can offer advice and assistance in using the course materials in this way.

For further information

○ To obtain further information and an application form for the rest of the course pack for *Parents and Teenagers*, or any course in the Community Education programme: write to – ASCO, PO Box 76, The Open University, Milton Keynes.
○ To purchase parts of the course materials; or to find out about when broadcasts will be shown each year; or to find out more about using course materials as a resource: write to – The Community Education Office, The Open University, PO Box 188, Milton Keynes.

Setting the scene

You may be expecting this book to focus on what happens to teenagers during the 'growing-up' process of adolescence, and to a large extent it does. But it also looks at what's happening in parents' lives, and in the family as a whole.

In this first chapter we take an overall view, looking at some theories of human development, which apply, not only to the teenage years, but to the whole of life. If you are to make use of these theories in everyday life – turn them into 'working knowledge' – you must relate them to your personal circumstances. We suggest in 'activities' how to do this. But *you* will have to put in the hard work of examining what is going on in your family. You will need to look at the personality, experiences, hopes and fears, of both you and your teenager.

Doing the activities will often involve asking your teenager to join in. As you will know by now, you can not *make* teenagers do anything. You can encourage, persuade, put your point of view and enlist their help, but demanding they do it is the quickest way to ensure that they opt out. This chapter begins with activities that require minimal involvement or personal disclosure for your teenager. Further on you can leave it to your teenager, if he/she does join in, to choose how far he/she is prepared to share his/her answers with you. Doing the activity – rather than disclosing the answers to you – is the useful part.

In most cases the participation of your teenager, though desirable, is not essential: after all, you probably know him/her very well. However, our parent testers reported that, if they chose the right moment, their teenagers were usually interested in joining in . . . provided they were treated as equals and their opinions were valued.

Your feelings

You will find that you are asked to do some hard thinking about yourself and your feelings towards your teenager. The importance of this is explained in "Parents' feelings" (pages 40–43). We emphasise there that reading this book without doing the activities will be a waste of your time. So we suggest you choose how you will read this chapter:

Read straight through: if you were expecting some theory, and feel more at ease starting with facts rather than feelings. But be sure to work through "Parents' feelings" before going on to other chapters.

Read "Parents' feelings" first: if you are already aware that your feelings and experiences play a major part in both helping and hindering you as the parent of a teenager. Then come back to other topics in the chapter which interest you.

Working knowledge and life skills

You need to help your teenager towards mature independence.

This may sound a daunting task – but you've been doing it ever since your teenager was a small child. It's a two-way process: you help your teenager on his/her way to becoming a 'self-managed' adult and having a teenager helps you to behave like an adult with grown-up children.

This book looks at some of the key issues in teenage development – which means looking at parents' lives too. In planning how you can help your teenager, it is useful to think in terms of three main needs:

1 the 'working knowledge' you each may want

2 the 'life skills' you each think are important to develop

3 the support and help that is available to each of you

This topic looks at knowledge and skill, the next at support and help.

Working knowledge

This is practical knowledge that is useful in everyday life. Some kinds of knowledge have little practical application: this is true of some theories of child and adolescent development. The guideline for including information in this book was – "As a result of knowing this, will parents be able to understand themselves and/or their teenagers better? Will it help parents help their teenagers towards independence?"

For example, it is important for parents to know that questioning authority is a vital, healthy part of teenage development. They are then less likely to take this questioning as a personal attack designed to undermine their values or to test their ability to maintain discipline. Parents who realise this are less likely to try using power to stifle what they see as teenage rebellion. They are more likely to recognise that questioning was the way they, too, acquired their values, and to leave the teenager space to find his own.

Equally teenagers need to know that such questioning is a vital part of development. Many teenagers become anxious when they reach the stage at which it is important for them to question and re-think their own beliefs about moral, political or religious issues. They may think they ought not to question the 'rights and wrongs' their parents have taught them. Yet unless they can question such beliefs, they may develop rather rigid ways of thinking about such issues.

Life tasks

While your child is a teenager he/she is moving into adulthood. The process of adolescence can be looked at in terms of the developmental tasks that are tackled at this stage of life. Looking at the teenager's life tasks is one of the main themes of this course. Teenagers are coping with major changes in their bodies and their minds. They develop new patterns of friendships and think out their life values for themselves. They start to plan their careers. And while doing all this, they must go on building up their everyday life skills, so that they become competent adults able to look after themselves.

Life tasks at all ages are outlined and explained on pages 20–23. Parents have them too. The chapters which follow provide you with working knowledge which relates to the different tasks. And they suggest activities which will help you and your teenager make use of this knowledge.

When we asked our parent testers about the areas in which they wanted more working knowledge about adolescence, their replies were very varied. Their concerns spanned the issues covered in this book and the course pack. For example:

"Should I continue to nag her – or should I let her find out the hard way?"
"Why doesn't he realise jeans won't do for every occasion?"
"She wants to spend all her time with her best friend . . ."
"Why on earth doesn't he get his hair cut?"
"I'm afraid he'll get into the 'wrong set', who don't work, or think the way we do . . ."
"Why does she put the minimum of effort into her homework?"
"He's got a one-track mind – electronics – and won't apply himself to his school work . . ."
"On holiday, why did she object to doing everything we did, without making any suggestions herself?"
"However will she manage when she leaves home?"
"Why does he push his younger brother around?"
"She thinks the world's problems would be solved if we became vegetarians . . ."
"I just don't know how to get through to him!"

A ⓓ Your concerns will guide you through this book. You don't have to start at the beginning and work through to the end, so spend a little time now thinking about the areas you want more working knowledge in. Use the chapter and contents indexes, and "What next?", to find your own particular areas of interest.

Life skills

Competent adults have built up a wide range of skills which help them to get on in life. Many people pick up a wide range of life skills without ever thinking of them as such. But unless you know you have them, you may not make the best use of them. And as you go on in life, there will be skills you want to improve or acquire.

Today, many schools are placing an increasing emphasis on helping teenagers to learn a broader range of life skills. You'll find that they crop up under many different subject names. The list of skills (right) was developed for use in a training course for young people. We suggest using this to review the skills that both you and your teenager are developing from experience.

Your life skills

A Do this activity yourself before asking your teenager to do it. Choose your time carefully – it can be counterproductive to look at a list of life skills when you are feeling rushed or not too good about yourself.

Look over the list of skills, and identify those you are already good at. Remember that most of them are skills that you go on improving throughout life. Every family has a total pool of skills which its members can usefully share and learn from each other. There's no need to be rivals, though parents and teenagers do sometimes find themselves in competition.

Avoid making a list of all the skills you think you are 'bad' at. Such a list is horribly depressing. In any case it is irrelevant to use the term 'bad' because all you are doing is identifying the skills you have had little chance to acquire or practise. There are many reasons in the family, and in society, why people don't acquire certain skills.

D Make a note of the two or three skills that you would most like to find out more about and to practise using. Start by thinking about what has prevented you from developing these skills. Many of the topics in this book and the course pack are concerned one way or another with life skills. "What next?" also lists several resources which help people to learn or refresh their life skills.

When our parent testers did this exercise, many of them were pleasantly surprised: "I hadn't realised how many skills I had". Equally, most of them said they were determined to brush up on some of their life skills. Many emphasised relationship skills – "how to manage conflict", "how to be assertive", and so on. Others focussed on personal skills which are needed to manage and grow: for example, "how to be positive about myself", "how to make the most of the present".

Your teenager's life skills

A An understanding of what life skills are, helps your teenager to take a more positive approach to acquiring them. And reviewing his/her skills should reassure you both that he/she is already becoming competent in many areas.

Suggest that, either alone, or with you, he/she goes through the list as you did. If he/she wants to discuss it, be prepared to share with him/her what you thought about your own life skills too.

Helping your teenager to build up his/her life skills is a powerful way to build up his/her self-esteem. The more competent he/she becomes, the more confident he/she will feel. The teenage years are a particularly important time for developing relationship skills. Getting on well with other people makes you feel especially good.

Many of the topics in this book will help you to help your teenager develop his/her skills. The course pack also includes a booklet for teenagers about life skills, and tapes on communication, decision-making and negotiation skills.

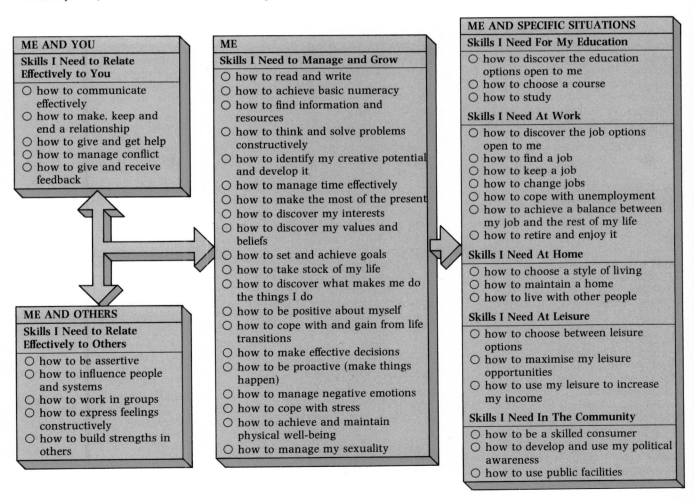

ME AND YOU
Skills I Need to Relate Effectively to You
- how to communicate effectively
- how to make, keep and end a relationship
- how to give and get help
- how to manage conflict
- how to give and receive feedback

ME AND OTHERS
Skills I Need to Relate Effectively to Others
- how to be assertive
- how to influence people and systems
- how to work in groups
- how to express feelings constructively
- how to build strengths in others

ME
Skills I Need to Manage and Grow
- how to read and write
- how to achieve basic numeracy
- how to find information and resources
- how to think and solve problems constructively
- how to identify my creative potential and develop it
- how to manage time effectively
- how to make the most of the present
- how to discover my interests
- how to discover my values and beliefs
- how to set and achieve goals
- how to take stock of my life
- how to discover what makes me do the things I do
- how to be positive about myself
- how to cope with and gain from life transitions
- how to make effective decisions
- how to be proactive (make things happen)
- how to manage negative emotions
- how to cope with stress
- how to achieve and maintain physical well-being
- how to manage my sexuality

ME AND SPECIFIC SITUATIONS
Skills I Need For My Education
- how to discover the education options open to me
- how to choose a course
- how to study

Skills I Need At Work
- how to discover the job options open to me
- how to find a job
- how to keep a job
- how to change jobs
- how to cope with unemployment
- how to achieve a balance between my job and the rest of my life
- how to retire and enjoy it

Skills I Need At Home
- how to choose a style of living
- how to maintain a home
- how to live with other people

Skills I Need At Leisure
- how to choose between leisure options
- how to maximise my leisure opportunities
- how to use my leisure to increase my income

Skills I Need In The Community
- how to be a skilled consumer
- how to develop and use my political awareness
- how to use public facilities

Support

Knowledge and skills are useful, but you need support as well.

Everyone needs support

Sooner or later many parents find themselves thinking things like: "There are times when I wish I'd never had children", "Some days I'd like to walk out of here and leave them to look after themselves. I'm sick to death of family life".

Everyone has everyday problems, so everyone needs a personal support system. Some people feel it is important to keep their problems to themselves and to manage on their own. Others feel they have to pretend that they don't have problems, if they are to live up to their own, or other people's expectations. It is much better for your emotional health if you can share your problems with people who can support you.

You need people who will listen in a sensitive sympathetic way. Once you have shared your feelings, you will find it easier to move on and plan how to improve the situation. Most people are happy to offer this kind of support – you should accept it. In the same way, despite your own problems, you will probably want to offer your support to others. In many cases, two people offer support to each other.

Your support system

It is a good idea, occasionally, to review your support system in a deliberate way. This will reassure you that you do know who can help you, or it may alert you to the fact that you are forgetting about your support system and need to give it more attention to keep it in good working order.

Some people think that talking about support systems in this way sounds cold and calculating. But in fact friendships build up simply because people do things you like – and you do things other people like. These things include listening and offering help when it is needed.

The following exercise helps you to review your support system, and suggests some ways to strengthen it if necessary. You may need to think carefully about this activity if you have a special need for support. For example, if you find yourself in any of the circumstances listed here:

○ have an unsupportive partner
○ have a demanding elderly relative
○ have a teenager who has difficulties at school, health problems, a handicap, or behavioural problems
○ are a single parent
○ are a 'reconstituted' family
○ are handicapped or have health problems
○ become unemployed and lose contact with supportive workmates
○ feel isolated living in your community – rural or town
○ feel isolated because you belong to a minority group
○ are under particular stress at the moment due to recent big changes in life, such as: move, new job, marital problems, divorce, illness.

Support system review

🅐 🅓 This activity is in two parts.

Everyday support

First look at your everyday support system: the kind of people listed in Checklist A.
1 Write down the names of people to whom you can go for support and en-

couragement, in as many of the categories as you can.
2 Now try to get a clear picture of your support network. Think back to the last time you talked things over with each of them. Make a note of what you talked about. Are there some people you talk to more often than the others? Why is this? Are there some you only talk to about certain problems?
3 Have you actually talked something over with someone during the last week? You should make regular use of your support network so that you don't get into the habit of bottling up your worries, otherwise you may find it difficult to approach them when the need arises.
4 Do you have at least four people on your list? If not, think around your circle of friends: is there someone who, from the way they talk about themselves and other people, sounds sympathetic? Try talking over one or two things with them to see how you get on.
5 If you or your support people move, then you should take care to build up your everyday support system again.

Professional help

Now look at the professional help you might need: the kind of support sources listed in Checklist B.

For special difficulties – like the ones listed in the text (left) – your everyday support network may not be enough and you may need to seek help from people who have had special training. You may need expert advice, or your problem may be swamping you so that it would make too heavy a demand on a friend or relative to ask them to provide all the support you need.
1 Think back over the times when you sought help when your child was younger – say aged five to eleven years old. Make a note of the people in Checklist B to whom you turned for help and how you felt about their help.
2 Now list the people who have already helped, or you think you might need help from, now your child is a teenager. Do your earlier experiences affect the type of help you will seek?

As you work through this book, you will be encouraged to identify the additional support you may need. "What next?" at the end of the book, tells you how to get in touch with various sources of professional help.

Checklist A: Everyday support	
Your partner	Your workmates
Your parents	Your neighbours
Your brothers and sisters	Other parents
Your other relatives	Your other friends
Your other children	Others

Checklist B: Professional help			
G.P.	School counsellor	Marriage guidance counsellor	Cruse – for widowed parents
Health visitor	Education welfare officer	Citizen's Advice Bureau	Psychiatrist
Community nurse	Vicar/minister/ priest	Police	Samaritans
Social worker	Educational psychologist	Gingerbread – for single parents	Youth worker
Form teacher	Child guidance clinic		Probation officer
Head teacher or Year head			Others

How do you feel?

Reviewing your support system is thought-provoking. Some of our parent testers said – "I never realised I had so many good friends". Others realised that they depended on just one person, or on people in just one place, for example at work. Doing this exercise prompted them to think about widening their network of everyday contacts.

Reviewing your support system can bring painful realisations too – "I'm upset to see how isolated I am." Without support it can be very difficult to make the kind of moves needed to get help, particularly if you're feeling low.

It can be useful to:
○ **think over why your support system has got rusty.** Is there a single reason or is there a pattern to your network failing? If it happens regularly, can you see why?
○ **talk it over with someone who can help.** This may be a time when a voluntary group or professional service really could help. "What next?" lists many support agencies for parents. Some of them, like marriage guidance, counselling, cover a far wider range of problems than their name might at first suggest.

Your teenager's support

Your teenager needs a support system just as much as you do. Some teenagers feel isolated because they don't know who can help them. You might like to suggest that your teenager does the "Support system review" activity on pages 16–17 for him/herself. This can help him/her be more aware of the need for a working everyday support system and of the possibility of professional help.

Your teenager may prefer to do this activity on his/her own – particularly if he/she feels you will expect him/her to put you at the top of his/her everyday support list. But you may like to share with him/her the conclusions you drew about your own personal support system when you did the activity.

Checklist B on page 17 will include people who may be of use to your teenager. Of course, help is available from magazines, books, leaflets, TV and radio as well as from people. "What next?", at the end of this book, lists many sources of specialised help for teenagers. Encourage your teenager to have a look at that list now.

What if . . .?

A Rehearsing how to get help makes your teenager feel more confident about using his/her support system when a particular need arises.

This activity may appeal most to younger teenagers. It suggests you look at a variety of situations in which your teenager might need help – and encourage him/her to talk about how he/she would get help or support.

The lists below give some ideas to start you off. They won't all apply to your teenager, so choose the most relevant ones, and add your own. Many situations could apply to anyone in the family, so it may be helpful to compare what you each would do. Are there solutions which would help everyone, such as leaving a spare key with a neighbour in case anyone gets locked out? What makes life easier for parents than teenagers – and what advantages do teenagers have in their support systems?

Things that might happen at school
○ You lose your dinner money
○ You're being bullied
○ Someone cuts their hand on a broken window
○ You're getting into trouble for not doing your homework
○ You're given a punishment for something you didn't do
○ You feel ill in class.

Things that might happen to anyone in the family
○ Your bike is stolen
○ You're worried about your skin
○ You have to decide what to wear to an interview
○ Your friend shoplifts
○ You've lost your keys and are locked out of the house
○ You've missed the last bus
○ You want to sound off about someone else in the family.

Support systems change

By the time your child is a teenager you are no longer the centre of his/her world. It's a slow process which has probably been going on from the time he/she was about five. Can you recall the first time he/she came home from school saying "Miss Smith said . . ." – and you realised that, on at least one issue, Miss Smith's opinion was much more important to him/her than your own?

Support and challenge

You should not expect to be your teenager's main source of support, but it is important for your teenager to know that if he/she wanted you to be, then you would. Often the best support you can offer your teenager is encouragement to go-it-alone – so long as he/she knows you will offer help if it is needed.

Of course, continual support without any challenge would become stifling and unhelpful. Your teenager needs to learn how to challenge him/herself, how to make things happen, rather than just letting things happen to him/her. This will involve understanding him/herself and inviting other people to help him/her do this.

Challenge often comes mainly from parents. At times you may suggest that your teenager does something, or thinks about something that will make demands on him/her. At other times you may help him/her to face challenges. Of course, challenging without support doesn't work – it just feels cruel and punishing. Challenging must be done within a supportive relationship based on love and trust.

Involving your teenager in some of the activities in this book is a form of challenge. You are inviting him/her to understand him/herself, to examine and possibly change his/her behaviour. In some cases you are also challenging him/her to examine what's going on between the two of you. Equally, by choosing to work through this book you are challenging yourself to become a more understanding parent.

New sources of support

As your teenager's life changes, so will his/her support system. For example, the teenager changes school, goes to college, or starts his/her first job. Perhaps a key support person is no longer available. Or perhaps the family moves to a new area leaving behind a network built up over the years.

A time of change is a good opportunity to talk with your teenager about support systems. Sometimes other help will be available too: for example, good schools provide a booklet and spend time, when new pupils start, explaining the support system available in the school.

Support from mentors

Another new source of support for the teenager is often a 'mentor' – a friend who can offer the intimate support that teenagers desperately need. Mentors are usually older than the teenager, but not as old as their parents. Mentors are usually responsible people, who are successful in at least one aspect of life important to the younger person. They share their experiences, provide advice, and model competent behaviour. A mentor might be:

○ older brother/sister – or young uncle/aunt
○ teacher, club leader, guide/scout leader, church leader

○ older pupil or student – or workmate
○ older boy/girl friend

Teenagers may have two or three mentors at one time, or a series of them. Mentors provide valuable support at the time a teenager is moving away from his/her parents but isn't yet too sure of going-it-alone.

In every case, mentors are powerful builders of self-esteem. When the teenager matures and no longer needs such support the mentor may become just another friend. However, if the mentor enjoys the role and doesn't want to give it up the teenager will break off the relationship: by now he/she prefers a more equal relationship with friends.

Your mentors

A Many people recall the mentors of their teenage days with affection, for the valuable support they provided. As adults, it is still useful to have mentors to help, for example, in establishing yourself at work, or in a new area.

D Stop for a while and think about the mentors you have had in your life. You may find it quite easy to write down a few key sentences about your relationships with them. These are just a few of the mentors our parent testers recalled:

○ Alf – who taught me to sail and opened up a whole new way of life for leisure time
○ The girl in charge where I first worked – who taught me how to organise an office full of different characters
○ Gran – who supported me when my mother objected to the boy I wanted to marry
○ The youth club leader – who was very supportive when I was trying to establish my own beliefs
○ My sister-in-law – who, as an outsider coming into the family, helped me sort out my feelings about my childhood

Your teenager's mentors

Your teenager may already have had mentors. He/she may be willing to talk to you about them. It will help him/her to know that you too had mentors, and appreciated their support – and are pleased if he/she has them too, for your teenager may think you might be a bit jealous of his/her mentors. He/she may be right – mentors provide the kind of support that only parents used to be able to give.

If for any reason you are the only parent actively concerned with bringing up your teenager, he/she may need mentors even more. Or if communication is particularly difficult between you, a mentor may sometimes be of more help than you. Occasionally, mentors provide a second chance for the teenager to be mothered or fathered by someone who offers non-possessive parental love.

Rehearsing what you would do makes it easier to cope with emergencies. Look at "What if . . .?"

Life tasks

At each stage of life, certain changes are important.

At each stage of life, certain kinds of biological and psychological changes need to happen. Knowledge and skills must be acquired. The ability to get on well with other people must be developed. These activities can be called developmental – or life – tasks.

Tasks at different stages

The idea of 'life tasks' is a useful way of looking at development because it increases a person's feeling of being in charge of their own life. It's often tempting, particularly for teenagers, to take a passive approach and think that life just happens to you. But this makes you feel helpless and depressed. Life task theory provides a map which gives an overall picture and can help to plan how to reach your destination.

The chart presents a developmental map for the whole of life, based on an analysis of life in a modern society. The cube (right) expands on the tasks for teenagers and shows where these are dealt with in the chapters of this book.

Some life tasks may be of importance at only one life stage. For example, physical maturation – the development of an adult body – is a concern of early adolescence.

Other life tasks are important throughout life but have key significance at a certain stage. For example, the need for close friends of more or less the same age is important throughout life, but, in adolescence, getting on well with peers is particularly important. Peers give the teenager the support he/she needs to move away from parental authority, towards being in control of his/her own life.

The ages in the chart are only a guide. The groups of tasks reflect a cultural pattern which may change: for example, some people start their families much later now, others find that early redundancy brings forward some 'winding down' tasks.

The tasks themselves are also a guide to the process of developments. Life is clearly not a specific set of achievements that must be managed at exact times and then ticked off on a list.

Parents' life tasks

A This book will help you look in depth at one of your current life tasks: being the parent of a teenager. But as the chart suggests, you will have other concerns at the same time, and the exact nature of these will affect how easy it is for you to parent your teenager. Many parents of teenagers are making a 'mid-life review' in early middle age.

D Look at the chart and make some notes about the life tasks which most concern you at the moment. The topic on family life maps (pages 28–29) will examine how your life tasks, and those of other members of the family, are interconnected.

Life stage	Life tasks — it is important to:
Infancy (birth–2)	○ feel attached to one or more people ○ know that people and objects still exist, even when they can't be seen ○ develop ideas through handling objects ○ develop movement skills
Early childhood (2–4)	○ begin to develop self-control ○ begin to develop language ○ explore and pretend in play ○ develop further movement skills
Middle childhood (5–7)	○ develop ideas about being male/female ○ begin to think about right and wrong ○ develop ideas of numbers etc. through practical experiences ○ play co-operatively
Late childhood (8–12)	○ develop co-operative skills ○ be a member of a team ○ begin to think about yourself ○ develop academic, artistic, craft and sporting skills
Early adolescence (13–17)	○ become used to a mature body ○ learn to use abstract ideas ○ gain support from same age friends ○ try out sexual activities
Late adolescence (18–22)	○ become independent and competent ○ make first decisions about work ○ set own behavioural limits ○ make close, intimate relationships ○ freely choose own values
Early adulthood (23–30)	○ develop patterns of family living ○ begin to be a parent ○ develop work plans ○ actively choose lifestyle ○ give to local community
Pre-middle age (30–35)	○ look anew at what's worth spending time on ○ be sensitive to the 'looking anew' done by people important to you ○ be the parent of an older child
Early middle age (36–50)	○ review commitments in mid-life ○ cope with children leaving home ○ develop relationship with partner ○ take an active part in community life
Late middle age (51–65)	○ develop community involvement ○ complete or wind down working life ○ acknowledge the prospect of death
Old age (65–death)	○ negotiate increasing dependence on others ○ evaluate one's own life ○ deal with the deaths of close friends and relatives ○ come to terms with one's own death

Teenagers' life tasks

The chart below summarises the life tasks of adolescence which are examined in this book. The book looks at adolescence as a whole, without separating it into early and late stages. The tasks of early adolescence are usually well on the way to completion by the end of the teenage years. The tasks of late adolescence are unlikely to be completed then – and in any event, parents have less influence on the final outcomes of these tasks.

Often a teenager seems to spend several months concentrating on one task before turning his/her attention to another. This allows the whole range of tasks to be accomplished smoothly over a period of years. Trouble can occur when several tasks pile up at once. A clear example of this would be a late-maturing girl, having to cope with a rapidly changing body, the start of menstruation, and a rising interest in boys, all in the six months before 'O'-levels. She will need a great deal of support from her parents. A working knowledge of life tasks could help both her and her parents.

Sometimes one or more of the teenager's life tasks may particularly worry the parent. The concerns of our parent testers ranged right across the issues in this book – although the choice and influence of friends stood out as having worried most of them at some point. At the same time, these parents recognised that their teenagers were coping well with many aspects of growing up. When you have such confidence in your teenager, it helps to tell him/her so.

A new body
Development of an adult, sexually mature body. Coming to terms with a new body image. Learning to use the 'new body' competently and to manage personal health. **Chapter 2**

Best friends
Intimacy involves the sharing of oneself with another person in a close, intense relationship. In adolescence this is usually first achieved with a best friend of the same sex. **Chapter 3**

Sexual relationships
Intimacy does not itself imply a sexual relationship. In moving towards intimacy with a sexual partner the two elements – intimacy and sexual activities – often get out of step. **Chapter 3**

New friends
Being close to a group of friends the same age provides the teenager with support while he is breaking away from parental authority and learning to run his own life. **Chapter 4**

A new mind
The teenager becomes increasingly competent to handle abstract ideas, solve problems, make choices. He needs motivation and skill to learn, and encouragement to do so. **Chapters 5, 6**

Initial work decisions
Subject choices at school can limit the work open to the teenager. He needs help from home and school in identifying his abilities and interests. **Chapters 5, 6, 7**

New rules
The teenager learns how to set his own behavioural limits. He needs to decide for himself what he sees as right and wrong, and apply his moral rules to his own life. **Chapters 8, 9**

New directions
The teenager begins to re-examine the 'absolute truths' learned from his parents. He needs to look at alternative views of life and to choose his own values. **Chapter 8**

Independent living
The teenager needs to become competent and autonomous – able to lead a 'self-managed' life, having formed an adult identity. This process starts long before leaving home. **Chapter 9**

Life tasks and settings

Life tasks are not the concern of the individual alone. He does not have to face them on his own. The individual develops in interaction with others, in a variety of social settings: for example, the family, school, work, peer groups, neighbourhood community groups.

Key settings for teenagers

The three key settings during early adolescence are:

Family This has been the most important setting since birth, but during the teenage years its influence wanes. The focus of this book is on the relationship between parents and teenagers, and so the family setting is explored in all the chapters, mainly through the activities in the topics.

Peer group The influences of peer group friendships reach peak importance during adolescence. It begins to wane as the teenage years end. For some teenagers the peer group setting will appear to have greater influence than either home or school. But peer group influence often only lasts for a few years. It's importance as a social setting is examined in Chapters 3 and 4.

School This should be the setting which provides both support and challenge to the teenager to develop him/herself to the full. The teenager must leave school and move on to college, work – or unemployment. The setting for a major part of his/her life changes abruptly. Chapters 6 and 7 of this book deal with school and work.

New body and new mind

These three key settings will affect the teenager's attitudes and behaviour, and shape the way he/she develops. Consider their effects on two important life tasks: developing and coming to terms with a 'new' body and a 'new' mind. Chapters 2 and 5 look at these aspects of development in more detail.

New body Teenagers who mature earlier or later than average may find that the extent to which they are supported and accepted in the three key settings varies. For example, within his family: are his/her parents keen to see him/her grow up? Or anxious to keep him/her as a child for a while longer?

At school teachers may have very different expectations of early and late maturers. An early-maturing boy is usually to be expected to be more responsible than a late maturer. The apparently 'childlike' late maturer may be able to get away with behaviour that would be punished in an early maturer, who, because he looks like a man is expected to behave like one.

Among friends, early maturers are usually admired for their size and strength and may become group leaders. Late maturers may compensate for their lack of size by taking greater risks or becoming the group comic and so earn the approval of the peer group.

New mind Teenagers may find that the ability to think about complex, abstract ideas is valued differently in the three settings. Most schools value it very highly, though some value skill at sport more. At your teenager's school who is most admired by the teacher, the captain of football/hockey or the cleverest person in the class? Who is most admired by the pupils? Which would you prefer your teenager to be?

Families vary a great deal as to how much they value intellectual abilities. The whole weight of the family may be brought either as support – or more likely pressure – for the teenager to do well academically. In other families, the teenager may be criticised for "always having his/her head in a book", or for being "too clever by half" when he/she begins to dominate family arguments.

Some peer groups exclude highly academic teenagers. Equally, some peer group leaders are undoubtedly very clever though perhaps not motivated to demonstrate this at school.

Settings change

Familiar settings provide security. You know where you are, even if you don't like it. But during the teenage years, major changes in the settings occur. Such changes can make getting on with life tasks more difficult. For example:

The school setting ends abruptly and further education may be far less supportive. College may provide little support for the student. He/she will be expected to organise his/her own life.

At work the teenager may find a variety of support or lack of it. He/she may be more or less apprenticed to an older experienced worker who will show him/her the ropes. If he/she is lucky he/she will find him/herself working as a valued member of a team whose members support each other. It can be difficult to know what is expected of you and how to fit in. Worst of all he/she may become unemployed – where no-one expects anything of him/her.

The family becomes much less important – yet it may be many years before a person settles down with a partner, and starts his/her own family. This secondary family will eventually provide many people with a stable setting for their middle years. For now, the teenager's close relationships are likely to be much less stable.

The peer group may be the only setting the teenager feels sure of him/herself in. Friends will particularly be important to him/her if support from his/her family setting has always been weak – or is now suddenly withdrawn on the basis that "it's time he learned to stand on his/her own two feet". The unemployed teenager may also turn more to the peer group for support.

Settings may conflict

Different settings may make the same – or conflicting – demands on the teenager. Our parent testers and their teenagers identified a whole range of issues, large and small, over which family, school and friends agreed or disagreed.

The most painful conflict for parents is often between the demands of family and friends. Teenagers may not share this view. They are not too worried about what their parents think of hairstyles, clothes or musical taste. On more serious issues, they are likely to agree with their parents – though they may not tell them so.

Family and school may find they disagree in many ways, particularly if there is little choice over which school the teenager attends. The culture of the family may conflict with the school. Schools may think they are not backed up by the family, while parents may come to feel that any problems their teenager encounters are seen as caused by the family.

Conflict between school and the peer group is likely to be over what is acceptable behaviour in school – and outside.

Family

School

Peer group

Your teenager's settings

A D Develop a list of personal examples – with your teenager if you can – of ways his/her key settings agree or disagree. Many of our parent testers pointed out that it is far easier to think of conflicts than similarities. However, trying to list both can help you to look at your teenager's settings in a fresh light – and to understand the pressures he/she may face.

Family and school

Agree	Disagree
○ We like the way the school encourages and helps to run after-school activities	○ We like to know what's happening at school, but there's a lack of communication
○ The school sets a lot of homework. We agree that studying is important	○ Our religion doesn't allow her to expose her legs, but the school expects her to do games in shorts

Peer group and school

Agree	Disagree
○ Her music teacher plays pop music to them in class – the sort of thing they listen to with their friends	○ The school has a 'no smoking' rule – but their group spends the dinner-break in the loos smoking
○ They both value doing things together rather than alone	○ They're set two hours of homework a night – but they meet outside the chip shop most evenings

Family and peer group

Agree	Disagree
○ She's learning to get on well with people – all sorts	○ At home he's sensible, with friends he is easily-led
○ It's nice to think of them out enjoying themselves	○ I distrust drinking, but my son and his friends think it's great

Transitions – times of change

Changes in lifestyle can cause great stress.

A transition is . . .

1 A time when a life change is being made – a bridging time between an earlier, more or less well-defined period of life and a new way of life.

2 A time of finishing or changing relationships – with important individuals and groups of people

3 A time for questioning – who you are, what's it all about?

4 A time for experimenting – the answers you find to your questions will suggest ways of running your life differently

5 The beginning of new patterns – of a new structure to life, and of commitment to new people and different types of groups

6 A time of slow acceptance – that life must move on

Is the teenager (right) having a wonderful time? Perhaps. Certainly a time of transition. What does she say that fits the six points above?

When do transitions occur?

Age-related transitions: These occur at definite times of life and everyone has to go through them. These times are a part of the natural sequence of development. At every stage of life certain life tasks have to be tackled. But certain stages involve changes of a more unsettling nature than the relatively stable periods of life on either side of them. At these times a major 're-think' goes on.

Dear Pam,   Oct 17

How's London? Life isn't all it used to be here in deepest Beds! It was more of a change than I expected starting Business Studies at the VIth Form College in Sept. I missed most of the old gang — you especially, though I bet you're having a super time in London. It's really odd at college — perhaps one of the best things is that no-one makes you go to lessons — sorry lectures!

I'm already thinking of switching to the computer programming course if I can. But then I ask myself — why work? How about coming to the Jazz festival in Nice — we could throw it all up (sorry!) and live a life of ease in the S. of France. Can you claim social security there? Did you know I could get more on S.S. than I do on my grant?

Hey — how about coming back for the mid-term disco the w/e after next? I'm going with Sylvie and Sharon (never thought I'd get thick with them did you?!) — there'll be quite a lot of blokes from the tech. course there — maybe I should P.T.O.

Adolescence is one of these major times of transition. The other two are the times of the 'mid-life review' (around 40–45) and 'preparation for retirement' (around 55–65). Parents of teenagers may thus find themselves in transition as well.

Life events: These do not occur at definite times or points nor do they happen to everybody. For some events there is

an advance warning which makes them easier to tackle. Life events are not always welcome.

Strangely, even desired changes can be upsetting. For example, you may have been eagerly awaiting the arrival of your first child, but you lost the freedom you had when there were just the two of you. Most people feel bewildered if depression hits them soon after their wedding or the birth of a baby. It helps to recognise that however much you welcome the new way of life you have also given up an old familiar lifestyle, which has to be mourned.

In coming to terms with a change or loss, a variety of strong feelings occur. Some common ones are listed below.

Denial – that the loss ever occured because you don't want to face the changes ahead. ("He'll come back").

Anger – you are angry at yourself, or with others, sometimes for no apparent reason. ("I could wring his neck").

Bargaining – you want to put off the changes for a while longer. ("He'll come back if I promise never to nag").

Depression – you feel low, tired and irritable. ("I'm so tired I don't have the energy even to brush my hair").

Uncertainty – you feel insecure, unsure what to reject and what to keep from the past. ("Shall I train for another job?").

Acceptance – you come to accept your losses of people and places, and see them as part of life moving on, without undue regret. Quite tiny things can be major steps forward. ("No more filthy overalls to wash!" . . . "Now I don't have to watch Match of the Day" . . . until finally "We had some good times but we'd have split up sooner or later anyway").

Life events list

Life events as a child/teenager		Life events as teenager/adult	
Start playschool/nursery school	Go on a long holiday	Leave school	Child starts school
New brother or sister born	Go away from home	Move away from home	Fall out with family
Move to a new home	Serious illness	Start a job	Teenager leaves home
Start primary school	Parents separate or divorce	Change a job	Marital problems – may become separated or divorced
Move up to a new class	Acquire step-parents	Become unemployed	
Pet animal dies	Mother returns to work	Get married	Move far from elderly parents
Change schools	Father or mother become unemployed	Become a family – birth of first child	Re-marry
Elder brother or sister leaves home	Parent changes job	Miscarriage	Win the pools
Friends move away	Grandparent dies	Move to a new town	Physical powers diminish
Fall out with best friend	First part-time job	Have another baby	Active sex life diminishes
			Retire from work

Your life events

A This activity helps you review your life events and recall the mixed feelings these transitions arouse. Such a review can cause you to think deeply about your life, and doing this should help you to understand your own transitions more clearly, so that you become more able to cope with them in the future. It will also help you to help your teenager with his/ her transitions.

You may like to do this exercise with your partner and/or teenager, to gain a family perspective on events. First, check through the list of events and tick those you have experienced, or are experiencing now. Now, focus on two particular events, one welcome and the other unwelcome.

A welcome life event

D From your personal list recall an event when you felt excited about the change – maybe when you got married or had your first child. When you are able to recall this time quite vividly, think about the other feelings you had. Was a part of you sorry to be losing the old way of life? Did you feel anxious about how you would cope with the new way of life? Talk about the event, and your feelings, if you can. Was what was welcome to you also welcome to the rest of the family?

An unwelcome life event

D Next think of a life event you did not want to happen: perhaps separating from your partner, or having to leave your well-loved home town to take a job far away, or being made redundant. Try to recall the feelings you had.

You will almost certainly recall a period of not accepting the change, thinking that you still might be able to go back to the old way of life. Did any of the feelings listed left apply? The beginning of acceptance is when you can make positive answers and plans in response to your feelings of uncertainty. Can you also recall the small discoveries you made which showed you were coming to accept your loss?

For some people it will be difficult to recall feelings. This could be because the whole painful episode is now deeply buried in your memory. For you it would be best to think of some other episode – something which you did not want to happen, but which was rather less painful. Equally, if you are in the middle of an unwelcome life event now, that may be too hard to think about. Thinking about another event, which you coped with well, may help you with the current event.

Talking things over

All our parent testers could tell us about at least one unwelcome life event. Most still felt upset or sad, looking back. At the same time, they felt that thinking and talking events over did help to come to terms with them. "I was annoyed to go back and think about it – and then surprised to find that it had taken its place in the past. It was just that, unwelcome – and not, as I had thought of it, tragic, momentous, overwhelming".

Half our parent testers wanted to talk about the event still – "talking would help me get it in proportion". Others felt they'd talked anough. Feeling upset is a helpful sign that you need to talk some more, otherwise those painful feelings may come back over the years to upset you. They may also upset your relationship with your teenager. If there's an event you haven't fully accepted, it can be difficult for you to help your teenager if he/she comes along with a similar problem.

It can be hard to talk if you are afraid that you will swamp the other person with what you've got to say, or if you are afraid that you'll look silly. If you don't feel you can tell people in your everyday support system, it may help to see a counsellor who has been trained to help people come to terms with their losses.

More than one at a time

At times of transition, people are confused about their feelings. This affects other people with whom they have relationships. Your teenager is in a major transition time – adolescence. This can be painful for him/her and painful to be his/her parent. What if the parent also faces a transition at this time? A vicious spiral can build up because each person's transitions have a knock-on effect on the other. The whole family, and people outside it, can be affected.

The following is an example of this knock-on effect. Bob is offered promotion to a job 100 miles away. He is excited about the new job but he knows it will be more difficult. He will miss his old workmates. He feels slightly guilty about uprooting his wife and teenage daughter Sarah, even though they think he should take the job. Bob's wife is

pleased he has got promotion, but sad to leave the garden she has built up over the last 15 years. She will miss the support of her neighbours, and will have to give up her part-time job. Sarah is just about to take her exams and was looking forward to a long relaxing summer with her friends before going back into the sixth form. She definitely does not want to move.

Making a move

Life becomes difficult if you have to cope with more than one transition at a time. For a teenager, already in the transition time of adolescence, moving house or changing school can be particularly upsetting.

Sarah, from the example above, is now in her late thirties and recalls the

family move: "We moved the week after my exams had finished. I spent a whole summer getting to know my mother – but no friends my own age. Starting a new school where everyone seemed old friends was tough – I felt really worn out for a whole term, and no-one (least of all me) understood why at the time. I left one area too soon, and didn't spend long enough in the next, to retain many friends from my adolescence."

If you moved as a teenager you might like to recapture your own feelings. What were the good things about the move? What were the bad things? Could anything have been done to increase the good and minimise the bad? Sarah now feels that: "Things would have been better if my parents had understood my moods and feelings better. I had strong feelings about losing my friends and home, but we moved quite suddenly and we all focussed on the new life so my losses got ignored." What about you?

Helping your teenager

There are four main ways in which you can help your teenager to cope with transitions:

1 Talk about transitions

Looking at the transitions you have faced can help you to be more aware of your teenager's own transitions. Thinking about how you felt during transitions should also make it easier to talk with your teenager about his/her mixed feelings. Tell him/her about things that have happened to you and how you felt.

Remember that during adolescence your teenager must give up being a child. It is natural to experience painful mixed-up feelings which will pass as he/she becomes an adult. Knowing this will help your teenager to understand his/her feelings. He/she might like to make a list of his/her own life events, from the chart on page 24, and to look at a welcome and an unwelcome event, as you did.

2 Accept your teenager's feelings

It's no reflection on you if your teenager feels angry or depressed. That has more to do with his/her loss. Anger with you may arise if you try to deny his/her feelings or tell him/her to "snap out of it".

It's very easy to misinterpret the teenager's feelings if you are not aware that they are normal feelings to have at this time. The way parents respond in each of the cases right reflects a belief that their teenager's behaviour:

○ has taken a turn for the worse
○ is not normal for his/her age, and
○ will continue into adulthood with dire results.

Fortunately none of this is true.

When you find it difficult to accept your teenager's feelings, try to stop and think why. Often, parents' own feelings get in the way of them understanding the teenager's feelings. Perhaps his/her feelings remind you of something which happened in your own adolescence, or conflict with what you want to happen now. "Accept his/her feelings" is easy to say, much harder to do. You may find it useful to read or reread the topic on "Parents' feelings" (pages 40–43) now.

Teenager's feelings	Parent says
Denial The teenager is putting off accepting that he must give up the advantages of being a child	"He's such a baby. I can't believe he'll be grown up in just a few years time."
Anger The teenager feels unrecognised anger at having to tackle the difficult tasks of becoming an adult	"She's always in a temper about something. Nothing suits her. There's always something she criticises. She'll be impossible to live with."
Bargaining The teenager wants to put off the changes for a little while longer	"He just can't face up to things. Leaves his homework till the last moment. Won't say which exams he wants to take, and won't think about jobs."
Depression Very frequent during adolescence but doesn't always show as typical adult depression. Feeling tired and lifeless all the time is a common sign	"She never gets up before midday. When she is up she just moons around. She needs to pull herself together. How will she manage when she gets a job?"

3 Look at the gains and losses

Making lists of the gains and losses in a transition is one way to get a clearer picture of the mixed feelings involved. After writing down a loss, you should put down a gain before adding another loss. This helps you to keep the balance so that all the losses do not swamp you with depression.

You might like to look back at your own adolescence using this technique. Or everyone in the family might use it to explore their feelings and concerns about a transition which will affect the whole family, for example, moving house or separation.

Encourage your teenager to look at growing up in terms of:

○ what I'm losing now I'm not a child
○ what I'm gaining by becoming an adult

Your teenager may want to keep his/her replies secret or he/she may like to discuss them with you. Most of our parent testers' teenagers did this activity. Their answers were very varied, but "independence" and "freedom to decide" cropped up time and again as gains. At the same time, the teenagers missed being able to 'muck about' in a childish way, and rely on their parents sort things out when needed.

4 Provide support

Look at practical steps which will help: For example, in Sarah's case, moving at the end of holidays rather than the beginning. Ideas for support often come from thinking about gains and losses. For example, if your teenager puts 'losing old friends' – how might he/she set about finding new friends? And – how will he/she keep in touch with his/her old ones?

Teach him/her to look after him/herself: Good habits of caring for yourself provide a stable routine during a period of upset. This helps to protect both physical and mental health. Caring for yourself includes giving yourself a treat when you feel low.

Seek help: You and/or your teenager may need to talk about the transition with someone you can trust. Help your teenager to find out where to get help for particular problems. And practise what you preach – share your problems and strong feelings with a sympathetic friend, or seek professional support.

What about you?

Your teenager is in a major transition time. Are you, the parent, also in a major transition time, of mid-life review or planning for retirement? And/or – are there major life events occurring for you? Acknowledging that all members of the family face transitions which have knock-on effects can make it easier to understand the strong feelings and stress that build up at these times.

Your family life map

A map can highlight the complexities of family life.

Life tasks and life events

The previous topics on "Life tasks" and "Transitions" explained what life tasks and life events are. You have looked at the tasks and events which you have to tackle yourself – and at the tasks and events which your teenager is coping with. How well you each get on will be affected both by your past experiences and by the life tasks and events of other members of the family.

The ways in which each person's life tasks and events affect – and are affected by – those of all the other members of the family can make a complicated picture. Making a family life map can help you to see these connections more clearly.

A family life map can also help you to identify:

○ why clashes can occur between members of the family who face different life tasks and life events

○ how choosing to make a life change – or an unexpected life event – may affect the whole family

Clashes and changes and special family circumstances are considered in the next two topics. Very often these will create a need for extra support, but it can be hard to make use of the advice of experts who do not know the life tasks and events of your whole family.

How to make a family life map

A 1 Review the list of life tasks on pages 20–21, and your thoughts about your own.

A 2 Review the list of life events on pages 24–25, and your thoughts about your own.

D 3 Write a brief description of the issues and concerns in your life. Divide them into tasks and events, as in the example, or make a list of key points about your life at the moment.

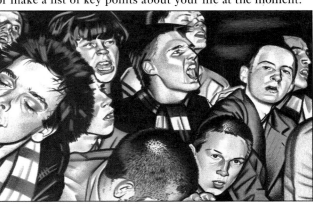

Age

10   20   30

Family cards

Janet age 11

Life tasks
○ Gets on well with school friends and teachers.
○ Conscientious about doing her share of housework.
○ Competent at housework and at organising her own life.
○ Shows signs of early physical maturation.

Life events
○ Has to have remedial maths and English. (Got off to a poor start at primary school. This coincided with her father leaving).
○ Is soon to represent her school in a swimming gala.
○ Now has to share a room with her mother.
○ Enjoys the chance to talk to her grandfather now.

Gary age 15

Life tasks
○ In the throes of adolescence.
○ Early maturation.
○ Average at school work.
○ Planning to take 3 'O'-levels and 3 CSE's.
○ Active member of peer group – supporter of Ipswich Town F.C.
○ Goes along with the group – has been involved in football vandalism.
○ Keen on girls – but hasn't yet had a steady girl. Not very good at being friends with girls.
○ Has best friend, Mike – whose parents are also divorced.
○ Can look after himself around the house. Will so do – if ordered – but prefers to leave it to his mother (and sister).

Life events
○ Still misses father, who he remembers as his pal.
○ Fed-up with grandfather moving into the home, because for the last few years he has seen himself as 'the man of the house'.
○ Is soon to go on school adventure holiday – rock climbing.

Major transition times ▶   **Adolescence**

4 Now repeat this process for each member of the family, whether they live at home or away. Use a separate card for each person. Where possible, encourage them to make their own lists.

5 Mark each person's age on their card. If their age falls into one of the major age-related transition times shown below – adolescence, mid-life review, or pre-retirement – ring their age to remind you that they may be facing a particularly trying time.

A life map is not a substitute for discussion and awareness of each others' needs. It is simply a tool which can help you to get started, or keep talking, or see things in a fresh light. If possible, make your family life map as a family activity. It will help everyone to realise just how complicated family life can be.

Below is a completed set of family life map cards as an example. They were made by one of the parent testers who helped with this book. Eileen is bringing up her two children on her own. Her widowed father has just moved in with them.

40	**50**	**60**	

Eileen age 37

Life tasks
○ Wants to get better-paid job, which may mean she must do some retraining.
○ Spends most of her spare time looking after the children.
○ Is worried about Gary's group – and the possible vandalism they get involved in.
○ Is coming to terms with her and her husband's decision to end the marriage.
○ Unsure of what she hopes for – or can reasonably expect – from the rest of her life.

Life events
○ Faces many practical problems as a single parent.
○ Taking her Dad into the family home seems to have revived old quarrels she used to have with him.
○ Flat needs re-decorating.
○ They are over crowded now that Dad has moved in. Janet has to share her bedroom.
○ Little time or privacy for herself.

Keith age 44 (absent)

Left six years ago. Pays maintenance regularly, but seldom sees his children. Now works 200 miles away.

Bill age 66

Life tasks
○ Has just retired.
○ Is worried about becoming dependent on others – sees moving in with Eileen as first step.
○ Wife died a year ago – has nearly come to terms with it.
○ Is worried about his chronic bronchitis.

Life events
○ Has several life events piling up the stress in his life.
○ No longer a breadwinner.
○ Moved away from his old home.
○ Is trying, on doctor's advice, to stop smoking.
○ Has started to do various jobs around the house. Feels good about this.

Mid-life review

Pre-retirement

Clashes and changes

Clashing life tasks or events make relationships stressful.

Clashes in the family

Look at each pair of your family life cards one at a time and consider how each of the two sets of life tasks and events may clash with the other. For example, when Eileen looked at Bill's and Janet's cards, she could see a major clash. Now that Bill has moved in, Janet has to share a room with her mother – just as she is reaching a time when she will want to spend more time alone.

Our parent testers identified a whole range of clashes in their families.

"The children and I clash because I find it hard to do a job, the housework and still have enough time to mother them".
"My son and his stepfather both compete for my interest".
"My husband and I clash over the amount of time he spends at work instead of with the family".

Between parents and teenagers

When parents and teenagers compare their life cards, two common, but painful types of clash often show up.

1 Teenager has an advantage compared with the parent
"My teenage daughter is slim and full of energy, while I have difficulty with my weight, and get tired quickly".
"My teenage son is bright and remembers things well. I sometimes feel patronised when I get things wrong".
"Our teenagers can go out more or less when they like, while I have to think about the money, and being fair to the rest of the family, before I go out".

2 Parent has an advantage compared to the teenager
"I'm old enough to be confident – my teenager is so shy".
"I've achieved a lot in my career. These days it's harder for my teenagers to gain educational and work opportunities".
"My daughter has eczema and she sometimes comments how much prettier her mother is".

The commitments of mid-life often restrict the choices open to parents. Many parents feel depressed or envious if they compare their lives with their teenagers'. Equally, highly successful parents can make their teenagers feel inadequate. Fortunately most teenagers and parents have advantages and disadvantages on both sides.

In your family

A D It can help teenagers and parents if they share their feelings about such issues. They may be unaware of how each other feels. Recognising and accepting feelings can go a long way to ensuring that they don't cause problems.

Think about your teenager – or discuss this activity with him, if you can. Can you write a pair of statements as in the examples from our parent testers, where:

1 your teenager has an advantage compared to you
2 you have an advantage compared to your teenager

Create as many pairs of statements as you can.

Discussing issues like these can be quite hard to do. You might like to read, or reread, the topic on "Parents' feelings"

(pages 40–43) at this point. In addition, the course pack looks at communication skills in detail. You might find it helpful to try structuring your discussion like this.

The person who feels at a disadvantage should describe their feelings first: "I feel unfit and overweight", or "I feel desperate about my spots". The other person needs to show they have listened to and understood the feeling: "You feel pretty bad about it". Statements of blame, such as "You need to get yourself in shape" or "You're a fat, spotty lay-about" would be a disaster. It would be helpful to say: "What do you think you can do about it? Can I help?"

Making changes

Supposing one person in a family wants or has to make a major change? It can help to look over your family life map and see how this change may affect everybody's life tasks. You can also see if any other person's current life events will make this change easier or more difficult. For example, Eileen was pleased to have her father Bill move into the house, but Bill was reminded that the older he got, the more dependent he would be. Eileen worried that she would find herself quarrelling with him the way she did when she was young. Janet had to share a room with Eileen. And Gary felt he was no longer 'the man of the house'.

All changes have their pro's and con's. But you don't have to keep things as they are just because there are disadvantages. You can do two things:

○ share your views about what the gains and losses are, so that you build up an overall picture

○ try to make the losses as few as possible – and work out ways in which family members can support each other to face the losses that remain.

Making lists of gains and losses is just a means to help you focus on the issues which are important to individuals. Each person prepares their own list, and then shares this with the family. You may find that what one person sees as a gain, another sees as a loss. Three examples of this are marked in the Walker's chart.

The activities below give further suggestions about what you can do with lists of losses and gains. It may sound as if you will take the lid off family quarrels – with explosive results – but feelings of loss will be around and it's better to look at them openly.

Gains and losses

A D This activity provides a chance for the family to look at the losses which always accompany a gain and to work together to see how such losses can be minimised. First make your individual lists of gains and losses, and compare them to see the patterns in your answers.

Then work through the whole list of losses, with everyone making suggestions as to how these might be overcome. It's best to have a brainstorming session, where everyone's suggestions – however 'way-out' they may seem – are listed without criticism. When you've run out of possibilities, go through and consider which are most practical.

If you're nervous about trying this in your family, practise

Should Clare Walker work?

Gains	Losses
Clare (Mother)	
○ more money will help everyone	○ there'll be more work to fit into the day
○ I'll have more interesting work	○ I'll get more tired
○ I'll have a wider circle of friends	○ I'll do less cooking, which I enjoy
○ I'll get out of the house	○ I won't be home when Sean comes in from school
Patrick (Father)	
○ more money will make life easier, pay for better holidays – and for someone to paint the house	○ I won't have a meal waiting for me when I come in and I don't cook
○ Clare will be less depressed and have more to talk about	○ the house will be less tidy
○ Sean will have to learn to look after himself	○ I won't be able to ask friends round so often
Sean (Teenage son)	
○ the house will be less tidy – so I won't get nagged so much	○ I'll have to look after myself more
○ mother won't be around when my friends come in after school	○ there'll be less of mother's homemade food
○ mother will look smarter, which will be nice	○ mother will have less time to listen to me
Rover (Dog)	
○ better tasting, more expensive dog food	○ fewer walks

by discussing Clare's family. What might they decide to do about their evening meals? What could happen about the housework? And what about Rover's walks?

You could also practise within your family by starting with small issues, or with just two of you together. Our parent testers used the gains and losses technique to help them discuss a whole range of changes – daughter leaving school, course of study for mother, moving house, and so on. One family who moved commented wryly: "We wonder what we'd have said if we'd had this talk before we moved!"

An unexpected change: redundancy

A Suppose the main breadwinner in the family were made redundant tomorrow? Or suppose you won the pools? We suggest you think about redundancy – unfortunately, it's the more likely of the two.

To get over your initial shock you would need to talk to family and friends about your feelings. You would also seek advice about what you could do. Of course political and economic changes are needed to improve conditions for the unemployed, and to reduce unemployment. But within your family, sharing ideas about gains and losses can help you all to come to terms with this change in your family circumstances.

You might like to make some lists of possible gains and losses now. If there is another 'unexpected' change your family is more likely to face, you may prefer to consider this.

Almost all our parent testers thought it worthwhile trying this exercise. Happily for most of them it was still just an exercise. Half of the families commented that it encouraged them to see a positive side to redundancy that they hadn't thought of before. This can be difficult if you hold strongly negative views.

Some families commented that the exercise made them feel worried. Would they be able to cope? It certainly isn't nice to think about losses, but thinking through a change in life before it happens can help you to manage it when it comes. Strong feelings are a natural part of handling changes (see "Transitions" pages 24–27).

Special circumstances

These family situations may make for extra clashes.

Certain family circumstances may increase the number of clashes between parents and teenagers over life tasks, so their need for support is greater.

One-parent families

"I wish they would go and live with their father (mother) and never come back!"
"Why did she have to die and leave me to cope on my own?"
"I'd rather he left than stayed around never lifting a finger to help!"

Parents are full of mixed feelings and unspoken thoughts about parenting. Anger, frustration and despair are mixed with love, pride and concern for the teenager.

In a one-parent family, the lone parent usually experiences such feelings more deeply. Lone parents have an incredibly difficult time. Eileen found that she was working all day and coming home to do the housework. At the same time, she was determined not to miss out on anything with Janet and Gary that mothers and fathers would be involved in. She often felt angry and depressed.

When a lone parent feels this way, it can be easy to fall into seeing everything about the teenager as different just because he lives in a one-parent family. Yet this is becoming an increasingly common experience: currently there are almost one million one-parent families in Britain. The vast majority of these parents are women. Most are divorced, but many have been widowed and some have never been married. One in eight children will spend some part of their life in a one-parent family.

Many people assume that children from one-parent families will have more problems than children from the standard two-parent family, but there is little hard evidence for this. Major life events such as a divorce do bring the kind of mixed feelings described in "Transitions" on page 24: the children will probably show some signs of disturbance, but the vast majority come to terms with the changes. They are no more likely to go on to become drop-outs, vandals, drug-addicts or delinquents than are children from standard families. Problems like these seem to be related to parenting style, and to general social and economic problems, rather than to the marital status of the parent. Indeed some 'standard' families, in which the marriage partners are more or less at war with each other, can be very damaging to live in.

Your family

A The main need of a lone parent is support. He/she needs financial, practical and personal help. Where there are two parents, they can often provide each other with this support – though this is often not enough. The lone parent needs particular support over his/her feelings. Looking over your family life map can highlight the tasks and events which cause the strongest emotional reactions in you.

As a lone parent, it will be particularly important for you to review your support system. Your teenagers may also want to think about the support they need and receive. The activities in "Support" (pages 16–19) may help you to realise the changes you might make in your support systems. "What next?" suggests a range of possible sources of support.

Reconstituted families

This is the official term for families where one or both partners have been married before and have children of their own. They are choosing to make a major change: to combine two families into one. Children may also be born in the new marriage. Latest figures show that in one out of every three marriages, one or both parents have married before.

Your family

A If your family includes children of former marriages, your pattern of family life will be more complicated. It becomes particularly important to have an ongoing awareness of each family member's needs. A family life map, as suggested on pages 28–29, can help you to compare the current life tasks and events of all family members.

Take care to consider each possible pair of people in your family in turn. You may need to include both parents and step-parents. Look carefully at how current life tasks and events may clash and affect everyone. Young teenagers, in particular, may see their parent's new partner as an intruder.

There are often money problems in reconstituted families too, because the man may be paying alimony and perhaps maintenance to his first wife. Sources of conflict need to be looked at. It is often all too easy to gloss over the life tasks and events of some members of the family, in an attempt to see the new marriage as being much better than the old one.

"What next?" includes books and organisations which reconstituted families may find useful.

When coping is hard . . .

A teenager has to tackle the life tasks of adolescence whether or not he or his parents have major problems which may make these tasks more difficult.

. . . for parents

Some types of parental problems can make it harder to provide the support the teenager needs. Parents who are handicapped in some way, who are depressed or anxious, or who have a drink problem, need extra support themselves if they are to help their teenager as well as they can.

Most physically handicapped people who become parents have learned to cope well with their disability long before their children are teenagers. But where the parent becomes physically disabled or chronically sick at a later date, their energies are bound to be used up in adjusting to their disability. They may feel that they are letting their teenager down by not having enough 'emotional time' for them.

Attempting to hide the seriousness of disabilities and problems may make teenagers feel that they are being treated like children. If they are taken in by the act, they may put other interpretations on their parents' lack of involvement that can be even more painful. There needs to be a balance. It's important not to go to the other extreme and expect the teenager to become so deeply involved in helping and caring for his/her parent that he/she lacks the chance to develop an independent life of his/her own.

. . . for teenagers

Physically and mentally handicapped teenagers will have special difficulties in tackling some life tasks. If your teenager is handicapped some of these difficulties may have been highlighted when you made a family life map. Coping with these difficulties may be made worse if the parents lack support. As well as practical help, counselling help is needed for the worries parents face when coping with their teenager growing up. Several of our parent testers told us how having such support made a vital difference to them and their teenagers.

Handicapped teenagers are often dependent on their parents for daily attention to their physical needs: feeding, washing, toileting, transport. This can make it harder for parents to encourage their teenager to be as independent as possible in other areas, such as decision-making and personal relationships.

They may have little personal privacy. And parents often feel particularly worried about coping with their handicapped teenager's sexuality. Yet support may be hard to find. On the one hand society professes to care and help – but on the other would prefer to think that the handicapped have no sexual feelings and no need for sexual relationships.

It can be hard for parents to allow teenagers who have needed special protection to take the kinds of risks involved in boundary testing. They want to protect their teenager from any other hurt at all costs. But, in truth, most people would rather be hurt than lead a cocooned life. The whole family needs encouragement to work towards the day when the teenager will lead a separate life away from his parents.

Your family

A The focus in this course is on understanding adolescence and building up parenting skills. Sometimes particular problems can make the parents' task more difficult. This book seeks to acknowledge the problems and to suggest sources of support. But although the parent's task may be harder – it is not basically different.

However, if you see your teenager's handicap as the most important thing about him/her it will be difficult to accept anything written about teenagers that is not entirely from a handicapped teenager's point of view. Such a view can lead to ignoring the 'whole person' behind the handicap.

At this stage you might like to review:

1 Your own responses to the approach of this book. Do you read it as applying to your family? Or do you find yourself saying "yes but, I/my teenager . . ."? You may need to reconsider what you think this book can offer you, or, more fundamentally, you may want to rethink your approach to your teenager as he/she grows up.

2 The clashes that occur between you and your teenager due to particular problems. Did you include all these in your family life map? How do they affect other members of the family?

3 The sources of support that you and your teenager can draw on. The activities in "Support" (pages 16–19) may help you both to do this. "What next?" may also direct you towards sources of extra support and help for your family.

Parenting styles

What is your general style as a parent?

Parents' ideas

A **D** What kind of an adult do you hope your child will become? Stop for a few minutes and write down your answer before reading on.

Our parent testers overwhelmingly hoped for happy, contented adults. Some of the other things they wanted their teenagers to be:

○ confident, honest, considerate, caring

○ healthy

○ able to get on with other people, a good friend

○ able to make and maintain family relationships

○ successful in his/her chosen way of life

○ not necessarily the most brilliant of people, but someone who enjoys life

○ able to be self-supporting financially

○ at ease with him/herself, doing what he/she wants to do

Some of these parents acknowledged, ruefully, that they hadn't achieved all this themselves. This is hardly surprising since what they describe is an ideal of maturity. It's something we strive after all our lives. It certainly can't be achieved by – say – age 21. But then neither is it ever too late to take active steps towards achieving most of it.

When younger teenagers are asked about the kind of adult they want to be, they are likely to describe a specific ambition or 'dream'. "Play football for England", or "Become the lead singer in a group" for instance. Some examples of work 'dreams' – and how they relate to reality – are given in Chapter 7.

Older teenagers (who are often asked this kind of question in school) tend to give answers which are very similar to their parents'. Because the details of the lives they want differ, parents may find it hard to accept that their teenager really wants that life, or that it will make them happy. Gradually, though, most parents come to see that their offspring are pursuing – in their own way – the same kind of ideal of maturity that they hold.

Tomorrow's adults

Many parents look at their teenagers and think: "Will this awkward/irritating/argumentative/dirty/lazy/unreliable/self-centred/wayward teenager ever become the kind of adult I would like him/her to be?" The answer in most cases is amazingly, "Yes".

Becoming a new adult person with a new body, new mind, new values and new friends is quite an upheaval. During this transition the teenager may often cause his/her parents to despair. But in the end they are usually pleased with the way he/she turns out.

The 'perfect' teenager on the other hand doesn't necessarily go on to a trouble-free adulthood. He/she may have to finish tackling the life tasks of adolescence later on in life. The process of forming an adult identity is considered in detail in Chapter 9. The focus here remains on the hopes and expectations of parents – and how teenagers match up to these.

A parent's view

Parents whose children are now grown up were invited to look back and tell us about the teenage years. The following account is based on the experiences of one mother. We are grateful to her for allowing us to draw on her letter in this book.

As you read about this family – where do your sympathies lie? Both daughters had a lot going for them. But still their lives did not go entirely as expected. The same story could undoubtedly be told by many parents from very different backgrounds and with other approaches to bringing up their children.

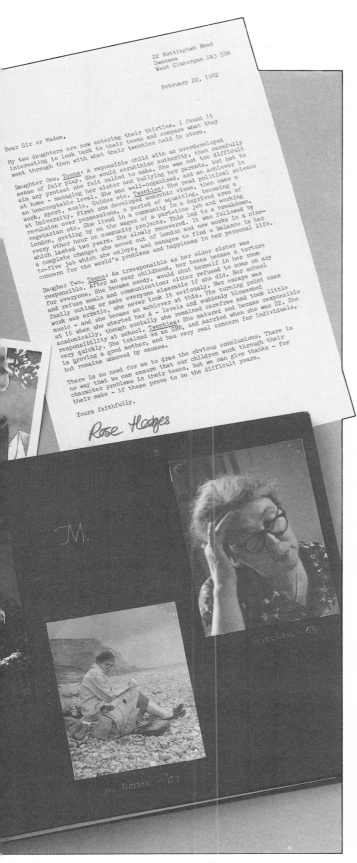

22 Nottingham Road
Swansea
West Glamorgan SA3 5DB

February 22, 1982

Dear Sir or Madam,

My two daughters are now entering their thirties. I found it
interesting to look back to their teens and compare what they
went through then with what their twenties held in store.

Daughter One. Teens: A responsible child with an overdeveloped
sense of fair play. She would scrutinise authority, then carefully
aim any protest she felt called to make. She was not too difficult
at home - managing her sister and bullying her parents, but not to
an unacceptable level. She was well-organised, and an achiever in
work, sport, music, Guides etc. Twenties: She read political science
at University. First she developed anarchic views, then came a
revulsion over possessions, a period of squatting, becoming a
vegetarian etc. She lived in a community in a deprived area of
London, getting by on the wages of a part-time job and working
every other hour on community projects. This led to a breakdown,
which lasted two years. She slowly recovered. It was followed by
a complete change: she moved out of London and now works in a nine-
to-five job which she enjoys, and manages to find a balance in her
concern for the world's problems and happiness in her personal life.

Daughter Two. Teens: As irresponsible as her older sister was
responsible. After an easy childhood, her teens became a torture
for everyone. She became moody, would shut herself in her room
and refuse meals and communication; either refused to come on any
family outing or made everyone miserable if she did. Her escape was
music - and she never took it seriously. The turning point came
at 16 when she started her A - levels and suddenly blossomed
academically, though socially she remained carefree and took little
responsibility at school. Twenties: She matured and became responsible
very quickly. She trained as an SRN, and married when she was 22. She
is proving a good mother, and has very real concern for individuals,
but remains unmoved by causes.

There is no need for me to draw the obvious conclusions. There is
no way that we can ensure that our children work through their
character problems in their teens, but we can give thanks - for
their sake - if those prove to be the difficult years.

Yours faithfully,

Rose Hodges

Your style as a parent

This may be something you've given a great deal of thought
to, or you may be almost unaware of what your 'style' is. It
may have just developed over the years during which you've
been raising your family.

Many of the activities in this book will help you build up a
clearer picture of your parenting style. Overleaf in this topic,
for example, we suggest that you:

○ take a fresh look at parenting, as if it were like gardening
○ identify the kinds of approach you take in explaining teenage behaviour, and in trying to help

The activities will also help you to identify why you use
the kind of approach you do. This is important, because the
reasons for your approach may also be reasons why you find
some of your own or your teenager's problems hard to handle.
For example, you might stress achievement above all, because
you were a scholarship lad and your family were proud of
that. This could make it particularly hard for you to cope
with, say, early redundancy for yourself or a teenage son who
shows no ambition in your terms.

The final topic in this chapter – "Parents' feelings" – looks
at some of the possible effects of parents' own life experiences
on the relationship between parents and teenagers.

Changes

The activities will also help you to identify what, if anything,
you would like to change in your approach. While feelings
get in the way, change can be difficult, so self-awareness is
the first step in change.

Flexibility is essential. Parents are not producers of new
adults, but rather enablers of growth. Their role is to help the
teenager become the kind of adult which is appropriate for
him/her. Trouble arises when parents are determined to
make their children grow up exactly the way they want them
to be. They may rigidly apply a particular style of parenting
in the hope of producing a particular type of adult. In so
doing, they may forget, or ignore, the facts that:

○ the style of parenting they chose may have undesirable
outcomes as well. It can even become counterproductive and
make the desired outcome even less likely
○ even within one family, teenagers have different personalities and needs
○ parents are not the only influence on their teenager
○ teenagers have every right to have a say in the kind of an
adult they want to become. And they will go their own way
once they are adults – even though their upbringing may
partly restrict them

Reflections

A D When you have finished this topic, try to summarise your reflections on your parenting style Write
yourself a description of your style in general.

You will tend to write about your ideals. So try also to
be specific about the actual approaches you take. Over the
years, how have you changed?

Theories of development

Theories of human development help to describe, explain and predict the way people behave. An outline of four theories is given in the next topic. They are:

A *Psychoanalytic approach*: instincts and desires
B *Self-actualizing approach*: striving towards ideals
C *Behavioural approach*: one thing leads to another
D *Socialisation approach*: the roles people play

The names may be unfamiliar. But what each theory teaches about understanding adolescence has to some extent become part of common knowledge. The approaches offer different ways of helping teenagers to cope with their life tasks. A combination of the approaches perhaps works best.

Insight and self awareness are needed:
○ into the origin of poor self-esteem if this prevents a person believing in his own ability to make changes, drawing on behavioural theory
○ into what makes people 'selfish' and how this affects the personal goals that they choose, which may harm others
○ into the way people relate to each other in groups, especially if people are to work together to change society.

An understanding of how to make changes is needed:
○ to put new-found insights into practice
○ to pursue personal goals
○ to bring about desired changes in society

An understanding of society is needed:
○ to prevent emphasis on personal behavioural change, when this isn't the solution
○ to give a wider perspective before choosing personal goals
○ to counterbalance the tendency to blame the family for every problem the teenager has

Parents as gardeners

A You've been involved in bringing up your teenager for years now. It can be difficult to stand back and think about what you're doing. This quiz may help you to distance yourself by looking at the relationship in a different light.

Imagine that you are raising a plant instead of a child. What kind of gardening do you go in for? Read the descriptions (right) – and tick the points you agree with.

The four styles A, B, C, D match the four theories described above and overleaf. Any one if used alone and in an extreme version – can have some extreme results. Can you match these types of adults to the four styles?

1 The perfectionist: self-centred, overstriving, easily depressed by failure of any kind. Values people for their achievements only. ☐
2 The timid type: not what he wanted to be, more the sum of his parents' ambitions. Finds it hard to relax and be natural, or to strike out in new directions. ☐
3 The toughie: aggressive or suspicious, unable to show his personal needs for care and affection. May ignore the feelings of others in trying to change society. ☐
4 The unambitious: not keen to stretch himself. Feels he can't – or there's no need to – change himself or society. ☐

Style A: The bedding plant

You believe that the plant/child has a built-in potential to develop properly. With suitable protection in the early years it will naturally become what it is 'meant' to be. So you:

1 Provide a lot of protection when the plant is young and tender; and gradually help it become tough and well-grown, able to thrive in the outside world. ☐

2 Allow the plant to grow naturally; but provide nourishment and give extra support when needed. ☐

3 Don't expect an orchid to grow from a petunia seed – but you like petunias anyway. ☐

Style C: The bonsai tree

You are concerned that – unless carefully watched and trained – the plant/child might get out of hand. Applying the rules of growth/behavioural control will help to ensure that it is shaped up properly. So you:

1 Provide just enough nourishment: too much would make the plant soft. ☐

2 Keep a close watch on development: nip unwanted growth in the bud. ☐

3 Shape and train the plant – using constricting wires if need be – to grow exactly the way you want it to be. ☐

Answers 1B, 2C, 3D, 4A

Style B: The flower show exhibit

You think that being top/best is very important. It is essential to develop the plant/child's full potential – regardless of the needs and demands of others. So you:

1 Lavish attention on the plant: even at inconvenience to yourself. ☐

2 Value the plant only for the size of its bloom. ☐

3 Constantly compare plant with others – you are determined to make it the best in its class. ☐

Style D: The windswept garden plant

You believe that the development of the plant/child is heavily influenced by the setting in which it has to grow. It must grow up amongst others who also have their own needs. So you:

1 Plant it out as soon as possible in the open ground: so that it can adapt to the environment and become tough and well-established. ☐

2 Consider the ability to grow well among other plants to be very important. ☐

3 Realise that the weather will play an important part in what the plant will look like when it is fully grown. ☐

Which theory applies?

A This activity asks you to look at the way your ideas may be shaped by your knowledge – formal or informal – of the four types of theory.

Imagine for a moment that a teenage girl has stolen some make-up (or a boy some aftershave) from a chemist's shop.

1 Which of the following points do you think might be part of the explanation for why teenagers steal like this? Tick as many of the points as you want in column 1.

2 Read the pages overleaf describing the four theoretical approaches in more detail, then check your grasp of the approaches by linking them to this example. Write the letter of the approach – A, B, C or D – which best fits each point in column 2. There are three points for each approach.

3 The answers below show the match between the approaches and the points. Ring in the answers the points you ticked in column 1. Do you tend towards one approach, or to a mix?

Why do they steal?

Explanations	Col. 1	Col. 2
1 The shopkeeper made it easy to steal by the open display of the goods		
2 He/she is unsure of him/herself as a developing sexual person – and wants to make him/herself more attractive		
3 Parents have turned a blind eye to/covered up for similar behaviour before		
4 Advertisers make teenagers desperate to have such things		
5 He/she hasn't yet decided for him/herself that stealing is wrong		
6 He/she is stealing to get attention		
7 He/she did it as part of exploring different values to his/her parents		
8 Similar behaviour was not punished in the past		
9 This sort of thing is a natural part of growing up. All teenagers do it		
10 He/she feels unloved and has poor self-esteem, so stole to give him/herself a present to make up for it		
11 He/she has not chosen for him/herself the 'image' (goal) that says "I'm not the kind of person who steals"		
12 There are no – or few – part-time jobs for teenagers today. So they are short of money		

A: 2,9,10; B: 5,7,11; C: 3,6,8; D: 1,4,12.

Approaches to adolescence

There are different ways of looking at teenager development.

Each approach is divided into four sections

1 Key points: the framework for looking at life that each theory provides.

2 Peer groups: a specific example of the kind of interpretation that each theory leads to, about friends.

3 Helping teenagers: the practical focus and emphasis of each theory for providing support to teenagers.

4 Pros and cons: some advantages and drawbacks of drawing on each theory to help.

A Instincts and desires

(based on psychoanalytic theories)

1 Key points

Emphasises that there is an inbuilt psychological process of maturation, of which we are usually unaware. Adolescence is a time of internal upheaval, reflected in outward behaviour: a time of storm and stress. The teenager may go back (regress) to earlier babyish behaviour and often has intense, mixed feelings about things. This is because rapid biological, social and psychological changes are going on and the teenager is unsure of who he is (identity confusion). If all goes well an adult emerges with a strong sense of who he is and what he wants to do (identity formation). This internal stormy period is called an identity crisis. Teenagers may show few or many signs of such a crisis.

The process of adolescence involves moving from a dependency on the family and a loosening of the early childhood ties, which frees the teenager to find new 'love objects' outside the family.

2 Example: peer groups

Peer groups are seen as providing essential support in the early stages of moving away from dependence on parents. The teenager relies on them less as he/she forms his/her own mature identity.

3 Helping teenagers

The focus is on developing *insights* – mainly by talking over the past – into the instincts and desires which prompt us to behave as we do.

The theory emphasises the importance of *significance* – the need for a person to believe that they are liked by, and important to, someone who is important to them. This is a crucial part of the development of self-esteem. Ideally children experience this in their relationships with their parents. But it can be experienced fully for the first time later in life.

4 Pros and cons

It does seem that at times we manage to delude ourselves about our motives. Or we are simply unaware of them. Developing insights into what's going on can help us be more in control of what we are doing. The trouble is that gaining insight may only be an intellectual activity. Teenagers – and parents – may need a great deal of help to decide what to do with their new insights. They then need to practise the new behaviour they have chosen to adopt. If these new behaviours succeed, they will encourage parents and teenagers to gain more insights – and generally enhance their self-esteem.

B Striving towards ideals

(based on self actualizing theories)

1 Key points

Emphasises self-awareness. The motivation for our actions is seen as a desire to strive towards developing our full potential. Building up self-awareness involves using an understanding of biological instincts, learning skills and social roles.

The focus is on self-actualization: initiating action yourself which helps you define and work towards your goals. Challenge – from oneself as well as others – is an important spur to encourage pursuit of these goals. Teenagers who have not had these challenges may feel confused about who they are, what are the important issues in life, and what is worth striving for.

The 'life tasks' approach set out in this chapter owes a lot to 'self-actualizing' theory.

2 Example: peer groups

Peer groups provide a setting in which teenagers can explore different sets of values from those their parents hold. They also enable the teenager to choose and set his/her own goals.

3 Helping teenagers

The focus is on challenging the teenager to become *self-aware* – to become in charge of his/her own life and set and pursue his/her own goals. This usually involves a good deal of exploration of values.

The theory emphasises *autonomy* – a self-directed lifestyle. A person should take the initiative to run his or her life the way he/she wants to rather than just letting life happen to him/her.

4 Pros and cons

Teenagers usually respond readily to the challenge to become more self-aware. It helps to encourage teenagers, who may be feeling passive victims of social circumstances, to examine what they can do to help themselves and how they can become involved in constructive community action. Self-actualization – striving towards personal goals – can, on its own, become a very self-centred view of life.

The approach for you

Most of our parent testers found this section useful and interesting, but quite hard-going. As you read, make it personal. Ask yourself: "Is the way I behave to my teenager based in any way on this particular theory?"

You may want to reject some of the approaches. Or you may find you incline towards one approach, or to a mix (see page 37). If you want to find out more, see "What next?".

C One thing leads to another	D The roles people play
(based on behavioural theories)	**(based on socialisation theories)**
1 Key points	**1 Key points**
Emphasises the connections between events. Any action, thought or feeling, closely followed by a 'reward' is likely to be repeated and become habitual. Actions, thoughts or feelings which are ignored – unrewarded – tend not to be repeated. We are often not aware that such learning is happening. So-called 'bad habits' are learned because something rewarding occurs at the same time. 'Problem teenagers' are seen as having been reinforced (rewarded) at the wrong time and for the wrong behaviour. It is important to remember that attention from a parent acts as a potent reward. Some teenagers who are desperate for attention have learned that 'bad' behaviour will get this attention. They will settle for annoyed, angry attention as being better than little or no attention.	Emphasises that we are what we are because of the pressures society puts on us to behave in certain ways. Behaviour is interpreted in terms of social roles which are learned from the models presented to us. People know what to expect of themselves and others in particular roles. A teenager may play many roles, for example: son, brother, pupil, friend, scout, consumer. Teenagers often feel unsure of their newly adopted roles. This is made more likely today because models are changing and people no longer 'know where they are'. The roles of women, for example, are changing. And work roles are changing for almost everyone, with rising unemployment and new technology. There can be external conflict if society demands that people play roles which they reject. Internal conflict occurs if people play roles which they find meaningless or inappropriate. They feel they are not being true to themselves, and this damages their self-esteem.
2 Example: peer groups	**2 Example: peer groups**
Behaviour which is not acceptable outside the group may none the less be strongly rewarded within the group. Many teenagers learn useful social skills – getting on with others – within their peer group.	Peer groups are seen as support for teenagers who need to free themselves from the oppressive power of their parents or other authorities. So-called 'deviant' groups are seen as an inevitable – and for the teenagers, appropriate – response to an unaccepting society.
3 Helping teenagers	**3 Helping teenagers**
The focus is on *learning skills*. Often, we need to unlearn ineffective, self-defeating habits, and learn new, more effective habits or skills. The theory emphasises *competency*, acquiring and using a wide range of life skills that the learner will value. The theory provides practical help for people who want to change their ways and build up their skills.	The focus is on *understanding society* – how it is changing, and how it may be changed. Society can both support and restrict the development of the individual teenager, who needs to be aware of its effects on him/her. He/she also needs to be able to identify what needs changing, and to take part in bringing about these changes. The theory emphasises *power* and *potency* – the inner feeling of power which helps to build self-esteem. People need to work together to bring about changes in society.
4 Pros and cons	**4 Pros and cons**
If you concentrate on building up one skill at a time, you very quickly get the reward of seeing that you can learn new skills. Small changes are quite easy but changing your whole lifestyle is much more complicated. For some people, making changes is difficult because of their poor self-esteem. They don't feel confident in their ability to make a certain change. They undermine their good intentions by running themselves down – to others and to themselves.	This approach avoids putting all the blame on the individual for any problems that he has. It explains why expecting the individual to change can not be the answer to all his 'problems'. It often shows the true target for blame to be the powerful 'shapers of society' – the structure of the economic system and the political beliefs of those in power. Taken to extremes this theory can emphasise the helplessness and impotency that many people feel when faced with the complex problems of society – and make them feel unable to help themselves in any way.

Parents' feelings

Feelings can get in the way of you helping your teenager.

It would be possible to read up all the books on adolescence, practise your skills, know where to go to get help – and still not be able to get on with your teenager. You need to be aware of your feelings too.

Your life experiences . . .

Without you realising it, your feelings can be getting in the way of your relationship with your teenager. Trying to ignore your feelings can only make things worse. You need to understand your feelings in order to use your life experiences to help your teenager.

. . . as a teenager

Memories of your own experience of adolescence will be revived by seeing your own teenager go through the same process. Hopefully you will remember times when you felt excited, challenged and competent to tackle life. However, this revival of old feelings is also painful because 'unfinished business' comes to light. You will remember things that you wanted to do but never had the chance to do. And, things you did, which you've regretted doing, but never had the chance to talk about.

Sometimes, although actual memories are not recalled, old feelings get stirred up and affect how you behave towards your teenager without your realising what is happening. Strong feelings such as envy and jealousy, which affected your relationship with your father, sister or friends, are revived.

Being the parent of a teenager is likely to make you more self-aware. It gives you the chance to rethink your own teenage feelings and behaviour. You will be able to see some of your feelings now as left over from the past and triggered off, rather than caused, by your teenager's behaviour.

Once you understand the origin of these feelings they may no longer interfere with how you get on with your teenager. If they still do, you can consciously decide what to do about them instead of unknowingly act them out with your teenager. You may choose to explain your feelings to your teenager so that he/she too can learn about old feelings getting in the way of present relationships. If you do this, be sure to reassure him/her that you don't intend to let your old feelings cloud your judgement now.

. . . as an adult

The life tasks and life events you have had to cope with since becoming an adult may also help or hinder you in your task of being a parent of a teenager. It would be unfortunate if this course gave the impression that parents' experiences were always negative and unhelpful. This danger really only arises because this book concentrates on the areas with which you may need help.

It's important for you to keep the balance and recognise your strengths as well as your weaknesses. Remember you will have built up a wide experience of life which will be immensely helpful to you as a parent. However inadequate you may occasionally feel as a parent, you do have an enormous amount of wisdom and skills to offer your teenager.

Self-awareness activities

Throughout this book there are self-awareness activities. These will help you to look at the effects of your past and present experiences on your relationship with your teenager.

Although these activities will increase your self-awareness, you may sometimes find them quite painful to carry through. However, since your feelings and attitudes can prevent you relating openly with your teenager, you may find that reading this book without doing the activities would be a waste of time. All the working knowledge in the world about adolescence is of little help if you don't also have a working knowledge of how your own life experiences can help or hinder you as a parent.

Helps and hindrances

A This activity asks you to review your experiences and see how they affect you in relating to your teenager as a person who is becoming sexually mature. It can take around an hour to do, so tackle it when you have time to reflect.

There are three sections. In each section:

❶ Step 1: Answer the questions in as much detail as you wish. Some sample quotes are given from other parents.

Step 2: Think about your answers in the light of the comments given. Rate your own experience as a possible 'help' or 'hindrance'.

Life doesn't often fall neatly into two such simple categories, so you will need to think about what different aspects of your

experience mean for you now. You may be aware of some conflict, where what you see as a help, your partner sees as a hindrance.

Step 3: Review the comments you have marked 'hindrance'. You will have been well aware of some of them, others may be new to you. In most cases we have made some suggestions as to what you might do about them. In general – and perhaps particularly where you and your partner disagree – talking things over with a supportive person is one of the best ways to come to terms with experience.

Step 4: Finally review your strengths – the experiences you know will help you as a parent. In the activities in this book it is just as important, if not more so, to focus on your strengths as well as possible weaknesses. Telling yourself about your strengths is a good way of building up your self-confidence.

Looking back

Recall your experiences as a teenager:

1 Would you say you were sexually inexperienced?

"Yes I believe you should 'keep yourself' for marriage."
"Yes – I concentrated on my studies and left sex till later."

If yes — because you chose not to: you probably had well thought out reasons for not doing so. This could be a *help* since you should be able to explain the values you held to your teenager. However it could be a *hindrance* if you simply try to impose, as an order, your opinions on your teenager.

"Yes – I was much more interested in motorbikes."

If yes — because you never thought of it: this could be a *hindrance* if you didn't realise that today's teenagers mature earlier and have many pressures from society to become sexually active. It could be a *help* if it prevents you from urging your teenager into too early an interest in sexual activities.

"Yes – I was tall, thin, spotty and painfully shy."

If yes — because you never had the chance: this could be a *hindrance* because you may want to encourage your child to have all the fun and excitement you think you missed out on – and so put pressures on him/her before he/she is ready. It could be a *help* if you now realise the importance of helping your teenager build up the social skills which will make it easier for him/her to get on with others.

2 Would you say you were sexually experienced?

"Yes – I think you should enjoy yourself while you're young."

If yes — and you enjoyed it: this is probably a *help* because you can pass on the idea that sex is fun and enjoyable. It may just possibly be a *hindrance* if you have a late maturing teenager who you encourage too soon.

"Yes – I used to try it on with every girl I met."
"Yes – I used to kid myself it was true love. I think I made myself really cheap."

If yes — but looking back you wish you'd not been: you may feel like this because what you were looking for was closeness and affection and you mistook sexual activities for true intimacy. This could be a *hindrance* if you pass on the

message that sex is cheap and/or nasty. It's definitely a *help* if you can now teach your teenager the difference between true intimacy, where you can share all your thoughts and feelings together, and sexual activities alone.

3 Were you made to think that sex was sinful?

"Yes – I was given strict advice about how far you can go. We used to keep pushing the limit back!"
"Yes – though it didn't stop me doing it. If anything, it made it more exciting. Funny thing is once we got married it wasn't as exciting any more."

If yes — but it made them all the more exciting: you may have begun to experiment too soon. Sexual excitement and guilt together can build up an anxiety that spreads over into everyday life. For these reasons it will be a *hindrance* if you pass this message to your teenager. If you now see things in a different light you could *help* your teenager think about why taking risks over forbidden activities are so tempting.

"I kept thinking 'Is this a sin?'. I could never relax."

If yes — and it put you off sex: this will be a *hindrance* and you need to talk over your problems with someone who can help you. It will be a *help* if you no longer feel like this.
You can explain to your teenager how to make his own moral decisions. Explain, too, why threats of sin are wrong because they can stop normal teenage sexual activities which are part of learning to live. They can also prevent the enjoyment of a vital part of a committed relationship.

4 Were you frightened about pregnancy?

"Yes – and I did fall. That's why we've a son of 14 and we're only 32!"

If yes: you were probably right to feel like that as you were unlikely to have been using an effective method of birth control. You are probably much better informed today. It will be a *help* if you can make sure that your teenager knows how to get advice and contraceptives if he/she does choose to have intercourse. However, your experiences may leave you anxious about your teenager taking risks. This may be true if you are still unsure about using birth control. This *hindrance* requires you to find out more about yourself.

Past feelings, present actions

A More or less unrecognised feelings from the past affect how you relate to your teenager today. Think carefully before you answer "No" to any of the questions below. √ Yes X No.

1 How do you respond to having a teenager now?

A Do you dress in teenage-style fashions? (Ask your teenager). ☐

B Do you almost compete with your teenager as to who has the most hectic social life? ☐

C Do you join in – or attempt to join in – your teenager's social activities? ☐

D Do you flirt with his/her friends? (Again – ask your teenager what he/she thinks). ☐

E Do you get worked up about the amount of money your teenager spends on clothes, hairstyles and make-up? ☐

Yes to any or all of these questions: suggests that you need to think carefully about another question: "Did you realise you were envious of your teenager?" The chances are that your first reaction will be to say "I'm not! It's just that . . ." and explain away your answer. In many cases, even if there is a grain of truth in your answer, you will almost certainly be trying to explain away a strong feeling that's too painful for you to own up to.

For example, you see your teenager looking lovely and dressed up in the latest fashion: this revives the old feeling of envy which you felt when your older, prettier sister was allowed out on dates when you were not. The feeling of envy may be revived without your remembering what originally caused it. If so, you may be surprised by the cutting remarks you make about your daughter's looks.

You may be tempted to explain this example away to yourself as just a typical psychologist's 'trick'. But try and take some time when you are on your own, or with someone who you can share such things with, and think back to your teenage years. You may recall being made to feel unattractive, inadequate or unpopular.

It's those old feelings that are making you so critical of your teenager now, or leading you to behave inappropriately as a teenager yourself. You need the chance to say to yourself: "Yes, it was rotten for me that . . . used to happen. I still feel hard done by about that". When you have talked, or thought over past feelings, it is easier to control them so they don't get in the way of your present relationship.

Unrecognised feelings that lead to inappropriate present actions are thus a major *hindrance*. Once explored – they can be a *help* because you will be able to help your teenager recognise and think about similar feelings. He/she will have fewer leftover feelings to be revived when he/she becomes a parent.

2 Do you encourage your teenagers to behave in ways of which your parents would have disapproved?

If yes: you may feel strongly that your decisions are right. But is there just possibly a little bit of defying your parents – 'getting your own back' – going on? You will need to detach yourself from such feelings and think about whether what you are encouraging is right for your teenager.

You may also need to talk over some of these issues with your own parents, if they are alive, and/or also talk with a supportive person who can help you come to terms with your differences.

Adult life events

A This section asks you to think about your adult life and how this affects the 'messages' you give to your teenager about sexual maturity. You may have experienced a supportive, committed, sexually-satisfying relationship with your partner. If so, you will probably want to pass on the value of such a relationship to your children. Even if you have every reason to feel bitter because you haven't had such a relationship, you probably hope that your teenager will.

For some parents, the questions in this section will prove particularly painful. This will certainly be true if, for example, you have decided that sexual relationships are not important. Many people who reach this conclusion do so because facing the alternative hurts too much. They would have to admit that "it was important, they had failed to achieve it, and the future was now too painful to look at."

Explaining away your feelings – in this case by denying the importance of something you want – is not a good way out. It's more difficult to admit that "Yes – it's rotten that I don't have a partner, life's not fair". But in the long run doing this makes you more self-aware, more open to other relationships, and more able to seek help. Knowing how to confront problems, and not shut them away, can be a great help to you as a parent, too. You can pass on to your teenager the value of such an approach.

Answer the questions in this section, and then review them in terms of helping or hindering. The comments should help you identify what you have learnt from your experiences that you would like your teenager to learn, too.

1 If you have a partner with whom you have a sexual relationship – how do you feel about this relationship?

Happy? This is obviously a *help* because you can talk about your own good experiences. But could be *hindrance* if you have little experience of, or sympathy for, the pain that unhappy relationships cause.

Unhappy? You should give top priority to getting help for yourself and your partner. Talking things over with an experienced, supportive friend should help. Or seek professional help from a marriage counsellor. Helping yourself is the best way to help your teenager.

Being unhappy will be a *hindrance* if it makes you envious of your teenager's happier relationships, and, if you are tempted to pass on messages that give narrow, unrealistic expectations of the opposite sex: for example, "Men always want one thing . . .", "Women never really mean 'no' . . .". Try to avoid "always" and "never" statements, and messages about not expecting much from relationships.

2 If you have separated or divorced, how do you feel now?

Has it made you disillusioned? As with the *hindrance* above, try not to let your bitterness be passed on to your teenager. Help him/her understand that the skills of personal relationships and love-making can be learned. Can you think it through and see what you can help your teenager to learn about avoiding relationships which will inevitably break up – or how to handle break-ups if they look like happening? Painful life events can be a *help* in that people often learn and change most as a result of them.

3 Has adult experience changed your views about subjects like:

○ faithfulness in marriage?
○ the rights or wrongs of extra-marital sex?
○ the morality of using birth control, or abortion?

It *helps* to review your values in the light of experience, even if you come to the same conclusion as before. It can be a *hindrance* to stick to values you adopted as a teenager, if these no longer fit your life. Here are two examples of changing values, provided by a marriage counsellor.

Changing a value which damages a relationship: Jill –
"We agreed in theory that ours would be an open marriage. When I want an affair, I think it's OK to be unfaithful. But when Paul had an affair, I nearly died of envy and hated him. When we talked about it, he admitted he felt the same about me. But he thought he'd lose me if he said so. I think we've settled down now because affairs aren't worth the pain they cause your partner. I'd like the children to understand this – without having to be too open about what we learned in our own marriage."

Changing a value which is hard to practise: David –
"We both thought that artificial birth control was wrong. But when we desperately wanted to make love and had to go without sex – because we were afraid of another pregnancy – we became very cold towards each other. I now think that the most loving thing to do is to express your love, even if it does mean using contraceptives. Keeping your marriage together is more important. That's what we'll teach our four children."

This activity

This activity has pushed you to examine in depth how your past and present experiences may help or hinder you in your relationship with your teenager. Sexuality was deliberately chosen as this can be a very difficult issue to examine. The whole area of the teenager's developing sexuality is discussed in Chapter 3 – 'Intimacy'.

There will be other areas of possible conflict with your teenager which you may find it helpful to look at along similar lines. For example:

○ how you feel about your teenager's new ways of thinking (Chapter 5)
○ the job you would like your teenager to do (Chapter 7)
○ how you feel about him/her taking risks (Chapter 9)

In each chapter there will be issues which relate to parents' feelings. Remember to ask yourself about:

1 Your experiences as a teenager
2 Strong feelings you have now which may have arisen when you were a teenager
3 Your current life events – and what you have learned from them

How do these all help or hinder your relationship with your teenager?

New body

At times, teenagers act like the children their parents have always known and loved – affectionate, considerate, close. On other days, there is a gap: sullen silence, leave me alone. Parents' reactions are equally mixed. Sometimes they feel warm and supportive; at other times, hurt, rejected and angry.

The reason for these intense feelings is not hard to find. As hormones begin to change the body, so the teenager needs to begin to move into his own world and live more independently. The problem for both sides is one of timing: when to hold on, when to let go.

The positive side of holding on is the support parents give to their children as they go through the physical changes of adolescence. The teenager's mind is full of questions about his/her 'new body', mostly unspoken. Information and understanding can reassure the teenager – and you, the parent.

Recognising and accepting mixed feelings will help too. It is quite common for both parents and teenagers to feel a little sad at the passing of childhood. But 'holding on' becomes destructive when it pushes parents or teenagers to deny changes. For example, some parents allow no make-up or freedom of action. And some teenagers unwittingly slow down development by keeping themselves undernourished.

At the other extreme, some parents push their teenagers too hard towards maturity. Yet letting go and giving responsibility needs to be a clear and gradual process. In some cultures, physical changes are marked by social ceremonies. It helps to acknowledge those changes in the family as well.

Your thoughts and feelings

A D This chapter asks you to become aware of your reactions to your teenager's 'new body'. Here are some typical questions which span the range of issues covered. You might like to spend a few minutes now, noting your immediate replies. After you've finished working on this chapter, review your notes and see if you think or feel differently.

○ How does your teenager's state of physical development now compare with yours at the same age?
○ What are your worries, if any, about your teenager's current state of physical maturity?
See Physical development, pages 46–49

○ When do you feel embarrassed by the clothes your teenager wears?
○ What do you think your teenager feels about the shape of his/her body?
See Body shape and self-image, pages 50–53

○ Compared with your teenager, how do you feel – fit and lively, or old and jaded?
○ What are your feelings about teenage masturbation – both generally, and in the case of yourself and your teenager?
See Enjoying the body, pages 54–57

○ Why do you think teenagers smoke and drink?
○ What are your greatest worries about your teenager's health?
○ How do you get on when you discuss health hazards with your teenager?
See Self-managed health, pages 58–63

2

Physical development

You need to understand feelings as well as know the facts.

Growing up fast

The time of fast growth and sexual development in adolescence is called puberty. For five years or so, changes in height, weight, co-ordination and sexual capability happen rapidly. The whole process is closely regulated by the body's internal time-keeping system. Chemicals called hormones control the growth and development of the body in all its parts. Sometimes physical growth feels smooth; at other times it can feel like a clumsy, runaway period of development.

Growth as a guide

It sometimes takes a while for parents to realise that their children have entered puberty. This is particularly likely with boys. Height, general build and voice may seem the same as ever, but in fact they will know that their testicles are growing bigger and that pubic hair is beginning to appear. But before long, they will begin to grow visibly much taller. In girls, this height spurt is the first sign of puberty.

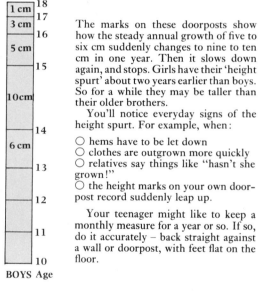

The marks on these doorposts show how the steady annual growth of five to six cm suddenly changes to nine to ten cm in one year. Then it slows down again, and stops. Girls have their 'height spurt' about two years earlier than boys. So for a while they may be taller than their older brothers.

You'll notice everyday signs of the height spurt. For example, when:

○ hems have to be let down
○ clothes are outgrown more quickly
○ relatives say things like "hasn't she grown!"
○ the height marks on your own doorpost record suddenly leap up.

Your teenager might like to keep a monthly measure for a year or so. If so, do it accurately – back straight against a wall or doorpost, with feet flat on the floor.

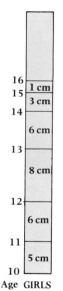

GIRLS

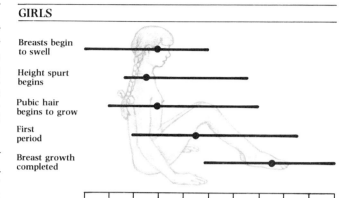

| | AGE | 8 | 9 | 10 | 11 | 12 | 13 | 14 | 15 | 16 | 17 | 18 |

Breasts begin to swell
Height spurt begins
Pubic hair begins to grow
First period
Breast growth completed

Is it the same for everyone?

There is a set order of events at puberty, which is different for boys and girls. Girls also tend to begin and end their sequence before boys. Some of the events are private to your teenager, so you won't know about them directly. But you can be assured by the latest visible sign that all earlier ones will have happened.

The charts (above) show that each event can begin anywhere along the line and be within the normal range of development. The blobs mark the average age of onset. Completion of events occurs up to five years later, anywhere between 13–18 years.

A You or your teenager might like to mark on the lines the age at which events occur for him/her. He/she is:

○ **normal** if events occur at any time shown
○ **average** if you mark near the blob
○ **an early maturer** if you mark far to the left
○ **a late maturer** if you mark far to the right

Remember these charts can only tell you *what* will happen next, not *when*. The order of the events may be fixed, but the timing of onset, and the gap between events, vary according to the individual.

Feelings about growing up

The charts in this topic describe the sequence of development and the actual events. Timing is important, for teenagers like to be the same as their peers. They may find it worrying to be bigger or smaller than their friends.

Accepting your teenager's thoughts and feelings – both positive and negative – about growing up, is important to aim for. As part of this process, parents need to become aware of how their own thoughts and feelings may affect their teenager. For example, you may be so proud of their growing up, that you leave them little room to be childlike still, or you may feel discomforted to have a sexually attractive teenager in the house. But it helps teenagers to know that – strictly from a parental point of view – their parents find them acceptable, attractive people.

Understanding the changes

When you try to understand what your teenager is experiencing, the first link you can make is with your own adolescence. But this can be misleading. Better living conditions mean that teenage development now starts earlier and goes further. Individual families differ, but on average, today's teenagers mature about a year younger than their parents did, and, age for age, they are several kilograms heavier and more than five centimetres taller. So when you find out that the attractive young lady opposite is only 14, your overestimation of her age isn't at all due to make-up.

One effect of earlier maturation is that adult needs begin to emerge earlier. Today's teenagers will feel the need for a private life with special friends, for some independence of action, and for some response to growing sexual feelings, at a

BOYS

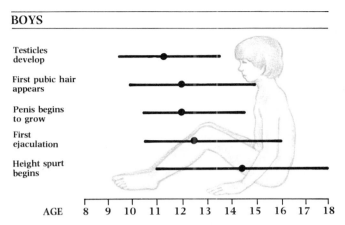

Testicles develop

First pubic hair appears

Penis begins to grow

First ejaculation

Height spurt begins

AGE   8   9   10   11   12   13   14   15   16   17   18

younger age than their parents did. The age and experience gap is usually widest between fathers and daughters. When father compares the behaviour of his 15-year-old daughter with himself at that age, he is out on two counts: one year due to the generation difference, and about 18 months due to the sex difference. He would be closer, and less surprised, if he compared his daughter with the way he was at 17.

Early and late

Some teenagers move into puberty very soon, others very late. Look at any class of 13 or 14-year-olds, and you will see a tremendous range of shapes and sizes. This is normal. When development is complete, there will be much less difference between them. But the differences during adolescence affect how teenagers come to see themselves.

Teenagers are influenced by comparisons with other teenagers, and by the opinions of other people. For early maturers, this is often an advantage: for late maturers, it can be a problem. Research studies suggest that:

Early maturers: look grown up for their age. As a result, they tend to get treated as more responsible by adults. They find it easier to compete and win at sport. Their self-confidence gets a boost, which is likely to increase their popularity. Sometimes the strain of being different, of being expected to behave, can tell. Boys may be less badly off than girls, because early maturity puts them in step with most girls of the same age. Girls, in particular, may find that their early maturity is sexually provocative – which can be a real strain for them.

Late maturers: look childlike for their age. They are more likely to be teased by their peers and – unless they are lucky – to be discounted by adults. Girls may be less badly off than boys because they come into line with most boys of their age. They may worry about breast development and periods starting, particularly if under pressure from apparently more-developed peers. Late-maturing boys seem to suffer the greatest pressure, and lack of self-confidence.

Your teenager

A **D** Over the coming weeks, you might like to note your own and your teenager's responses to their state of maturity. Some examples are given in the extracts below. In particular:

○ how does your teenager feel about his/her current state of physical development?
○ how does he/she compare him/herself with his/her peers?
○ what range of behaviour, from most childlike to most adult, does he/she show?
○ what do *you* feel about his/her changing body?
○ can you see times when you respond helpfully, as Paul's parents did, to your teenager's need for information and acceptance?
○ can you see times when your responses reflect your own concerns – past or present – more than those of your teenager? (See Sue and Richard)

Points of view: early and late maturers

"Susan is mature for her age - although occasionally her behaviour belies her appearance. She is responsive in class and I have enjoyed having her as a member of my form. She lacks a little confidence, perhaps because she is aware of being much taller than most of her 11-year-old classmates, but I am sure this will soon pass."

"I was giving Sue a cuddle the other day, when I suddenly became aware of her breasts against my chest. I told her to get off my lap because she was too heavy. I don't suppose I ought to do that sort of thing now she's a growing girl." (*Sue's father*)

"I get really pissed off, because I'm always supposed to set an example. Teachers say things like 'The whole class takes its tone from you. I'm relying on you to set the right atmosphere'. Then when I muck around, like anyone else, they go all hurt and make me feel I've let them down."

Here's the family photo I promised. You'll notice what a lot Richard has grown since you saw us last summer. He's 14 now, and almost a man already. I sometimes feel old, having such a big son. He's been captain of his rugger team and a class monitor this year - doing well...

"Paul is a hard-working boy who should do well in his 'O' levels. However, he seems to feel the need to compensate for his size by making more noise than most. He is co-operative rather than competitve."

"I sometimes felt rotten about being small. I wasn't good at sport or exams. I worried a lot about my body. Luckily my parents were good at praising things I did do well. I'm pretty together now."

The shape of things to come . . .

This spread charts the general sequence of changes at puberty. The pictures do not show an ideal or standard body – simply one girl and one boy. Each teenager is unique.

A You may find it helpful to show this topic to your teenager and to discuss it with him/her. The information can reassure you about what is happening. It can answer common questions, for example:

Girls growing up

1 Hips broaden and a thin layer of fat under the skin begins to round the body outline. Skin and hair may get oilier as oil glands become more active. A few pimples may appear if pores get clogged.

Soon after, breasts begin to change. The nipples often get larger and stand out more. The circle of skin surrounding them may get thicker and darker, and hairs may grow there. The breasts may take 3–4 years to reach their full size. They may grow unevenly.

2 Suddenly the girl grows faster, putting on up to ten cm within 12 months. This rapid growth can make her feel conspicuous and clumsy while she gets used to her new dimensions.

Pubic hair begins to grow – light, straight and fine at first. Gradually it gets darker, thicker and curlier. It spreads over the pubic area and back between the legs, often onto the top of the thighs. The clitoris and inner lips of the vagina grow larger. The inner lips may be different sizes and may come down between the outer lips. Body hair also begins to grow: in the armpits, on the legs and arms, maybe on the face. The pattern varies from family to family.

3 The first period happens – a shedding of the lining of the womb. It can start unexpectedly, or be preceded by a few days of stomach cramps or headaches. Headaches, irritability and cramping pains are linked to hormone changes. Usually a girl starts her periods about two years after her breasts begin to develop, and about one year after her pubic hair first appears.

If the girl has not discovered her clitoris before, then to do so now and begin to masturbate can be increasingly enjoyable. (See pages 56–57)

○ how will he/she know when puberty has started?

○ how tall will he/she grow?

○ how will she know when to expect her periods?

It is better to tackle any concerns you have promptly, because some problems of development are easier to deal with if detected early. If you are worried about the pace of your teenager's physical development after reading this topic – see your G.P. "What Next?" gives further sources of information.

Boys growing up

1 Testicles begin to get bigger, and fine, downy pubic hair appears. Testicles may grow unevenly, and it is perfectly normal for one to hang lower than the other. The area round the boy's nipples may get larger and darker and there may be some temporary swelling of one or both breasts.

2 The boy starts putting on weight and muscle, especially about the shoulders. His penis grows rapidly and erections become more frequent. They may be brought on by any kind of excitement – not just sex. At this age, boys worry a lot about the size of their penis. It may be helpful to know that penises are more alike in size when they are erect.

The boy suddenly grows much taller. Hair grows thicker on his face, in his armpits and round his penis, testicles and anus. Skin glands produce more oil and he may get pimples on his face, neck, chest and back as oil glands respond to changing levels of hormones. This may pass away and does not necessarily lead to full-scale outbreak of acne.

3 By now he will be able to ejaculate – producing a clear sticky fluid at first, which later becomes milky as the testicles start to produce sperm. His first ejaculation may come in his sleep – a 'wet dream'. This may happen fortnightly or monthly from then on. Most boys masturbate, some quite a lot – in which case he won't have wet dreams. (See pages 56–57 on fantasy and masturbation).

More hair appears – on the chin, legs, chest and maybe on his back. The thickness and spread of body hair isn't a sign of virility. It is a family or racial characteristic and in some boys body hair may be very scanty.

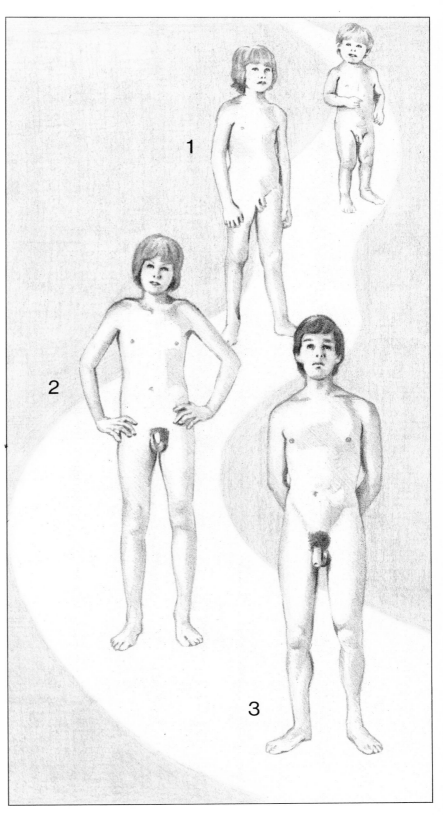

Looking good?

Appearances matter. They reflect self-image.

Looking right

Part of looking good is looking right. In the three pictures above, the couples are dressed correctly for their type of wedding. Looking right depends very much on cultural factors – on what groups in society you want to belong to. Your clothes send out a message about you as a person: "I belong here". Or, in the case of teenagers dressed defiantly for school, or a family outing: "I'm only here under pressure – I belong somewhere else".

It's not only clothes that send the message. Body language is involved too – the way people stand, move, look at others, gesture etc. Think of a person sitting elegantly, legs crossed, twirling a wine glass. Now think of a person sitting comfortably crosslegged on the floor, holding a beer-mug. These are different self-images. Body language can also tell you how the person is feeling – confident, nervous and so on.

All sorts of people and pressures help to shape a person's appearance and how they feel about themselves. For teenagers, peer group fashions and opinions are clearly very important. Here are some of the influences our parent testers mentioned as affecting the way they themselves look today:

"I had little money for clothes when I was younger – so I tend to buy lots of casual clothes now"

"I mostly wear neat 'classic' clothes and tint my hair to cover the grey – my husband prefers it that way"

"As chairman of the school governors, I feel it is necessary to dress 'safely' for certain functions. At other times I please myself"

"My figure doesn't encourage elegant clothes"

Body image

The way people feel about their body shape is very important. Build cannot be altered except by surgery or drastic weight change. Even then, the mental image – positive or negative – that the person has of their body is more important than the actual reality.

Body image often has little to do with reality. It is tied up with the way a person feels about themselves. Although that may be influenced by the way they look, how they feel will be reflected in their appearance. For example, a girl who *feels* confident in high fashion, will probably *look* more fashionable than the girl who isn't so sure of herself.

Pressures from all kinds of sources can make it hard for a person to like, or at least learn to live with, their body the way it is. Sometimes people find their bodies, or parts of them, so unacceptable that this colours their whole image of themselves. For example, a boy with slightly round shoulders may take no account of his strength or his curly hair: to himself, he's a hunchback.

Teenagers have to come to terms with a whole range of changes in their body and its shape. At the same time, they are re-defining 'who they are'. Small wonder if they are particularly vulnerable to comments and pressures about their appearance. The body image they develop in adolescence can last a lifetime. See overleaf for more details.

Your style – and your teenager's

A D Can you think of influences – job, money, body shape, age and so on – which have helped to create the way you look today? In particular, can you recall remarks from other people:

○ *helpful remarks* like "you look good wearing blue"
○ *restrictive remarks* like "no-one round here wears a suit"

Now think about the influences on the way your teenager dresses. Are these as reasonable in their own way as the influences on you? And in particular, what kind of remarks do *you* make to your teenager?

Most of our parent testers were fairly tolerant about clothes. Every now and then they'd 'have a go' about something. Many said that they tried to comment only when they liked what their teenager was wearing. The only trouble with that is, teenagers often interpret silence – usually correctly – as parental disapproval. Settling your differences openly is probably a more helpful thing to do.

Settling differences

A D Teenagers test the limits they can go to – sometimes deliberately, sometimes unintentionally – in the course of experimenting to find their own style. The following step-by-step approach can help you to settle differences of opinion with your teenager about appearance. It assumes that teenagers, as emerging adults, have the need and the right to be consulted on matters which directly affect them.

Before you approach your teenager:
Step 1: Try and sort out your own feelings about the situation. Completing this sentence can help to clarify it in your mind.

○ *I feel* ————————
(describe your feeling – embarrassed, angry, amused etc.)

○ *when he/she wears* ————
(describe the situation)

○ *because* ————————
(describe why you feel that way).

Step 2: Decide whether the particular situation is worth bothering about. List three or four reasons why the issue may be worth raising – and why it may not. If it helps, mark your reasons with one to four stars, according to how important you feel they are (**★★★★** = very important). Overall, do the reasons for saying something outweigh the reasons against? Often it's finely balanced.

Example
Reasons for talking to my son about dress:
He may lose his holiday job otherwise ★★
He's setting a bad example to his brother ★★★
Reasons against:
There'll be an almighty row between us if I do ★★★
He needs to find things out for himself ★★★

Step 3: Decide on the spirit in which you want to bring the matter up. The previous two steps should have helped to clarify how strongly you feel. Complete this sentence:

○ *I want to deal with it* ————
(describe your style – firmly, gently, mildly etc.)

Approaching your teenager:

Step 4: Begin by telling your teenager how you feel, and why. You have prepared for this in Step 1. You are telling him/her how you read his/her 'message'. It may not be what he/she intends. Avoid phrasing your feelings as criticisms which will make him/her defensive and unwilling to listen.

Step 5: Listen to his/her reply and check that you've got his/her message – both *his/her* feelings about the situation and *his/her* reasons for them. You might say something like: "You feel ———— because ————" and see if you have it right. If not, go over it again until you can both see each other's point of view.

Step 6: Work out a practical agreement. You should be able to put it into a few words, for example, "when we go to Gran's, you'll be cleanly but casually dressed". Make any vague words clear – for example, "casually" may mean cords and shirt to the parent, denims to the teenager. Agree on as broad a definition as you can and leave the final choices to the teenager.

This kind of step-by-step approach is developed in greater detail in the sections of the course on communications, decision-making and negotiation. Chapter 9 also looks at teenage limit-testing in a broader context.

Do you see what I see?

Parents and teenagers can clash over clothes because they want to send different messages about themselves. They may also read each other's messages differently. What you think of positively as your style (respectable, confident?) may come across as something else to your teenager (unimaginative, pompous?). Equally, your teenager's appearance may not look as good or appropriate to you as it does to him or her. For example:

Have you ever felt embarrassed by:
○ the way your teenager dressed when relatives came?
○ the way he/she dressed to go out?
○ what's printed on his/her T shirt?

Has your teenager ever criticised you for:
○ what you wear to his/her school?
○ wearing clothes too young for you?
○ what you wear to go to work in?

A You might like to talk over these points with your teenager, or discuss the two pictures below together.

○ what messages do you think father and son are sending about themselves?
○ what makes you read these messages – face, clothes, posture, hairstyle . . .?
○ who is each message mainly aimed at?
○ which message do you prefer?

Unspoken doubts and self-criticism are part of teenage development.

Judging yourself

Directly or indirectly, parents' views can affect how their teenager feels about his/her body. Directly, parents can make remarks which show liking and acceptance. Or they can make remarks which make teenagers feel they have something to be ashamed of. (The same goes for liking bodies of the opposite sex, too.) You may well be able to recall remarks made to you by your own parents, when you were a teenager. If so, that's a measure of the power of comment.

Teenagers are particularly sensitive to remarks about appearance and how these reflect on them as people. A careless joke about spots can really bruise the self-image. If you do say something which you later realise was hurtful, it will help your teenager if you can apologise and let him/her know you understand his/her feelings.

Indirectly, parents' own body image may affect their teenager. If you feel bad about your body, it can be hard for you to make positive remarks about theirs – particularly if they seem to have a 'body beautiful'. So it's important to take a look at your own body image – and how this may affect what you say to your teenager.

Got a clear outline?

🅐 🅓 Drawing yourself is a way to see how accurately your body image reflects your body shape. It doesn't matter what sort of an artist you are. Get a plain sheet of paper and without looking in a mirror, draw your outline without clothes. Then look at yourself in a full-length mirror, either naked or wearing underwear only. Notice the shape of your head, the slope of your shoulders, the length of your arms and so on down.

Did you get the shapes and proportions of your body more or less right? Did you have any surprises? Here are some things our parent testers said:

"I think of myself as shorter than I am"
"I made my hands bigger than they are"
"My shoulders droop more than I thought"
"I made myself look fatter than I am"

What are your feelings about your body-shape drawing and any surprises it gave you?

You may find it helpful to tell your teenager about this exercise as a way of talking about body image and pressures to look a certain way. If you share what you feel about yourself – be sure to remain positive in your remarks about your teenager. He or she may like to do a body-shape drawing for him/herself.

Fat and thin

Girls in our society tend to be under much greater pressure than boys to be slim and to conform to an ideal shape and size. For example, almost all magazine articles and advertisements for slimming are directed at women. It becomes harder for girls to accept themselves for what they are. Slimming pressures also often contradict other pressures a girl may be getting about maturity. Should she be slender or voluptuous? Childlike or womanly? Rigidly controlling the shape of her body can be a way to assert herself against all these pressures.

About one in every two hundred teenage girls suffers from a condition called *anorexia nervosa*. This is sometimes called 'the slimming disease' because the most obvious sign of it is a drop in weight due to excessive dieting. But this name gives the wrong impression. It puts the emphasis on slimming when the more basic problem is to do with self-image and how the teenager feels about herself.

At the other extreme are overweight teenagers who feel bad about their bodies and console themselves with eating. Being overweight and feeling bad about yourself is a double problem that isn't solved by diets which ignore feelings. In order to successfully reach a desirable weight, the person needs to understand her self-image as it is now, and as she imagines it could be. Many compulsive eaters have secret fears about being slim. They also feel there are advantages in being overweight. For example, one young woman said: "I'm a bit frightened at being thought of as sexy. And if I were slim, people might not take me seriously like they do now".

Other pressures

Parents' view and slimness are just two of the pressures on teenagers to judge their body in a particular way. The range is endless – to have clear skin/pale skin/straight hair, to look macho/tender/romantic and so on. Fashions change and so do cultures.

What's important is what each of these pressures means to the teenager personally. For example, thin is often thought of as "good", fat as "bad". It is these meanings which colour how the teenager feels about him/herself.

Buy yourself a new person

Advertising is another source of pressure on the teenager's body image. Some ads play on teenagers' worries about how acceptable they are physically. They suggest that they might be more sexy if they buy a particular spot cream, or use a particular razor, for example. And they may carry a clear message about what ideal maturity is – "you can tell a real lady by the way she shaves", for example.

A Your teenager needs to decide for him/herself what is a likeable adult body. So it can help to discuss the messages he/she is getting from advertising.

1 Find six advertisements for products which in some way affect a teenager's appearance. Try to find ads which are aimed at boys, or both sexes, as well as those for girls. (This can be difficult, for while ads directed at women often stress appearance, advertisements for men more often emphasise being 'manly', or socially at ease.)

2 Cut the ads out if you can, and stick them on a piece of paper with room to write notes. Note by each one the message you think it gives teenagers. In particular:

○ what kind of person can you be if you use this product?
○ what kind of person are you if you don't use this product?

3 Then invite your teenager to comment on your answers – and on the products. Would they like to be like the person in the ad? Do they think they might need to go out and buy this product?

Some examples from our parent testers are shown below.

Your teenager's replies may tell you something about how influenced they are by advertising. Do daughters differ from sons? Don't mock if they seem gullible, but do continue to question and discuss the ideals shown. If there is an ad which offends one or both of you, consider making a complaint.

Your teenager's replies may also reveal some of the things they'd like to change about themselves, and why. If you don't get an answer – don't press the point. It may be years before a teenager can admit to not liking something about their bodies, especially to their parents. The best thing you can do is to help them learn to live with their body – and hopefully get to like it better.

Enjoying the body

Sensuality, sport and sex provide new sensations for teenagers.

Using your senses

The teenager's new body demands new experiences, new activities. He needs to experiment, to try out different things to find out how they feel. The disappointments will be dropped, and the pleasing sensations repeated, until they form stable patterns of behaviour as habits and hobbies.

Parents have their own established ways of behaving. You may find it hard to try out exploratory activities with the gusto of a teenager. And you may feel just slightly envious of your teenager's fresh approach and youthful vitality.

Every once in a while, it helps to jolt yourself into reviewing the things your senses normally ignore. The following two activities may help to refresh you and to put you more in sympathy with teenagers' typically intense preoccupation with sensations.

What's going on right now?

A D The picture right shows a flood of sensations. There are things to see, hear, touch, taste and smell. And here's a mood or atmosphere.

Even in everyday settings there's plenty to be aware of. Stop for a moment, right now, wherever you are, and list all the different impressions you are gaining:

I can touch: —————————
I can taste: —————————
I can hear: —————————
I can see: —————————
I can smell: —————————
I can feel (mood): —————————

You may have quite a long list. Which sense(s) were you using most? Did anything surprise you? If you like, you might go on and imagine some other situations. Our parent testers suggested laying a fire, soaking in a bath, sitting in the garden, riding on a bus, for example. Or explore your own or your partner's face again. Look closely and carefully and describe what you see. Use your other senses too. There is always something new to discover even in the most familiar things.

Habits and hobbies

A D Many habits and hobbies give pleasure through the senses. Examples are listed under the main sense used. Do you regularly use each of your senses?

You and your partner or teenager might each like to see if you can note something you do in each of the categories. Again you may get some surprises.

Using sight: painting, drawing, photography, birdwatching, TV watching
Using hearing: singing, playing in a group, enjoying silence, listening to the radio
Using taste or smell: cooking, drinking beer, wearing perfume, smelling flowers, home brewing
Using touch and manual skills: DIY, sculpture, bread-making, knitting, sewing, car repairing
Using body sense and movements: sport, dancing, massage, yoga, mime

Family work-out

A D The teenager's new body sense means that – given the opportunity – he/she will get extra enjoyment from sport and exercise. Equally, there may be times of awkwardness or poor co-ordination, when some parts of the body are developing faster than others. You may need to encourage your teenager to help his/her new body in trim. As a parent, you are an important model for your teenager's behaviour. What you do – and don't do – will influence the way he/she views exercise and body sense. Studies show for example that:

○ only 40–60 per cent of school-leavers play any active sport
○ even fewer parents take active exercise, and overall they have less leisure pursuits

Look at the many benefits you and your teenager may get from any activity. In the chart:

Tick under **A**: The benefits you each already get

Tick under **B**: The benefits you would like to have

See where you disagree: This exercise may highlight where you find it hard to value each other's concerns. For example, a stay-at-home father may feel jealous of his son's sporting successes. A slim mother may daunt her chubby teenager daughter. In Column A, have you ticked benefits that your teenager does not have? (And the reverse). In Column B, are there benefits that your teenager wants that you do not? (And the reverse).

See where you agree: If you both leave the same items blank in Columns A and B, talk about why this is. Is there a family tradition, for example, that "our lot are no good at sport?" If you have both ticked the same item(s) in Column B, you may want to develop new activities separately or together. You'll need to consider your abilities and interests – and constraints in terms of time, money, family routines, local resources. See "What next?" for ideas on new things to do.

	Becoming more active can help you to:	Parent A	B	Teenager A	B
PHYSICAL	1 work hard for long periods without tiring too quickly				
	2 have plenty of energy for everyday tasks				
	3 have muscle strength for lifting, pushing etc.				
	4 bend down and stretch up for things easily				
	5 be agile and graceful				
LOOKS	6 trim your·figure by toning up your muscles				
	7 lose some weight				
	8 keep your body feeling young				
HEALTH	9 ward off heart disease				
	10 have a feeling of well-being				
	11 beat the stress in your working life				
RELAXATION	12 relax and feel refreshed				
	13 meet people and socialise				
	14 enjoy yourself				

The S in Sport is for . . . . .

Suppleness
the ability to move freely. You need exercise which moves your joints

Strength
the ability to lift and push. You need exercise which makes your muscles work.

Stamina
the ability to keep going at an energetic activity. You need exercise which helps your heart and lungs.

Sensation
when suppleness, stamina and strength are used in a sociable, enjoyable activity such as swimming or dancing.

Sexual pleasures

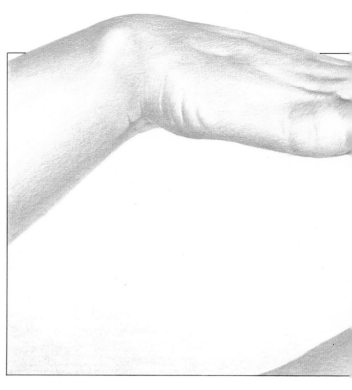

It's OK to congratulate yourself on being fit. Enjoying using your body in sports and hobbies is fine. But what about enjoying the sexual powers of your body?

Some people have concerns about enjoying – or admitting to enjoying – sexual activities. They may have learned from their parents that sex is not to be talked about – or only to be referred to in dirty jokes. Or they may have been so inhibited that they have never discovered just how much sexual pleasure the body can give. When our parent testers looked back over their own youth, here are some of the things they said:

"I was brought up that only men should enjoy it – I find it hard to relax in case of enjoying it too much."
"I was always told that masturbating was harmful and should never be indulged in."
"I wasn't allowed to be alone with a boyfriend in the evening – though somehow it was OK in the daytime."
"Physical contact wasn't part of our everyday life."

Your own views and values will affect what you say to your teenager. They will also affect your response to this topic. Some of our parent testers found it reassuring. Others were embarrassed. A few found it virtually unacceptable. What do you think about discussing sexual pleasures?

Many parents find it hard to talk to their teenagers about sex in direct, personal terms. But many teenagers interpret silence from their parents as disapproval.

When talking to teenagers about sex, it's important to respect their privacy – and to protect your own. You shouldn't expect to share the details of your sexual activities. The main thing is 'giving them permission' – reassuring them that it is OK to explore how their body responds and to look forward to enjoying an active sex life.

Of course you want to make clear the values you hold about what are appropriate adult sexual activities. But equally you need to be clear that your teenager will eventually choose his or her own values. Parents' own concerns and problems should remain just those. It doesn't help to pass them on to the teenager. One of the best ways to help your teenager may be to take time to sort out your own feelings. The activity on pages 40–43 may help. And "What next?" lists sources of information and counselling.

Giving permission

A ◑   The chart right will give an indication of how you respond to your children's sexual activity.

Column A Tick √ if you think the situation is morally acceptable in principle. Put an x if not.

Column B Tick √ if you would allow this situation for your own children, when the time/occasion arises. Put an x if not.

Column C Tick √ if you have already permitted such a situation – or at least turned a blind eye to it. Put an x if not.

You might like to explore your thoughts and feelings with your partner, or a close friend, about situations you mark x. In particular, look for two patterns to talk over:

1 *You're unable to allow something which you believe is generally acceptable* (√ *in* **A**, x *in* **B** *or* **C**). This may be a leftover guilt from your own youth. Or you may be worried about how other people would react if they knew you permitted this. Talking over how you would actually handle the situation, may help you to have the courage of your convictions.

2 *You're going along with something you believe to be wrong* (x *in* **A**, √ *in* **B** *or* **C**). If so – have you just kept quiet about it, out of respect for your teenager's freedom? Or have you discussed it and told him/her how you feel? Disagreements of this kind are better faced. Both of you may change your views in a discussion where you are open with each other.

As a parent would you:	A	B	C
Let toddlers play with their genitals			
Let young brothers and sisters share a bath			
Let young children see you naked			
Turn a blind eye to soft porn in your teenager's room			
Accept a teenage son masturbating			
Accept a teenage daughter masturbating			
Leave a teenage couple alone in the house			
Let your teenager sleep with boy/girl friend at home			
Accept your teenager using birth control			

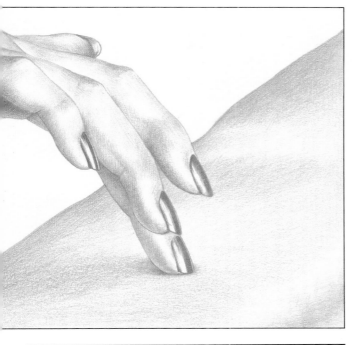

Fantasy and masturbation

Fantasy and masturbation are major sexual activities for most teenagers. This worries some parents. But they can be helpful ways by which teenagers learn to enjoy their bodies and to build up pictures of their own sexual identity.

Daydreaming is a part of life. In their imagination, teenagers can safely try out roles they don't have, or don't actually want, in real life: the revolutionary, the hero, the great player, the amazing lover. Sometimes fantasies are sparked off by books, music or watching TV. Very often they take over at unexpected and inconvenient moments. The teenager finds him/herself staring out of the window when he/she should be working, or suddenly silent in conversation. The fantasies that fill his/her mind are fascinating, but they may be frightening.

This can be especially true of sexual fantasies in which the teenager experiences new, intense, sexual feelings. Sexual fantasies are important because they are a way to rehearse what it's like to be a sexually active adult. It's helpful for teenagers to know that fantasy is a very common activity. Equally, fantasies are highly personal and private, *certainly not to be shared with parents*. Sometimes they are shared in a limited way with friends of the same sex.

Boys may discuss their fantasies using the current sexual words crudely and aggressively: jerking off, banging, screwing and so on. Girls are more likely to talk in romantic, emotional terms of their dream boy. The magazines they read exaggerate this difference – 'true love' stories for girls, explicit sex in adult magazines for boys.

Such differences reflect society's traditional views of the roles of men and women. These can make it hard for boys to value or put into words their need for tenderness and shared gentleness. Girls can find it just as hard to be open about the sexual side of their romantic dreams.

Many people now believe it would help development if girls had a bolder, and boys a broader, view of sex. This might make it easier to reach sexual maturity, in which excitement and tenderness go together. Such an approach is used in therapy to help adults improve their sex lives. Masturbation is also seen as important in helping people explore and understand how their body responds.

Masturbation

People of all ages masturbate. Sometimes instead of, and sometimes as well as, sex with a partner. How they masturbate –and when and where – varies from person to person.

Masturbation is now seen as a normal part of development. It is one way in which teenagers learn to know and accept their bodies, and get started on a happy sex life. They learn what gives them pleasure and can later share this with a partner. Masturbation can also provide comfort that has little to do with being turned on by sex. It can be a way to relax or to get to sleep. Or to console yourself when you are temporarily feeling 'fed-up', lonely or depressed. There is nothing wrong with this – many couples use love-making for exactly the same purposes.

Acknowledging that masturbation is OK, can help a teenager take a positive approach to building up an enjoyable sex life. It can help him/her feel relaxed and prevent him/her feeling guilty. Sexual pleasure mixed with guilt can be an anxiety-provoking combination. If a person learns from repeated experience to link sexual excitement and guilty feelings together, it can be very difficult to unlearn, and may even be carried over into sexual relationships with a partner.

During masturbation, you learn to associate the exciting feelings with the time, place, fantasy or technique used. So there's something to be said for teenagers learning to masturbate in ways which will not limit their sexual response with a partner. For example, it may occasionally be fun to masturbate while looking at erotic pictures, or to imagine that your partner is a famous film star or sex-symbol, but it's miserable if that's the only way you can get turned on.

Another sort of problem would be if you could only have orgasm in a position that can exclude intercourse with a partner. For example, a girl may learn to have an orgasm only with her legs pressed close together. Similarly, it could be a problem if a boy got into the habit of masturbating only in the presence of other boys.

Your views

Your own experiences and attitudes will affect how you react to this approach to masturbation. After reading this topic, several of our parent testers wanted to think over their own views further: "I'm not sure I agree – but it's refreshing to have another opinion". Some decided to talk it over with their partner – "their father should be aware of this topic" – or with someone close. Others decided to talk to their teenagers, though sometimes saying "I feel I need more information first".

If you want information or support – see the listings in "What next?". Chapter 3 explores values about sex in more detail, and looks at the 'how' and 'when' of sex education.

Self-managed health

Are risks worth taking?

When your children were younger, you were probably pleased and proud to see them begin to do things for themselves. During adolescence, the milestones of independence may cause you worry rather than delight.

Taking risks

🅐 🅓   It is a vital part of teenage development to experiment and take risks. Teenagers need to discover what they really do like and who they really are. Experimenting with different activities, lifestyles, views and feelings is part of this process. Without taking risks your teenagers will not find their own sense of what is and is not safe and sensible.

Some parents think that some things in life are just too risky to experiment with. You might put drink, or drugs or pre-marital sex in this category – it depends on your values. The problem is, forbidding something always makes it more attractive to teenagers, and unless you keep them under lock and key, you have no sure way of enforcing your opinions.

Equally, it is hard to stand by and watch your teenagers come under influences that you dislike. They may, for example, put their health at risk by smoking, drinking or dieting. This topic looks at how you can discuss with your teenagers the choices they face, and how they can learn to manage them in a way that, it is hoped, will satisfy you both.

What risks did you take?

Think back for a moment to your own adolescence. Tick which of the following you tried at any time:

smoking more than five cigarettes a day ☐

drinking beer more than three times a week ☐

drinking spirits regularly ☐

riding a motor bike ☐

hitch-hiking ☐

staying at a party all night ☐

mountain-climbing/pot-holing with a friend ☐

trying marijuana ☐

going on a crash diet ☐

sniffing glue or other solvent ☐

having sex without using a contraceptive ☐

riding a bicycle in a busy street ☐

There are risks – some greater than others – attached to each of these activities. You almost certainly took some yourself, even if your teenage days were different from now. All our parent testers could tick at least one item in the list. They said that what they'd found helpful were adults who'd said "OK – if . . ." and suggested acceptable compromises. Can you recall what adults said to you about the risks you took? Which of their approaches were helpful – and which weren't?

Looking at your own experience can help you see that risk-taking is a part of living: you probably still take some risks now. It's a particularly important part of growing up, and the approach adults take can make a great deal of difference.

You might like to go over the list again, and mark the activities you think your teenager may try. What approach will you take now? This topic looks specifically at dealing with the risks involved in smoking, drinking and dieting. But whatever the risk you are trying to deal with, here are some 'ground rules' you may find useful to follow.

Ground rules

1 Remember that risk-taking is an important part of teenage development – even if it worries or frightens you at times.

2 Make sure you and your teenager are well-informed. If you want more information, see "What next?" for details.

3 Model your preferred way of life. If you expect your teenager to say when he/she'll be home, make sure *you* don't roll home hours later than you said you'd be.

4 Discuss risk-taking with your teenager. Try to agree what he/she can do to make the experimenting relatively safe. Think about what you can do to help make it safe.

5 Negotiate and bargain if you need to. For instance, you might get agreement on no motorcycling, if you are prepared to give way on other risks.

6 Don't pry. Your teenager will manage many risks unaided. But tell him/her of any behaviour you would find serious enough to seek outside help or inform the police, for example.

7 Remember that your aim should be for your teenager to learn to manage his/her own life and health.

Smoking

Most teenagers are well-informed of the dangers of smoking, but the risks to health seem a long way off. It's most helpful to focus on how you discuss the subject – and on the practical help you can give.

What would you do?

A John, 15, is doing a CSE course at school. His mother has recently found out that he is smoking. If you were John's parents would you:

A Tell him not to smoke?
B Not mention it?
C Talk to him about why he smokes?

Circle the option you would choose.

John's father circled (**B**). In his view, smoking was a phase every teenager went through. He thought John was a "sensible lad who'll grow out of it left to himself".

John's mother circled (**C**). But when she tried to talk to him, John became angry, said that it was his life and that she just didn't understand. She replied just as angrily that it might be his life, but it was her money he was spending and she wouldn't stand for it. They glared at each other. John went out to meet his friends – and to have a cigarette.

How do the three options meet the ground rules (left)?

(A) Tell him not to smoke: John's parents were quite right to think that telling him not to smoke would be ineffective. This approach does not meet the ground rules for dealing with risk taking.

(B) Not mention it: John's father was right in thinking that many teenage habits are phases that will be grown out of naturally, if the teenager is left to get on with it. Unfortunately, smoking is not one of these habits. It quickly becomes addictive. Smoking is one of the hardest habits to break, and one of the most damaging to health. So while this option would meet the ground rule about not prying, it would meet none of the others.

(C) Talk to him about why he smokes: John's mother was right to circle (**C**). Talking to your teenager is the only way you will find out *why* smoking has become important for him or her. Through discussion you may be able to influence him/her a little or give him/her the support he/she needs to refuse cigarettes. This option is the only one likely to meet the ground rules for dealing with risk taking. John's moodiness and his mother's temper combined to produce a row. Afterwards, John's mother realised she'd failed to explain her real concerns – or to find out why he smoked. She resolved to try again.

Why do teenagers smoke?

A If you are to give your teenager real help in giving up or refusing cigarettes, you need to know why he/she smokes. Some possible reasons are listed below. If your teenager smokes, ring the reasons which you think are most important for him or her. If he/she doesn't, ring the reasons you think apply to most smoking teenagers.

1 He/she enjoys a cigarette
2 It's something to do when bored
3 It helps him/her concentrate
4 It's something to do with his/her hands
5 He/she doesn't want to feel left out
6 It helps him/her feel relaxed
7 It helps him/her to feel grown up.

Check your answers with your teenager. The comments below suggest ways you might help. If you smoke yourself, you may find this hard. You may be ashamed of your own example, or feel that you haven't a leg to stand on in asking him to give up. Try to admit your feelings, and your own smoking problems. Use yourself as an example of what to avoid. And perhaps strike a bargain – you'll cut down, or not smoke indoors, if they do too.

Reason 1: If you circled this, your teenager may have the habit already. See "What next?" for help in giving up.
Reasons 2,3,4: If your teenager is willing to give up, these reasons can be the easiest to tackle. Help him to think of other solutions to problems of boredom, concentration, nervousness.
Reasons 5,6,7: These are the reasons why most teenagers smoke. They are social reasons. The pressure of the teenage group can be very powerful. If your teenager would like to refuse cigarettes you may need to build his/her confidence so he/she feels able to.

Refusing cigarettes can be hard. Suggest that your teenager develops his or her own line for times when just 'no thanks' won't do.

Drinking

By the age of 14, most teenagers have tasted alcohol. By the age of 17, 98 per cent have done so. It is parents who usually first introduce their children to alcohol, on special occasions. But a large minority of teenagers learn alcohol use from other teenagers.

Some parents feel that even though moderate drinking is the social norm, that does not make it morally right. But while parents can make their own choices clear, they cannot insist that their teenager follows them. The teenager must choose his own moral stance – which will almost certainly involve some experimenting with drink.

Research suggests that drinking in the home is likely to be under parental supervision, and controlled. Forbidding alcohol in the home increases the chances that teenagers will learn to use it elsewhere. Licensing laws do not prevent teen-age drinking outside the home, merely force it underground. So drinking outside the home often comes to involve more drink than other situations. It is also more likely to carry with it anti-adult, anti-authority attitudes.

It may go against the grain of your own beliefs – but it is reasonably clear from research that parents who treat drink-ing as moderate, ordinary behaviour, are most likely to have teenagers who do the same. Heavy teenager drinkers tend either to come from tee-total families or from families where there is heavy drinking within the family. This is often within a society which admires heavy drinkers as being able to "hold their drink".

What would you do?

A Inevitably, mistakes occur in learning alcohol use. For example: Carol is 16 and enjoys the occasional drink with her parents – especially on family occasions such as birthdays. One Saturday evening she went out with friends and arrived home noisily after midnight. The next morning she felt ill and confessed to spending the evening in a local pub trying various spirits. Carol's father was distressed by this episode and worked out that he had the following options:

1 To speak sharply to her and forbid her to drink
2 To suggest that she try different drinks at home
3 To remove all alcoholic drink from the house
4 To invite her friends in and provide alcohol at home
5 To make her drunk again to "teach her a lesson"
6 To do nothing
7 To give her a chance to discuss what she might do in the future

Carol's father decided to try a mix of options **2** and **7**. Circle the option(s) that you would choose.

Discussing drinking

There are also some ground rules for discussing risks.

Choose your time: Teenagers easily become defiant, angry and cornered. Even if they want to, they find it hard to climb down in an argument. So – if you want a discussion – find a way to open it in a relaxed way. In particular:

○ Keep an open mind and don't make accusations. High spirits may be just that – not a sign of drunkenness.
○ Find out the size of the problem. One drunken night doesn't mean you have an alcoholic on your hands. A brief chat may be all that's needed.
○ Try not to be judgmental. Moral judgements and good advice don't usually go down too well with teenagers.
○ Try to be supportive. Help your teenager to make up his/her own mind about what he/she wants. It's his/her life, even if at times what he/she does distresses you.

Carol was willing to accept her father's suggestion and on a number of evenings tried various drinks with him. In the relaxed atmosphere of a shared glass of sherry she was pre-pared to discuss what she felt about drinking, with her father.

Share your concerns: That means really listening to your teenager's views, as well as discussing your own.

It turned out that Carol was quite well-informed about the risks of drinking – though she hadn't bargained on the added ill-effects of mixing drinks. The danger of alcoholism seemed remote to her, but she did worry about driving with

someone who had been drinking. She also worried that she might one day drink so much as to fall asleep and choke on her own vomit. A fear Carol felt unable to discuss with her father was that drink made her more easily aroused sexually. She worried that she might be tempted to sleep with someone without using contraception.

Carol's father explained that he was worried that she was breaking the law by drinking in pubs. He was worried about the kind of people she might meet there. He was worried that she might get so drunk as to be unable to get home – or that she might accept a lift from someone who had been drinking.

Come to an agreement: Make sure your discussion comes to some conclusion – even if it's that you can't agree yet.

Carol and her father struck the following bargain. Carol would only drink fruit juice or coke in pubs. In return, her father would make sure there was alcohol at home that she could try and that she could offer her friends when they came round. Carol also agreed not to accept lifts from anyone who had been drinking. In return, her father agreed to share the cost of a taxi with her, if that was the only way she could get home. They discussed ways she could refuse drinks and lifts home.

Reviewing your options: the options Carol's father chose helped him to keep all the 'ground rules' for dealing with risk-taking. Option **4** might also have done this. Options **1,3,5,6** would be unlikely to do so. If you have chosen these in the past – try again, following these guidelines for discussing drink.

Why do people drink?

A In discussing alcohol with your teenager, remember that his/her reasons for drinking may be just as good as yours. You might want to compare your reasons, using the checklist.

On the whole, these are accepted reasons for drinking. For teenagers, social reasons for drinking can be particularly important. There may be few places to go except the pub, where there are pressures to buy rounds and drink alcohol. And research suggests that, within reason, teenagers see drinking as tough and sociable. Heavy drinkers are seen as

Reason	True for me	True for my teenager
I like the taste		
It makes me feel relaxed		
It makes me feel good		
All my friends do it		
I need to buy a round like everyone else		
It makes me feel grown-up		
You can't sit in a pub and not drink alcohol		
Other		

cynical, mature, while abstainers are seen as weak. Both are regarded as unsociable.

It can be useful to discuss these aspects of drinking. You may be able to offer a new angle. For example, you might look at alternative benefits to be had from money now spent on alcohol, or at the positive sides of people who drink little or nothing.

No-one knows when to stop drinking once they've started – so it helps to discuss the limits beforehand. Legal limits are best explained in terms of the effects of drink, rather than the age of the teenager. If you don't drink yourself, can your teenager try drink under the supervision of other adults? If you think your own drinking behaviour is a model to avoid, can you explain to your teenager why?

What worries many parents most is the kind of behaviour that heavy drinking can lead to – rowdiness, aggression, dangerous driving. So in your discussions, concentrate on finding safe situations where your teenager can experiment with drink without it leading to other risks.

Eating

Peculiar or faddish dieting is a problem that mainly affects girls. But both boys and girls need to learn to take control of their own eating habits. They need to stop relying on *you* to decide what they eat and when they eat it. They need to develop their own ideas about reasonable eating.

The risks connected with bad eating habits are less dramatic than those connected with smoking or drinking. Some you might consider are these. If your child doesn't take over responsibility for his own eating he may reach adulthood:

○ unable to plan a healthy diet
○ unable to choose and decide what he/she likes
○ unable to cook for him/herself
○ unable to budget and shop for him/herself
○ unable to maintain a reasonable weight

These risks may seem paltry compared with your fears about other teenage habits. However, your child may develop real health problems over food if he/she doesn't learn a healthy diet for him/herself. He/she will also be socially at a disadvantage if he/she can't cook, budget or shop.

In discussing eating with your teenager try to follow the ground rules given on page 58 for all risks. They can be just as important here.

Eating patterns

A Eating patterns are learned at home. Some parents:

1 Use food as a reward: "Well you've tidied your room so you can have an ice-cream."
2 Overeat at mealtimes: "Well I shouldn't – but I will just have another roast potato."
3 Offer constant snacks: "Have some milk and a biscuit – lunch isn't ready quite yet."
4 Withold food as a punishment: "You'll go to your room and don't think you'll get any supper."
5 Give food instead of affection or attention: "I'm busy – get yourself some cake and don't bother me now."
6 Force children to eat without choices: "I cooked it for you and you'll eat it all."
7 Don't help teenagers to build a positive body image: "You're getting fat, just like your mother."

○ Which of these happened to you as a teenager? Circle the numbers of any that did: **1 2 3 4 5 6 7**
○ Which of these happen in your family now? Circle the numbers of any which do: **1 2 3 4 5 6 7**

All these situations happen in most families from time to time. If they happen all the time, they will make it hard for your teenager to develop his own ideas about sensible eating. In numbers **1,4,5** for example, the child is learning that food can be used as an exchange for good behaviour or as a substitute for feelings. In numbers **2,3,6** the child is learning that food is something that he has little control over. In number **7**, the child is learning to connect the desire for food with being unattractive.

SELF Alice Brown		PARTNER Paul Brown		CHILD Sue (12)		CHILD P
What did you eat?	Who decided you eat this?	What did you eat	Who decided you eat this?	What did you eat?	Who decided you eat this?	What did you eat?
BREAKFAST tea one crispbread	self	tea 2 slices toast	self	cereal 2 slices toast tea	self	cere ban coff
MID-MORNING coffee 2 biscuits	self	coffee	self	bag of crisps apple	self	cok chi bisc
LUNCH (too busy)		lager 2 sandwiches	self	salad with meat pie	school canteen	ham chi fru cus
TEA TIME cup of tea 2 biscuits	self	cup of tea	self	tea & biscuit	self	tea bis
SUPPER Meat pie potatoes cabbage fruit salad cream	self	Meat pie potatoes cabbage fruit salad cream	Alice	meat pie potatoes cabbage fruit salad cream	Mum	mea pota cab fru
SNACKS —		peanuts & a beer	self	chocolate	self	pe

Who decides what you eat?

A D Look at who makes the decisions about food in your family. Pick a day that you think is fairly typical, and draw up a chart like the example above. Ask each member of the family what they ate, and who decided this.

When the Brown family looked over their eating patterns they found it was, on the whole, Alice who organised the food for the family. She was responsible for the weekly shopping. She planned all the evening meals. To some extent she decided what everyone ate for breakfast by what choice of food she had in the house. Susan pointed out that her mother never took into account that she might choose something at lunchtime, which her mother might cook in the evening. Alice noticed that she herself had developed a habit of eating sugary snacks during the day.

As a result of talking over their chart, the Browns made several changes in their eating patterns. Susan suggested that Alice and she planned the meals for a week, so that everyone would know what they would be eating in the evenings. Alice agreed to this idea and suggested that perhaps everyone might take a turn at doing the cooking and shopping. Peter and Paul said they'd organise weekend breakfasts. Alice decided to try and change what she ate as snacks, and maybe lose a pound or two.

About half our parent testers resolved to let their teenagers have more say, or to give them more responsibilities. The others said that their teenagers already took a full share – or that there were 'good reasons' why not. It's worth looking twice at your own good reasons. For example, it may seem most economic for you to do all the family's shopping and cooking, but is that most helpful in terms of your teenager learning to care for him/herself?

Healthy eating

Your teenager may be well-informed about diet. Many schools teach nutrition in biology, home economics or general studies classes. Some general rules for a good diet are:

○ cut down on animal fats
○ eat plenty of wholemeal bread
○ eat more raw fruit and vegetables
○ cut down on red meat and eat poultry, fish or pulses
○ eat fillers like potatoes in their jackets, pasta or rice (without oily sauces or dressings)
○ cut down on sugar

Daughters in particular may be influenced by the food and diet suggestions they read about in magazines. Some of this advice is good. Some is not. "What next?" lists some reliable sources of information about diet and nutrition. But information alone is not enough; choices about food are bound up with the way the family organises itself and the relationships parents have with their children. If your teenager helps to:

○ choose and shop for the food the family eats
○ prepare and cook food
○ make meals for him/herself or the whole family

then he/she is learning to make his/her own choices. You may need to talk further with your partner or teenager about why they need to choose – and how you will let them.

Of course, there are constraints: money, time, what's in the garden, who's where, and so on. But you manage these, so they must learn to. Be prepared for both mistakes and surprises. The more you can talk about the choices and decisions you each are making, the more likely you are to arrive at a plan of healthy eating for the whole family.

Rarer risks

So far this topic has looked at some very common areas of experimenting which can affect teenagers' health. There are a variety of other risks which a minority of teenagers may run. Some of these are described briefly below. Further sources of information and support are given in "What next?"

Extreme eating habits

A minority of teenagers – especially girls – develop eating habits which may reflect their concerns about themselves and which can seriously affect their health.

Fast and binge: is a pattern of gorging alternating with dieting. It occurs in all weight groups. It seems to happen when a bout of overeating combines with anxiety to shake the teenager's self-confidence in her control of her own eating habits.
Bulimia: may develop from fast and binge eating. The person rapidly learns how to make themselves sick after eating. They may also use laxatives. The problem seems linked with poor self-image. It can be difficult to detect because the girl usually just looks slim and doesn't have apparent problems with the opposite sex.
Anorexia nervosa: is a condition where the teenager refuses to eat and starves herself in the belief that she is unattractively fat. She may lose weight to the point where her periods stop and her health is in danger. Anorexic behaviour can be seen as the result of not wanting to grow up physically, or of trying to control your body because you have no real control over the rest of your life.

Glue sniffing

Glue sniffing is a teenage habit which worries many parents. Unlike drinking and smoking, it is something none of your generation thought of. Its very strangeness can make it seem one of the most dangerous things your teenager could get into.

The main risks in glue sniffing are that:
○ fumes from glue can cause damage to the liver and brain
○ using plastic bags to increase inhalation can cause suffocation or lead to choking on vomit
○ because it is so unacceptable, glue sniffing tends to be done alone or in isolated places. If something goes wrong, the teenager may not be found or rescued easily
○ the teenager may do something else dangerous while under the influence of the glue

If you are worried about your teenager experimenting with glue, forbidding it – or ignoring it – are probably not the most helpful solutions. The ground rules for dealing with risk-taking still apply. Try to discuss the risks with your teenager; and possibly suggest ways of minimising them, for example: don't do it alone/with a bag/in an isolated place.

Drug taking

Yet again, the ground rules apply to experimental drug-taking. There is a clear difference between this and using drugs as a solution to identity problems. See Chapter 9.

Intimacy

What are you expecting to find in this chapter? Try answering the above question quickly – 'off the cuff', then spend enough time to give a considered answer to this question: "What are you hoping to find?"

What you are *expecting* to find will probably depend on what you have seen and read elsewhere about sex and relationships. Many books when considering teenage relationships concentrate on the physical side and what can go wrong. They give the impression that the mechanics of sex, birth control, pregnancy, abortion and VD are the *key* topics. It is hoped that by now you are used to the rather different approach of this book. It asks you to spend time thinking about your own feelings, attitudes and values, and deciding, in the light of what you know about your teenager, how best you can help. This is particularly true for this chapter.

Many of our parent testers said they were *hoping* for an emphasis on:

○ the importance of friendships
○ sexual activities as part of a caring relationship
○ the need to consider emotional as well as the more obvious sexual risks.

Perhaps the title – "Intimacy" – has raised questions in your mind?

Our approach

There is no way a chapter like this can be written so that everyone agrees with it. We focus on helping you decide what you think is important and 'right'.

However *our* values underlie our approach and should, perhaps, be made clear:

○ intimacy, in its true sense – a warm caring relationship in which you know you can be completely open about yourself – is important throughout life
○ a close friendship with someone of the same sex is valuable in its own right
○ teenagers should not be pressured into sexual relationships before they have learned how to be intimate with people
○ good sex always involves caring; not just getting good feelings
○ that intimacy is vitally important in long-term committed relationships, not just the sexual side.

Talking to your teenager. This needs to be handled particularly sensitively. Teenagers sexual *activities* are a private area: *respect their privacy*. They need this privacy – it's an important part of establishing their separate identity. Unfortunately asking their opinions and trying to understand their values is often interpreted by teenagers as prying into their sex life.

Your feelings. The subject matter of this chapter can arouse strong feelings. Working your way through this chapter will help you examine these feelings. They are important. They affect the way you behave. Some of the activities are about linking your own experiences, past and present, with the stage your teenager is at now. They aim to give you a feel of what your teenager is preoccupied with, and to help you see things from their point of view. If you look at your own experiences before studying the theory, the theory often makes more sense to you.

Best friends

Everyone needs friends to share their lives.

"We go almost everywhere together. She stays at my house sometimes, and we talk half the night! Sometimes we talk on the phone too, if we can't get out. I know she can keep a secret. She's honest and tells me if I sound like an idiot or look a mess. We like the same things and have a laugh together. She's my best friend."
Mandy, 15.

"Nick, my brother, and I were sitting at home with Mum and Dad one night. Nick looked out of the window and said, 'Look — here's Lorraine and John coming'. Quick as a wink my mother said suspiciously — 'What have they come for?' I tried to explain 'They're just our friends' — they don't have to have a reason to come round!"
Kathy, 15.

Do you remember?

A **D** Spend five minutes recalling what you were like as a teenager. Can you picture your best friend at the time? Perhaps you met at school or at a club. You probably shared some secrets together, like who you had a crush on and didn't dare tell. What did the two of you do when you were together? Where did you spend most of your time? Did your parents influence it at all? What did your parents do or say about the friendship?

Perhaps you've re-awakened the excitement of a special friendship, and spent much longer than five minutes thinking about it. You might be feeling quite nostalgic about the happy times, or sad that things have changed. You might have regrets or feel angry that your parents interfered. A whole range of feelings are natural. Although you might recognise the things you have lost since you were a teenager, you might also be aware of what you have gained. What's nice about being mature, for you? When you have finished, you might want to discuss your memories and current feelings with someone close to you.

Everybody needs friends

A friend is someone who likes you for who you are. We all need friends to talk with about our thoughts and feelings, to share everyday matters and special events.

Young children tend to have friends who are just convenient and pleasant playmates. Parents meet their emotional needs giving praise and love. Young teenagers try to have a large number of friends.

During teenage years friends become particularly important. Deeper friendships are possible at this age because teenagers are now more able to see another person's point of view and sense how they feel.

One of the great things about friendship, particularly for teenagers, is that it helps you to learn about yourself. Friends help you to discover yourself, your identity. You learn the skill of disclosing things about yourself. Friends support you, and in some ways take over from your parents. They can give you information and advice as well as emotional support and companionship.

What kind of friendship?

The word 'friendship' is often loosely used. It can refer to different levels of relationship. At one extreme is the relationship with the person you say "Hello" to at the bus stop. At the other extreme is your love for a person who you'd trust with your deepest secret. People who we only know casually are *acquaintances*. *Friends*, on the other hand, show strong mutual support and loyalty to each other. They tend to have a similar view of the world. The deepest level of friendship is *intimacy*, the relationship between best friends.

Intimacy does not necessarily imply a sexual relationship. Unfortunately, intimacy has come to mean sex in many films and books. For example, the television lawyer who asks a witness "Were you intimate with Mrs. Smith?".

We sometimes know a person first as an acquaintance and later the relationship deepens. It's good to have relationships at all different levels. Best friends can open themselves up to each other. They share their thoughts, feelings, values and experiences. In doing so they can be hurt. You just can't be intimate with someone without risking being hurt. Parents are often upset to see their children hurt in this way. It's a risk anyone takes if they want a deep and sharing relationship. The rewards of friendship usually make it worthwhile.

Areas of intimacy

You may say that there's no-one you hold all the same values and views as. Dan, for instance has a good relationship with his wife, but they disagree on politics. He has a good friend who is a member of the same political party, but they only meet at political functions and they talk politics all the time. They know little about each other's home lives. Their political friendship is very important to them both. Most of us have intimate relationships something like Dan's, built on particular activities or values. A common example is a friend at work. You may confide in each other about worries over relationships and tasks at work, but never meet socially. Both of you value your intimacy. In short, with some people such as "work friends" or "church friends" we share only certain areas of our lives intimately.

Different types of friends

Our friends tend to be people who are about the same age as us, and live nearby. They tend to share our attitudes and values. But we may be completely different to our friends in personality, intelligence or popularity.

Friendships with older people can be valuable too. Often in these friendships the younger person benefits from the older one's knowledge and experience in a subject they're both interested in. The older person, too, benefits from the satisfaction of passing on knowledge and experience. It's also stimulating to be with someone full of youthful energy and excitement.

Best friends are usually of the same sex, particularly among teenagers. We have more in common with people of our own sex, so they're sometimes easier to understand and get to know than the opposite sex. Usually they're easier to confide in, and this is accepted in our culture. Confiding in someone of the opposite sex doesn't seem right to some people. A close friendship with someone of the same sex is valuable in its own right throughout life.

Teenagers' relationships with their same-sex best friends help them learn what it means to be a man or woman. It also gives them practice in close relationships. This practice can later benefit them in their intimate relationships with members of the opposite sex. A teenager who doesn't have a best friend or who drops their friend for a member of the opposite sex early on may miss out on learning these things. Particularly if this relationship becomes sexual before the couple have become intimate in the true sense of the word.

Are friends better than family?

Friends can do some things that the family can't. Younger teenagers' friendships are often very intense. Their friendships help them find the answer to "Who am I?" and "What are the different ways I can be me?". When they have a more confident sense of their own identity they can be more tolerant of other people's differences in their friendships.

In many areas teenagers consider their friends to be more expert than their parents. They might value their friends greater expertise and advice on things like:

○ events at school
○ what to wear to a disco
○ which bike to buy.

Can you think of five things which your teenager's friends know more about than you do?

What about your friends?

🅐 🅓 We have already given a description of friends and acquaintances. Now give your definitions in your own words by completing the following sentences:

1 To me, an acquaintance is _____
2 To me, a friend is _____
3 To me, an intimate is _____

Think about your own pattern of friendships for a few minutes. Look at your pattern of friendship in terms of:

○ the acquaintances you have, of both sexes
○ the friends you have, of both sexes
○ the intimates you have, of both sexes

Then think about the kinds of friends you want, but don't have. This is what Joe said about his friendships:

"My only close friend is my wife. I lost contact with my best friend, Bob, after I married. It's a shame, because I used to enjoy the occasional evening out with him. He's a mechanic, too, so we sometimes talked shop and always knew that the other person understood your problems. I have a lot of male acquaintances and a few women ones. I met most of them at work. Some of the men are real friends, but I wouldn't be totally open with them. I know they'd stick up for me and lend a hand if I needed it. My 19-year-old son has friends of both sexes. I'd like that too, but I suppose I think a married man shouldn't. I think I'll try and contact Bob. I'll be a bit more friendly with the women at work too."

When you have thought about your own pattern of friendships, see how they compare with your teenager's. Styles and patterns of friendships often change as you grow older, so don't expect your teenager's friendships to be like yours. And of course, your teenager is an individual with a personality of his/her own. You may have loads of jolly friends and be very outgoing. He/she may be quiet and prefer a small circle of friends. If he/she's happy, that's fine. Also, the situations you are in and the roles you play might influence how you behave, and the friends you have. In some jobs it's easy for workmates to become friends. In others, you may be expected to keep a certain distance from people.

Your feelings

A What do you feel about your teenager's same-sex best friend? Tick your answers, and then discuss with your partner, if possible.

I wish he/she'd spend more time with a group of friends.	————
I don't know what they spend all their time doing together.	————
I'm pleased he/she has such a friend.	————
I'm worried he/she'll be led astray.	————
I think he/she's missing out on opposite sex friendships.	————
I'm afraid it means he/she might be gay.	————
I'm pleased he/she isn't showing any interest in the opposite sex yet.	————

Your hopes for your teenager's friendships

A **D** Our hopes for our teenagers say something about our own lives both past and present. We hope they'll succeed where we failed, or that they'll succeed as much as we did. Complete the following sentence to sum up your hopes for your teenager's friendships.

"As far as friendships go, I hope my teenager . . ."

Ask yourself:
○ Are your hopes for your teenager's friendships realistic? For example, you might be wishing your daughter would settle down with a nice young man. She needs time to get to know herself and might have several boyfriends before having a 'steady'. And, in any case, she will always need same-sex friends. Another unrealistic hope might be if you wanted your boy to stick with the buddy he had when he was nine or ten. You might think "He was such a *nice* little boy!", but he'll have grown up too, and they may have grown apart.

○ What would you have thought if your parents had had the same hopes for you? Perhaps you can remember your parents criticising every friend you brought home. It was as if they had to pass a test.

Discuss your answers with your partner, if possible. You might find you have different expectations. You might even find that you're judging all friends of the opposite sex as if they were future sons- or daughters-in-law!

Teenagers' comments on their parents views:
"My parents don't seem to think I can pick my own friends sensibly. My mum thinks they're older, so they're bad." "My mum's bothered about age. It's not age that's important. It's your own child and how they behave. Whether they're responsible or not." – both girls, 15.

What do you think your teenager thinks of your views of his/her friends?

Help or hindrance?

The purpose of this activity is to get you to think about the ways in which you can help or hinder your teenager in the way he/she spends his/her time with friends.

D In the left-hand column are several ways in which teenagers spend their time with friends. Make your own list and write down the ways *you* could help them get on with these occupations in the 'help' column. Write down the ways *you* might hinder them in the 'hinder' column. We have filled in examples from our parent testers, but you may disagree with their answer in your own circumstances.

Teenage occupation	How parents can 'help':	How parents can 'hinder':
A Sitting chatting in the bedroom	*Leave them to it*	*Insist they sit with the family*
B Going to the disco	*Give them a lift home*	*Say it's too late to be out or go as well!*
C Staying overnight at a friends' house	*Trust to behave*	*Keep phoning and checking*
D Trips out with friends	*Encourage provided we know the friends*	*Point out all the things that could go wrong*
E Holidays away from home with friends	*Say OK if part of an organised holiday*	*Keep on about not getting into trouble*
F Hanging around on street corners	*(Ideally) give them a 'cosy room' for personal use*	*Say "I FORBID THIS"*
G Teenage parties in your house	*Stay in the house*	*Want to stay around*
H Conversations about heroes	*Listen*	*Mock them*

Comments: Some of our parent testers couldn't think of things they did that might be a hindrance. Do you too consider that everything parents do is 'for the best'? In some cases when 'helps' were discussed with their teenagers the teenager didn't see them in the same light. Often the 'helps' were interpreted as 'hindrances'. What the parents thought of as well-meaning, they saw as interference. This certainly seems to be a tricky area for some parents and teenagers.

What is a help in some circumstances might be a hindrance in others. For example, if your daughter is trying to get rid of an over-attentive boy who she isn't keen on, she might be relieved when you appear and ask for her help with something. If she's interested in the boy, your appearance might be unwelcome.

Ask your teenager what he/she thinks of your answers and if he/she can think of any alternatives. A discussion with your teenager might be quite difficult if you disagree strongly about how you should respond. This exercise will be more constructive if you both agree to listen to each other's point of view without criticising it, before discussing the pros and cons of both of your suggestions.

What is important to your teenager?

A D Think about your teenager with his/her best friend. To get a broad view of them, picture them having a lark, talking seriously, engrossed in an activity . . . Imagine them in a wide range of activities. Then write down at least five ways in which you might complete this sentence:

My teenager's friend is important to him/her because . . .

Here is what two of our testers wrote:

Parent A
1 They have the same sense of humour and can laugh and joke together
2 They are both 'tomboys' and enjoy similar activities
3 They have known each other a long while
4 They are intellectual equals
5 Though basically similar in outlook the two families have different lifestyles and the girls enjoy sampling each other's.

This mother adds: *"My teenager agrees with these points"*.

Parent B
1 They laugh together
2 They enjoy the same kind of music
3 They support each other
4 They advise and encourage each other
5 They are company when needed.

Are *you* right about the importance of your teenager's friend?

Mistakes

Children often look at their parents and decide what they will copy or try to avoid about the way they relate to other people. In this way, by observation, they can learn from their parents' mistakes without actually being told what to do differently. But even if their parents could tell them, seeing for yourself is far more effective. Looking back at your own parents, can you remember:

○ what you liked about their relationship and tried to copy; for example, they paid a lot of attention to each other
○ what you disliked about their relationship and tried to avoid; for example, their relationship was very unequal. "He took all the decisions and treated her like a child."

If you were brought up in a one-parent family, or a two-parent family where both partners quarrelled most of the time, you may find it difficult to answer these questions. Perhaps you knew another family well enough to recall how the parents got on together?

It's not always easy to take a different course from the last generation. There are many people who've said, "I'll never behave like that" but then find that they do.

Even if your teenager has an unhappy relationship, he/she'll probably learn something from it. He may decide not to try to make friends with someone so bossy again. Or she may decide she was too submissive and she'll try to stand up more for herself in future. One mother, talking about her 17-year-old daughter's first boyfriend said: "I objected, but only because he treated her badly. But I thought, perhaps she'll learn from her own experience. If she happens to like the boy, then let her get on with it and then perhaps it'll wear out. And it did."

Looking back at your own friendships, can you see any mistakes that you made? What did you learn about what you might do differently? It's worth discussing these with your teenager when the opportunity arises. Even if he/she doesn't learn from your mistakes he/she will learn that he/she, too, can learn from his/her own mistakes.

Values about relationships

Most people have strong views about relationships and sex.

It's important to explain to your teenager the values you hold about relationships and sex. Understanding how you came to hold your values, and how your values may have changed since you were a teenager, will help you do this.

Values – a mind of your own

Personal values give meaning to life and arouse deep feelings. Parents try to pass on the best of their conclusions and guidelines for life to their children.

Teaching values isn't simple, because the essence of a value is that it is thought about and freely chosen. You can't just accept another person's values wholesale. Teenagers tend to scrutinise the attitudes and traditional beliefs of society. They challenge your values, and experiment with new ones. This is what choosing your own values is all about. You may have looked forward to the stimulation of a questioning teenager. Or perhaps dread having all you hold dear rejected. Chapter 6, "New Directions", looks at the whole field of values. In this topic we focus on values about relationships and sex. These are frequently challenged by teenagers, as demonstrated by these remarks made to parents:

"Whatever you say, I'm not going to get married. I'll just take lovers and get pregnant when I feel like it." (16 year-old-girl)

"I think you're awful the way you spend so much time sitting around in the house instead of living it up with friends." (14-year-old boy)

"I don't see why I should visit Gran in hospital. I'd rather play football." (13-year-old boy)

It's vital for teenagers to question values. They see a whole array of different standards around them, and they experience new sexual feelings inside themselves. This might be particularly difficult for parents to cope with. For example, you might see your son's or daughter's new approach to sex as a direct attack on the way you have tried to bring them up and on all you hold dear about family life. It can be very painful to have your values questioned, attacked and maybe rejected. Maybe your teenager just seems to ignore your values in favour of their own or their friends' values. You may feel confused, angry or sad. On the other hand, a parent might flush with pleasure to hear their teenager express a value which they hold themselves. This is particularly true if the teenager has reached that conclusion themselves after a thorough investigation of its implications and alternatives.

You need to explain why you hold the values you do. But you also need to practise what you preach. Really what you do may be more important than what you say.

If dad preaches about marital fidelity and then leaves his wife for his lover, what do the children learn about the value of fidelity? Your teenager is highly likely to learn this kind of a lesson from other adults. You need to point out the hypocrisy of such actions. Otherwise, by your silence, your teenager may deduce that saying you hold one value, but acting as though you don't, is OK provided you don't get found out.

If your teenager is to form his/her own values successfully it is important that *you* stick by your own values. It isn't helpful for you to agree with everything your teenager says, just for peace and quiet, nor to rant on about how right you are. A good policy is to say where you stand on whatever the issue is, but be prepared to help your teenager sort out the value he/she wishes to hold; then do your best to understand and accept what he/she decides on.

Sources of influence

A **D** This activity helps you think about how you came to hold your present values. The boxes show possible sources of influence. For each box write:

○ a brief description of how it affected you – or –
○ quote something said to you which has stayed in your memory.

We have added comments from our parent testers to start you off thinking.

Your teenager has grown up in a different world to you, possibly under a different set of influences. He/she may like to work through this activity on his/her own. If you are willing to share your responses it would start off a good discussion about values.

Marriage
'You can't live together in harmony until your two sets of values are sorted out.'

Work
'Value of co-operation!'

Friends
'Don't betray your friends.'

Divorce
'Knowledge I could cope as a single parent. My mother did and made a good job of it!'

Films, T.V., books
'Oklahoma – fantastic! Rod McKuen's poetry.'

School
'Self-discipline is important.'

Values

Others
'In-laws made me question values of my own family.'

Boy/Girl friends
'Boy friends certainly put your moral values to the test!'

Parents
'My mother used to say "Don't let the buggers get you down." It taught me to value assertiveness.'

Religion
'One can be Christian without going to church.'

Adult education
'Gave me confidence and a goal to work for. I realised I had something to give.'

Family
'Grandma gave me a feeling for the past and a desire to keep what was best of her attitudes.'

It's OK to undo the package

A whole bundle of values often comes wrapped up into one package. "This is what the church teaches" package, or "Here is my package of values". Some values do seem to go together. But most people examine each one separately taking into account their own experience and circumstances.

Even after twenty-odd years *you* might still be wondering about some important questions to do with sex. Your behaviour, if not your values, on this subject might have changed over the years. Certain circumstances might have put your values to the test. For example, you valued faithfulness until you met someone you fancied much more than your spouse. Or perhaps you thought abortion was always wrong until you were faced with the anguish of someone dear to you who desperately wanted an abortion.

Have you changed?

A **D** This activity helps you review how your values about sex may have changed. Below are some questions concerned with values about sex. You may find that the values you hold about your own behaviour (column A) are different from what you feel should apply to other people (column C). If you agree with the statement put a tick. If you disagree put a cross. For columns **B** and **D** put a tick if your values have changed since you were a teenager.

	A	B	C	D
1 Is it OK if people kiss and embrace in public?				
2 Is it OK to have homosexual relationships?				
3 Is it OK to masturbate?				
4 Is sex before marriage OK for men?				
5 Is sex before marriage OK for women?				
6 Is it OK for a woman to ask for what she wants in lovemaking?				
7 Is it OK to get a divorce?				
8 Is it OK for a woman to be unfaithful?				
9 Is it OK for a man to be unfaithful?				

Comments

Your values Look at your ticks in columns B and D, which show where your values have changed. They will give you some idea of how much you have changed your original package of values.

For each change:

1 Can you remember what influenced your initial values on the subject?
2 Why did you change your views?

You and others Consider how the values you apply to yourself differ from those you would apply to other people (✓'s and X's in columns **A** & **C**)

1 Ask yourself why you believe something may be OK for you but not for others, or not OK for you but OK for others.
2 In general would you say your values are more 'permissive' for yourself – or for others?
3 How many ticks do you have in column **B**, and in column **D**? If your totals differ – how would you explain this difference?

Values change towards acceptance of divorce and homosexuality were the two changes most often identified by our parent testers. Here is what two of them said about homosexuality:

"Have changed values on most things. Attitude to homosexuality changed after seeing *The Naked Civil Servant* some years ago on TV. I was most moved by John Hurt's sensitive performance as Quentin Crisp – really made me re-think my attitudes."

"I changed my values about homosexuality because, as I grew older and met homosexuals, I realised that they weren't a threat to me at all (I did feel that they would touch or try to seduce me when I was a teenager), and that they were just as entitled to their choice of relationship with other people as I was to mine. As long as they don't force themselves onto people who don't feel the same way – then live and let live."

Your values and your teenager

You may well have noticed that you have undone your original package of values about sex and relationships. Now that you have reviewed your values, which do you want to pass on to your teenager? Have you been offering a whole package which you expect him/her to accept? Perhaps even more importantly – are you offering a package of values that is 'higher' (more idealistic) than those you live up to yourself? If so – what do you hope to achieve by doing this?

In the first stages of value formation young teenagers will usually accept the whole package that is offered to them. As they become older they will re-think these values and choose for themselves. They will do this by:

○ looking at values from a variety of view-points
○ listening to the opinions of others
○ considering the problems posed by holding certain values
○ putting their values to the test.

The original package you offered your teenager will undergo a long process of remodelling before it becomes something that belongs to him/her and that he/she is happy with.

How do their values compare with those their parents hold? Will the couple be acceptable to either of their families?

Clash of cultures

To some extent most teenagers are brought up in a different culture to their parents. They grow up about a quarter of a century later, for one thing. The differences are most obvious in families where the parents were brought up in a different country to their own children.

Children may be exposed to two very different sets of values at home and at school. In some families, for example, girls may be expected only to prepare themselves for marriage, by learning the skills of a good housewife and mother. This can clash with expectations from school that pupils will do homework in the evenings. The family values the traditional female role of home-maker, wife and mother: the school values academic progress. Another clash might occur between parents and teenagers, where parents put loyalty to the family above everything else, and the teenagers don't.

Even if teenagers may rebel against their parents social and cultural values in their teens, they are unlikely to accept their peers' views wholesale. They work out a middle course, making the best of both worlds as applied to *their* situation.

Many parents fear that their teenagers will discard their clearly held sexual values. They see the younger generation

as loose-living, immoral and lacking in self-control. However, despite the popular – and long-held – view that there is a generation gap, recent surveys show that most teenagers respect their parents' ideas and opinions about major life issues and respect them as people. On the whole, the values of peer group cultures are more likely to reinforce the values of the adult world than to oppose them.

Although superficial expressions of the values may differ, underlying values may be the same. For example, adults may prefer a particular hairstyle or a style of dress. Teenagers may prefer something wildly different. Both generations usually conform to what their friends like. So if conformity – in this case showing you are part of a group by dressing in a similar way – is the important underlying value, then both adults and teenagers are expressing this value in their own way. Of course, they might also be valuing "make yourself look attractive to the opposite sex", and just be expressing it differently.

Fill in the spaces in the story below to show how you would respond to your teenager's imaginary relationship.

My teenager announced that he/she was going to bring home a new 1 _____ friend. They had known each other for 2 _____ already, so I was 3 _____ meeting the friend. I want to know if my teenager's friend 4 _____. I was 5 _____ to learn that the friend was the kind of person who 6 _____. The friend came from 7 _____ so I was 8 _____. Their friendship seemed 9 _____. I thought this would be 10 _____ for my teenager.

Ask someone else (your partner, friend or teenager) to complete the activity too. When you have both finished, discuss what your responses say about your values concerning relationships and people. You may find that your teenager 'sends you up' if he/she fills it in. If so he/she is probably telling you a lot about what he/she sees as your 'hang-ups'.

Here are some questions you can ask about your particular answers. The answers they refer to are given in brackets after the question.

A Was the sex of the friend significant to you? (1)
B Do you want to meet your teenager's friends early on in the relationship? (2,3)
C What kind of friends do you want your teenager to have? (4,5,6,7,8)
D What sort of friendships would you like your teenager to have? (9,10)
E Would you have answered differently if you had made the friend a boy instead of a girl? Or a girl instead of a boy?

Dating teenagers: the parent's role

What is the parent's role?

You may be clear about your values when thinking of them in theory. But what happens when your teenager starts dating?

The parent's role

When your teenager is dating what is your role:

○ chauffeur?
○ chaperone?
○ educator?
○ guardian of morals?
○ shoulder to cry on?
○ advise on where to get help?
○ keep out of the way?
○ turn a blind eye?

This list isn't complete. Add any others you think are relevant.

These roles cannot be simply defined. They will depend on the people involved and the situation. You will feel very different about a shy 13-year-old going out with the local wolf for the first time, compared with a 16-year-old girl and her steady boyfriend whom you know and like. The next activity looks at some of your possible roles.

What would you do if . . .

A This activity gets you thinking about your role in a number of different situations. If they later occur, you will be less likely to be caught unawares.

You might like to try role-playing these situations as a way of rehearsing them before, or in case, they happen to you. Ask your partner, or a friend, to pretend to be your teenager, while you experiment with what you would say. Try out first of all what your immediate reaction would be and ask 'your teenager' to give you some feedback about what it feels like. Swop roles some of the time so that you play 'your teenager' and your partner has a try.

For each case try to sum up what you would do. Would your partner tackle the situation differently? Would one of you deal with it better than the other?

1 Jane, 14, doesn't have a boyfriend. All her friends have. She feels left out. What does she do or say to let you know?

2 Your son, 16, wants to entertain his girlfriend in his bedroom. They've been going out for six months. (Does your answer depend on what time of day it is?)

3 Mandy, 16, has known her boyfriend for three weeks. They say they are in love and want your permission to marry.

4 It's 11 p.m. and Winston and Linda have been kissing goodnight on the front doorstep for half an hour already!

5 You arrive back home earlier than expected and walk into the living room and find your 14-year-old daughter only half-dressed. You have burst in on a petting session with a young man you've never met.

6 Your son, 17, has love bites on his neck.

7 His girlfriend lives ten miles away. There are no buses. You are spending a lot of time driving him to her house, or taking them out somewhere.

8 They've had their first row. Your daughter is very upset.

9 Sarah, 14, has been seeing a lot of Dave recently. She still hasn't brought him home to meet you.

10 Your son Stefan, 18, and his girlfriend Gill, 17, have been going out for 4 months. You suspect they sleep together. They ask you if they can sleep together in your home.

11 He's painfully shy with girls and wants to talk to someone outside the family about it.

12 Paul is meeting his girlfriend's parents tomorrow for the first time. He's nervous, and wants to make a good impression on them.

Your answers

Would your answers have been different if all the boys were girls and vice versa? Your answers will depend on your own values and attitudes. Perhaps you feel you should turn a blind eye to some of the situations altogether. For example you may feel that 4, 5 and 8 are best ignored. With 5, why did you come back earlier than you said? And why didn't you knock on the door before going in? May be *you* need to apologise?

You may need to ask yourself – "Are there things about my teenager I *shouldn't* know?" Teenagers want (quite rightly) to keep large areas of their lives private, particularly from their parents. To parents who say "But my teenagers tell me everything", it's tempting to suggest that either the teenager is good at telling lies or else the relationship is inappropriately close. Teenagers should be growing away from their parents and establishing their own identity. Of course it's difficult for parents to 'win' in these situations because they have the delicate task of respecting their teenager's privacy whilst also offering a listening ear whenever it's needed.

Some of the situations require you to be a good listener and to be willing to negotiate. In other cases you may need to know where your teenager can seek advice. "What next?" and the course pack will help you build up your listening and negotiating skills, as well as sources of help for both you and your teenager.

Our parent-testers thought that situations 5 and 10 were the most difficult to cope with. It seemed for situation 5 that their embarrassment at finding their son or daughter like this would make it difficult not to burst out with something which they felt they might regret once they had cooled down.

With situation 10, many parents felt they would face the dilemma of having previously taught their son that he should not 'sleep with a girl'. If chastity *is* an important value to you, then it's also important you should say so and you've every right not to allow them to sleep together in your own house. But many parents felt that they needed to think over in advance just what they did believe. It seems that it is one thing to privately suspect what he is up to and quite different to openly condone it in your own house.

This was also one of the situations in which partners were likely to disagree. There isn't an easy solution to such disagreements. A lot of talking and listening is always involved where parents disagree with their teenagers.

Style-talk

One of parents' roles might be to discuss with their teenagers the meanings people can read into their appearance or behaviour – their style-talk. Perhaps your daughter doesn't realise that wearing a tight, low-necked black dress is seen by some as sexually-provocative. And if she does, can she handle the consequences?

A young girl may be clear about the 'messages' she wants her appearance to send to young men. But the responses of older women – which may, indeed, be partly based on jealousy – can be very hurtful. And if older men must translate the message as "I'm making a pass at you" – or – "I'm sexually available", then the young girl may find herself in a frightening situation with which it's difficult to cope.

This issue can perhaps be best approached by considering how we often choose our clothes to convey certain messages about us. Think about what you're wearing now. What do you hope it says about you? "I'm fun!"? "I'm serious"? "I'm responsible"? "I'm sexy!"? "I'm rich"? Even if we don't consciously mould our appearance to give a particular message, other people might read meanings into our hairstyle, make-up, clothes or posture.

Can you remember what you wore as a teenager to attract the opposite sex? What does your teenager wear now for the same purpose? Styles might change, but the idea or the cues remain the same. Teenagers are experts on the subtleties of fashion, and the finest details of what to wear to look just right. Why not look through some old family photos with your teenager, and discuss the style-talk you see in them.

Sex

What do you think? What do you feel? What do you know?

Mention sex and you'll normally get some kind of reaction. A laugh, a blush, a frown. The subject brings out all kinds of strong and varied emotions in people. But what is sex? It's more than just the mechanics of keeping the human race going.

How do you feel?

This topic will help you sort out your own feelings and opinions and examine how they may affect what your teenager learns from you about sex.

It's a good idea to air your feelings and thoughts about sex. Your feelings are particularly important: they influence the way you see and think about things. They will also influence your teenager. You need to remember that although your feelings are genuine and important to you, they are not a universal truth. Other people do not necessarily feel the same way.

Many people confuse their feelings and their opinions. It may help you get a clearer picture if you check that when you say *"I feel"* you are referring to an emotion or sensation that you have: for example, "I feel – sad, depressed, excited, aroused, disgusted, guilty etc.". When you say "I think" this should reflect your opinion: for example, "I think that today's teenagers are not as experienced as people say they are" – or – "I think there should be heavier fines for selling pornography".

Your opinions may be affected by both your feelings and by the facts you know. For example: "I think that casual sex should be discouraged" (*opinion*) may be based on "The very thought of it makes me feel dirty" (*feeling*) and/or "Casual sex has been shown to be related to increasing risk of catching V.D., and sterility in women" (*facts*). Not everyone would share the feelings, but the facts can not be ignored.

When thinking about sex – and in discussing it with your teenager – it helps to be clear as to what your opinions are – and how they are affected by your feelings *and* knowledge or lack of it. Ignorance of the facts is easily remedied.

Knowing the facts of sex does help. Of course, you don't have to know *all* the answers to be someone a teenager would feel happy to ask questions of, you just need to be approachable. But the chances are you may still be too embarrassed to discuss them with your teenager. Even more likely he or she will be too embarrassed to come to you. Far more important than the actual information is knowing where to advise your teenagers to go to find out more from knowledgeable adults or books. (See "What next?")

The vital thing to learn as a parent is not to be angry, or feel a failure, if your teenager does go elsewhere.

Your answers

A D For each of the topics below complete these three sentences:

1 I think (my opinion is) _____

2 I feel (my gut reaction is) _____

3 I know (the facts are) _____

Your answers can be as long or as short as you like.

The topics

○ sex before marriage
○ casual sex
○ pornography
○ different standards for each sex
○ pressures to have an active sex life
○ male *and* female homosexuality

If you are working with someone else use this list to start a discussion. Take it in turns to have your say. If you don't understand what the other person says, ask them to talk about it further. "What do you mean by such-and-such" or "Tell me more about that" might help sort things out for both of you.

Remember your opinions and your feelings are personal to you. There aren't any right answers. In some cases you may realise that you don't know much about the facts. If this is so, you may find your opinions change when you know more facts. Of course, if your feelings are particularly strong you may ignore or discount the facts.

Are you unsure of some of your opinions? This may be because you lack information.

It may also be an honest sign that facts cannot help you be absolutely sure about a moral or ethical dilemma. For example: you may know all the facts about abortion – but they would not help you be 'certain' it is a good thing in every circumstance.

Sex and intimacy

There is a difference between sexual activity and sexual intimacy. Whether it's holding hands and kissing, masturbating or intercourse, *sexual activity* has several benefits. It can be entertaining; it can be a form of physical release and help you sleep. It can assure you that you're normal and attractive. *Sexual intimacy* can be all of this and more; it is a way to express love and closeness to your partner, and it makes you feel loved and whole. Your relationship is more than just friendship. Like best friends, you share yourselves at the deepest level, and you are vulnerable.

Some people think they can only be intimate in a sexual relationship. They haven't experienced intimacy without sex. They might go into a sexual relationship looking for intimacy, and feel terribly let down when they don't find it.

Think back to your responses to the topics in the activity above. Are some of your replies concerned with sexual activity, and others concerned with sexual intimacy? Your replies might show that you feel differently about these two aspects of sex. Many people feel good about the idea of sex as an expression of love, that is sex as intimacy, but not as an activity otherwise. Perhaps you can recognise the importance of them both in your own life.

Changes all round

There have been many changes during the last twenty-five years. Much more is known about sexual activities, family planning and sexual problems. Attitudes have changed and so has behaviour. We are not suggesting that *all* these changes are for the better. But they are important because they affect the world in which your teenagers are growing up.

All the changes are bound to affect teenagers. It's not surprising that they are more open and honest about sex and less ridden with guilt.

Are teenagers more sexually experienced these days than twenty years ago? Recent surveys say "Yes". This doesn't mean that they are all sex-mad. Far from it. Most sex occurs in loving and steady relationships.

These surveys show that compared

with you they will probably begin their sex lives earlier. Today's teenagers are likely to have a more varied sex life, with more than one partner. More teenagers say they will live with someone before marriage, but most want to marry and have children in the end. Fewer feel they *have* to marry.

Getting hurt

Many people are afraid that young people might be hurt or exploited if they start a sexual relationship too soon. It can be difficult to maintain a sexual relationship if you haven't already learned about intimacy in a non-sexual relationship.

And of course, many teenagers who are looking for love settle for sex, which doesn't satisfy the same needs. Teenagers can be left feeling inadequate and with damaged self-esteem if an early attempt at such a relationship fails.

Helping your teenager think about intimacy, sexual activities and sexual intimacy *and the differences between them* will help protect them from getting hurt. But really we all learn a great deal from painful experiences. It is more important to help your teenager learn from them rather than avoid them.

What do you think?

A D Write down the four main things which are better about sex today. Then write the four main things that are worse. Use your own experience, or the information from this section.

Ask your teenager if he agrees.

Of course not everyone will see the same things as 'good' and 'bad'. Here are the points which our parent testers considered most important:

Better: More open discussion. Constructive advice more widely available. Development and acceptability of contraception. Removal of premium on virginity. Increasing equality of the sexes.

Worse: Pressure to experiment with sex – without waiting for a suitable relationship. Weakening of marriage because of sex before marriage and easy divorce. Exploitation of sex commercially. Casual sex – disconnected from love. Still double standards.

Sex education

How should it be done?

Your opinions

A **D** Read the descriptions of what the four teenagers are being taught and make written lists of the items of which you:

A approve
B are dubious about
C definitely disapprove

Now compare your opinions with those given in the far right column. Pick out the points in their arguments with which you agree or disagree.

Evidence from recent surveys suggests that:
○ school sex education programmes do not change pupils' own sexual values or behaviour, but pupils do tend to become more tolerant of others
○ teenagers who know how to use birth control are less likely to have an unwanted preganancy than those who have never had any education in birth control methods.

Different approaches

A criticism made by our parent testers is that sex education is too often divorced from personal relationships and values. This might suggest that more than one teacher must be involved at school, or that perhaps some aspects are best taught in school and others learned within the family.

What do you think? Now make a final chart. For each subject area listed below say whether you think it should be taught by parents and/or teachers. Which teachers should do it? When should it be taught?

1 Biology: Birth, conception, changes at puberty, intercourse.
2 Attitudes and morality (sorting out values): Use of contraceptives, sex before marriage, abortion, homosexuality, masturbation, divorce.
3 Personal relationships: Getting on with others, communication skills, dating, what makes for a stable partnership?
4 Problems: Birth control, abortion, sexually transmitted diseases (VD), homosexuality, rape, incest. Any others?

Comments: Where in all of this will your teenager learn that sex is highly exciting? And that it can be a lot of fun, the source of consolation when you're feeling down, and a way of expressing your deepest love?

Discussion can often be linked to recent TV programmes or newspaper articles which will have aroused interest.

Occasionally arousal of interest in this way makes it important to discuss the subject regardless of the age of the child or teenager. If this interest is ignored the child may be left confused and worried. Accurate information must be given but the approach must suit the age of the young person. Consider what you would say to an 8-year-old, a 12-year-old and a 16-year-old about: indecent assault, rape, homosexuality and incest.

But what if you feel too embarrassed to talk? If you really feel stuck give your teenager one of the books listed in "What next?". Say something like "I'm not good at talking but here's a useful book". A smile can suggest you feel good about sex even if you find it difficult to discuss. Finally, encourage your teenager to talk to more experienced adults.

Margaret, 15, at a mixed comprehensive in Yorkshire, had lessons based on *Learning to Live with Sex*, published by the Family Planning Association. It was part of a series of classes that dealt with community development. The book, which is illustrated, is directed at a wide range of teenagers, and covers, in a matter of act way, almost everything from adolescence to marriage, from the menopause to wet dreams.

AN FPA PUBLICATION FOR TEENAGERS
Learning to Live with Sex
85p
Revised Edition

Nicholas, 12, of Bromley, Kent, learned the facts of life as part of an integrated science course evolved by staff at Wreake Valley School, in Leicestershire. Before turning to the chapters on sex, Nicholas had already learned about heating water, and electric circuits. It is a straightforward, scientific method, with clear drawings and explanations of the human body and its reproductive functions. Nicholas' homework (above) shows he knows about the anatomical differences between men and women, how babies are 'made' and born, care of newborn babies, menstruation, birth control . . . The aim is to approach sex as a regular school subject, so the children treat it without embarrassment.

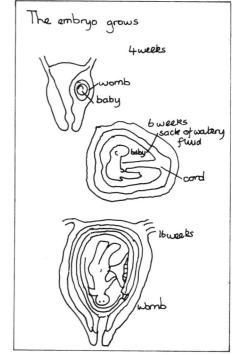

The embryo grows
4 weeks
womb
baby
6 weeks
sack of watery fluid
baby
cord
16 weeks
womb

Roberta, 16, who goes to a girls' comprehensive in north London, learned about sex on her day release course at a further education college. The lessons, part of her child development course, were based on the controversial award-winning book *Make it Happy*, by Jane Cousins, published by Virago. It is the boldest of all the teaching aids, has frank illustrations and uses teenage language, including four-letter words. Chapters on love-making techniques, masturbation, homosexuality make some parents feel it is too direct. Others find it refreshingly frank.

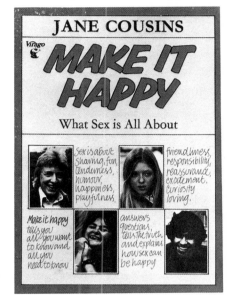

Kathy, 14, at a mixed comprehensive school in Middlesbrough, learned about sex as part of a family-care course, and one of the teaching aids was a 'comic strip' from the Family Planning Association called *"Too Great a Risk!"* It tells of a girl's fears that she is pregnant, how it affects her relationship with her boyfriend, the impact on their families, her visit to the doctor, followed by advice on contraceptive methods (these are the only mildly explicit drawings) and the good news that her pregnancy test is negative. It's a good method to get the message over to young girls of 12 upwards, who like reading romantic comics.

What people say

Opinions are divided about the usefulness and the morality of different kinds of sex education.

Alastair Service, speaking as the secretary of the Family Planning Association, says that "any sex education programme has to cope with society as it is now.

"We see our priority as making sure that youngsters don't become pregnant. We make no apology for that. Good sex education should get across the message that no-one should be pushed into sex. But if they're having intercourse they must not cause suffering."

Ray Hutchinson, as medical director of the Brook Advisory Centre, which advises young people on sex problems, birth control and pregnancy, says "Demystifying sex can only make for a healthier and happier generation.

"Children absorb their parents' attitudes long before they see any films or pictures. In my counselling work I find that the more responsible youngsters are the ones who have had a good background instruction and the chance to discuss the whole subject openly."

Valerie Riches, as secretary of the Responsible Society which opposes permissiveness and pornography, condemns "the message of the sex educators" that it's fine to have sex at any age, as long as you use contraceptives.

"Of course children should have sex education, but it should be in the context of their future lives, as something beautiful and dignified.

"Sex education reached a new low with *Make it Happy*. It's disgusting and dangerous – yet the *Times Educational Supplement* gave it an award."

Charles Stuart-Jarvis, headmaster one of the judges to give *Make it Happy* the *Times Educational Supplement* award, says, "I'd rather see teenagers reading straight information about sex and its deviations than much of the stuff that's easily available. *Make it Happy* is an antidote to all that. It's frank, tells the facts in plain language and gets rid of myths and misery. Anyone who thinks today's teachers can convince teenagers there's something wicked about sex is totally out of touch.

"In the third year our pupils learn basic biology, see a film of a birth and the Health Education Council film, *Loving and Caring*, about a girl in the 'should I – shouldn't I?' situation with her boyfriend. This sparks off a discussion.

"The fourth and fifth year courses cover the whole field of health education, including contraception.

"Our job is to help boys and girls emerge happy and secure through adolescence. Most parents are pleased with our balanced, scientific approach."

Your teenager's school

○ Ask what they do
○ Remember you *may* withdraw your child from sex education classes. But should you?
○ Suggest resource materials (See "What next?")
○ Request a P.T.A. discussion meeting. You might use this topic in discussion groups.

Taking risks

Emotional risks concern parents as much as the physical ones.

Deciding whether or not to take a risk depends on:

○ how likely you believe the possible outcome to be
○ how important the outcome is
○ how much you have to lose.

The necessity for teenagers to try things out for themselves is a recurring theme of this book. Learning about relationships and sexuality by trial and error is one aspect of this. An element of risk is bound to be involved. If something is new to you, you can't know the exact outcome. This kind of uncertainty may be a risk. For teenagers this can be exciting or frightening. They might see things as risky which their parents don't consider to be risky, and vice versa.

What is the risk?

A **Case study 1** Jenny fancied Stan. She guessed he fancied her, too. Stan used to hang around a group of boys who always seemed to be playing practical jokes and making fun of people. She was more and more sure Stan liked her because of the way he looked at her. She didn't think he had a girlfriend, so she decided to take a risk and ask him out.

Case study 2 Tony, aged 17, wanted to impress his new girlfriend with how sophisticated he was. He thought he could pass for 18, so he decided he'd try and take her to the local nightclub.

The problem was, if anyone he knew saw him there, he might get chucked out for being under-age. What would she think of him then?

Answer the following questions for both Jenny and Tony.

> 1 What happens if the risk pays off?
> 2 What happens if it doesn't pay off?
> 3 What is he/she likely to lose?
> 4 How do you as a parent feel about the risk?

For example, Jenny may:
1 Gain a new boyfriend
2 Find her life a misery if Stan and his friends tease her
3 Lose her self-respect and damage her self-confidence

A parent might feel that it would be better if she waited a bit to see what Stan would do but that it wouldn't be much of a worry if she decided to go ahead.

Have you ever been afraid that your teenager was taking risks in his/her relationships? Ask yourself the same four questions for each risk you can think of.

Sometimes a person's behaviour will be less risky if they:
○ know all the available facts about the possible outcomes of their behaviour
○ have a chance to talk to someone about it beforehand.

Sexual and emotional risks

There are some risks that always spring to mind when parents think about their teenagers. They are afraid their teenager may take a chance with birth control, seek an abortion or catch a sexually transmitted disease. Parents may deny their fear – and console themselves – by saying "It couldn't happen to my teenager". Teenagers, too, may feel it couldn't happen to them. But it might! So it's worth thinking about your feelings and what you would do if these risks did happen. These three particular issues are dealt with in the second half of the topic.

However, we have been trying to emphasise that intimacy in a relationship is important in its own right and is not necessarily connected with sex. So it would be a pity to end with the focus on the unfortunate outcomes of sexual risk-taking. Of course, intimate relationships carry emotional risks and many of our parent testers thought that these could be even more difficult to help with.

They were often anxious to protect their teenagers from the pain of rejection when friendships fail. The trouble is that you can't really do this. Leading a full life does involve

taking emotional risks. If the emphasis is on protecting a teenager from getting hurt the danger is that he or she becomes too timid to become involved in intimate relationships. What you can do is to help your teenager learn more about him/herself – and other people – from such experiences.

So perhaps the most useful points to discuss with your teenager might be:

People do sometimes get hurt: They feel rejected or guilty for having rejected someone. It's worth thinking about the skills of finishing relationships so that both parties emerge with as little damage as possible to their self-esteem.

People want different things from relationships: lots of fun, plenty of cuddles, someone to take care of them, spending a lot of time together, sharing interests, the chance to "open up their heart" to this partner, are what many people need. But not everyone wants the same things.

So the early stages of a relationship need to be spent on exploring how you match up with your partner. There are two possible problems here:

1 spending all your time on one part of the relationship; for example, making love whenever you can, can leave little time for finding out how well matched you are across the wide range of your needs.

2 expecting all your needs to be completely met by your partner, with no need for other close friendships.

Sure of your reasons?

A Ⓓ One parent tester said: "I'd like her to be sure about when and why she would say 'No' or 'Yes' to sex (intercourse)". Some parents also worried about times when a young person wants an intimate friendship, but feels that sex has to be accepted as part of the 'bargain'. Or – worse still – where what is seen as only a sexual encounter by one partner is mistaken for intimacy (love) by the other.

Again, we would suggest that you consider what you think about the following points. Then, when a good opportunity arises, discuss the issues with your teenager. By all means, say what your opinion is, but keep the discussion open. Don't ask what sexual experiences your teenager has had. (Remember your own teenage years?)

Do you think these are wrong reasons for saying "Yes"?

○ to prove you love someone?
○ to keep your partner?
○ to feel loved?
○ to prove you're not frigid/impotent?
○ to please your partner (though you don't enjoy it)?
○ because you don't know how to say "No"?
○ because you can't stop – although you meant to say "No"?

These *are* common reasons why both girls *and* boys do agree to have sexual intercourse, but they do carry heavy emotional risks. Helping young people be aware of their 'reasons' helps to avoid them acting on them, perhaps unwisely, without even being aware of what they are.

Good reasons for saying "Yes"?   Which of these statements would you agree with?

Sexual intercourse is OK provided:

1 the couple use effective birth control (and have seriously considered what they would do if it failed).
2 both enjoy it (no persuasion needed).
3 it's done within a loving, caring relationship.
4 it's done within a long-term committed relationship.
5 it's done within marriage.

Of course, however much you may have thought about it beforehand a decision about risk-taking made in 'cold blood' doesn't always hold up in the heat of the moment. Teenagers who have not yet been faced with just how powerful their sexual drive can be, can be amazed to find they soon reach a point beyond which it's very difficult to say "No".

Taking a chance with birth control

A D In her survey of young people and sex, Christine Farrell found that, although most teenagers who had sexual intercourse used a method of birth control, only a third used it every time.

A few people, even these days, don't know about birth control or where to get help or supplies. Sadly, some girls don't have the confidence to say "No", even if they don't want intercourse.

No contraceptives are 100 per cent effective, but contraceptive failure, as it's called, and ignorance about contraception account for only a few unplanned pregnancies. The majority are due to people taking a risk with contraceptives, or not using them correctly.

Can you honestly say that you have never risked an unplanned pregnancy? Most people have at some time. What were your reasons for taking a chance? Compare your reasons for taking a chance with the list of problems (right). Then think about the method of birth control you use now. Why have you chosen this method?

Why might your teenager take a chance?

Marie and Phil's case is not at all unusual. It wasn't just one thing that made them decide to risk it. There was a sequence of events that added up.

There are several broad categories of events which lead people to risk pregnancy. Some are shown right, with examples. Write down the problems your own teenager might have in these areas. How can you help your teenager so that, if he/she has decided to have intercourse, he/she won't risk an unwanted pregnancy?

Taking a risk with birth control is perhaps particularly serious with teenagers for two reasons.

Firstly, they are much more fertile than adults. So on any single occasion when teenagers have 'unprotected' intercourse, the girl is more likely to get pregnant than if an older woman had unprotected intercourse.

Secondly, they have so much more to lose. Abortion or adoption causes worry and anguish – no matter how sure they are that this is the best thing to do. Coping with a baby – either alone or within a premature teenage marriage – is no easy task.

Help your teenager – Make sure he or she has up-to-date facts about birth control and knows where to get help. More importantly – but more difficult to do – encourage your teenager to consider why he or she might be tempted to take a risk.

Should parents be told?

If a girl is under 16, intercourse is illegal. But that doesn't stop many young couples from having intercourse. Doctors are advised that prescribing contraceptives for under-age girls may be justified as preventing damage to the health – from a possible pregnancy. *But should the doctor inform the girls parents?* Technically the parents' consent is required for medical treatment for under-age girls. However, doctors may

Problem area

Assertiveness

○ Doesn't want sex but can't say "no" ☐

Ignorance

○ Doesn't know what kinds of birth control available ☐
○ We've got away with it so far – I must be infertile ☐
○ I'm not fertile at this time of the month ☐

Morals/Values

○ I think using contraception is wrong ☐
○ We didn't mean to go all the way, but couldn't stop ☐

Availability

○ It's too far to the local clinic ☐

Embarrassment

○ I don't want to be examined by a doctor ☐

Self-image

○ Only promiscuous girls go on the pill ☐
○ It's up to girls to take precautions ☐

Secrecy

○ I don't want my parents to find out ☐
○ The doctor might tell my parents ☐

Spontaneity

○ If I take them with me it looks like I planned it ☐

Advantages of pregnancy

○ He'd have to marry me ☐
○ If I had a baby I'd have someone to love – and to love me ☐

Side-effects or problems with birth control

○ I couldn't stand the mess of that foam ☐
○ I'm scared to take the pill ☐

take into account the possibility of the girl refusing to use contraceptives if she thinks her parents will be told, but still continuing to have unprotected intercourse. In this case he may decide that telling her parents would cause an additional risk to her health.

What do you think? The danger is that if parents *had* to be told, teenagers wouldn't seek advice. Since most teenagers who seek advice have already had unprotected intercourse, they would probably just go on taking the risk.

Teenagers and abortion

Jean's mother was at first very upset that Jean was pregnant. Jean's father was ready to go out and thump her boyfriend. Both parents had long talks with each other and with Jean and her boyfriend. They soon rallied round and told Jean they would support her, whatever she decided to do.

Carol was too frightened to tell her mother she was pregnant, so she left her a note instead. She was frightened, too, at the idea of having a baby. But her mother very much wanted a grandchild.

How do you think you would react? There's no point in disguising your first emotional reaction. But hopefully most parents *would* want to support their teenager. You need to know what the law says and how to get help.

The law

The consent of two doctors is needed for an abortion. They can consent if they believe continuing with the pregnancy has more risk:

○ to the life of the pregnant woman
○ of injury to the physical or mental health of the pregnant woman or any existing children of her family.

They can also consent if there is a substantial risk that the child would be born seriously handicapped. The doctors can also take account of the woman's actual or forseeable circumstances.

A girl cannot get an abortion just because she is under 16, but at the time of writing about 60 per cent of pregnant under-16s do have abortions. Girls under 16 normally need the consent of a parent or legal guardian. If they refuse, doctors can still carry out an abortion if they feel it is necessary. A girl cannot be forced to have an abortion. Girls over 16 can consent to their own medical treatment.

Seek advice

Many people are concerned with the medical and emotional risks of abortion to the girl.

The medical risks involved in abortion depend on the length of the pregnancy. Abortion during the first twelve weeks is the safest. At this stage the risks are less than the risks of childbirth. So it is important for a girl who might want an abortion to see her doctor, or contact a pregnancy advisory service (see "What next?") as soon as she thinks she might be pregnant. If your daughter wants an abortion, she or you should ask the doctor to explain the risks in her particular case.

Emotional risks. Will she feel bad about it afterwards? This risk can be greatly reduced by counselling.

Counselling should help a girl considering an abortion to explore all her options – to look at how she would feel and manage if she had an abortion, or if she had the baby.

Counselling can help her talk to her parents and boyfriend about what is probably a very painful subject for them all. It can also help her and her boyfriend understand why they took the risk they did take, and help prevent them taking the same risk in future. Plans for future use of birth control are usually discussed.

After the abortion. Reactions to having had an abortion cover a wide range of feelings:

"What a relief!"
"I feel much better now."
"I regret it."
"I've done something awful."
"I'm depressed."

How any one girl reacts depends largely on what she was like *before* the abortion, and how sure she was about her decision. If she was unsure or was pushed into it by someone else, she's more likely to feel bad about it.

Most research has looked at negative feelings after abortion, because that is what people are worried about. There is evidence that, if the decision to have an abortion is carefully taken, most patients react well afterwards. They express relief, or say they have no regrets.

With a teenage girl, a number of things are likely to happen at the same time as an abortion. And each of them could cause an emotional reaction. She might finish with her boyfriend when he finds she's pregnant. Her parents might have an almighty row with her, because they've just found out she's been sleeping with her boyfriend. These could be enough in themselves to make her feel depressed.

Sexually transmitted diseases (S.T.D.)

This is the new medical term for venereal diseases (V.D.). If everyone only ever had one sexual partner, or remained celibate throughout their whole lives, there would be no S.T.D.

S.T.D. is still a very embarrassing subject, and no parent likes to think their child might catch it. But it is important to discuss the possibility with teenagers, so that in the event they are sure to get early treatment. They're then less likely to suffer permanent damage, and less likely to pass it on to someone else.

Even if they are not personally at risk, they might know someone who is and can advise them to seek help. ("What next?" suggests books which will explain the symptoms and effects of S.T.D., and what happens at special clinics.)

Some important facts they should also know are:

1 For your own protection – never have 'casual sexual intercourse', with someone you hardly know. But if you do – use a sheath which will give some protection to both people *and* go for a check-up at a special clinic afterwards.
2 Some diseases are at work even if you don't have any symptoms.
3 If untreated, some diseases can make a woman sterile.
4 Untreated S.T.D. can damage the baby if the mother is pregnant.
5 You can't diagnose them yourself: the symptoms vary a lot.
6 You can catch them over and over again.
7 Partners should always be treated – even if they have no symptoms.
8 The more quickly you seek help the easier S.T.D.s are to treat. Treatment isn't painful or particularly unpleasant: but as yet there is no real cure for genital herpes.

Your local "Special Clinic" (This is what clinics for S.T.D. are called). You don't need a letter from your doctor and can go to the one which is most convenient for you. Find where it is by:

1 Looking in the phone book under Venereal Disease.
2 Visiting (or telephoning) the casualty department of any hospital and asking for the "special clinic".
3 Asking your G.P.

New friends

Many parents worry about what their teenager gets up to in groups. Do you need to?

Parents' concerns

A These are typical worries about peer groups from parents, grouped according to their main concern. Which strike a chord in you? The comments suggest topics you might look at first if these are your main concerns.

Group influences on opinions and values:

○ "I thought I'd brought them up to know the difference between right and wrong"
○ "All those silly clothes!"
○ "These street riots – he thinks it's fine to be running about the streets making trouble"
○ "He's becoming rude and slovenly now".

Feeling that friends are replacing you, that they reject the things you hold dear, is upsetting for parents. "The good things about friends" and "Whose values?" look at what peer groups do for teenagers, and at the 'generation gap'.

Your own feelings:

○ "I'm scared to death, when he goes out to those political group meetings, that he'll get done over"
○ "It's awful they treat me as if I came out of the ark"
○ "I half expect a policeman to turn up on the doorstep to say they've had an accident".

Afraid, embarrassed, ashamed, envious, worried – these are just some of the feelings parents have about their teenager's peer group activities. The topics "Thinking about friends" and "Talking about friends" look at coming to terms with your own feelings.

What they get up to:

○ "It's the old story – where are you going? Out! What are you going to do? Nothing!"
○ "I'm sure they've been shoplifting – but when I ask, he just laughs."
○ "Going into pubs like that – she's only 16, but she probably drinks all sorts of things."
○ "God knows what they get up to!"

Not knowing – and not being told – are a maddening part of being the parent of a teenager. Yet a growing adult needs some privacy. "Getting into trouble" looks at the more serious side of teenage groups: delinquency and deviancy. "Peer groups and society" looks at involvement in a broader range of community activity.

Not belonging to groups:

○ "He's such a loner."
○ "She spends all her time with Julia."
○ "He dresses up like a punk, but spends his evenings listening to awful music in his room."
○ "She spends ages putting on her 'war-paint' in the bathroom – but doesn't go out anywhere."

Despite their concerns about what teenagers get up to in groups, parents also worry when their teenager is *not* involved in groups, or has problems belonging. "Not belonging" and "Learning about groups" look at these issues.

4

The good things about friends

Your worries can make you forget the good points about friends.

Peer groups

Peers is the term used throughout this chapter to talk about small and large groups of friends who:

○ are about the same age
○ share similar interests
○ are of about equal status in society
○ value, and often share, each other's opinions.

It is natural for teenagers to become less reliant on their parents and move into a widening range of friendships and groups. For teenagers, an intense involvement in a peer group can provide support while they establish a new identity. Breaking away from your parents feels safer if you're one of a crowd. Certain personal and social skills are easier to learn and more enjoyable to practise in a peer group. These skills are useful in later life.

Although many adults eventually come to have an intimate relationship with a partner they love, they remain members of groups who work, drink or pursue other leisure interests together. Peer group support remains important throughout life. But it is of key significance – a 'developmental task' – during the teenage years.

Why peer groups are important

Being part of a group builds up:

1 A sense of identity: discovering the 'real me'. The teenager can try out different attitudes and ideas among friends, to see which suit him/her best. Being valued as a friend, and feeling 'one of the gang', gives a boost to self-esteem. On the other hand exclusion from a group can damage self-esteem.

"I was so proud to belong to the group"
"It was important to show I was one of the gang"

2 Security and stability: adolescence is a disturbing time, the teenager is full of doubts and mixed-up feelings. It is comforting to know that others are going through the same things. There is also safety and strength in numbers when arguing with adults. It helps to be able to say that "everyone's doing it".

"I fought hard to have my hair the way I wanted it – all my friends had it done like that"
"It was great fun all going off together"

3 Shared interests: it is often easier to talk to people of your own generation about things that are important to you – sex, clothes, music, careers. Other age groups may not have the same interests, or talk about them in the same way. The teenager can compare ideas and views and find, reassuringly, that they are shared.

"We all liked the same kind of music"
"We used to all go round the shops together: and try on each others' clothes"

4 Social skills: the teenager learns to mix with and get on with others, to share and to give and take. As one among equals, he learns when to put himself or others first. Belonging to a particular group often gives a special social status.

"I learned how to make friends and listen to other people's points of view"
"We used to go to dances together to pick up girls/boys"

5 Code of conduct: being part of a group means keeping to common rules, helping those you like and accepting the judgement of your peers. Peer group members often look, and act, alike. However, it is rare for peer group opinion to overrule parents on the basic values of life.

"We were always ready to stick up for our friends"
"We all hated another group."

6 Practice and feedback: endless chat sessions replace the pretend games of childhood as rehearsal for adult activities. Peers give instant, objective feedback – they tell you what they think of you. This can help the teenager to try out and modify his 'style'.

"I could air my views, no matter how immature and was listened to"
"We argued about politics – endlessly"

Parents and peers

There is a strong case for thinking that such personal and social skills as these can only be learned among equals. Because adults and teenagers rarely see each other as equals, it may be difficult for teenagers to learn such things from their parents.

Unfortunately, parents often find it impossible to believe that teenagers are learning anything positive and good from their friends. They are more likely to focus on things that worry them. It is important to assess peer influences on your teenager for what they are, not the worst you fear they may be. Just because your daughter dyes her hair pink and wears bondage trousers, does not necessarily mean that she will go on to put a safety-pin through her nose, sniff glue and carry a chain and knife. The whole of life is rarely taken over by peer group activities.

Talking about friends

A D The pictures and quotes here may have helped you recall what belonging to a teenage peer group meant to you.

Compare your recollections with what your partner, or a friend, remembers. One parent tester who shared her teenage memories with her husband said – "It was interesting to discover how similar our teenage backgrounds were. We did not know each other then and were brought up in different parts of the country".

Some of you will, of course, recall unhappy experiences of being isolated or picked-on by a group. Another parent tester recalls: "My teenage years were very lonely – lack of money isolated me from most peer groups at school, (school was some distance from home) – and different interests isolated me from neighbourhood groups. Certainly home was a safe base; but to have had the kind of parents who I could really open out to would have been even better".

If your teenager is interested, suggest that he/she does this activity too. Can the two of you share together how you feel about your own teenage group?

Remember, talking about what peer groups *do* is easily seen as prying. Rather, this activity suggests that you think and talk about what peer groups *do for* teenagers, how they make them feel. The same parent tester as quoted above said: "We often chat like this over family meals. It's a way of building up a 'family history' – and it's fun. Several friends I know spend a lot of time, like us, on a two-way discussion with their teenage children, in which reassurance, comfort and intelligent talk have a part". She also made the point that she decided to do this because of her own teenage experiences.

Comments:
○ self-disclosure – telling someone about yourself – can be a difficult skill to get right. See "What next?" if you want to learn more about *appropriate* self-disclosure. There does need to be a bit of a generation gap – see next topic.
○ if your teenager faces problems – see "Not belonging" and "Learning about groups". These topics may resolve some problems for you too.
○ if your teenager doesn't want to talk – don't push him/her. You may be making things harder for him/her – see "Thinking about friends" and "Talking about friends".

Whose values?

Parents, peers and society affect teenagers' choice of values.

Teenagers and parents

Teenagers need to choose for themselves what to believe in and the rules and standards by which they will live. Friends appear to be a major source of influence. Sometimes teenagers seem to go through a phase of throwing all their parents' opinions and values out of the window. They may spend several years re-thinking their own approach to life.

Parents often feel upset by the apparent power of friends. However, surveys suggest that they needn't be too upset:

Agreements – surveys show that – "Yes there *is* a conflict over differences of taste and everyday domestic issues". *But* teenagers, on the whole, agree with their parents over the really important issues. For example, studies show that:

○ teenagers and parents both share the same important basic values, such as honesty and perserverance.
○ two in three students say that parents are the most important people in their lives. They value their parents' good opinion and do not want to disappoint them.
○ by their mid-twenties, most have settled down to a life-style – and a view of life – remarkably like parents'.

Disagreements – parents and teenagers *do*, frequently, disagree on matters such as clothes, hairstyle, make-up, music, time of coming in or going to bed. These relatively minor areas of independence are probably best granted to the teenager. Parents who fight head on will almost certainly fail. It is more productive to:

○ reserve energy for the differences which really matter.
○ negotiate limits when you or others are involved: for example, over what to wear for an interview or family wedding.
○ discuss the impact your teenager may make on others, who stereotype him according to the way he looks or behaves.
○ support your teenager when peer involvement goes further than he had intended: for example, taking more than his fair share of the blame for causing trouble in school, or where the group is 'daring' him to do something he considers to be 'wrong' or dangerous.

Rebellion: most teenagers who go through a phase of discarding all their parents' values soon come out of it. They may fly in the face of parents from day to day; but are likely to accept their views on decisions which will matter for life.

It is older teenagers, who are still dependent on their parents, who rebel most against parental discipline and decisions. At all ages, teenagers are more likely to rebel, if they don't get on well with their parents. Teenagers depend more on their peer group, for security and values, if they don't have a warm relationship with a parent or if there is no sense of 'equal rights' at home.

Relationships: as many as one in three teenagers say they find parents or teachers the most difficult people to get on with at some point during their teens. However, only about five per cent of parents and teenagers report a real worsening of relationships during adolescence. If there **is** a really poor parent-child relationship, this is most likely to have started in early or middle childhood.

If the parent and teenager don't get on they may need help from their own support system to try to improve matters. See Chapter 1 and "What next?".

A generation gap?

Minor conflicts may obscure the major agreements, and parents and teenagers may spend much of their time criticising each other. Some parents may become more restrictive in order to slow down the pace of change. Some teenagers will turn to their peers to speed things up. But there is little evidence, from surveys which have examined family relationships, to suggest a major generation gap within the family. There does however seem to be a gap between society, in general, and certain groups of teenagers. (See right.)

Your family

A **D** This topic has looked at the issues in general terms. What about your family? We have included quotes from the parent testers who did this activity to serve as comments.

1 Look back to your own teens. Your teenager may not seem so different from you if you can share with him/her some memories of your own teens. What you got up to may not seem so outrageous now, but the chances are you, too, annoyed your parents.

"I recall frequent accusations of untidyness, which is now a frequent source of dissension with my daughters. I had arguments about the amount of time I spent on homework and 'long-haired idiots masquerading as musicians' – again history repeats itself."

"Arguments with mother about make-up, and father about where was I going and who with: going places, like dance halls, where I knew I was not allowed, X-certificate films, smoking, and enjoying it because it was forbidden."

2 Look to your teenager. Is there anything you've learned from him/her recently? Parents today often recognise that they don't always know how best to advise.

"When my daughter applied for a part-time job while doing A-levels, I thought she would not have enough time and energy for studying. She assured me that being under more pressure of time she could work better, and proved me wrong."

"Yes – often. I tend to think the worst, but later, or in talking about it etc., I discover I was wrong. They do have lots of common sense, sensible values, kindness etc., and don't *want* to do all the awful things I get anxious about!"

3 Look to yourself. What part do you play in shaping your teenager's values, and the way he/she behaves when you disagree?

"I try very hard to give and make sure he understands the *reasons* for our disagreements, even if we have a bit of a slanging match first. When the atmosphere is cool, I am prepared to re-open the discussion. It does not always work but when we can 'agree to disagree' I feel I have achieved something worthwhile."

"I get too anxious too fast, I know in my *head* what is the best way to handle teenage upsets, arguments etc., but with my own children everything I know seems to be swamped by the way I feel – it sounds neurotic and probably is!"

Teenagers and society

Adolescence is now longer than ever before. Puberty begins earlier, and formal education lasts longer. A host of laws make many adult activities legal only after a certain age. So relatively mature young people are kept in a state of powerlessness and dependence. Such freedom from responsibility *can* help teenagers to experiment with and choose their identity. But that depends on there being options to choose among. For the teenager who does not have many options open to him or her, the delay in achieving adult status can be alienating and depressing. Youth cultures are an alternative to an adult world which has closed all doors to the younger generation.

Peer groups may well take on a wider role in the future than they have done in the past. Unemployment excludes teenagers from the key arena in which they feel "now I'm really an adult" – work. No job means no adult status. So reference points by which you judge yourself outside the adult world of work become increasingly important. Peer groups confirm that you are at least 'one of the gang'.

If unemployment leads to a longer period of dependence on the peer group, it is also likely to deepen and lengthen the phase of rejection of 'adult' values. Many black youths – so often seen by society to be rejecting it's values – have already entered this phase. They have long experienced adverse social and economic circumstances, but as opportunities for young people decrease right across society, white youths are facing the same experiences.

Again, in the absence of access to the adult world via work, teenagers are likely to be more strongly attracted to radical political/religious groups, such as The British Movement, Rastafarians, The Socialist Workers Party. These groups offer a form of power to young people. Within these groups they can stand up and air their opinions and join in demonstrations and community action.

'Society' disapproves of – and therefore often labels as 'deviant' – the behaviour of certain groups. However, 'deviant' teenage groups are often rebelling against the structure of a society, in which there is little going for them. Their behaviour may be taken as evidence for a generation gap, but, in truth, they are not rebelling *against* their parents. Their parents may also feel that society is letting them down.

In a way, it is surprising that so few teenagers do get into trouble or violence. After all, there is little you can do with no money, no job, few rights and little community provision. Many teenagers' needs remain unmet by an older generation, which enjoys teenagers as consumers, but gives them little real power or resource. Some writers see this as the real generation gap – one generation exploiting the next.

Thinking about friends

How to learn to live with your teenager's friends.

Just a phase

Deep involvement with peer groups is only a phase in development. But, as with other phases, parents can make it longer and harder for themselves, or they can make it relatively painless.

When it seems as if it's going on forever, it can help to remember that it is just a phase. Detecting some of the minor changes within the structure of groups, can help you to know that the phase is passing. You may like to identify in the descriptions which follow where your teenager is now.

Stages of group development

1 Unisex clique: single sex groups which include the teenager's best friend, if he/she has one. Activities are mainly sociable – larking about, doing things. Groups do not mix with groups of the opposite sex.

2 Initial mixing: the sexes begin to mix, relationships are diffident, sometimes apparently hostile. Activities focus on 'picking up', although other things may still be popular.

3 Initial dating: more mature teenagers start to 'date'. Girls now seek security and loyalty from one or two close friends. They worry more than boys about acceptance by peers.

4 Mixed sex cliques: dating poses a problem, for the teenager finds he/she has a foot in two separate camps. The group changes a lot. Mixed cliques of couples and their friends emerge.

5 Couples: gradually the peer group breaks up as couples pair off and 'go steady'.

Conflict

Negative attitudes towards everyone in authority seem to increase throughout adolescence. This starts with a marked turn for the worse in the early teens.

Boys tend to feel more open conflict. Conflict with parents also rises from the early teens on. Girls tend to reach a peak of conflict around the age of 15 – usually over not feeling able to 'be myself' or 'reveal my true thoughts". Conflict tends to go on longer with boys, peaking around the age of 17 and focus-

sing on frustration at being tied down and dependent. Much of the conflict is about peer group activities.

Activities

Peer group activities are often irritating as much as worrying. Most of the time teenagers are not really up to much, even though they make a big mystery out of it. Few teenagers join really way-out, socially-deviant groups. Despite media stories, research studies show on the whole a sedate pattern of interests. Watching TV, going 'out', going shopping, dancing, youth clubs and sport are the most common activities.

The music scene is one of the major influences on the growth of cult peer groups. Pop groups change rapidly and your teenager could (and probably does!) give you a long lecture on the minute differences of dress, style and values between the groups. But while he/she may want you to be interested, the last thing he/she needs is a parent who wants to behave like a teenager. There needs to be a gap between members of a family in order for everyone to have space to grow. If adults have teenage interests, they should think over carefully why this might be.

What can parents do?

A This activity looks at what you can do if you are worried by your teenager's activities with friends. It suggests a way of thinking over the problems before you talk.

Parents use phrases like "the wrong crowd", "being led astray", "just want to hurt us", when they feel their values and lifestyle are under threat. Yet in breaking their parent's code of behaviour, teenagers are probably obeying their group's code. 'Deviancy' depends on your point of view. It also depends on your emotions. When they feel calmer, parents will say of the same behaviour "it's only a bit of fun", "they've got to find out for themselves", "it's just high spirits".

Separating the facts from the feelings is essential if you are to get through to your teenager. We suggest four steps which will help you think things over. To make it easier for you to use these steps with your own problems we take the case of Danny.

Thinking it over

Four steps to prepare you for talking with your teenager about his or her peer group activities:

Step 1
Identify the attractions for your teenager

Step 2
Identify your feelings and worries

Step 3
Identify ways you can help your teenager – with **A** information, **B** practical/emotional support, **C** discussion of values.

Step 4
Identify ways you can help yourself by **A** negotiation, **B** reviewing your values, **C** changing your behaviour.

First read about Danny (right), then follow how we have applied the above steps to his case.

Step 1 – Attractions for the teenager (Danny)
○ thrill of speed
○ friendship and shared interest
○ spending money as he chooses

Step 2 – Parents' feelings and worries
○ afraid of accidents
○ afraid of fights
○ annoyed by appearance

Step 3 – How the parents might help the teenager
○ with information: for example, talking about local safety training.
○ with practical/emotional support: such as buying Danny some safety gear.
○ with discussion of values: for instance, talking about the fights – is it an image, or does he get involved? Why does Danny's father expect him to get into fights?

Step 4 – How parents can help themselves
○ negotiating over the teenager's behaviour: what Danny will do when he's going to be later than he said.
○ reviewing their own values: discussing between themselves the amount of independence they encourage in Danny.
○ changing their own behaviour: giving up criticising the jacket, as it is not really that important.

Before you try out these steps on your own problems, practise by applying the steps to Jackie and Mick. Then compare your comments with ours.

Danny and his motor-bike

Dad: "We finally gave in and let him have his own bike. Well, we didn't have any choice really, he was earning and could buy it himself. Then it was the black leather jacket and crowds of boys outside the house at night on their bikes. I worry about fights. And then there's accidents: that worries me sick if he's late coming in."

Danny: "My bike is the most important thing at the moment. There's nothing like being out with your mates. I'm thinking of buying my mate's bike from him – it's faster . . ."

Jackie, the good-time girl

Mum: "I know for a fact she's drinking and smoking, and if she's not on the pill, she ought to be. We never meet the boyfriends – she doesn't want to bring them home. Out at a party every other night; all her money goes on records and clothes. She dyed her hair and it looks dreadful. Of course, if I say anything, all I get is abuse."

Jackie: "They're so stuffy. They always think I'm getting into trouble when I'm just having a good time. Who wants to watch the telly every night? And why shouldn't I dress as I like?"

Political Mick

Mum: "Ever since he's taken up this 'cause' he's been a different boy. He and his father are always having terrible arguments. He's always off on some demonstration. There's leaflets and posters all over his room, people calling at all hours. And the things they talk about sound awful to me – overthrowing the government, smashing this group and that. It frightens me."

Mick: "They're incredibly materialistic, my parents. All they worry about is the state of their bank account and whether the place is clean and tidy."

Comments on Jackie

Step 1 – Experimenting with self-image and behaviour.

Step 2 – Envy and the anxiety/fear of not knowing what she's up to.

Step 3 –
○ talking about the risks involved in her activities. (See pages 58–63 and 80–83).
○ talking about the reasons for their strong feelings.
○ discussing and trying to accept her views of the issues involved.

Step 4 –
○ negotiate what Jackie will tell them.
○ review how they spend their time – does she have a point?
○ find more positive things to say about her behaviour (See right).

Comments on Mick

Step 1 – Exploring and expressing new ideas, finding his political voice.

Step 2 – Fear of violence; upset by arguments; hurt by his rejection of their values.

Step 3 –
○ talking about the legal aspects of his activities.
○ offering sympathy when at last he finds his idols are not perfect.
○ talking about the 'grey' areas of values and morals – where values may conflict or not be clear-cut. (See Chapter 8).

Step 4 –
○ negotiate about which activities he may take part in.
○ review their own political values in mid-life.
○ in arguments stress the process of choosing values rather than telling him which ones he must choose.

Putting up with them positively

❶ Here are 10 guidelines drawn from this topic and parents' experiences. We've put "keep your behaviour under review" as the last point to remind you to keep doing it. But you may need some practice in doing it – so, try keeping a diary of the comments you make about your teenagers' friends over the next weekend. It may give you a surprise.

1 Be patient – it is a phase that will pass if you let it.
2 Keep calm – it is mostly relatively harmless behaviour.
3 Take a cool look – at the risks, and at the knowledge, skills and support your teenager needs.
4 Recognise your own feelings – and find ways of coping with them.
5 Allow them to experiment – to take informed risks and make informed choices.
6 Avoid constant criticism – of the way they look, the things they like and do; or they'll bite back.
7 Show love and affection – even when you don't agree, it's important they know you care for them.
8 Appreciate their point of view – if you want them to respect yours.
9 Accept you haven't got all the answers – and that you could learn from them.
10 Keep your behaviour under review – it's easy to think you are more, or less, accepting and helpful than you are.

Talking about friends

Your views and feelings affect the way you talk about friends.

Your initial remarks and even the way you listen are important. If you criticise their friends you won't get told much about them. If you leap in to try to solve their problems with friends, they may clam up because they want to think things through for themselves. If you are convinced they are *always* up to something, or *never* doing anything worthwhile, then you won't be tuned in to hear when they try to tell you differently.

Parents' feelings

D Your feelings will also affect what you hear. It may hurt to be no longer the centre of your teenager's world. You may also feel upset if your teenager seems to be discarding all you've ever taught. You may feel jealous of the fun he/she is having, or feel old when faced by his/her youthful high spirits. It is natural and fair for parents to react like this, but it isn't fair to blame these feelings on the teenager, or pass on the anger he/she creates. When parents explode over something their teenager has done, there are usually some mixed-up parental feelings behind the outburst.

Completing the sentences below can help you to identify the events that provoke an emotional response in you. You may be only too well aware of your responses by now, but doing this activity can help you in two other ways. Firstly, you may realise that the feelings you have are to some extent an over-reaction to the situation. This is nearly always due to old feelings being revived. It's as though your teenager hit you on a spot where you already had a bruise. When you find yourself over-reacting, try asking yourself: "Are the strong feelings I have linked in any way to what happened to me as a teenager?" And also – "Is there something that has happened recently that makes me more likely to react so strongly?"

This activity also helps you practise 'owning your feelings'. So often, we find ourselves saying "you *make* me feel so . . .". It is more accurate to say – "I feel . . .". In this way, you are not using feelings to blame the other person. If you say "when you do that I feel . . .", it is then possible to negotiate some changes in behaviour. The other person can consider changing what they do and you can consider changing what you feel. At the very least you can expect the other person to respect how you feel, now that the situation has been spelled out clearly. You must, of course, respect the other person's right to explain that – "when *you* feel like that, *I* feel . . . (hurt, surprised, annoyed?)".

Complete these sentences:

1 I feel *powerless* when my teenager _____

2 I feel *disappointed* when my teenager _____

3 I feel *frightened* when my teenager _____

4 I feel *envious* when my teenager _____

5 I feel *puzzled* when my teenager _____

6 I feel *cheerful* when my teenager _____

7 I feel *happy* when my teenager _____

8 I feel *proud* when my teenager _____

9 I feel *sympathetic* when my teenager _____

10 I feel *confident* when my teenager _____

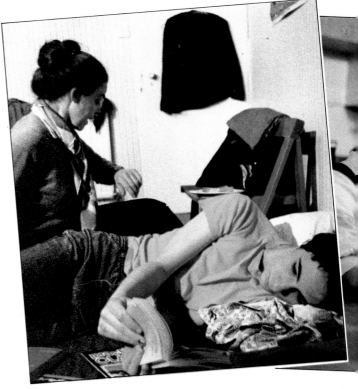

Scenes from a series: feelings about friends arise in each of the TV programmes which are part of the course this book is a part of. The

Translating feelings

A Teenagers rarely tell their feelings about groups directly to their parents, but they often drop heavy clues, if you listen for the feelings behind what they say. Your translations of their concerns won't always be right, but if you sound interested, not opinionated, your teenager will talk on, if he/she wants to. Practise by translating what the teenager is saying in the situations suggested in the table (right). Write in the feelings the teenager might have.

Comments: in real life, body language and other things your teenager says, would give you further clues. Likely feelings are:
1 discouraged, inadequate; 2 wants to, afraid – mixed; 3 hurt, rejected; 4 uncertain, unsure; 5 resentful, conforming; 6 angry, unloved; 7 proud, pleased.

How can you show your teenager that you have an idea of how he/she feels? You need to use the kind of phrase that sounds natural to you. We suggest you try something along the lines of – "I guess you must feel – lonely and left out" or "That suggests to me that you're feeling – lonely and left out" or just "Do you feel lonely and left out?". If your teenager had made the statements 1 to 7, how would you respond?

Showing that you are *trying* to understand how someone feels is a good way of encouraging them to talk to someone. Don't worry if you get it wrong sometimes. The other person will usually correct you – and again the conversation is opening up.

parents' body language shows as to whether they are listening to the teenager and accepting his/her point of view – or not.

Teenager says	Teenager feels
(*Example*) *Everyone else has gone to the beach and there's no-one left around here*	*lonely left out*
1 I'll never be any good – I practise and practise and the twins are still better than me	
2 I can't just phone her up, she might laugh at me for asking	
3 I'm not going to go around with them any more; they're dopes and creeps	
4 What do you think I ought to do, go with them or stick around here?	
5 I want to wear my hair like the others – it's my hair isn't it?	
6 You don't care where we go anyway	
7 Did I tell you we finished painting the whole of Mrs J's house in the community action scheme?	

First remarks

A First remarks can be vital in whether, or what kind of a conversation takes place. In the following situations, ring the response that would be closest to your first remark:

1 Your 16-year-old comes in late from a party. Do you say something like:

A "hi, you look happy/tired/ . . ."
B "I've had enough of waiting up for you; you'll be in on the dot next time."
C "Who do you think you are – out this late?"

2 You suspect your teenage daughter has been shoplifting make-up. Do you say something like:

A "I see you've lots of new make-up."
B "Where did you get all that stuff then?"
C "You look fancy all of a sudden . . ."

3 Your teenager wants to go on an 'Adventure Holiday'. There will be rock climbing, pot-holing and canoeing. Do you say:

A "That sounds exciting – and a bit scarey!"
B "Could you afford it? Wouldn't you need special boots and clothes?"
C "That's much too dangerous. I'd never have a moment's peace while you were away."

4 Your teenager wants to go to a concert in a town many miles away. Do you say:

A "Tell me more about it . . ."
B "OK, provided you go with a friend."
C "I didn't know that was your scene."

5 Your teenager comes home bruised and shaken from a protest march. He's been in a fight. Would you say:

A "Sit down and have a coffee."
B "Look, we can't have this happening again, what I think you must do is . . ."
C "Serves you right. I told you so."

Comments: Did you choose mainly:
A responses? These show you're ready to listen. In effect you're saying "I'm interested, ready to hear if you want to talk".

B responses? These suggest you're ready to move in with a solution or interrogation, without giving your teenager much time to explain himself or make suggestions. Yet these are all problems for the teenager to sort out. It might be better – after you've made an A-type response – to ask something like – "What do you need to sort out?". Put the responsibility on your teenager to do the planning.

C responses? These suggest you tend to cut off conversations before they've started. This kind of response is usually made when your own strong feelings threaten to swamp you.

You need to take time to sort out your feelings. If you possibly can – play for time by making an A-type response. If a stormy row seems likely delay discussion by saying something like "I feel too angry to talk about it now, let's discuss it after a cup of tea."

Not belonging

Parents worry if teenagers do — or don't — belong to groups.

Group activities

Teenagers often go through phases of concentrating on one area of their life at a time. If a teenager doesn't have time for peer groups at the moment, he/she probably will do so later on. Just because the average teenager gets deeply involved with friends in his early teens, doesn't mean that all teenagers will do so, or need to do so, at that age.

In any case the whole of teenage life does not revolve around group activity. Rehearsing possible roles alone in the bathroom or bedroom is part of deciding who you are. Absorbing personal hobbies are needed throughout life. And having just one or two close friends of the same sex is an important part of learning to be intimate.

A change of scene

Not being part of a group can be more uncomfortable when it is forced on the teenager as a result of a life-event. Moving house, changing school, parents divorcing or re-marrying into different circles, are all transitions which can affect the teenager's social life at a critical point. It is important for parents whose lives are changing also to ensure that they give their teenager the knowledge, acceptance, skills and practical support he/she needs to move from one social scene to another (see "Transitions"). Settling into a new peer group takes time. Like all transitions, it can be stressful. Your teenager may find, for example, that with a new group of people, he/she occupies a different position within the group.

Popularity

What makes for popularity? Research studies suggest:
○ cheerfulness
○ friendliness
○ enthusiasm
○ enjoying jokes
○ initiating games and activities
○ skill at games
○ good looks, physique, dress.

Other studies have looked at characteristics of the 'elite' in schools, as seen by their peers. Most important seemed to be:

○ sporting ability for boys
○ success in social relationships for girls.

Not that popularity, or lack of it, is a straightforward issue. For example, while physical attractiveness is important in determining popularity for the most – and least – good-looking teenagers, it has little effect for the large majority in the middle. Equally, school achievement on its own is unlikely to turn a teenager into a 'star'. Athletes are more popular than scholars, – but athlete-scholars tend to be most popular of all.

If your teenager is concerned about not belonging, he may welcome the chance to talk over this topic with you. Before you do so, reflect on what made for popularity within and between the sexes in your day. Prepare yourself to find that things have changed, and that your experiences and opinions do not conform with those of today's peer groups.

Missing out

Teenagers who, for whatever reason, are isolated from people their own age, may find it more difficult to make relationships with others. They may develop a lack of self-confidence, low self-esteem, a feeling of being 'different', which can last into adult life.

Sometimes parents are the best source of help: we suggest some further guidelines below. Sometimes a school counsellor, social worker, GP or youth worker outside the family may also provide support.

Anyone trying to help an isolated teenager needs to:

1 set up an understanding relationship
2 take time in discussions to develop trust
3 identify the teenager's strengths and needs
4 give the teenager a new way of looking at him/herself
5 encourage practical changes in behaviour.

Here is an example from a social worker's notes of how she helped one boy:

Case notes – Stewart

Background: Stewart is a child with an exceptionally high IQ. He has played in chess tournaments since age of eight and is in a class a year above his age. He seems to prefer the company of adults. He suffered a nervous breakdown during adolescence. He seems lonely and has problems relating to others. He likes listening to classical music.

Discussing the problem. I had great difficulty in establishing a good relationship with Stewart. He seemed ashamed of having had a breakdown and didn't want any outsider trying to help him. Eventually he confided that his great fear was of being 'different' and 'abnormal'. It was suggested to Stewart that his high IQ had helped to shut him off from other areas of life. Once he understood and accepted this, he was ready to try some of the suggestions made to him.

Practical support. Stewart was encouraged to develop his hobby – music – and became an accomplished double-bass player quite quickly. Now he has a girl-friend who plays in the same orchestra. He is considering going abroad for a year before University.

Joining in

A D Here are 10 steps which may help you get your teenager through not belonging. Make notes of your own possible answers as you work through these questions.

1 Are you doing anything which encourages loneliness? For example: Do you frown on friends dropping by? Do you make rude remarks about his friends? Or is he/she, by nature, a shy person?

2 What is he/she interested in? However unusual, there will be others, somewhere, who share them. Take a positive view of your teenager. Look in particular for groups that will bring him/her into contact with young people.

3 What might put him/her off? For each group you can think of review: their purpose and activities, the skills they develop, and the rules they have. If your teenager is put-off by any of this, the group is unlikely to be a success.

4 Are there practical difficulties? For example:
A Where do they meet? Can he/she get there?
B What time do they meet? Can life be re-arranged so that he/she can go?
C How much does it cost? Are there fees, special clothes or equipment, or travel costs?
    There may be imaginative ways round the difficulties: for example, sharing lifts with other parents, changing your arrangements so that he/she can go, buying second-hand gear.

5 What are the gains and losses? "I might not be any good at it", "I might not like the group leader", or "Will I be able to get my homework done as well?". What is the best as well as the worst that might happen from your teenager's point of view? How might the losses be kept to a minimum?

6 How might he/she cope with the 'first time'? How the first meeting goes is often a key factor in deciding whether to go on. Rehearsing possible events will help it to go well. For example, ask – "What could you do if – no-one spoke to you when you arrived?" "Do you need to take anything?" "Is there someone you already know who you could be with to start off?"

7 How did he/she get on? Talking it over with you afterwards may help him or her to take a more positive view. New people, places and activities can all be unfamiliar experiences and sources of stress.

8 Can you encourage him/her to give it a while? Even joining a group to which you want to belong is a transition. Understanding that all changes – even welcome ones – are stressful is important for everyone to understand and learn how to cope with.

9 What else might you do? You might like to brainstorm further options and alternatives. Include everything you can think of and sort them out later. Are you discarding many of them because you or your teenager thinks they involve risks? Are either of you being too timid?

10 Can anyone else help? Encourage him/her to seek it if this is what he/she decides. Cast your net widely – school teachers, youth workers, aunts and uncles, brothers and sisters may all be able to help. A quiet word from you may enable them to make suggestions that he/she will find more acceptable from them than from you.

Getting into trouble

Can parents prevent a brush with the law?

Delinquent is the commonly used label for teenagers whose behaviour is considered to be deviant or anti-social. It has an exact meaning too. Delinquency is that *behaviour which is punishable by law of under-17-year-olds.*

Theft and damage to property are the most common offences which reach the courts. Crime statistics for teenagers *are* horrifying. However about 50 per cent of first offenders do not offend again after their first court appearance. Apart from those offences which reach the courts there is a whole range of behaviour which adults see as anti-social or deviant. The question often asked is: Why is it that so many teenagers seem attracted to this kind of behaviour?

Social background

Teenage deliquents are more likely to live in inner city areas where there is overcrowding, poor housing, and few leisure facilities for young people. In these areas there is often a tradition of petty crime and vandalism.

Coming from a broken home, or one where there are frequent family fights, also seems to make a young person more likely to get into trouble.

These two factors are largely outside the control of individual parents. But not all teenagers with these backgrounds do get into trouble. The third and perhaps most important factor is parenting style. If the parents are lax and do not supervise the activities of their teenagers outside the home, then the teenager is more likely to get into trouble. Parents need to know where their teenager is and what he or she is doing when out at night.

Schools and delinquency

Different schools, despite taking children from the same kind of backgrounds, show different rates of delinquency. Some schools seem to provide an environment which positively encourages delinquency, whereas others seem able to prevent potential delinquents getting into trouble. Where there is a low rate of school attendance and low academic achievement delinquency is likely to be high.

Where you do have a choice of schools in your own area, one will probably have a better reputation than the others. Below we describe three problems which parents of teenagers may encounter at school. Put the letter next to each that best describes your approach to these problems.

Problems

1 Your teenager has fallen in with a crowd at school always in trouble. Now he/she is too.
2 You understand your child has been labelled difficult and a trouble-maker by the teachers and you know this isn't the whole story.
3 Your teenager used to enjoy school and work hard. But there's so much mucking about in his/her class, that he/she's stopped trying and joins in with the others.

Approaches

A Accept the situation thinking there's little you can do to change things.
B Wait and see. If the problem goes on, you might do something.
C Discuss the problems within the family, but not outside it.
D Go and see the teacher or Head to talk about it.
E Look around for another school to send your child to.

Comments: Parents react in different ways to problems like these. Some want to keep right out of the school world, others want to be involved, or try to influence what their child does at school. If you're the sort of person who normally rushes straight in, stand back for a while and see what happens. If you tend to be the other way inclined and are reluctant ever to get involved, then make an effort sometimes to go and talk to someone at the school. Changing schools is difficult and may not be the the answer; the same problem could crop up in another school. Schools and school-home relationships are examined in Chapter 6.

Nick and Nicholas

Here are two imaginary but typical case histories. Both of these boys have been involved in deliquent or deviant behaviour. Think about their backgrounds and also about how 'Authority' – teachers and police – are likely to label them. Who is more likely to become set in this pattern of behaviour?

Nick Jones wants to leave school on his 16th birthday in a few weeks time. His mother would have liked him to stay on as she thinks he's quite bright. But Nick has other ideas – and none of his friends will be staying on. He has played truant a couple of times this year, smokes a lot and can drink in pubs, as he looks older than he is. Out with the gang recently, he broke into an empty flat on the estate, just for something to do. His mother worries he's mixing with the wrong crowd. His father is unemployed.

Nicholas Harrington-Jones is at a boarding school. He is not academically inclined, but he will stay until he is 18, and his parents are insisting he goes on to college. He has been caught smoking at school and has been warned about it, and he also brought drinks into the dormitory which is against the rules.

During the school holidays, he used his brother's car, which he is not taxed and insured to drive. His parents are happy that Nicholas's doing well and getting a good start in life. His father works in the City.

Comments. It's pretty obvious that Nick is likely to have a brush with the police before long. He will soon get labelled delinquent. Nicholas's activities may be frowned on by his parents and the school authorities, and he may be punished by them if found out. But this behaviour is more likely to be excused as 'high spirits' and won't label him for life.

There are still double standards in our society. The socially disadvantaged pay a full price for their misdeeds. Similar behaviour on the part of others is treated differently. It might be said that, in general, the 'poor' get blamed, the 'rich' get excused. What do you think about this issue?

Peer groups and rituals

In many societies the passage from childhood to adulthood is marked by certain rituals. So-called primitive tribes may have had colourful ceremonies and perhaps painful ways of

proving adulthood. Many religions still have ceremonies which show public acceptance of the new adult. Coming-of-age parties are still held.

These ceremonies used to be a powerful way of announcing that the young person is now an adult. Often the group of young people being initiated were kept apart or made to look different. They were often required to prove their strength, courage and endurance.

In most industrial societies there are no longer any such rituals. In some ways this is a pity. These rituals were great for building up the young person's sense of identity and belonging to society.

Yet, in a way, teenage peer groups often create their own rituals. Peer group members dress in a way that sets them apart from all other age groups. They also set themselves tests of daring to see how far they can go. This may involve breaking the law, getting into fights, and taking risks with speed, alcohol and other drugs and sex.

However, with traditional ceremonies the standards are set by adults and the teenagers strive to live up to them. Peer groups today want to rebel against society. They make the rules of the ritual games they play.

How to help

○ Make sure you know what your teenager is doing and where he/she is going. You need to be firm about this. (See "Setting limits" in Chapter 9.)
○ All teenagers take risks. Help them to take 'informed risks'. Providing information, helping sort out values and being more aware of what's behind their attitudes all help minimise the risks.
○ Discuss delinquent and anti-social behaviour. Look at who gets hurt and why it upsets people.
○ Make them feel accountable for their actions – so that they accept that acting in a certain way will lead to consequences which they are responsible for.
○ Try to ignore outlandish appearance and high spirits. Concentrate on being firm about criminal or morally wrong behaviour.
○ Work at building a good relationship with your teenager where you actually talk and listen to each other.

Learning about groups

Knowing how groups work helps teenagers to feel more confident.

Conflict and conformity

Coping with the pressure to conform, and with conflict within the group are the two main challenges for teenagers. How much each is a problem depends on age and personality, as well as on the circumstances. Conforming in dress is quite different from going along with stealing. In both cases, much depends on whether the teenager has an ally in refusing to conform, and whether they have the communication skills to do so. Can you remember examples from your own teenage years of going along with the crowd willingly – and less so? Our parent testers often mentioned 'learning to smoke' as something they went along with unwillingly.

Typical patterns

It is difficult for researchers to study real events in teenage groups. But a whole range of experimental studies does suggest some probable patterns in conflict and conformity.

Group pressure: This type of experiment looks at group pressure on a task such as judging the length of a line. The experiment is rigged in that everyone, except the teenager who has to judge the line, has agreed to say the line is longer than it is. Will this make him agree? Results suggest that conformity:

○ is low at 7–10
○ is highest at 11–14
○ decreases again steadily from 15–21.

Leader pressure: Other experiments look at pressure from the group leader. The teenager is asked to choose a picture he prefers – and then he is told that the group leader chose a different one. 'Low status' members of a group – particularly younger girls – are more likely to change their minds to agree with the leader.

Emotional pressure: Another experimental method is to ask teenagers to complete sentences such as: "If someone is not part of the group . . ." Negative replies indicate that it is bad not to conform: "he's looked on as an outcast", "he feels inferior". These decrease from age 15 onwards. Positive replies indicate there are advantages to being independent: "they are admired or respected", "he enjoys not being a sheep". These kind of replies increase dramatically at age 17.

The urge to conform grows to its height in early teens (11–14), and decreases as teenagers come to value independence more highly.

Your teenager

A Do these findings ring true for your teenager? You might like to explore their own reactions in potentially tricky situations. For example, what happens when:

○ three teenagers are together . . .
○ one of them plays truant . . .
○ someone is not part of the group . . .
○ some of them damage something . . .

Remember your teenager is free to tell you only what he or she wants to in discussing these situations. Do not force the topic of conversation. If his/her replies suggest he/she finds problems in balancing personal freedom with belonging to the group, it may help to look at rehearsing responses to situations which worry him or her. For example, how to:

○ refuse a cigarette
○ get out of going to a party
○ prevent a class joke going too far.

In such situations it can help to look at the *facts and opinions* which will carry weight with the group. It may be easier for the teenager to invoke you – "my mum fusses if I don't phone home first". It can also help to identify someone else in the group who will *support* your teenager's action or point of view. And it will help to practise *looking assertive*, as if you mean what you say.

Roles in groups

People usually only think about what's going on in the group – the process – when things start to go wrong.

In the chart (below right) the phases of a discussion group are outlined. There are three different phases of activity, and a matching role which is of key importance for each of the phases. Every member of the group plays a useful part, but they usually feel more confident and skilled in one of the phases. There can be problems, as noted in the chart.

The cycle of activity described for a discussion group can apply to lots of other activities too, for example:

○ specific family events, such as mealtimes and holidays
○ the general pattern of your day
○ the life of a group, such as a group which gets together to put on a show.

Often, though, activities do not have this satisfying cycle of stages or they get stuck in one particular stage. Production

line work, for example, expects people to be at peak energy all the time. Sometimes a group gets disrupted or wears itself out and needs to be renewed by different members with new ideas if it is to continue.

Family talk in

A **D** Which roles do each member of your family feel happiest in during family discussions? Looking at this can help to

○ pinpoint problems
○ highlight differences between you and your teenager which need taking into account
○ give your teenager a working knowledge of group processes which he can apply in his own grounds.

Look again at the descriptions of roles in the chart. Mark the role you are best at as 3, second best as 2 and worst as 1. There's nothing good or bad about what you are best at: all roles are needed. Make a chart for the whole family, and get each member to rate themselves, if you can.

The Campbells	Nurturer	Energiser	Relaxer
Dad	1	3	2
Mum	3	1	2
Sue (18)	2	1	3
Bill (16)	1	3	2
Jeannie (12)	1	2	3
Total	(8)	(10)	(12)

In the Campbell family

○ Mum and Sue are good at encouraging people to open up and talk about what interests them
○ Dad and Bill are full of ideas, suggestions – and arguments
○ Sue and Jeannie are good at keeping the atmosphere light-hearted and ending up with some jokes and laughter: but they didn't add much to the discussions
○ Dad and Mum complement each other: between them they can keep discussions going well through all three phases.

When you add up the score down the lines you get a picture of the group as a whole. The highest score is the group's best phase. The lowest one is likely to be the phase it finds most difficult. The Campbells get better as they go along. But they do have trouble getting settled down to talk.

Improving a group: Once you are clearer about the patterns you may be able to help the group by:

○ Taking care to make each person feel welcome and settled during the Nurturing stage.
○ Encouraging people to plan which points they would like to raise in the Energising stage. Help the less skilled 'Energisers' to have their chance to get into the argument.
○ Avoiding the group splitting up rapidly at the end. People need time to wrap up their ideas, take up final points and relax for a while together.
○ Once you know which roles you are good at – make use of them *at the right time*. For example: just as the discussion is working up to a (heated?) peak, the 'Nurturer' in the group often dashes out and makes a cup of tea. They often feel 'hurt' when the group sees this 'caring' activity as a disruption. Or what about the 'Energiser' who is still making his discussion points when everyone else is arranging the date of the next meeting – or even putting their coats on?

A group in discussion

	Warm up	Energy peak	Relaxing
Phases of activity	People chatting, settling down, finding things, exploring the topic up for discussion.	More talk, conflict, new ways of looking at things. At some point energy 'peaks' the group seems satisfied with what they have done.	The atmosphere lightens, there are jokes, chat, laughter. People go away feeling satisfied and looking forward to more.
Role of members	**Nurturers** Warm, friendly, open people. Good listeners. Make sure everyone is welcome and included; may help to start things off.	**Energisers** Enthusiastic, active, quick-thinkers. Good at argument. Have lots of ideas and may be good at rousing people emotionally.	**Relaxers** Calm, reflective, good-headed, good at summarising. Usually draw conclusions and round the activity off, expressing satisfaction.
Possible problems	Too long spent on this and people feel they're not getting anywhere; too little and they feel confused. An energiser's introduction may be too excited; a relaxer's too closed.	May feel locked in argument, frustrated by too many ideas. Or people with the good ideas may be relaxers, or nurturers, who are less fluent in putting ideas across.	The group may finish too soon or too late to feel satisfied by the activity. Nurturers or energisers may be reluctant to let go and pull the threads together.

Peer groups and society

How do teenagers and peer groups fit into society?

Four systems

The diagram shows the four main systems of which any teenager is a part. They are shown as circles widening out from the teenager. At the centre is the teenager him/herself, and those closest to him/her – his/her personal settings (1). These personal settings affect each other and make up a network of personal settings (2). Round the outside are those aspects of society where the teenager often has little power or effect: larger institutions (3) and culture (4). This topic looks in particular at politics and culture. These are both powerful areas of influence, in which teenagers are allowed little say, but they are also areas in which the teenager is sorting out his/her own values.

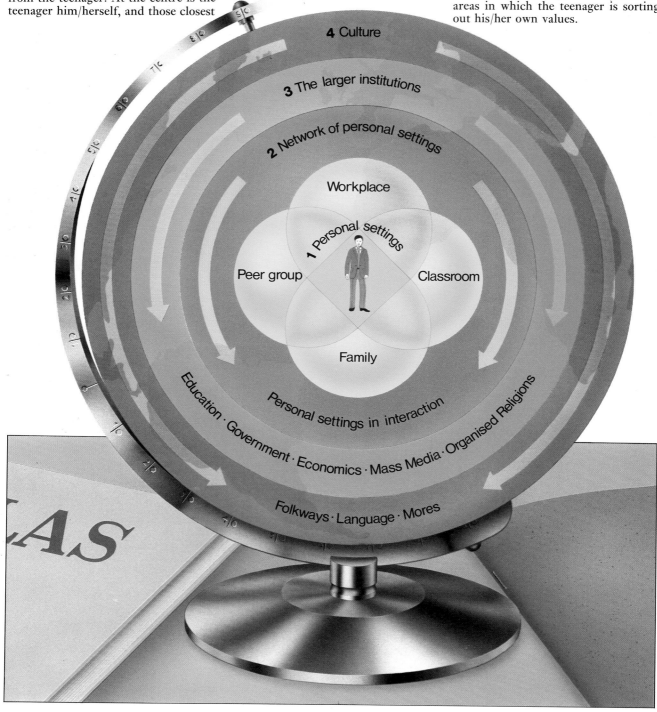

4 Culture

3 The larger institutions

2 Network of personal settings

Workplace

1 Personal settings

Peer group

Classroom

Family

Personal settings in interaction

Education · Government · Economics · Mass Media · Organised Religions

Folkways · Language · Mores

System 1: personal settings

Personal settings are all the groups the teenager is actually part of. There are two main types of personal setting.

Groups based on relationships. Here there are strong emotional ties between members. They are heavily involved in each other's life. They remain loyal to each other even if one does break the 'rules'. The most important example is the family. For teenagers, the peer group is also an important group of this type.

Groups based on performance. Members know the kind of behaviour expected of them and what duties they must perform. They need not be involved in each others' lives in other ways. A school class, the work place, a sports club are typical groups. The teenager joins many new performance groups. Involvement in these groups with their strict regulations is not always comfortable. But learning to participate in them is an important part of growing up.

Mixed groups. Many community groups are a mix of these two types. They are settings outside the family where people are involved together in a number of activities. Church groups, youth clubs and political groups are often examples of such mixed groups. For the teenager, they can be a supportive halfway house type of group.

A D Your teenager. Think about your teenager's personal settings. Include groups of all types and purposes. Make a list and see if each personal setting tells you something about the values he/she holds. Why is belonging to each group important for your teenager? How do you feel about his/her belonging to each of these groups?

System 2: networks of personal settings

Within any one personal setting, what happens between two or more people affects others in the group. For example:

○ Bob drops Gill and starts going out with her flatmate, Liz, which puts a strain on the girls' friendship

○ Gerry's parents continually row at home, which helps put Gerry off the idea of marriage

○ Fred is always on at work about his good sales' figures: this doesn't endear him to his workmates.

Such problems are especially important in shaping the development of teenagers who are taking on their first flat, relationship or job. In the same way, what happens in one setting can affect the teenager's behaviour in others.

The knock-on effect. The teenager goes to a late night party, which causes a row in the family and a headache and hangover in the classroom the next day.

Push and pull. The teenager's family expresses strong disapproval of his friends, which pushes the teenager towards them. Alternatively, the family may give so little support that friends give an irresistible pull.

Balancing acts. Each person needs to weigh the needs of the various groups they belong to, and act on what they consider to be most important. For many adults, the most difficult balancing act is between the needs of work and family. For many teenagers, the most important balancing act is between family and friends.

A D Your teenager. Can you think of examples where settings worked against each other, in a knock-on or push-and-pull way? What was your part in each case?

System 3: large organisations and institutions

These are things like government, the media, the economy. Teenagers aren't part of them directly, but they and their families are certainly at the receiving end of such systems. Relatively few major institutions include young people in their decision-making. They may not even be open to them. Main political parties, trades unions, local authorities, Parliament, rarely include those in their late teens or even early twenties. Alongside other groups in our society – women, the elderly, the poor and black people – teenagers sit on the sidelines while others wield the power. They are likely to be blamed when things go wrong, and to get a poor press.

Unemployment is a case in point. It is these marginal groups of people who suffer most. Yet to date government response has been merely to create a few retraining and job opportunity schemes. The underlying causes of unemployment remain unsolved – a depressing prospect for teenagers today.

The apathy of these groups, caused by lack of power, often needs to change into anger before they take action.

A D Your teenager. What does your teenager think of society's institutions: government, police, media, education, the law, work? Which, if any, of the three stages – apathy, anger, action – apply to your teenager for each of these? What has – or might – make him/her angry? Our parent testers' teenagers tended to be under 15 and were usually apathetic. They were often angry about the educational system. Some groups of testers from inner city areas identified anger against the police and the law as common. In general, unless prompted by parents, it was only the older teenagers who were involved in taking action.

System 4: culture

People who share the same beliefs and values belong to the same culture. Within a particular culture people will, to some extent, think, feel and act in the same way. A teenager's cultural background will affect all areas of his/her life. He/she may accept, reject or modify what his/her culture passes on to him/her but he/she can not ignore it.

Culture will affect the kind of family he/she lives in, the groups he/she joins, and how he/she values work.

However, with a particular culture there will be many individual differences. Any statement which begins "*All the Irish*" – or "*Skin-heads are . . .*" is simply stereotyping, seeing a person only in terms of the group to which he/she belongs. These statements are likely to be highly prejudiced.

A D Your teenager. Think of a family with teenagers who have different values to you. How have you, the parents, brought them up differently with regard to: roles for girls and boys; attitudes to authority; attitudes to other cultural groups? Most of our parent testers compared themselves favourably to other families. Here is one example:

Roles for girls and boys. *Our family:* any interest in any subject encouraged equally. Girl is expected to be more capable domestically but demands *are* made on boy. *Other family:* Girl – to be beautiful. Boy – to be good footballer.

Parental authority. *Our family* – respect demands. *Other family* – no respect shown.

Law and policing. *Our family* – questioning. *Other family* – try to outwit.

Other cultural groups. *Our family* – interested. *Other family* – slanderous.

Systems 2/3: Politics with a small 'p'

Politics, as we look at it here, is about power in any setting. Youth clubs, schools, workplaces, folk clubs, community groups are just as political as the parties and organisations which aim to govern society.

Political behaviour is anything to do with the organisation and control of the decisions and actions of any group of people. Young teenagers are only just starting to be interested in political thinking. Whether your teenager couldn't care less or whether he/she is hooked by a particular cause – you can help to develop his/her ideas by talking about practical politics.

What do you do?

The chart right describes various levels of involvement in politics. There are many ways of looking at political involvement. This one is used because it relates politics to your personal life. It asks – "what do you do?".

Any group or society needs people at each of these levels. The one you chose will depend on your interest in any particular group. You may find you adopt the same role in most of the groups in which you are involved. Certainly no-one is expected to progress over the years from bottom to top. That's a matter of individual choice. Many teenagers follow their parents in these matters. For example, 'Activists' tend to bring up their children to be 'Activists', though their teenagers may have a rebellious phase as 'detractors' or just members. Children of politically disinterested parents tend to remain uninvolved, unless encouraged by friends or groups outside the family – which may cause dismay to their parents.

Your teenager's reactions

Teenagers' reactions to political and social systems will probably fall somewhere between these two extremes.
The naive idealist – "everything would be fine if only . . ." Idealists avoid getting demoralised by not facing up to the facts. There is of course a difference between the teenager who has not yet learned about the world and the teenager who protects himself by avoiding the facts.

The younger teenager will usually see, or want, simple, global solutions to the problems of the world. A small upset to his view may swing him to the opposite extreme, rather than make him modify his solution just a bit. Idealism is a positive reaction, to be encouraged and channelled, not mocked. It is welcomed by some political groups.
The hopeless cynic – "only fools think they can change this rotten world." Like the idealist, the cynic protects himself from having to do anything. The cynic quickly surrenders to hopelessness. He is quick to say "I told you so" when the idealists fail to create a change. A cynical teenager is open to exploitation and manipulation by government and political organisations.

Talking politics

A D Here are some aspects of politics you might talk about with your teenager.

1 For social and political changes to be brought about people must work together in groups. Review which groups you are involved with. For each group decide what level you are involved at?

2 What do you think your teenager is learning from what he/she sees you do? Within your teenager's groups there will be the same levels of involvement. Here are some examples of what teenagers say, which reflect the level at which they are involved. Can you match the following quotes with the levels of political involvement? For example, "I read the school newspaper but that's all." Level = observer.

A "I went to the Peace March, and took the petition into school."
B "I've never been anything special in the form. Not captain or anything."
C "We took down all the opposition posters we could see."
D "No one knows – but I voted for Pat in the youth club election."
E "I helped set up the computer club, and I'm president this year."

Can you deduce from what your teenager says some examples of his/her political involvement? He/she may be interested to make a list like the one above.

(Answers: A – activist; B – member; C – detractor; D – participant; E – leader.)

3 Help your teenager to have a realistic view of society by:

○ Encouraging him/her to keep him/herself informed: TV, radio, magazines and newspapers
○ Avoiding mocking his/her dreams, or belittling his/her complaints
○ Talking about what he/she thinks about local and national events
○ Encouraging him/her to take part in groups.

Which of these have you done in the last week? Are there problems when you discuss politics?

Levels of political involvement

Detractors: people who hold up the work of a group by disruptive behaviour. Non-detracting members of the group will find it subversive. Other detractors, or members of an opposite group, will probably support it.
Just members: people who do not detract but who do not take part either. They are not well-informed and do not vote – but that does not prevent them from griping at times about services and policies. They obey the rules and pay their dues.
Observers: people who are relatively well-informed from the media. They have developed political opinions. However, their involvement ends at observation. They do not act on their views in any way, such as by campaigning or belonging to groups.
Participants: people who take basic political actions. They join groups, vote, give donations, sign petitions. However, they do not go as far as to encourage others to take part also. They do not, for example, collect signatures or run fund-raising events.
Activists: people who take the initiative and get practically involved in politics. Some may be more interested in policy, others in organisation. They register and vote without being reminded. They often support a number of campaigns, and encourage others to join or take part.
Leaders: are people who have an impact on the government of a group, and on its effectiveness. They may be politicians, administrators or party representatives. Some make the decisions; others carry them out.

You will have noticed how well the NF ...ve been doing, but why? Much of the success ...due to the fact that many of the white youth ...ho buy *NF News* and *Bulldog* at the football ...rounds, are the whites who come from the big ...nner city areas. The self same areas where the ...coloured immigrants live and work. So to us ...whites football is a one day in the week outlet. ...This way the youth are showing loyalty to ...something, their team.

But for the other six days a week, our youth have to work and live with the coloured immigrants in their area. In those six days white youth have to endure a race-mixing nightmare. A race-mixing Hell where blacks rule the roost at youth clubs, discos, schools and football pitches on council estates.

For those six days the white youth are outnumbered and continually harassed by the mafia type gangs of blacks and Pakis. They take over the youth clubs and turn them into havens for prostitution and drug addicts. They stick together at school and violently suppress any white opposition – often with the backing of left wing teachers.

Systems 3/4: Politics, youth and race

When cultural groups are in competition for scarce resources, social problems can arise. In the 1950's racial violence flared among youths. Blacks were blamed, as scapegoats, for unemployment, the lack of housing, the break up of old communities. Or the young were blamed as vandals looking for an easy target. Little or no attempt was made by the government to tackle root causes – lack of jobs, poor housing and lack of amenities within the community. The emphasis was more on maintaining law and order by stricter policing and prosecution.

Your own memories of these events as a teenager may be stirred by events today. The social and economic problems are still with us, and the age-old 'solution' of blaming the 'outsider' is still invoked.

Your views

A If you are worried by your teenager's views (or he/she by yours) then this course may help you to challenge him/her effectively. It also challenges you to review your level of involvement.

1 Look at the extract from an extremist youth publication. It is typical of leaflets meant to sway young people's views. You might find it helpful to discuss with your teenager:

○ the emotive language used
○ the lack of evidence for the assertions made
○ the underlying values held

In this way you are challenging your teenager not to accept uncritically what he/she reads.

2 Do you do anything to oppose these racist ideas? What is your level of involvement? (See opposite page.) What about your teenager?

Most of our parent testers taught their teenagers that "people, regardless of colour race or creed, should have equal opportunities and be allowed to live in peace free from harassment".

Some parents made positive attempts to involve their teenagers in a multiracial community:
"We have friends of all shades! We hope that we have brought them *(our teenagers)* up to take a balanced view."
"Her views are influenced by her acquaintance with individuals of other races – as personalities rather than belonging to another race."

Mainly our parent testers considered their teenagers to have sensible views:
"They discuss it sensibly and have a very open-minded attitude to all these problems. They are sympathetic generally to minority groups. As a teacher, I find this generally so. The proportion of children expressing racist views is small. However, children are often given racist leaflets as they leave school. Many react by tearing them up or dropping them without reading them.

So only a few may be influenced."

Teenagers may ignore racist propaganda but how about teaching *your* teenager to argue the opposite case? "He did have a school friend who was a NF supporter and he thought he was an idiot. They argued constantly." Although all condemned it, only a few of our parent-testers were actively involved in opposing open racism, like the NF party. Few mentioned the less obvious racism involved in immigration, employment and housing policies.

What are your reasons for being involved *at the level you are* in anti-racist activities?

3 In a growing number of inner city areas, youth unemployment is very high, and provision for the young unemployed low. Racist groups are active, distributing leaflets and encouraging young people to join. White youths attack black people and the open expression of hostility is increasing. You might like to discuss with your teenager:

A how can young people be contacted to put an anti-racist view
B what information is needed
C which organisations can help
D what groups could offer alternative involvement and excitement
E how far do you think news reporting – particularly in newspapers – contributes to racist attitudes?

Is there any way you can use your own involvement in local life to pursue anti-racist aims?

New mind

One of the major changes you may notice in your teenager is that he/she shifts from thinking only in practical terms to being able to think in the abstract. This allows him or her to try out all sorts of possibilities in his/her mind. For example:
Personally – he/she can fantasise, examine his/her own thoughts and feelings, experiment with new images. Teenage learning is closely bound up with self-image. He/she does things because they confirm or change the way he/she sees him/herself (pages 106–107).
Intellectually – he/she can analyse, predict, conclude, and so on. Some of the new thinking skills teenagers develop through school subjects are reviewed on pages 108–115.
Socially – he/she can criticise, rebel, form ideals. Chapter 8 looks at the new directions and values your teenager may be choosing. You may have noticed some of these signs of the 'new mind' already: your teenager pours scorn on what you stand for, gets 'into' things, argues any point for hours . . . Overall, the teenager's new self-consciousness – What do I value. What am I good at? – is reviewed on pages 116–123, with an eye to future jobs.

New ways of thinking need practice to develop. When your teenager was young, he/she may have gone through a phase of collecting things. This helped him/her learn to count, order and group objects. Now, as a teenager, he/she is likely to develop skills through a period of absorbed interests in and intense questioning of, anything and everything – including him/herself.

Parents need to help their teenager make a realistic assessment of him/herself, and develop his/her own skills. But giving help can be hard if your own feelings get in the way.

Parents' feelings

A **D**   The teenager's 'new mind' can leave parents feeling:

○ **negative** – threatened by a superior brain, irritated by a know-all attitude, at a loss to know how to help
○ **positive** – proud at the teenager's achievements, pleased to see him/her developing a mind of his/her own.

The range of possible emotions is wide. The teenager's fresh, questioning mind can cause parents to do some uncomfortable rethinking for and about themselves. Here are some of the things our parent testers said:

"I feel irritated when expected to enthuse over things that don't interest me – and guilty if I let this feeling show."
"I sometimes feel nostalgic about my relationship with my own parents – which included long debates on all subjects. I don't seem to have created the same for my teenagers."
"I feel inadequate, I haven't helped my 17-yr-old more."

You might like to think through your most common reactions to your teenager's 'new mind'. The "I feel _____ when _____ because _____" form of sentence can help you to pinpoint some of the situations which trigger off strong feelings, and why. Your feelings may relate back to events and emotions you experienced during your own schooldays, or they may relate to your current life concerns. The teenager's new mind is clearly a sensitive spot with many parents. You may find it helps to look back over the topics in Chapter 1 ("Parents' feelings" and "Support") which look at your emotions and what you may need to cope with them.

5

NUMERACY
SPATIAL
REASONING
ORIGINALITY
10
50
100
150
350
400
Midway's
GOLDEN

What's a turn on?

What makes a teenager want to learn.

Motivation and self-image

Learning isn't just – or even mostly – about school work. It's about all the things that contribute to the teenager's self-image – about becoming the kind of person they want to be. To understand a teenager's motivation to learn you need to look at how they see themselves. For example, two teenagers might want to learn to play trumpet in a band for different reasons: one may be primarily motivated by the idea of being able to play music, the other by the idea of taking part in the band's social life.

Adolescence is a time of rapid development in self-image. The things teenagers are most keen to do are things which enhance their view of themselves. Activities which leave their self-image untouched, or damaged, will not be as motivating. You can usually tell when something is motivating by the rapid learning and absorbed activity which takes place: for example, when your teenager decides he or she wants to find out all about computers, or dyeing hair.

What turns your teenager on?

ⓓ This activity looks at what currently motivates your teenager.

1 Overview: first, look at the aspects of self (opposite) which provide most of your teenager's motivation to learn. Make a table like the one shown on the right. Fill in the 'parent' columns as follows:

Column **1**: think about the range of activities your teenager engages in. Which aspects of self do they mostly relate to? Mark each one as very/fairly/not very/barely important.

Column **2**: try to decide how confident your teenager feels in each aspect of his/her self. Mark each one very/fairly/not very/barely confident.

Column **3**: try to decide who your teenager is learning most from for each aspect. Mark in: parents/school/friends etc.

If your teenager is interested, ask him/her to fill in his/her own responses too. If you and he/she do not agree – why might this be? In this exercise it is his/her view of him/herself which is the most important thing to reckon with.

Your teenager may be taking risks in aspects of self which are important for him/her, but where he/she is not particularly confident yet. Aspects which are apparently not important, and in which he/she is not confident, may suggest he/she is deliberately avoiding certain activities for a while.

It can be painful for parents to see that they are no longer the most important source of learning for their teenager. But in developing their own views and values, teenagers often need to explore different views from those their parents hold. For a while, the views of friends may be the most supportive – though not, in the long term, the most important.

Self	1 Importance		2 Confidence		3 Learning from	
	Parent	*Teenager*	*Parent*	*Teenager*	*Parent*	*Teenager*
Physical						
Sexual						
Social						
Vocational						
Philosophic						

2 Specific activities: Now ask your teenager if he/she will take a more detailed look with you at, say, six of his/her activities. Some of these should be formal subjects such as those taught at school, others should be things he/she learns about informally, at home or with friends. Make a chart like the one below from a parent tester and her teenage daughter. Mark in the following gains and effects.

○ short term gains (satisfaction, praise etc.)
○ long term gains (qualifications, job, purchases etc.)
○ the effects of these on self-image (status, confidence etc.)

Which activity does your teenager like best? Which least? The differences between these may highlight the gains in self-esteem that are major sources of motivation for your teenager.

Activity	Short term gains	Long term gains	Effects
Needlework	*Satisfaction*	*None*	*Confident*
Household chores (least)	*Good conscience*	*Small wage to spend*	*Confident*
Pet care – family cat	*Affections from pet*	*Broadened knowledge*	*Feels knowledgeable*
Typing	*Praise*	*Qualif. job*	*Confident*
History	*Satisfaction and interest*	*Qualif. job*	*None really*
Badminton (best)	*Relaxing*	*Fitness*	*Feels good*

Main source of motivation: good, happy feelings – physical sense of achievement.

Five aspects of self

As the central chapters of this book suggest, there are five key aspects of self: physical, sexual, social, vocational, philosophic. During adolescence there is a lot to learn about each of these aspects. In each, the teenager is exploring the question (rarely asked directly): "Who am I?" At times he/she will be uncertain, and may well react differently from one occasion to another.

The physical self: concern over looks is displayed in many ways – interest in clothes, testing strength, sensitivity about height, skill in sport and so on. Many teenagers want to learn how to present themselves well. They also have an interest in learning more about their health and how their bodies work.

The sexual self: teenagers are often uncertain about some of the biological aspects of their sexuality. But they are more strongly motivated to find out how this aspect of life can be integrated into their relationships. Nowadays there is a range of beliefs and approaches as to what a sexual relationship should mean. So there is much to decide – in an area which is often difficult to discuss.

The social self: learning how to get on with other people is a key motivation in adolescence. The teenager will want to develop social skills to handle a variety of situations: starting a conversation, coping with embarrassment, how to say 'no thanks', making new friends, needing to be alone, for example. He will also be developing an understanding of other people's points of view.

The vocational self: teenagers are still strongly motivated to have a job, for the independence and sense of personal worth it brings. This can raise difficulties when it is hard to get a job. Teenagers want to learn about what working life is like, how to get on with workmates – and how to balance work with other interests. They also want to learn those things they think will help them get a job which will suit them.

The philosophic self: teenagers are learning to make their own decisions about what gives meaning to life, and to develop their own beliefs about what is moral behaviour. Personal relationships, politics and religion are often areas where teenagers are clearly seeking to 'find themselves'.

At school . . .

"What's the point of taking exams? I'll never get a job, even with 'A' levels." "My dad earns more than a teacher, and he hasn't got any qualifications."

Teenagers like these don't seem motivated for school-work. They don't see the point. They can't see prospects in terms of a job, or money; and they don't mention day-to-day enjoyment of learning for its own sake. They're just biding their time until they can leave school. This may be because they've had repeated failures at school or, currently, they may be more motivated by learning how to mend motorbikes or play in a band.

Schools vary a great deal in the effects they have on teenagers' motivation. Immediate praise for good behaviour and work has more impact on the teenager than long-term treats or displaying work on the walls. Democratic forms of teaching, where pupils are involved and interested, are more effective than authoritarian ones. Punishment has only a weak effect on motivation, and may actually worsen behaviour.

To some extent, teenagers live up or down to what is expected of them, in terms both of behaviour and performance. Activity – being involved – and responsibility – being trusted – seem to be the key to motivation at school. Good teachers can build up an atmosphere of sharing and confidence to which their pupils respond whatever their ability.

. . . and at home

What applies in school applies equally at home. Parents need to look at the praise, involvement and responsibility they offer their teenager over a whole range of activities. If these things are missing at school, it becomes even more important that they happen at home.

Mixed feelings and uncertainty about what is motivating are a normal part of adolescence. The real tragedy is the teenager who can't get turned on by anything, who feels cut off and depressed. Prolonged inactivity may be a sign of depression – see pages 200–201.

Parents have mixed feelings too. They no longer know where they are, as they did when their teenager was a child. It can be frustrating to see the teenager apparently waste good opportunities, and it can be difficult to let go and show that you trust your teenager to manage his or her own life.

What you say to your teenager is important. Parents can give messages which boost self-confidence and motivation. Or they can limit the teenager or make him/her feel a failure. Messages may be about the teenager themselves: "you stupid boy", "you clever girl". Or they may be about what's OK or not in the family: "our lot never were much good at school", "all our family are in the bakery trade". What messages do you give your teenager?

Mature thinking

Teenagers need skills in language and logic to work things out.

The activities

The activities in this topic and the next explore the growing intellectual abilities of the new mind. They are *not a test* of your teenager's abilities. By now you and your teenager may have a fair idea of these; and they are a subject best discussed individually with your teenager's school.

Instead, these exercises are intended to give a degree of insight into some of the problems and pleasures of beginning to think in new ways. They are simply a small selection of everyday materials and exercises drawn from research into thinking. It's up to your teenager to decide whether he/she wants to try them with you. His/her – and your – reactions will affect your responses to the exercises. Here are some of the things our parent testers said. ❶ You might like to note your own reactions under the same headings.

Looking back, this topic made me realise:
"how much I missed out on as a teenager"

This topic reminded me of:
"Difficulties doing maths at school"
"What pressures we were under at school"
"Problems doing English – I read very little and couldn't spell"

It made me realise about my teenager:
"that I've been thinking she is more mature than she is – I've tended to talk over her head"

When we did the activities:
"the formula problem made *me* feel inadequate"
"my daughter went all feminine at the battery problem, and lost interest."

Meanings

A To get the most use out of a word, you need to be confident that you know its meaning clearly.

Here's a typical quiz that you might like to try with your teenager. Which words do you each think you know the meaning of? Do you agree?

1 Cull *means* **A** understand **B** gather **C** deduce **D** kill

2 Pervades *means* **A** is found throughout **B** influences **C** escapes from **D** attacks

3 Edifice *means* **A** illness **B** boatyard **C** building **D** executive

4 Irascible *means* **A** flamboyant **B** noisy **C** irritable **D** phlegmatic

Comments

The answers given are **1B, 2A, 3C, 4C.** Of course, you could get the answer right by guessing, or without being able to use the word in a sentence. And it would be perfectly reasonable to query the answer for 'cull', and suggest that **1D** is also possible (as in seal culling).

Such quizzes are meant mainly for fun. The more serious skills your teenager needs to learn are – how to use words in context . . . and to use the context to work out meanings.

Using the context

A A way of working out the meaning of new words is to use their context – to guess in the light of the words and sentences which surround the unfamiliar word. Older teenagers may be quite skilful at this. Younger ones may take a limited or a wild guess.

You might like to try the following paragraph with your teenager. It contains a nonsense word – *malmir*. Can your teenager work out and explain the meaning of *malmir* from the rest of the passage given in the book?

The years that followed the victory at Waterloo were some of the worst that Britain had ever passed through. The false and bloated prosperity of the war, as Cobbett called it, gave way to a terrible *malmir*. The government no longer needed to buy huge quantities of munitions and clothing for the army and the allies; the people of Europe, after more than twenty years of war, were too poor to buy the goods that British manufacturers would have liked to sell; instead, the foreign governments often used their discharged soldiers to make their own goods.

Missing words

A The ability to understand and use abstract words develops slowly. In this quiz, **Version A** asks your teenager to pick out another concrete example of a given idea, from a list of words. He/she will probably find this easier than **Version B**. This asks your teenager to think directly of the abstract word which sums up all the concrete examples listed. Follow the samples given to check that you and your teenager know what to do.

Version A
SAMPLE: Fill in from the list the missing word which is like these three:

Lager Beer Vodka _____
Is it: Lime / Coke / Liquid / Whiskey
Answer: Whiskey

1 Anthracite Coal Wood _____
Choose from **A** Gas **B** Firelighter
C Grass **D** Radiator

2 Jamaica Bermuda Majorca _____
Choose from **A** Morocco **B** Corfu
C Scotland **D** Cornwall

3 Beetle Fly Cockroach _____
Choose from **A** Creepy crawly
B Virus **C** Grass snake **D** Ladybird

4 Netball Football Badminton _____
Choose from **A** Chess **B** Squash
C Athletics **D** Leisure

Version B
SAMPLE: Fill in the missing word to sum up the three words given:

Lager Beer Vodka _____
Answer: Alcoholic drink

5 Anthracite Coal Wood _____

6 Jamaica Bermuda Majorca _____

7 Beetle Fly Cockroach _____

8 Netball Football Badminton _____

Comments
The expected answers are: Version A – **1A, 2B, 3D, 4B**; Version B – **5** fuel, **6** island, **7** insects, **8** games/sports. Your teenager might suggest some alternative possibilities – for example, that the answer to **2B** could be Morocco, it is another seven-letter place-name.

This shows how difficult it is to devise foolproof test questions. It also shows why it is important in tests, essays and exams for your teenager to explain his/her reasoning. He/she may not give the answer expected, but his/her explanation will show whether it is a reasonable choice or not.

Younger teenagers most often use concrete examples, and confine words to particular meanings. Older teenagers are often more able to generalise and to use abstract terms. Part of mature thinking also is learning to use the level of language which fits what you are trying to do.

Comments

The meaning of *malmir*, as used here, is a depression or slump. A nonsense word like this one forces the teenager to rely wholly on the context, and what he/she understands about that. With real words, the teenager can also think about related words that he/she knows.

Overall, teenagers' replies show four broad stages in understanding. These stages are described in more detail in the next topic. Here, some typical answers are given, stage by stage. How much did your teenager understand?

Stage 1: Little or no understanding: Teenagers who do not understand much of what they have read may make a rather desperate attempt to answer, for example: "It meant a terrible disaster to the people of Britain, it gave way to a terrible disaster." *(Graham, 13)*.

Stage 2: Limited understanding: Teenagers at this stage tend to focus on only one part of the information available. For example: "It is a disease, because the soldiers that came back from the war might have bought back diseases with them." *(Donna, 14)*. Or "Loss, because the people of Europe were too poor to buy the goods." *(Lynne, 14)*.

Stage 3: A general grasp: Here teenagers are beginning to link up several pieces of the evidence – although they may still focus on specific aspects rather than the total situation. For example: "Redundancy, I think so, because it said that Europe was too poor to buy things that Britain made because of twenty years of war. Also it said that European people used to make their own clothes." *(Joanne, 15)*.

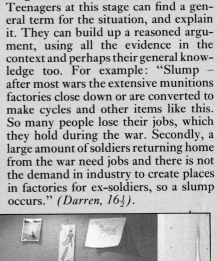

Stage 4: A full understanding: Teenagers at this stage can find a general term for the situation, and explain it. They can build up a reasoned argument, using all the evidence in the context and perhaps their general knowledge too. For example: "Slump – after most wars the extensive munitions factories close down or are converted to make cycles and other items like this. So many people lose their jobs, which they hold during the war. Secondly, a large amount of soldiers returning home from the war need jobs and there is not the demand in industry to create places in factories for ex-soldiers, so a slump occurs." *(Darren, 16½)*.

What's the idea?

The activities so far have concentrated on language skills. The activities here give a few examples of the kind of logical thinking skills your teenager may need to solve problems. The same cautions apply.

Abstract thinking

In each of the problems presented here, abstract thinking can help. Abstract thinking is sometimes called 'formal operational thought'. This is because it lets you 'operate' on a problem in any 'form', not just in specific versions. It involves being able to explain and apply ideas, general principles and formulas; and to consider possibilities and probabilities in problem solving.

At the start of adolescence, many teenagers still prefer practical problem-solving. It takes time to learn to develop ideas without practical experience, or to change ideas in the light of evidence which is given.

Not all people get to thinking in the abstract, certainly not for all problems, all the time. One aspect of mature thinking is finding out what level of thinking is appropriate in any particular instance. So you may notice times when your teenager generalises unnecessarily; or confuses ideas in practice; or works laboriously at a problem which could be solved quickly with a formula.

Your teenager also needs to work out which ideas are interesting enough – or vital enough – for him/her to want to get to grips with them. There are, after all, many times when you can get by with practical methods, or a calculator, for example.

Many teenagers are only just beginning to reach more mature levels of thinking, and then only in some areas. There may be other developmental tasks which currently are more important for them: developing social skills, for example. The important things are that your teenager realises he/she can develop his/her thinking at his/her own pace – and that he/she gets help to do so.

How parents can help

Our parent testers suggested a range of everyday ways to help develop both language and logical thinking skills. Are any of these appropriate to try with your teenager?
○ doing crosswords, puzzles, quizzes
○ helping the teenager to buy – or use the library for – books he/she wants to read or needs for homework
○ encouraging the teenager to write – letters, diaries, notes, lists, etc.
○ discussing news items and articles
○ talking about documentaries on TV
○ valuing and discussing your teenager's views and efforts, even when they strike you as immature
○ reading through homework, if asked
○ encouraging the teenager to fill in forms for him/herself – with a pencil draft if needed
○ talking about what's wanted in exams
○ talking about what the teenager feels about his/her abilities – and your own feelings about intellectual achievement.

Avoiding confusion

A Teenagers can sometimes give definitions without being able to apply ideas correctly in practice. For example, you might like to look at these practical questions about electricity with your teenager. Can your teenager explain his/her answers?

Comments

A common mistake in **A** is to confuse the idea of electrical current with electrical potential; for example, "Yes, if it has not all been used up" *(Gwen, 16)*. In fact there is no current, until a circuit has been completed, as in **B**. If your teenager says there is no current "because there are no wires connected", he/she is beginning to get the idea.

A full answer to **A** and **B** explains what is happening; for example, "I don't think there is a current in battery **A** until the light's connected up – like in **B** – because it needs a circuit all joined up for the electrons to go around" *(Anna, 15)*.

If your teenager is not clear about the idea of an electric current, he/she is likely to be confused in **C**. A common mistake is "No. 3, because it has the

current from the other two batteries passing through it" *(Steven, 14)*.

The correct answer is that all the batteries have the same current through them when the light is on, because the

current travels in a complete circuit and is the same at all points on it. Other electrical properties do vary at different points, which may be why confusion arises. Sorting out ideas takes time.

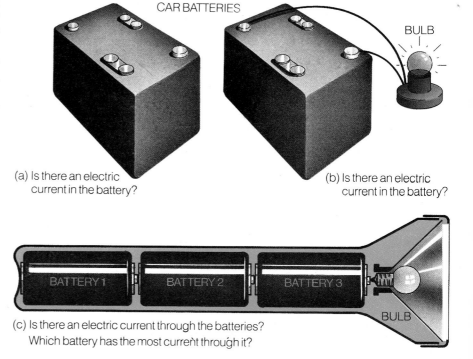

CAR BATTERIES

BULB

(a) Is there an electric current in the battery?

(b) Is there an electric current in the battery?

BATTERY 1 BATTERY 2 BATTERY 3

BULB

(c) Is there an electric current through the batteries? Which battery has the most current through it?

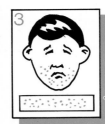

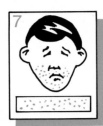

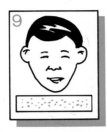

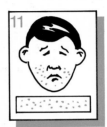

The most likely answer

A Not all problems have a clear cut answer. Nonetheless, there is a need to find the most likely answer under the circumstances. This is true, not only for school problems, but also for everyday decisions – whether to buy something, for example.

The problem which follows is difficult, because parts of the evidence conflict. What's interesting is not how right or wrong your teenager's answers are – but how he/she tackles thinking about probabilities and explaining exceptions.

Problem – doctor's diagnosis: The cards represent some patients in a small, rather isolated community. Some of them have a rash on their faces. Blood samples are taken from each person. Six of these samples show the same new germ. Discuss with your teenager:

A Do you think the germ causes the face rash?
B How sure are you about this? In other words, how likely is it that a person with the germ will develop a rash?
C How could you explain patients 5 and 9, who show a germ but no rash? And patients 6 and 10, who show a rash but apparently no germ?
D After discussing **B** and **C** – do you want to change your answer to **A**?

Comments

If your teenager examines all the cases carefully, he/she will see that there can be no straight answer to **A**. On the evidence, only four out of six patients with the germ also show the rash (3, 4, 7, 11 – 5 and 9 are exceptions). So in **B** there is a probability that 2 out of 3, or 67 per cent of people with the germ will develop the rash.

In **C**, perhaps the rash is simply slow to appear in patients 5 and 9. And perhaps patients 6 and 10 really have the germ, but something went wrong with the blood test. Or perhaps anti-bodies have killed it off fast, and the rash is slow to go. Any of these possibilities could increase the likelihood that the germ definitely causes the rash. They need further investigation. In complex problems, it's being able to see the possibilities and probabilities which counts.

Using a formula

A When your teenager can hold general principles in his/her head, as distinct from solving specific problems, he/she can begin to make sense of formulas. A formula is a general rule which – if correctly applied – will give a fast and accurate solution to any example of the problem. Such rules are often found in science and mathematics. Here are two examples you might like to look at with your teenager:

1 Car numbers: How many different four-digit car plates can you make using only the four digits 1,2,3 and 4? Each digit must only be used once in each number plate.
2 Flags: You have fabric in six colours – red, blue, brown, green, yellow, black – to make up into flags. Each flag is in two pieces. How many different pairs of colours can you make up into flags? You can have pairs of the same colour (brown/brown), but not repeats (for

example, brown/black is the same as black/brown).

Comments

It's more interesting to see how your teenager tackles these problems, than whether he/she got the right answers. Younger teenagers in particular usually need the practical experience of writing out all the possibilities. In so doing they may make errors; duplicating sets of numbers or colours, or missing some out, perhaps.

Older teenagers, or those who are familiar with this kind of problem, may use formulas instead as a short cut to finding the total number of possibilities. Or they may recognise the formulas afterwards, without having been able to transfer what they have learned in maths to practical problems presented in words.

The car numbers problem involves the permutation formula: $N!$ where N

is the number of digits and $!$ means multiply up all the digits: $1 \times 2 \times 3 \times 4 = 24$ different possibilities. The flag problem involves the combination formula: $\leq \frac{N}{1}$ where N is the number of colours (6) and $\leq$ means add up all the numbers from 1 to N: $1+2+3+4+5+6=21$ different possibilities.

The actual answer for number plates is:

1234	1243	1324	1342	1423	1432
2134	2143	2314	2341	2413	2431
3124	3142	3214	3241	3412	3421
4123	4132	4213	4231	4312	4321

The possible colour combinations for the flags are:

red + red/blue/brown/green/yellow/black
blue + blue/brown/green/yellow/black
brown + brown/green/yellow/black
green + green/yellow/black
yellow + yellow/black
black + black

Understanding school subjects

Different subjects at school develop different thinking skills.

Thinking skills

This topic looks at three different aspects of teenage thinking. It is by no means a full review – which would also include physical/manual as well as intellectual performance. Simply, three typical subject area problems are presented for you and your teenager to work through if you wish. Here, as in later life, it is the way of thinking that is important, rather than the subject content. Even if you don't know much about the subject – there will be ways you may be able to help your teenager develop his/her thinking.

The topic may throw some light on the way subjects are presented at your teenager's school. These days, teenagers are often encouraged to gain knowledge and skills from working out problems. Some schools provide curriculum evenings or booklets, which explain the kinds of thinking they are trying to develop in different subjects. If your teenager's school doesn't do this, you might like to raise the matter through the PTA or governing body. (See "What next?"). You might also like to encourage your teenager to ask why he/she is learning things. It is usually a reasonable request and it will help him/her to know.

The topic may also highlight problems your teenager may face in class or with homework. You may want to talk these over with him/her and his/her teachers. Equally, the topic may prompt you to talk with your teenager about the pleasures and enjoyment he/she gets from learning. It's also important to talk about what you each think is important to learn. Academic performance and what you need to get on in life may be two different things.

Warning!

The activities are *not* a test for your teenager. They are simply examples used to demonstrate development in teenage thinking. If you have two or more teenagers, you may see a difference between the younger and older ones in their replies. You will need to pick your time to try the activities with your teenager. If he/she has dropped the subjects concerned, or has left school, he/she may not be interested.

They are not tests for you either. You may feel disappointed in yourself if you don't know all the answers, or annoyed if your teenager does. But the examples may not relate to your own education, or to what interests you now. You may also find your own preferences surfacing. "I never did like poetry" or "I disliked geography at school", as two of our parent testers said. Try to avoid pushing your views on your teenager, or competing with him/her. Rather, support him/her in developing his/her new skills.

Stages of thinking – and helping

Research studies show four broad stages in the development of teenage thought. Individual teenagers will develop at their own rate – which may vary from one subject, or way of thinking to another. They cannot be forced – but they can be encouraged, by parents as well as teachers.

Stage 1: Little or no understanding. What the teenager calls "boring" may in fact be temporarily beyond his/her grasp; and he/she may need rescuing from defeat. It helps to boost his/her confidence in the skills he/she already has, and to reassure him/her that in time he/she will be able to cope with more complex problems. Practical experience, in addition to talking will help, as it did when he/she was younger.

Stage 2: Limited understanding. Here the teenager is often focussing on only part of the problem. Discussion can be a helpful way to get him/her to look at more of the evidence, and to think through his/her answers. Questions can help him/her to move from descriptions to explanations: for example, "Why would that happen . . .?" "What's important here . . .?" Stages 1 and 2 often coincide with times when subject choices must be made at school.

Stage 3: A general grasp. Here the teenager is learning to make use of all the evidence. He/she is likely to give detailed answers, but he/she may need help in sifting out the key points, or in explaining why he/she has chosen to say what he/she does. It is the process of thinking, as much as the actual solution, that teachers and examiners want to see. A tape recorder may help the fluent talker to transcribe his/her thoughts into written words. A patient listener may help the good writer put his/her thoughts into words more fluently.

Stage 4: A full understanding. Here the teenager can link evidence to existing ideas and suggest answers which go beyond the particular problem and relate it to the wider world. Often the temptation with the teenager who excels is to stretch him/her yet further in the same subject. But it is better to help him/her acquire a range of thinking skills in a variety of subjects: these are more likely to be useful to him/her in later life. It may also help to look for challenges outside school – in reading, clubs, holiday jobs and so on.

Reflecting on yourself

Poetry – whether classical, modern or song lyrics – often has a particular appeal to teenagers. The 'new mind' enjoys the flights of imagination, and the freedom to interpret the poem in a personal way.

Poetry and literature help the teenager to reflect on him/herself, to have the confidence to experiment, change and grow. They feed the imagination and suggest a range of possible roles and outlooks on the world. They can also stimulate the teenager to create his/her own 'personal fable' – the story of him/herself, as told to him/herself alone, in diaries, dreams, poems and fantasies.

Helping: Encouraging your teenager to take part in a variety of arts can be a practical way to help. It is important for the teenager to try a wide range, so he/she can decide for him/herself what he/she enjoys. It doesn't matter if he/she doesn't take to the classics. It matters more that he/she finds authors he/she likes who help him/her to reflect on the question: "Who am I?". This self-important phase can be irritating for the rest of the family, but with time and support the teenager will move on to reflect on how much he/she shares with others.

The reader and would-be writer may enjoy sharing discussions about books, poems and words. However, anything they write themselves is likely to be private, not for parental comment or criticism.

What does it mean?

A If you and your teenager are at all interested in poetry, you might like to suggest he/she reads through this poem with you. What does it mean to each of you?

Not Waving But Drowning

Nobody heard him, the dead man,
But still he lay moaning:
I was much further out than you thought
And not waving but drowning.

Poor chap, he always loved larking
And now he's dead
It must have been too cold for him his heart
   gave way,
They said.

Oh, no no no, it was too cold always
(Still the dead one lay moaning)
I was much too far out all my life
And not waving but drowning.

(Stevie Smith: *Collected Poems of Stevie Smith*.)

There are many possible personal interpretations of a poem. All are equally acceptable. It is possible also to see developments in teenager's thinking about poetry. Here are some typical replies at different stages. What kind of understanding does your teenager currently seem to have?

Stage 1: Little or no understanding. For example: "The first verse is about a man who is dead in the middle of a river or lake, the second verse does not mean much to me nor the third verse." *(Gordon, 12½)*.

Stage 2: Limited understanding. This kind of answer may not clearly grow out of the poem itself. But it shows that the teenager has grasped the fact that interpreting poetry involves going beyond the words on the page. For example: "This poem means to me that if something ends it still goes on in another place, like if a man dies he still has a sort of life afterwards and goes on normally in another world." *(Luke, 12)*.

Stage 3: A general grasp. These answers are more detailed and complete. The teenager discusses the whole poem, in more general terms. For example: "This is a strange poem. It is the life story of a man who lived well, who was always in the middle of things. He had plenty of friends, a hectic social life, was unmarried. He was the sort you never seemed to care about anything. Yet he was struggling to fight against loneliness. He was desperately alone. Only when he's dying does he realise this. He realises his life has been wasted and there is nothing he can do. I liked this poem very much." *(Kim, 16)*.

Stage 4: A full understanding. These answers often go on to relate the poem to life. The teenager provides an interpretation which goes far beyond the actual words on the page, to the feelings and meanings the poem conveys to him/her. For example: "This is well written and shows how someone may appear to be doing all right, but is really in trouble. It illustrates the deceptiveness of appearances. It could be compared to school work, how someone might seem to do all right during the year, but get a very poor exam result, and no-one knows why, except the pupil, who knew he was out of his depth." *(Chrissie, 16½)*.

Making connections

Scientific understanding depends on being able to connect evidence with existing ideas, and develop a logical answer. The teenager's increasing ability to imagine things means that he/she becomes more able to work out connections and predict consequences.

Helping: science problems can get quite complicated, requiring the teenager to juggle with several ideas at once. Even without knowing much about the subject, you can help your teenager with the thinking process. For example:

○ asking about possible connections, forgotten pieces of evidence, other ideas which might be relevant
○ linking the problem to things the teenager knows about in everyday life – "it's a bit like . . ."
○ gently challenging the teenager to explain his/her answer, and helping him/her to think through the consequences of what he/she says
○ being prepared to be a partner in finding out.

A typical problem: the food chain

A The idea of the 'food chain' is almost bound to come up at some point during your teenager's study of science. Like many scientific ideas, it can take the teenager quite a while to see all the connections. He/she has to link the problem with what he/she already knows about the nature of the creatures involved; and he/she has to imagine what the consequences will be over a number of seasons.

You might like to discuss the problem as set out below with your teenager, and see what he/she thinks about it. Compare his/her comments with the ones below.

Problem: Greenfly are caught and eaten by blue tits. Blue tits are caught and eaten by sparrow hawks. This series of events is called a food chain. Which – greenfly, blue tit or sparrow hawk – would you expect to be the most common and found in the greatest numbers? Why?

Stage 1: Little or no understanding. For example:
"Greenfly, because they live off plants in the summer." (*Cheryl, $11\frac{1}{2}$*).
"Sparrow hawk, because if the greenfly is eaten there won't be many left, and if the blue tit is eaten by the sparrow hawk, there won't be many of them, so the sparrow hawk is the commonest." (*Darrien, 13*).

Cheryl happens to be right, but the reason she gives is quite irrelevant to the problem. Darrien has not thought about the need for the food chain to renew itself. His parents might suggest he thinks about what the sparrow hawks would go on living on.

Stage 2: Limited understanding. For example:
"Greenfly, because you can see lots in a garden so there would be thousands in only a few gardens." (*Julia, 13*).
"Because it is small and cannot be caught as easily as the blue tit or sparrow hawk." (*Mike, 14*).

Both these teenagers have the correct answer, but nothing like the full explanation of it. Teenagers at this stage tend to describe bits of the problem without making connections, or they only use one piece of evidence. Here Julia and Mike focus on what they know about the greenfly, rather than considering it in relation to the food chain.

Stage 3: A general grasp. For example:
"Greenfly, because if they weren't as common as they are, the blue tit wouldn't be able to catch and eat enough to feed him and so he wouldn't go after something else." (*Justin, $15\frac{1}{4}$*).
"The mother greenfly knows she has to produce more because she knows some will be eaten and also they eat each other when young." (*Mira, 15*).

Teenagers at this stage use more than one piece of evidence. They may also draw on other knowledge and experience as Mira does. They are beginning to consider the consequences as well as the immediate problem.

Stage 4: A full understanding. For example:
"Greenfly, because more of them are needed to feed the large animals which need them to survive. As there are a lot more greenfly, the blue tit can eat them and there will still be enough greenfly to go on breeding so they will never become extinct. If the greenfly died out, the blue tits would decrease in number. The same applies further up the food chain, to blue tits and sparrows." (*Diana, 16*).

Explanations like these use all the evidence, plus other knowledge the teenager has, to give a full and accurate explanation.

Understanding sources

Your teenager's studies will certainly include people and places of which he/she has no personal experience. He/she needs to be able to take 'second-hand' sources of evidence – maps, photos, tables, records, objects, etc – and to translate these into pictures in his/her mind. He/she also needs to be able to imagine why, given these circumstances, people who live there behave the way they do.

Helping: Some everyday ways to help are:
○ finding similar tasks which give practice in everyday life: for example, translating camp guide symbols, reading bus timetables, navigating in the car or on walks in the country.
○ encouraging visual thinking: for example, making visual notes, drawing route maps
○ encouraging an interest in local geography and history, where the teenager can relate what he/she sees to maps, pictures and other sources.

A typical problem: prairie farming

Prairie farming in Manitoba, Canada is a good example of something taught at school, not so much for the usefulness of the knowledge, as for the way it helps teenagers to think through a specific kind of problem. Typical questions which might be set for teenagers to work out from the maps and photo below are:

A Is it wise for the farmer to grow one crop only over such a very large area?
B Why has this small town grown up just here, where the main road and railway cross each other?

You might like to discuss these questions with your teenager, to see how he/she tackles them. Typical replies at different stages of thinking are given below. Which stage does your teenager seem to be at? Would any of the ways of helping suggested left be useful?

Stage 1: Little or no understanding. For example: "Canada is where they grow lots of grain." *(Sean, 11¼).* "They built the town there because the land is flat and they build on flat ground usually." *(Sarah, 11).*

These teenagers find it difficult to sort out what is relevant to the problem in the information given: for example, the whole of the area is flat, so Sarah doesn't even begin to answer the question. It is hard for them to combine the information from the maps and the aerial photo, each of which is on a different scale.

Stage 2: Limited understanding. For example: "The flat plain means they can use big combine harvesters to cut the grain." *(Andy, 12½).* "The town would be in the middle and have the same amount of land on either side." *(Gemma, 13).*

These answers take one aspect of the pictures and discuss the problem in terms of that. They do not take account of other information, such as the map which shows how vast the prairies are; or of other aspects of the problem, such as the fact that transport is needed.

Stage 3: A general grasp. For example: "The land would make the grain easy to harvest, being so flat. Mass production would be profitable so long as there

was a demand for it." *(Sadiq, 14½).*
"The road and the railway go through the town, so the farmers can send the grain off to the coast and then abroad, perhaps to Britain." *(Simon, 14).*

These answers are reasonable, and contain more detail.

Stage 4: A full understanding. For example: "Normally it wouldn't be wise. For something could easily go wrong with the crop in a particular year, and they would lose everything. A great demand for it would be necessary before they can grow on a scale like this, and they would need transportation to get it away to a world market." *(Kirk, 15½).*
"The town has grown up where the road and railway cross because all the farmers bring their grain in and put it on the railway to go off and be sold, it can reach the world market via the Great Lakes and ships across the ocean, even though it is grown so far inland. There must be a big demand for the grain to make it worth while sending it so far." *(Wendy, 15).*

These answers are more sophisticated versions of Stage 3 replies. The teenagers use the information given, and also draw on their other knowledge, and relate the problems to general, world-wide issues.

Tinker, tailor, soldier, sailor . . .

The job for the person: Introduction/Assessment 1

The teenager's 'new mind' lets him/her stand back and look at the kind of person he/she is becoming. Work will be an important influence on his/her self-image. So this topic offers some activities to help your teenager think about him/herself in relation to the kind of work he or she would like to do.

The self-assessment charts are adapted from a workbook for teenagers prepared and tested by the Careers Research and Advisory Centre. You can use them in several ways:
1 Your teenager may like to work through them on his/her own, and just discuss his/her views with you.
2 Your teenager may like to work through them with you.

3 You may simply like to think them through in terms of your teenager, to find new ideas for talking together.
4 You may like to do them yourself, as part of your own 'mid-life review'.

Your own knowledge and experience of work, and your contacts with people in different kinds of jobs, can be a great help in discussion. However, as a parent, your main purpose in using these assessments is to challenge your teenager to take a fresh look at him/herself. They do take some time. Our parent testers and their teenagers took an average of four to five hours, often working over several days. So clearly you

A   Education: what you enjoy in school/college work

I like using tools, utensils or technical instruments ___ I like working with my hands on something useful ___ I like working with things or objects rather than books or ideas ___ I like learning things of practical use to me ___ I like subjects which will help me get a job ___	I like being taught in an orderly, organised way ___ I like subjects where you know exactly what you are expected to do ___ I like teachers who keep students under control ___ I like subjects where I know that I am going to be able to cope ___ I like subjects which are about facts ___	I like subjects where the teacher encourages a friendly atmosphere ___ I like subjects which are about the way people think, feel and behave ___ I like working in groups ___ I like to hear other people's views ___ I like subjects where the other students are friendly ___	I like taking part in class discussion or plays, readings or exhibitions ___ I like unusual subjects ___ I like my work to be good, so that it can be used as an example ___ I like or would like people to think I am good in certain subjects ___ I like to have my work praised ___

B   Leisure: what you enjoy in your spare time

I like learning things that are useful ___ I like collecting and keeping things ___ I like looking after equipment or machinery and tools ___ I like making extra pocket money ___ I like keeping fit and healthy ___	I like sorting things out and keeping them orderly ___ I would rather spend my time alone than meet people I'm not sure of ___ I like to keep my leisure life within respectable limits ___ I feel more comfortable in familiar surroundings ___ I like to plan ahead ___	I like helping the needy ___ I like doing things in co-operation ___ I like doing things which are companionable ___ I like activities where I am with a lot of friendly people ___ I like listening to my friends telling me about themselves ___	I like wearing clothes or a uniform that people find attractive or smart ___ I like unusual activites ___ I like the chance to perform ___ I like activities where you can win prizes, cups, medals or badges ___ I like the chance to show-off a bit ___

C   Opinions: your views about individuals and society

A lot of people have impractical ideas ___ I admire people who focus on useful things ___ Man has benefited most from the invention of tools and machines ___ Money spent on the needy is wasted unless it provides them with food and shelter ___ One of the first questions to ask of any new venture is "Is it practical?" ___	We should all have more respect for parents, teachers etc. ___ Wrongdoers should be made to conform ___ Military strength and strong government are basic needs ___ Society is becoming a bit too chaotic, there is not enough stability ___ Law and order is more important than most people seem to realise ___	What the world needs now is love: not sex but caring love ___ People don't listen enough to each other's points of view ___ I admire people who are kind and sympathetic to others ___ The courts should at all costs be fair to every individual ___ The worst part of being in need is the loneliness ___	I admire people who gain and keep attention or admiration ___ Having the respect of other people is more important than anything ___ When I see a cheering crowd I wish they were cheering me ___ The way you dress and behave publicly tells others a lot about you ___ Most people are anonymous and dull ___

| 1 Practicality   Total ___ | 2 Security   Total ___ | 3 Sociability   Total ___ | 4 Attention   Total ___ |

will need to present them in a way – and at a time – which will make your teenager want to get involved. For example:

○ if your teenager is facing subject choices at school, thinking about personal interests can help him/her to decide
○ younger teenagers may not have very specific ideas about jobs – but they like to have a closer look at themselves
○ older teenagers may have clear ideas about what they want to do, but find the assessments a useful check
○ teenagers who get surprise exam results may want to reconsider their view of themselves and their future.

Assessment 1 : Values

A D *The rows* of the chart below look at your views in different areas. Work across each row: tick the statements which you agree with. Tick √ as many or as few as you like. If any seem especially important to you – put two ticks √√ – or three ticks √√√ for really key statements.
The columns of the chart represent different things you may be seeking from work. Add up the total number of ticks in each column – and then read on overleaf.

I like taking part in class debates or arguments ___	I like finding out things by experiment or research ___	I like subjects where I can create something ___	I like having to use all my concentration and ability to work ___
I like writing essays where I must argue a case persuasively ___	I enjoy subjects which involve thinking, memorising or reasoning ___	I like subjects which deal with attractive or beautiful things ___	I like doing subjects that I can do really well
I like subjects which are important to my plans ___	I enjoy subjects where there is a lot to read ___	I like to present my work attractively ___	I like subjects where I am in competition ___
I like subjects where I can work in my own way ___	I like subjects where I can satisfy my curiosity ___	I enjoy subjects that develop my understanding of the arts ___	I like being kept up to the mark ___
I like subjects where I can be asked for my advice or opinion ___	I like working with an intelligent and expert teacher ___	I like working in attractive surroundings ___	I like subjects where I can discover and use my own capabilities ___

I like the chance to be in authority ___	I have a lot of curiosity ___	I like making beautiful or artistic things ___	I like activities where I must stand on my own feet ___
I like being on an organising committee ___	I like documentary TV programmes best ___	I like keeping in touch with the arts ___	I like things that I can do in my own way ___
I like getting things done effectively ___	I like libraries, museums and other places of educational interest ___	I like the chance to appreciate beauty ___	I only really like doing things I know I do well ___
I like making decisions for myself ___	I would like to be an expert or authority on some subject ___	I like developing my artistic, music or literary understanding ___	I am a competitive person ___
I like activities which will develop my leadership qualities ___	I like non-fiction books best ___	I feel more comfortable in beautiful surroundings ___	I like attempting challenges where I have to work hard ___

I admire people who get things done, influential people ___	I admire people who are well educated and intelligent ___	It is art, music and literature which have contributed most to the quality of life ___	People should not rely on other people ___
A good leader must be able to persuade others to accept his way ___	Mankind has benefitted most from the invention of writing and books ___	We must preserve the beauty of nature ___	I admire people who face challenges and do not give up ___
Politics are very important ___	Expanding our knowledge of the universe justifies any new venture ___	Pleasant design in clothing is more important than fashion ___	The happiest people are those who use their abilities and work hard ___
The world needs more 'doers' and fewer 'dreamers' ___	Man's ability to learn and solve problems is his most important characteristic ___	More attention should be paid to building and landscaping design ___	People are not given enough opportunity to do what they are capable of doing ___
Many of the problems of our society needs strong, forceful solutions ___	Schooldays are the happiest days of your life ___	Artistically creative people are not paid enough ___	A person is worth only what he achieves ___

| 5 Influence Total ___ | 6 Knowledge Total ___ | 7 Beauty Total ___ | 8 Achievement Total ___ |

The job for the person: Assessment 2

In Assessment 1, your teenager and/or you looked at personal values by identifying what's enjoyable in education and leisure – and your opinions about other people and society. Most people will have ticked statements from several, if not all, of the eight columns. But there are likely to be some that stand out as more important to you than others. For example, when Richard did this exercise, his total ticks in each of the columns showed the following range:

What's important to Richard	What's important to me
1 Practicality 8	1 Practicality
2 Security 0	2 Security
3 Sociability 4	3 Sociability
4 Attention (12)	4 Attention
5 Influence 8	5 Influence
6 Knowledge 4	6 Knowledge
7 Beauty (20)	7 Beauty
8 Achievement (11)	8 Achievement

Assessment 2: Matching values and jobs

A D This section asks your teenager to think about how their personal values may be matched – or not – in the kind of job they are looking for. The instructions are written to the teenager. Adapt them as needed to suit the way you are using these activities (see pages 116–117).

First, carry forward your own totals from the chart in Assessment 1. Enter these on the scorecard above, and ring the three which score highest for you. Then read the descriptions (right) of people who hold these values. Do these:

○ confirm your ideas about the sort of person you are?
○ give you some new ideas – or some suprises – you'd like to think over?

If on reflection you do not feel these descriptions fit you, review your answers to Assessment 1. The descriptions are simply stated, so you also may find that they are not all exactly true for

you as an individual. When you are fairly confident that you have identified your current three main values – see how these apply in work.

Read the general descriptions of jobs, and examples, which match your three main values. The 'jobcards' clearly don't cover everything. And of course many jobs – like people – fit more than one value. But they may give you a general feel for different types of work, and perhaps suggest new ideas for the kind of work you'd like to do. They can also help you to compare the satisfactions offered by different jobs. When you find out about a job you may be interested in, ask yourself two sets of questions:

○ What are the main value or satisfactions in this job? What kind of statements would a worker in this job make about him/herself?
○ Are these the same things that I value highly? If not – will this job suit me as a person?

1 Practicality

For some people, a well-paid job, a comfortable home, or eating has greater value than almost anything else. That doesn't necessarily mean that the practical person is good at making things, cooking, building or things like that – although such a person would probably like to have such skills. He will work hard to keep a job that gives him what he wants. He will be unhappy in a job that doesn't. He will find a job that has to do with producing useful things especially worthwhile.

2 Security

For some people, the need to feel safe and secure is especially important. Such a person will do a lot of checking to make sure that their families, homes, jobs and lives are as free from danger as possible. He will suffer more anxiety than other people in an industry where there are a lot of redundancies. But, provided it was secure, he might get a lot of satisfaction from a job which was itself about making life more secure.

3 Sociability

The social person may not necessarily be the most sociable or popular type – but he will probably be the one most prepared to listen to others, including

1 Practical jobs
Society needs this job done in order physically to survive
It means working mainly with things rather than people
It is a practical job, useful to people
It is well-paid
It is a convenient job – travelling would be cheap and easy
The skills learned could be used to make money outside
Examples: bricklayer, machinist, dustman, hospital ward orderly, milkman, oil-rig worker.

2 Security-oriented jobs
This work makes life safer
The job stays the same
It is a secure job
A person with abilities like mine would not be taking on more than he could cope with
It is a job where you can easily find out what to do and how to do it
It is a job where the employees are properly looked after and protected
Examples: police officer, machine-tool operator, car-park attendant, prison officer, shop shelf-filler.

their troubles. In his work he likes to feel that he is offering a service which other people want and appreciate. He is likely to be very unhappy in a job where he could not be on friendly terms with his colleagues and workmates, or get on well with clients and customers.

4 Attention

The attention-seeking person will enjoy work where he can be with other people who will notice how well he works. Or he may look for jobs which have a great deal to do with holding other people's attention. He may worry about humiliation at work. He is likely to find his work tedious if he is isolated from other people.

JOB CENTRE

3 Social jobs
The job is about helping people
It involves knowing and understanding clients or customers
It involves listening to what people have to say
The work is done in a friendly atmosphere
There is plenty of company
You can talk to colleagues or workmates while you work
Examples: shop assistant, probation officer, careers officer, air hostess, receptionist, interviewer.

4 Attention-seeking jobs
It is a job which many people consider important
It involves a certain amount of leadership
The work done is looked at or noticed by seniors
The public sees you at work
It is a job that a worker can be proud of in our society
It is an unusual job
Examples: actor/actress, teacher, doctor, lawyer, hotel manager.

5 Influence-seeking jobs
The job carries real responsibility
It means working persuasively with customers or clients
If it is not done properly the consequences can be serious
You get a feeling of achievement
A person with qualifications could be put in charge of something
The work could mean persuading workmates what has to be done
Examples: project controller, sales director, financial journalist, time-and-motion-study expert.

6 Knowledge-seeking jobs
It is scientific work
The work requires a good educational background
It involves finding things out, getting information
It involves providing information to others
It is concerned with books or ideas
Further study is required
Examples: research worker, librarian, information officer, museum creator, advice-centre worker.

7 Beauty-oriented jobs
The job involves being artistically creative
It is concerned with decorating things – making things attractive
It takes you into the countryside
It involves handling other people's creative work
It is done in attractive surroundings
Some sense of what is good in music, art or writing is involved
Examples: silversmith, editor, window dresser, graphic designer, photographer, guide in stately home.

8 Achievement-oriented jobs
The work is hard and demanding
You get on by your own effort and ability
You can do this kind of work in your own way
The work involves competition
A person with ability could get on in this job
A lot of people would be unwilling to attempt taking on this job
Examples: self-employed craftsman, advertising executive, bank manager, newspaper editor, politician.

5 Influence

The influence-seeking person will enjoy and work hard at tasks where he has real responsibility. He will find it irksome to work as a tiny, insignificant cog in a massive machine. He will enjoy a job where he has real decision-making. His nightmares may be about being dependent on others, being manipulated by others or being entirely ignored by people in charge.

6 Knowledge

Curiosity is a stronger drive for some people than for others. The knowledge-seeking person will gain great satisfaction from becoming an expert in his job, or an authority on his subject. He will find work frustrating where he is not told what is going on, or what contribution his work is making to the overall enterprise. He will not enjoy jobs where there is nothing very much to think about or learn. Scientific work, and also a range of other jobs are concerned with facts and discovery.

7 Beauty

The 'aesthetic' person has a keener sense than others of what is beautiful in art, music, literature or his surroundings. He will get satisfaction from his work if he can use an artistic skill in it, or work with the artistic productions of other people. He will want to work in pleasant surroundings, since anyone who appreciates beautiful things will find it unpleasant to work in an ugly, noisy or unattractive place.

8 Achievement

The achievement-seeking person goes out of his way to prove himself. Such a person will want a job that he can do well in, and will work hard to succeed in it. He will find repetitive work boring because there are no new challenges to overcome. He needs the scope to improve his performance. He may want a job where there are clear ways in which he can measure his own achievements – like professional qualifications, or set promotion ladders.

119

The job for the person: Assessments 3/4/5/6

Assessment 3: Job demands

Assessment 2 looked at the satisfactions a job may have to offer the teenager. Assessments 4,5,6 look at what the teenager may have to offer a job in terms of qualifications, mental abilities and physical qualities.

Stop at this point and do Assessments 4,5,6. All instructions are written for the teenager. Adapt them as you need.

A When you have a clear picture of your own strengths and weaknesses, return to this assessment. Ask yourself about any job you are interested in:

○ What qualifications are needed for entry? How do these match the ones I expect to gain?
○ What mental abilities does the job seem to call for and why? Do these match mine?
○ What physical demands may the job make?

You may need to get further information on the job in question to answer all these points. Where there is a mismatch, you do not necessarily have to give up the job idea entirely. There may be a different grade of job which would suit your likely qualifications better. Or you may be able to find the satisfactions you seek (Assessments 1,2) from a related kind of work which is better suited to your mental or physical capabilities. With luck you will be able to match what you have to offer, with a suitable job you will also enjoy. All that remains then is to see how well the style of the job will fit your personality (see Assessments 7,8 overleaf).

Assessment 4: Qualifications

School-leaving qualifications are clearly important when looking for a job. Younger teenagers (11–13) may not yet have much idea about their exam chances. If this is the case – leave this section for a while. Older teenagers and their parents may need to talk to teachers; or the last school report may give an indication.

A ⑩ The questions in the chart help you and your teenager to think through the likely chances of success. For each subject being studied, make a column in a chart of your own, and answer the questions below. You can then pick out all the subjects in which a pass may be expected, at what level (questions 1 and 4).

As a result of doing this assessment, you may want to talk over the subjects being taken at exam level in more detail with the school.

1 My teaching group for this subject is:
A non-examination **B** CSE **C** 'O' level **D** 'A' level
E other (specify)

2 In relation to others in my group, I am near the:
A top **B** middle **C** bottom

3 Between now and the examination, I can expect to improve:
A a lot **B** somewhat **C** barely at all

4 So the best guess about an examination result is:
A good pass **B** fair pass **C** borderline **D** fail **E** not entered

1 **Verbal ability**

2 **Numeracy**

3 **Spatial ability**

4 **Originality**

5 **Word fluency**

6 **Memory**

7 **Perception**

8 **Reasoning**

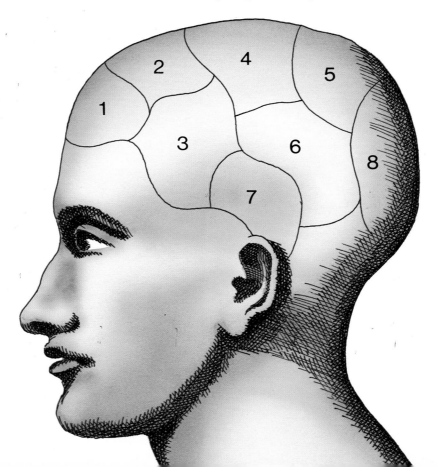

Assessment 5: Mental abilities

Qualifications are one measure of ability. It can also be useful to take a more general look at basic aptitudes and interests. Eight of these are described in the chart below. Alongside are just a few examples of jobs which draw on such abilities. Careers Advisory Services can offer more detailed information and guidance. This assessment does not help to assess general level of intelligence, but it can help to highlight patterns of strengths and weaknesses.

A ⓓ Make your own list of the eight abilities. Read the descriptions in the chart below and think how these relate to things you do well at in school/college; or things you enjoy in your leisure time. Note these beside the relevant ability, with a √. If you want, also make a note of things you dislike, or do not do well, with an X. For example, you might put:
√ English and the drama group beside word fluency
X Maths and being on the till in beside Numeracy.

Ring the abilities which seem important for you to try and use when choosing a career. For instance, you might realise word fluency and originality were two of your strong points.

Example jobs	Abilities
Telephonist Secretary Editor Shop assistant	**1 Verbal ability** Can you understand words? Verbal comprehension is the ability to 'take in' accurately the meaning of written and spoken words. How well do you understand speech and writing?
Accountant Computer systems analyst Cash till operator Banker	**2 Numeracy** Are you good with numbers? Numeracy is the ability to understand and express ideas by way of numbers. Being good at arithmetic or remembering mathematical formulae is not necessarily an indication of your ability to understand.
Surveyor Window dresser Archaeologist Engineer	**3 Spatial ability** Are you good with shapes, diagrams or objects? Spatial ability is the ability to understand two- or three-dimensional shapes or objects. It is a mental ability, not to be confused with being good with your hands.
Dress designer Architect Advertising agent Illustrator	**4 Originality** Are you creative? Originality may or may not be closely related to intelligence. It is the ability to produce a flow of new and useful ideas, though not necessarily in every area of thinking. You may be original in the use of words, numbers, shapes and objects, or pictures.

Assessment 6: Physique & health

A ⓓ All jobs make physical and mental demands. This is as true of an office job as of manual work – though clearly some jobs make greater demands than others.

The list below sets out 12 main aspects of physique and health which may be relevant in choosing a job. Make notes about your own assets and problems. Your assets may be points in your favour when it comes to particular jobs.

You may be able to improve some of these aspects, if you need to, on your own or with medical or other support. If you are worried about any part of this assessment now, think about seeing the school doctor or your own GP. Or perhaps talk the problem over with the careers teacher or school counsellor.

1 Good general health	7 Strength
2 Height	8 Fast reactions
3 Clear breathing	9 Good eyesight
4 Clear skin	10 Dexterity
5 Clear speech	11 Good co-ordination
6 Good hearing	12 Pleasant appearance

Example jobs	Abilities
Broadcaster Demonstrator Driving instructor Salesman	**5 Word fluency** Are you fluent? Word fluency is the ability to 'give out' your meaning in the right words readily. Do you enjoy talking because you know you do it well?
Linguist Librarian Information officer Solicitor	**6 Memory** Do you remember well? Memory is the ability to retain and recall material from the past. Even if you have a good memory you may find it operates better in some areas of thinking than others.
Policeman Cartographer Investment analyst Administrator	**7 Perception** Do you notice things? Perception is the ability to notice things in detail, not to be confused with good vision or hearing. Like memory, good perception can operate differently in various areas of thinking – in written or spoken material, numbers, shapes and diagrams or objects.
Forensic scientist Radiographer Work study officer Scientific technician	**8 Reasoning** Are you good at working things out? Reasoning is the ability to move surely from the known to the unknown taking what is known and then drawing conclusions logically. Like memory and perception, it can operate with varying degrees of efficiency in areas such as verbal, numerical or diagrammatic reasoning.

The job for the person: Assessments 7/8 and Summary

The job style		Personal style	A	B	C
Not taking any risks Paying close attention to detail Working slowly and methodically Doing the work very precisely Doing everything thoroughly *Example jobs:* craftwork, research	**1 Careful**	Careful – tries to avoid mistakes Thorough – sees a task right through Gives attention to detail Takes pride in work Concentrates closely Perfectionist – dislikes shoddy work			
Being very co-operative with everyone Working closely with others Waiting to be told what to do Fitting in with the team or group Getting along with others *Example jobs:* personnel or social work, armed forces	**2 Cooperative**	Co-operative Loyal – will not let friends down Polite – does not like to offend Responds well to suggestions Adaptable – can fit in well with others A 'joiner' of clubs, projects, whatever is going on			
Using initiative Telling others what to do Taking responsibility Exercising leadership Seeking to influence others *Example jobs:* teaching, management	**3 Dominant**	Dominant – wants to be out in front Influences others Takes initiative Accepts responsibility Elected representative by colleagues Can handle limelight – even enjoys it			
Being very active – never pausing Always working quickly Working vigorously and energetically Working to the point of exhaustion Working under pressure *Example jobs:* teaching sport, oil rig work	**4 Dynamic**	Active – is always on the go Hard-working Keeps up to date with work Vigorous – plenty of energy Plenty of drive Can manage part-time job without hindering studies			
Remaining calm under pressure Not worrying when things go wrong Being detached, not too involved Coping with others' unhappiness Being consistent under stress *Example jobs:* nursing, publishing	**5 Resilient**	Resilient – stays cheerful Overcomes all kinds of difficulties Accepts criticism calmly Not easily upset or discouraged Consistent Relaxed, not the type to panic			
Being prepared to carry on alone Not waiting to be told what to do Working alone Being prepared to answer criticism Working out problems on your own *Example jobs:* research work, any form of self-employment	**6 Self sufficient**	Self-sufficient, stands on own feet Resourceful Usually knows what he/she is doing Prefers own decisions Thinks for himself/herself Independent, prefers to handle things alone			
Listening to people Being tactful Being influenced by feelings Understanding unspoken needs Keeping confidences *Example jobs:* counselling, social work	**7 Sensitive**	Feeling – reacts to atmosphere, mood Aware of other people's feelings Wanting to please Tactful – doesn't like to hurt others Interested in others			
Making people at ease Talking to people in a friendly way Working in an easy-going way Being good-humoured Developing personal contacts *Example jobs:* Sales, PR	**8 Sociable**	Sociable Easy-going, not quick tempered Friendly, likes to be with people Popular, is well-liked by others Wide range of friends Good-humoured			
Always being honest Always being reliable Sticking to the rules Always doing what is expected Following a set routine *Example jobs:* warden, postman	**9 Trustworthy**	Trustworthy Honest Punctual whenever possible Rarely absent except through illness Works well unsupervised Reliable			

Assessment 7 : Personal style

A **D** It helps to have a job which suits their personality. So it's useful to look at personal style. The right-hand side of the chart (left) lists statements which describe behaviour. This is the 'visible you' – in contrast to the values in Assessment 1, which may or may not be clear to other people.

The instructions and comments in this topic are written for teenagers. Adapt them as necessary for yourself.

○ In Column C, tick the statements which – honestly – you think describe your own behaviour.
○ Then ask a friend to tick the descriptions they think apply to you, in Column B. (Cover up Column C.)
○ Ask a friendly adult (parent, teacher, relative) to tick their views of your behaviour in Column A. (Cover up B and C.)
○ Look at the overall patterns of ticks – how far do you all agree with each other?

Where you disagree, your personality is coming over to other people in a different way. They may see more or less in you – or a different you – compared to how you see yourself. This may give you cause to think about your behaviour.

Some of the styles in the chart don't really go with others: for example, it would be hard to be both dominant and co-operative. So although you may have ticked several styles in the chart – you may well have to choose some styles at the expense of others. You might like to ring what you see as the three most important styles for you.

Assessment 8 : Job styles

A In the left-hand column of the chart, the personal styles have been turned into a list of briefs which jobs may involve.

When personal style matches job style, the job is likely to be done well, and the person who does it to be satisfied. When the job is done by a person in a mismatched style, this can cause friction or conflict, and may mean the job is not done well. For example, someone who always "does things by the book" would be suited in a job where trustworthiness or co-operation are important, but they might be mismatched with jobs where self-sufficiency is needed.

Analysing your personal style can help you to look out for jobs in a matching style. Each time you find out about a job you may be interested in, ask yourself:

○ What sort of working brief is involved? What kind of things would be said about the type of person likely to do this job well? Try to identify the job style. Then ask:

○ Does this match my own personal style?

Summary

A **D** Finally, make a summary. In the right-hand column, note a picture of yourself based on Assessments 1,4,5,6,7. You may want to revise this if you do it first at 13, say, and again at age 16. Each time you find out about a job you are interested in, assess it in the left-hand column, along the lines of Assessments 2,3,8. What is required, and why? How well does this job fit the person you are?

The job	Assessment	The person
The satisfactions offered are:	**Values** (Assessments 1, 2) 1 Practicality 2 Security 3 Sociability 4 Attention 5 Influence 6 Knowledge 7 Beauty 8 Achievement	My three most important values are:
The qualifications required are:	**Qualifications** (Assessments 3,4)	I expected to gain the following qualifications:
The mental demands of the job are:	**Abilities** (Assessments 3,5) 1 Verbal ability 2 Numeracy 3 Spatial ability 4 Originality 5 Word fluency 6 Good memory 7 Perception 8 Reasoning	My own abilities are as follows:
The physical demands of the job are:	**Physique and health** (Assessments 3,6) 1 Good general health 2 Height 3 Clear breathing 4 Clear skin 5 Clear speech 6 Good hearing 7 Strength 8 Fast reactions 9 Good eyesight 10 Dexterity 11 Good coordination 12 Pleasant appearance	My physical assets and weaknesses are:
The job involves being:	**Style** (Assessments 7,8) 1 Careful 2 Co-operative 3 Dominant 4 Dynamic 5 Resilient 6 Self-sufficient 7 Sensitive 8 Sociable 9 Trustworthy	The three most important styles for me are:

Schools

Schools vary too much for this chapter to give detailed information. Instead, the emphasis is on the *processes* that parents can help with. Parents always have the most individual knowledge about their children, so you are well placed to help in the *process* of getting the right kind of schooling for your teenagers (pages 126–129). You can also sense the moment when your particular teenager might like help in the *process* of learning (pages 138–143).

As the three-way relationship between parents, teenagers and teachers, does not always run smoothly, the central topic in this chapter looks at feelings about school, and the *process* of exchanging information, in the context of home-school relationships (pages 130–137).

Parents often say that school has changed so much since their own day that they don't know where to begin helping. Subjects are different and there is likely to be a more developed system for 'pastoral' care as well. Your own experiences at school may also have left you feeling unable to help. More information can be useful – and this chapter should help you to find out more of the things you'd like to know, but information alone is not enough. You need also to examine your feelings – in particular, how feelings left over from your own schooldays may colour your present attitudes and behaviour.

Past feelings, present actions

A **D** Think back for a moment over the last meeting you had with your teenager's headteacher or form teacher at school. What were your feelings . . . and why?

Feelings about the subject: Did your feelings about the topic you were discussing have anything to do with your own schooldays? For example, you might be cool about your daughter's success in French because your own teacher put you off the subject. You might feel uncomfortable discussing truanting if you regularly – or absolutely never – did this.

Feelings about the setting: Could your feelings about the discussion have anything to do with the set-up in your own school days? For example, did the teacher sit opposite you, and give you the impression that he barely knew who you were – and didn't care much?

Sometimes our parent testers' experiences put them in sympathy with their teenager:

"I hated games too – so I dish out 'excuse' notes readily"
"I worry about him not making friends, as I had this problem"

Other parent testers appreciated the differences for their teenager today – although these could also be cause for concern:

"I was definitely a 'plodder', so I'm pleased he's doing well, especially in maths, which I was hopeless at"
"I've always felt I'd have done better going to a mixed school, so I'm pleased my teenager will have this experience"
"I think perhaps we push too hard – but I didn't do well in exams, and I realise they are necessary now"

This chapter covers many situations where events at your teenager's school can push you back into feeling like the teenager you once were. As you work through this chapter, be alert to your feelings as well as the facts about school.

Secondary schooling

What's right for your teenager?

Schools are different

Secondary schools have changed since your day, so what's best for your teenager can be difficult for you to decide or to agree on. This topic looks at choosing a secondary (upper) school for your teenager at age 11–13, but it may also provide a useful review of your teenager's school after he/she's been there for two or three years. And, if you have to move house, you may also find it helps you to find a school well-suited to your teenager's needs.

These two pages of the topic look at your opinions generally, while the next focus on the specific issues of school transfer, pastoral care, and subjects in the curriculum.

What makes for success?

Clearly, the size of a school, its facilities, organisation and so on, will have an effect on pupils, but there is no simple, single recipe for the general success or failure of a school. Researchers can often identify clusters of factors which seem to relate to good achievement and behaviour in the schools they study, but it is very difficult to demonstrate cause and effect. A recent major research study into the effects of secondary schooling made the point clearly that equally effective schooling is possible in schools that vary a great deal in resources, organisation, disciplinary approach, and so on.

So the important questions for parents are: What's most likely to make my teenager happy and successful at school?

And what does the school he/she goes to now – or the schools he/she could go to – have to offer in this respect?

You can find out about schools from a variety of sources: booklets, visits, local papers, talking to teachers, to other parents (including parent governors), to pupils – and to your own teenager, of course. Each of these may give you a slightly different point of view, with a bias you need to consider.

Some facts are easy to find out, others are more a matter of judgement. Ultimately, it isn't merely the facts that are important, it's how you interpret them, and the conclusions you draw, which matter.

Girls' performance: a case in point

For example – there is growing evidence that girls of all ability levels do less well than they could in science and maths, at mixed secondary schools. Your opinion may be that this doesn't matter, if you think girls aren't suited to technical jobs, but if – like a growing number of parents – you do think this matters, then you need to look at what can be done.

Often, girls perform better in maths and science in single sex schools. But mixed schools are also finding ways to help girls, for example:

○ making maths and one science compulsory to age 16
○ providing careers guidance which points out the job options girls may be closing if they don't take maths or science
○ developing teaching methods which keep girls more involved
○ separating boys and girls for maths and science classes
○ putting more girls than boys in teaching groups, so that boys do not dominate the lessons

So if maths and science are important for your daughter, you don't have to conclude that single sex education is essential. Discussing the issue can reassure you that she can have the benefits of coeducation *and* the support she may need in these subjects.

1 Size of school.
Large schools may have more resources. What efforts does the school make to avoid pupils feeling lost in the crowd?

5 Pupils' background.
Do you and your teenager think it is important that he mixes with pupils from a variety of backgrounds?

2 Mixed or single sex.
How might you compensate for any disadvantages you see?

6 Handicapped pupils.
If your teenager is handicapped, can the school cope?

9 Sports facilities.
Is there a wide range? Does your teenager have a choice? What's the school's attitude to non-sporting types?

4 Catchment area.
Most pupils will come from the defined catchment area. Free transport – if needed – is provided within the area.

7 Average class size.
May vary a lot; but is not nearly as important as the skills of the teacher.

10 Arts facilities.
Are music, art and other creative subjects seen as an important part of a good general education?

12 Range of subjects.
Does your teenager have specialised interests like computer science or Russian?

3 Religious links.
Any – or none? What's important to you? Do you need to complement or counterbalance the school's approach?

8 Uniform.
Is there one? Does the school fuss about it?

11 Science facilities.
Do the students *do* the experiments themselves? Are they encouraged to *discover* the answers?

13 Academic groupings.
Are pupils taught in mixed ability groups or by ability in sets or streams? Ask the school *why?*

Choices and compromises

A D This activity can help you and your teenager to sort out what you want from a secondary school.

Read through the items and questions in the chart below. Make a note of the ones which concern you most:

○ if you are trying to choose between schools, note the top priorities you want to obtain.
○ if you are reviewing the school your teenager attends, note the areas where you'd like to see a change.

Then take a closer look at your opinions. You may find it helps to work through the following steps:

1 State your opinion, and the reason for your concern. For example, "I disapprove of setting because it damages the confidence of the lowest group".

2 Find out more about the school's policy and views. What are their reasons, and basis for, grouping pupils by ability? How do they try to overcome difficulties?

3 Discuss your opinions with the school, including what you'd like to see happen. Can you persuade the school to make changes? Or can they persuade you to change your mind?

4 If you have to accept something you disapprove of, there are still several things you can do:

Explain to your teenager. For example, "I don't believe that setting helps all pupils equally – but the school thinks that overall it's better for teachers as well as the pupils".

Stay interested in what happens. If your teenager is in the bottom set, what help is he/she given with difficulties? If he/she's in the middle – when will there be a review? If he/she's in the top set – does he/she get enough support?

Plan what you'll do if things get much worse. For instance, you might decide to discuss your teenager's difficulties with the Head of the relevant Department.

Look for compensations for things you can't change.

You might decide to encourage your teenager to take part as well in mixed ability groups or clubs outside school.

When parents and teenagers disagree

When you and your teenager consider schools, you may well disagree about what you think is important. The chart can help you each to list your main reasons in favour of a particular school. Then you can see more clearly the differences you have to sort out.

Where you clash – hold opposite points of view on the same issue – how important is the clash point to each of you? Can you agree to differ?

Where you disagree on what you emphasise – how far can you each find what you want in the other's choice of school? What priority do you place on the things each other find important?

Remember that it is your teenager who has to go to the school for the next few years. If you try to impose a decision, you need to be aware of what the best, worst and most likely consequences will be for you and your teenager. Negotiating the final decision together can be an important step towards adulthood for your teenager.

No school is perfect, and in the end the choice is likely to be a compromise between the two of you, and what you each want. However you come to a decision, you will need to find ways to cope with any negative aspects of your choice.

14 Special help in learning.
Do they provide remedial help? Do they stretch the high-fliers?

15 Academic record.
You can't tell much from the bare exam results. Ask the Head to talk to you about them.

16 Pastoral care.
Do some staff have special responsibility for pupils' personal problems? What counselling training have they had?

17 Homework.
How much? How well-marked is it?

18 Clubs and outside activities.
What? When do they meet? Are there school trips?

19 Conditions for pupils.
Is there a pleasant working environment for pupils?

20 Participation by pupils.
Do many of the pupils have special responsibilities? Do pupils have a say in the way the school is run?

21 Conditions for teachers.
Are they involved in decisions about what goes on? Do they get clerical help and support from more experienced teachers.

22 In lesson time.
Is most of the time spent on the subject rather than keeping order? Are a variety of teaching methods used?

23 Discipline.
Is there plenty of praise and not too much punishment? Are bullies dealt with firmly? What about corporal punishment?

24 Parent-Teacher Association.
Is there one? How active – and powerful – is it?

25 Home-school communications.
How much do they tell you? How easy is it to talk to the teachers?

HOME PARK COMPREHENSIVE

127

Going up – and moving on

Teenagers changing schools have a range of concerns. Most secondary schools now have special arrangements for new pupils and parents to see round the school and ask questions. Such a visit can give you both insight and reassurance:

"It gave a foretaste of how formal the school was."
"It was interesting to meet the Headmaster and get some idea of his personality."
"Our queries were adequately dealt with, to the extent that we were happy for our daughter to go there."

Schools may also produce an information booklet for new pupils, and make special start-of-term arrangements: for example, new pupils may start a day or two early, with an older pupil to act as their guide.

Studies of pupils' attitudes to secondary school transfer suggest that the majority experience some problems of adjustment. Happily, these seem mostly to disappear after a term or so. Some of the more frequent problems relate to changes of classroom, different school rules and punishments, and having more than one teacher. The more similar the type of school, the easier transfer seems.

However, all school changes – even from class to class, or to a new subject – are transition times, and as such, they can be a source of stress.

Topics in Chapter 1 look in more detail at age-related transitions, and the support your teenager may need to cope with them. They also discuss life events such as moving house, which can have a knock-on effect into other areas of life, such as school.

The teenager who changes school for reasons other than simply 'going up' faces additional stresses. He/she lacks the mutual support which comes from transfering with friends, or at least a whole class of new pupils. And the school may provide less information and support to the odd newcomer than it does to the annual intake of new pupils. It becomes doubly important for parents to help the teenager acquire the information, skills and support he/she needs to cope with the change.

Your teenager

A Encourage your teenager to:
1 Find out as much as possible about the school. What information is available beforehand? Is there a map of the school? Being lost and having to ask someone from a sea of unfamiliar faces is daunting. If your teenager's school doesn't provide a map ask if some pupils could make one for newcomers.

2 Ask when he/she needs help. Even apparently confident teenagers may feel nervous about this in new surroundings. Can you help him/her improve these skills? See the topic on "Support" in Chapter 1.

3 Get to know the teachers. Talk to him/her about what he/she thinks of the teachers and encourage him/her not to stereotype them as 'strict', 'boring', 'silly' etc. They are just like other people with a wide range of strengths, weaknesses and personality types. He/she needs time to get used to them – and they to him/her.

Pastoral care

Each pupil will be put into a form or tutor group with a teacher responsible for his or her welfare. This may be a form group where pupils are all the same age. The form may have a different teacher each year, or the teacher may move up with them. Alternatively, the tutor group may have pupils of all ages in it. Here the teacher stays with the group for several years. The younger pupils have the support of the older ones and in turn have the responsibility of helping younger new members.

Each 'Year' will probably have a Year Head who is skilled in coping with problems of that particular age group: for example, Third Year Heads have experience in helping pupils chose which 'O' level or CSE examinations to study for.

In addition some schools have a specially trained School Counsellor or Deputy Head to whom both pupils and parents can take personal matters. Problems disclosed to school counsellors will be treated in confidence and not discussed with other teachers in the school without the pupil's agreement.

Your teenager's school

A Teachers who provide pastoral care should have good counselling skills. They also need support in their work from someone who provides them with pastoral care. What happens in your teenager's school? This topic might be discussed at a parent-teacher meeting. Some questions to ask are:
1 Is there a School Counsellor? If not does one teacher deal with specially difficult or confidential problems?
2 What in-serve training is provided in pastoral care skills? Which teachers receive training?
3 What support is provided so that teachers can discuss any problems that arise with a more experienced person?
4 Does your teenager know who to seek help from? School counsellors often hear, in confidence, about problems between parents and teenagers. You need to encourage your teenager to seek help if he/she needs it. This can be hard for some parents to accept. But, of course, skilled 'outsiders' can often be more helpful than 'family'.

The curriculum

Sian's timetable for Monday

Period 1	9.15–10.10	Technical studies
Period 2	10.10–11.05	(double period)
Period 3	11.25–12.20	Humanities
		Lunch break
Period 4	13.35–14.30	Computer studies
Period 5	14.30–15.25	English
	15.25–15.30	Registration, school ends

This probably looks quite different from the kind of timetable you had when you were at school. So what did Sian actually do on Monday?

She began with a double period of car maintenance. Other subjects which come under the heading of Technical Studies could be cookery and needlework, wood, plastic and metal work. After the mid-morning break she went to the Humanities building for a lesson in the sex education course being given by the teacher responsible for Social Studies. The class had a fairly animated discussion on the subject of schoolgirl pregnancies. Geography, history and religious education are also Humanities subjects.

In Computer Studies, after lunch, Sian got on with writing a programme which will help her and her fellow pupils to plan what subjects they will take at 'O' and 'A' level. Before registration in her own classroom at the end of the day, Sian has a period of English, when she studies modern poetry. In the course of her day she has done one subject which may sound familiar – English – and three which may not:

○ an 'old' subject with revised contents (Technical Studies)
○ a 'combined' subject (Humanities)
○ a relatively new subject (Computer Studies).

Most subjects you don't recognise from your own school-days will fall into one of these categories. Today the curriculum tends to be broader, with a greater range of choices, or options. A wider range of media and teaching techniques are used – TV, group discussion, role play, surveys, projects, worksheets are just a few of the things you may hear about. The emphasis tends to be on ways of thinking rather than merely on the facts of a subject (see "Understanding school subjects" p 112–115).

In addition to academic and practical skills, many schools these days also aim to teach a range of personal and social skills: for example, how to study, make decisions, be assertive, express feelings, take an active part in the local community.

From the age of 13/14, your teenager may begin to specialise in the subjects he/she studies, with a view to the examinations he or she will take at 16. Most schools expect all pupils to study certain basic subjects which are considered essential: maths, English, physical education, religious education, careers, guidance, for example. These usually take up about half the week. The remaining time is spent on a number of subject options chosen from the range available.

Options

A Subject options are important because they help to determine your teenager's whole future. Wise choice depends on discussions between parents, teenager and teachers. Choosing is too important, and too individual, an issue to cover in detail in this book. But there are some general guidelines:

1 Keep informed: about when choices need to be made. Try to read all the booklets the school provides, and go to meetings. Take up the option of individual advice if you need it.

2 Discuss all your teenager's talents and interests: Your teenager needs to choose subjects he/she is interested in and good at. Reasons like "I hate Miss X" or "Sharon's doing it" aren't in the long run, such good reasons for choices.

3 Consider careers: Your teenager may not yet know much about what he or she wants to do, or what different jobs require. The key thing to check is that he/she doesn't close off too many work options with the subjects he/she chooses. He/she may end up doing some subjects because he/she needs them more than likes them.

4 Challenge the school if you need: The school will probably suggest some general guidelines, which reflect their idea of a rounded education: at least one language, one science, one humanities subject, for example. If you and your teenager can argue a good case for doing something else, they will probably permit it, if it is possible.

5 Look for alternatives if you need: Sometimes there may not be a teacher, or space in the timetable, for a subject your teenager wants to do. If so – could he/she do it at an evening class, or pick it up later, in the sixth form?

Teenagers' feelings about school

How teenagers feel about school will affect how well they do.

Teenagers' feelings about school don't come out of the blue. There are always reasons for them. This topic looks at:

○ *the effects of pressures from home – and from school:* Does the school stretch your teenager? Do you push too hard?
○ *how school affects the teenager's self-esteem:* does it make him/her feel important, involved, positive about him/herself? Or is your teenager sufficiently turned off to truant? Does he/she play up teachers to get their attention?

Feeling bad about school may be reflected in the teenager's attitudes, behaviour and even real physical complaints such as headaches or stomach upsets. Success and failure at school – both academic and social – will affect the teenager's whole view of him/herself both now and in the future. Parents who feel they failed at school may understand this well.

Equally, the teenager may be depressed and unable to concentrate at school because of problems at home. Home, school and teenager make a three-way relationship. Each side needs to keep the other in the picture. The next two topics look at ways of raising concerns with the school, and improving relationships. Even if you are all satisfied now – it never harms to make a review.

Pressures from home

Achievement is important to everyone. It feels good to do well. The right amount of support and challenge from parents can help a teenager to do what he/she wants. Too much or too little – or inappropriate pressures – can be unhelpful. Can you see anything of your own family when you were a teenager, in the following case histories?

Living up to expectations: Jo's mother had to leave school early to earn her living. She'd wanted to go to college and was determined Jo would have the education she missed. Jo did well at school and knew she made her mother proud – especially on the day she was accepted for teacher-training. But she found she disliked the course, the college, and small children. To cap it all, her mother was planning her career ahead. Jo left college and took a job as a gardener. She was happy, her mother disappointed. Their relationship became strained.

Living down to expectations: No-one in Derek's family had ever done well at school. His teacher told his parents that he was bright and could do well, but they didn't see the point of schoolwork and exams. They had done alright without any qualifications. When Derek started secondary school and

had homework to do, his Dad would often say "Leave that and give me a hand in the garage". His parents never praised him for his good school reports. After a while, Derek lost interest in schoolwork and his marks declined.

Second place – second best: Amin was walking on air as he came home with his first report from secondary school. He'd worked hard all term and come second in his form. His teacher was very pleased. Amin was hurt and then bewildered when his father said "Well that's alright, I suppose. But why didn't you come first?" Repeated blows to self-esteem like this can make a teenager give up trying altogether.

So long as you're happy: Lynne's parents didn't want to push her too hard. They thought it best just to let her follow her own interests. That way, they told each other, she would be happy. To begin with, Lynne was happy and developed at her own pace. But she didn't get any encouragement to keep up with her schoolwork. By the fourth year, it was clear that she hadn't developed the self-discipline to concentrate on a task, or to fit in with what the rest of the class were doing.

Practise! Practise! Practise! Early on, Sarah showed a talent for playing the violin. Her father had great hopes that she would make a career of music. He paid for her to have lessons from the best and most expensive violin teacher in town, and made her practise for two hours each day. He frowned on Sarah's other interests – sewing and discos. By her early teens, Sarah had begun to hate the violin – and her father's restrictions.

Parents' messages

Parents always say they are trying to do their best for their children, but sometimes they put pressures on the teenager to provide what they want themselves, not what the teenagers want. Some parents send the message "be like me". Others say "do better than me, do the things I never did".

Teenagers are highly sensitive to their parents' ambitions for them. A survey of 16-year-olds found that only a minority didn't know what their parents' feelings were, or said that their parents didn't mind how they did.

Parental pressures of all kinds can influence how teenagers feel about school, or about specific subjects. As the case histories show, what parents 'mean for the best' may not always work out as intended.

You and your teenager

A D You might like to write a brief case history of the influence your parents had on your education. What feelings do you recall? If you want, go back to "Parents' feelings" in Chapter 1, to think over how your teenage experiences may be helping or hindering your teenager's achievement at school now.

Try to write a case history also for you and your teenager now. What kind of pressures and support do you provide? How do you feel about your teenager's school performance? And how do you think he/she feels about your views?

If you can, ask your teenager for his/her impressions of your views. Does he/she interpret your behaviour in the same way? Or, for example, does he/she see your insistence on regular homework as an undue restriction? Sharing your views can help to clear up misunderstandings.

Pressures from school

From the day children enter school they are grouped and labelled. Even if the categories remain unspoken, they exist in the teachers' heads. Teachers begin to predict success or failure. These predictions are based on the teachers' views about how girls/blacks/lively children/the fourth year/etc. behave, and how they perform in a variety of tests.

Sometimes, expectations can be poorly grounded. For example, a recent survey of West Indian pupils in a Midlands school showed that many teachers 'misread' them. The teachers confused their identities long after they had learned the names and faces of white pupils. And they saw a turning away of the eyes as a failure to respond, rather than the sign of respect intended by the pupils. The teachers tended to estimate ability according to behaviour, rather than to judge the two things separately. In response, the girls often tried to minimise misunderstandings between themselves and the teachers. The boys were more likely to turn away from the school and seek the support of friends – with the result that their exam results were below their capabilities.

The more teachers rely on their expectations, the less they may actually think about the individual child. Research has shown that children of all abilities can live up to or down to their teachers' expectations.

Grouping teenagers into ability sets, bands or streams is intended to enhance their motivation to learn, by creating a close match between teaching and level of ability. In practice, it can also create unfortunate expectations and stereotypes: for example, "*all* the D stream are thick"; "you can *always* trust 3S to be good". Some studies suggest that there is a relationship between ability grouping and the development of pupil 'sub-cultures' which encourage or discourage achievement. Moves between ability groups are infrequent. Some people take this as evidence that grouping is efficient. Others say it shows how efficient pupils are at adjusting to what is expected of them.

Just like families, schools often operate on a set of assumptions and attitudes which are never made entirely open. They may encourage boys and girls to specialise in different subject options, or pupils may find that they are expected to hold certain values or that only certain beliefs are acceptable. Low and high achievers may be treated in subtly different ways.

Discussing pressures at school

A All these pressures can affect your teenager's feelings about school. They're worth discussing openly.

School attitudes which may influence all pupils' are best discussed at general meetings of parents. These might be arranged by the school or by the Parent-Teacher Association. It will help discussion if information is available (for example, numbers of boys and girls doing different subjects) and you can draw conclusions about what might be done.

Pressures on your teenager are best discussed individually, first with your teenager then with the teachers concerned. You and your teenager might usefully talk about:
○ whether the school's assessments of the teenager's personality, behaviour and abilities are fair, in your view?
○ how is the teenager affected by these assessments?
○ what, practically, might the school do to improve matters?

What teenagers need from school

A **D** Learners need to feel positive about themselves. How far does your teenager's school make him/her feel:

○ significant – he/she matters and is accepted
○ influential – he/she has a say in what happens
○ competent – he/she is able to learn

The quiz which follows explores these feelings. It is loosely based on research questionnaires. Ask your teenager, if he/she is interested, to tick the statements which are true for him/her. Of course, 'self-discipline', say, will mean different things to first and to fifth formers, but good schools will encourage it, as appropriate, at all levels.

A degree of significance
1 I know at least one teacher very well
2 When I have a problem, there's a teacher I can go to
3 I feel teachers respect me regardless of the marks I get
4 I have an opportunity in class to discuss a range of things that are important to me
5 I am recognised for my special talents and abilities
6 I feel that teachers understand my needs and interests
7 I am generally enthusiastic about going to school

A degree of influence
1 I am encouraged to develop self-discipline and to take responsibility for my own learning
2 I have the opportunity to make some decisions about what and how I learn
3 I can voice a concern openly
4 My parent's opinions are valued by the school
5 When I don't understand something, most teachers will adjust their class activities to help me
6 I have influence on decisions within the school
7 I feel I can have some effect in getting changes made in school policy or courses

A degree of competence
1 I mostly feel involved and interested in lessons
2 I have the skills to find out what I want to know
3 I can discuss ideas
4 I can use what I learn to solve problems
5 What I learn helps me understand myself more
6 I can comment on what, and how well, I am learning
7 I can achieve my learning ambitions

Comments

Many parent testers commented on the surprises this quiz gave their teenager:

"My daughter says she sometimes feels taken for granted. This made her realise she has more influence than she thought"
"The twins were surprised that the things they didn't tick could actually exist in a school"
"Doing the quiz made him feel more positive about school"

Do you and your teenager agree on how important feelings about school are? If he/she ticked less than half the items in each section you may need to look together at how things could be improved. When a person feels insignificant, un-influential, or incompetent – however briefly – he/she is unlikely to learn much. Good pastoral care (p 128–129) and home-school relationships (p 134–137) become of key importance.

Truancy

Truancy naturally concerns most parents – although sometimes you may feel helpless to know what to do about it.

Your teenager is truanting if he/she repeatedly misses school:

○ without having the school's permission
○ without being ill
○ or without an acceptable reason for staying away.
It *isn't* truancy if:
○ your teenager is sick
○ his/her religion forbids attendance on certain days
○ there is no transport and school is too far away to walk.

School registers are legal documents and teachers are obliged to keep records of school attendance and reasons for absence. So your teenager needs a note in advance if he/she must be away for special appointments. And he/she needs a note to explain school time missed for 'good reasons' such as illness.

Truants can be made the subject of a care order, or their parents can be fined or imprisoned. But most authorities today realise that threats and punishments rarely solve the problem. These days the emphasis is more on trying to under-

Is Gill prepared to reveal why she doesn't do her homework?

stand *why* the teenager is truanting. The school pastoral system, and perhaps the Educational Welfare Officer, are likely to be in early contact with parents, to see what can be done.

Why do teenagers truant?

One survey found a high level of occasional truancy, with up to half the pupils in their final year of compulsory schooling staying away at some time. Their reasons varied:

○ being fed up with school
○ having to help at home
○ wanting to do something special out of school.

For such teenagers, occasional truancy probably seems a 'reasonable' risk to take to do something else. School attendance is an easy limit to test (see pages 190–193).

The minority who truant persistently may be 'turned off' by school. Generally they may lack feelings of significance, influence, or competence. Or they may be running away from specific difficulties at school. Some teenagers never get to school because early morning hassles and arguments at home leave them feeling too upset to face school. Teenagers need help to sort out for themselves what to do about such problems.

Besides truanting proper, turned off teenagers may also roam corridors, hide in the loos or sit in class and do no work. Or they may 'play games' with their teachers to get attention of some kind.

Games teenagers play

Gill's homework was late. Her teacher tried to offer some helpful suggestions to prevent it happening again.

Teacher: "Why don't you stay on after school to finish it?"
Gill: "Yes, but I have to get home."
Teacher: "Well, why not do it as soon as you get home, while you're still in the mood?"
Gill: "Yes, but I'm always hungry, so I eat then."
Teacher: "Why don't you work later in the evening?"

Gill had an answer for that too, and for every other suggestion her teacher made. After a frustrating ten minutes they parted, problem unsolved.

Without fully realising it, Gill was playing a game with her teacher. Or, rather – since it takes two to play – they were playing a game with each other. Gill presented a problem, which the teacher tried to solve. He offered suggestions which Gill promptly rejected. And so on.

"Why don't you – yes but" is just one of the many repetitive loops that parents and teenagers, or teachers and teenagers, can get into. Always, at least one person ends up feeling bad.

People of all ages play games. They do so to get some kind of response. Anything – even feeling bad – is better than being ignored altogether. People also play games to set other people up to confirm their views. Gill, for example, was reassured that teachers couldn't tell her what to do. And the teacher began to see Gill's answers as confirmation of the view that Gill was beyond help.

Teenagers may play games at, or about school, to get a response from parents, teachers, or authority figures. On the surface, they may provoke a reasonable discussion. But the real reason for the exchange is found at a deeper level, and affects the *feelings* of the people involved.

What parents can do

A You can help yourself, and your teenager, by:
Recognising games: It's a game when you notice that the same kind of exchange has happened before; and you realise that there is more going on than appears on the surface. The teenager (or you) gets a predictable response, and the usual bad feeling, confirming his/her (or your) view of things.
Stopping games: You are most likely to do this by treating the teenager as an equal, and seeking his/her views. Avoid talking down, or one or other of you behaving as if you are being victimised. Games are the opposite of negotiation.

Gill's teacher stopped their game the next time Gill brought up a problem, by saying "That seems to be a problem for you, Gill. Can you see how you might solve it?" He was genuinely interested. His tone of voice was calm, matter-of-fact, without any malice.
Preventing games: This means finding a way the teenager can obtain, or you can give, satisfaction in a more useful way. For example, Gill's teacher realised how good she was at sport. He made a point of congratulating her on her frequent sporting successes. Eventually, she stopped bringing up problems which she wouldn't let him solve.

You may find it helps to talk over these points with your teenager. "What next?", and the course booklet on negotiation, offer further help.

School–home communications

What do schools tell parents about their teenager's education?

Keeping you in the picture

Schools try to set up a dialogue so that:
○ parents can find out more about the school in general
○ parents can discuss their teenager's progress

Booklets and regular school newsletters should keep you informed about rules and regulations, future plans, meetings and events. There are also general points and information about decisions – which subjects to study, which exams to take, whether to stay on – that can be usefully set out in writing. Reports are written for individual teenagers.

Written documents are most usefully followed up by a variety of parent-teacher meetings. There may be open days about the school, parents' evenings to discuss reports, discussion evenings to talk about the curriculum and subject options. And parents can make arrangements for individual meetings with members of staff.

Checklist A (below) lists things parents must now by law be told about their teenager's school. But there are still many other things which rightly concern parents, which you don't have to be told. Checklist B (below) lists some key points parents may also like to know. In practice, what schools communicate varies enormously. The examples (below right) come from a school which provides a great deal of clear information on both the school and individual teenagers.

Do communications do any good?

The key question of course is: do communications really help the teenager? The school from which the examples are taken was one of six in a research study into the effects of good communications. The study suggested that:
○ Parents like good communications, and believe that they help their teenagers' education. Parents are more likely to back up the school when they are fully in the picture.
○ Parents like to know not only about the curriculum but also about everyday things like lost property arrangements – even if information can sometimes seem overwhelming.
○ Parents like long, detailed, constructive reports about their teenagers "They're better than the reports we used to get – just a mark and you didn't feel they knew you".
○ Parents welcome the chance both to read and to talk. Discussion can make the information in booklets clearer and more personal. "We saw the Deputy Head, and chatting to him we got it. The booklet was quite difficult – but it was sorted out by the time she had to choose."

The teachers in the study were committed to giving information about the school, and to sharing concern and decisions about the individual teenager's education. But they thought decisions about school policy should rest with the school. What do you think?

Checklist A

Information that schools/LEAs must publish each year

1 Address and phone number of the LEA's offices ☐
2 Name, address and phone number of the school ☐
3 Status of the school (county, etc) and whether it is mixed or single sex ☐
4 Age range covered ☐
5 Name of the headteacher ☐
6 Availability of members of staff for consultation ☐
7 Times at which staff are available for consultation ☐
8 How parents should arrange visits to the school ☐
9 Teaching organisation within the school ☐
10 Subjects and options available and the arrangements for consulting parents on these matters ☐
11 Arrangements for religious education ☐
12 Special facilities offered in particular subjects or activities, including careers guidance ☐
13 Public examinations for which pupils are prepared ☐
14 Brief outline of the organisation of the school (family grouping, mixed ability, streaming) ☐
15 Brief statement of policy regarding homework ☐
16 Organisation within the school for pastoral care ☐
17 Statement about discipline in the school ☐
18 List of school rules and procedures including details of sanctions taken: (detention, suspension and expulsion) ☐
19 List of games, clubs, societies and any extra-curricular activities, and to whom they are available ☐
20 School policy regarding uniform and PE kit ☐
21 Summary of the information available to parents about free meals, uniform, grants, transport etc. ☐
22 Arrangements for transfer between one stage of education and the next ☐
23 Address where further information is available ☐

Checklist B

Useful information that does not have to be given

1 Plan of the school showing car parks and buildings ☐
2 List of teaching staff ☐
3 List of non-teaching staff (caretaker, secretary) ☐
4 Name and address of the chairman of the governors ☐
5 List of governors with their nominating bodies ☐
6 Address for contacting the parents' representatives ☐
7 Election procedures for governors ☐
8 Frequency of the governors' meetings ☐
9 Details of any internal methods of assessment and whether these are held termly or annually ☐
10 Frequency and ways in which parents are informed of their children's progress (reports) ☐
11 Special arrangements for enabling parents to discuss their children's progress ☐
12 Medical facilities within the school ☐
13 What parents should do when their children are ill ☐
14 How parents are told of illness in school ☐
15 Dates and nature of medical/dental inspections ☐
16 Details of lunchtime arrangements including free meals, and facilities for eating packed lunches ☐
17 Costs likely to arise from studying certain subjects ☐
18 Whether pens, pencils and similar basic equipment are supplied by the school free of charge ☐
19 Details of home/school organisations and the name and address of the secretary ☐
20 Ways developed by the school to involve parents ☐
21 The school fund, including parental contributions ☐
22 Details of internal school consultative arrangements that involve pupils (sixth form councils) ☐
23 Details of any school/community liaison (community service schemes, use of premises for adult education) ☐

School and your teenager

A The following questions review the communications you get from your teenager's school.

1 Do you think you are told everything in Checklist A now? Mark items you don't recall being told **X**.
2 Which items from Checklist B are you told? Tick them. Put **L** by the ones you'd like to know as well.
3 Are there other things you'd like to know, which aren't on either checklist? Include situations you're not sure how to handle, like how to get an emergency message to your teenager.
4 Do you like the style in which your teenager's school presents information and policy decisions? Is it straightforward?
5 What about the style and detail of your teenager's reports? Are they an improvement on the kind you used to get?
6 As the examples suggest, some schools now provide:
A a mark for effort, so you know how hard your teenager is trying, as well as a mark for attainment ☐
B reports and letters which give constructive criticism about what might be done to bring about improvements, as well as degrees of praise ☐
C encouragement to parents to come and discuss matters ☐
D a chance for parents to comment on the teachers' comments. ☐

Which of these does your teenager's school do? Tick them √. Mark with an **L** those you'd like to see happen.

Comments

While all our parent testers knew some of the information in Checklists A and B, everyone had a good sprinkling of 'X's and 'L's where they'd like to know more. They also added a variety of other questions, such as: what are the benefits of school trips? what's the school exam record? In general, the style and detail of the example communications went down well. Parents who didn't have such reports wanted ones like them.

Your own answers to the questions may suggest that you'd like more information, or that you'd like to see improvements in home–school communications. Some of our parent testers were satisfied. Others said that this topic reminded them of things they wanted to know or take up, now or later. It helps to be concrete and specific about what you want to find out, or what you want to see happen. Be clear about your reasons: for example, if you want to know more about exam results – what conclusions will you draw from them?

Matters which concern most parents can be taken up with:

○ the Head
○ the Parent-Teacher (or Parents') Association
○ the parents' representatives on the board of governors

More individual concerns can be talked over with your teenager and the appropriate teachers. (See next topic). "What next?" lists information sources and groups concerned with secondary schooling.

Smoking

This is a very difficult problem for schools to deal with. Most parents are very anxious that we should try to do something about it. We do not allow it for two main reasons:
a If it takes place in the buildings, there is a very real fire danger, as many schools have discovered at their cost.
b Smoking is a serious health hazard.
Having made our rules for sound reasons, to allow people to ignore it threatens the discipline of the school, so this is what we do . . .
a The first time a student is caught smoking on or near the school premises they are fined 25p and the money given to Cancer Research.
b We keep a central register of people found smoking including anyone within a group where smoking is clearly taking place. No one can say 'It wasn't me'. We treat all people within the group in the same way.
c The second time we find a student smoking we increase the Cancer Research funds by another 25p, but we also send a letter to parents saying what has happened and telling them that on health, safety and discipline grounds, if it happens again, the student will be suspended from school until we have had a chance of talking together . . .
d . . . and if it happens again, that is exactly what we do.

SUBJECT FRENCH	EFFORT B	ATTAINMENT 3

I am very pleased with D.....'s standard of work and attitude. He now has more confidence in himself and can at times produce exactly the type of written French which is needed in the essay component of the examination. He may well obtain a very good grade in C.S.E. for which he will be entered.

Dear Mr. and Mrs. G.,
C....'s progress so far has been disappointing on the whole—although it is pleasing to find that she is working as hard as she is in mathematics.
I know that she finds school work difficult and not **very** interesting, but there is no doubt that the progress she could make during her remaining time at school would be of great benefit to her and that at present she is largely wasting the opportunity.
Apart from her lack of effort in the classroom, C.... is also making things difficult for herself by her tendency to be late and by her frequent absences. In addition she is **very** inclined to be unco-operative about

135

Home–school communications

What do parents need to tell schools?

Keeping the school in the picture

It can help the school to know about both changes in the teenager and changes in his or her family.

Family changes

Unless the school knows a little about your teenager's family background they may misinterpret his/her behaviour, or jump to unjustified conclusions as to what his/her home life is like. This is particularly true if there are major family transitions or life-events which may have a 'knock-on' effect on his school work and behaviour. For example:

○ parents have marital problems, separate, divorce, or remarry
○ parent becomes redundant, family finances change
○ new baby is born, or brothers/sisters have serious problems

Unfortunately, many teenagers keep up an air of unconcern about family changes. The more unconcerned a teenager seems at home about such things, the more he/she may show some kind of reaction at school.

Deciding what to tell the school can be difficult. Families vary as to how open they like to be about family life. Parents may also be worried as to what use the school will make of their confidences. Justified – or not – parents may worry that:

○ too many teachers will be told – and they might 'gossip' about it.
○ teachers' judgements may be coloured by the information. They may 'label' the teenager as 'broken home' or 'delinquent family' and adjust their expectations accordingly.
○ the information may be used to explain away other problems, when in fact other explanations should be explored. For example – "she's not keeping up with maths because there is a lot of trouble at home". But – is the teacher having trouble with the whole class? Did the teenager miss a crucial explanatory lesson? and so on.

Your best line may be to share these worries, along with information about family changes, with the headteacher, school counsellor, or home–school liaison worker. You may feel that they will only give you bland assurances that none of the staff would behave like that. But explaining your concerns should ensure that they check that the information you give in confidence is not misused.

Changes in your teenager

Changes in your teenager may be easier to understand and to offer help if you can discuss them with a teacher who knows your teenager well.

You may be worried about his/her relationships. For example you suspect he/she is isolated, teased, or getting into 'bad company'. Or that he/she finds it hard to get on with certain teachers.

Or perhaps you are concerned about his/her studies. He/she may seem to have too little or too much homework to do. He/she may have become uninterested in school work – or obsessed and worried about studying.

You need to be open with your teenager about what is causing you concern. Don't talk about him/her behind his/her back. If you decide to go against his/her wishes – tell him/her your reasons for doing so. For example, you may suspect – or be certain – that your teenager is being bullied. It can help to work out ways of avoiding, or dealing with, bullies with him/her. But even if he/she doesn't want you to, you probably need to see the school as well. They need to be able to deal with the bullies too.

Individual advice should be available to help you all to decide whether to seek further help for problems over school work or behaviour. The educational psychologist, the educational welfare officer, the family and child guidance clinic are just some of the possible sources of support beyond the school.

Talking to teachers

A Many parents feel anxious about talking to teachers. It helps to identify what you – and your teenager – hope to get out of an interview. Here are some guidelines to think over:

Playing the blame game

If something goes wrong at school, many parents almost automatically jump to the conclusion that "It's all the teacher's fault" or "It's all my teenager's fault". Stop for a moment and consider which conclusion you tend to choose. For example:
Your son falls behind in maths. Do you think:
A "he's so lazy"
B "his teacher's no good"
Your daughter is rude to the Head. Do you think:
A "she's getting out of control"
B "the Head really must have provoked her"

Taking sides doesn't get you very far. A more useful focus for an interview would be: *how can parents, teenager and teachers work together to improve things in the future?* Before you go to the school, discuss with your teenager what suggestions you will make. If he/she's going with you – also decide beforehand who will talk about what. During the interview, keep focussing on what's going to happen. At the end, recap on what you've each agreed to do.

Afraid of being thought fussy

Many parents worry that their teenager may suffer if teachers see them as having 'fussy parents'. And many teenagers say "Oh, don't make a fuss". But you are only really likely to come over as 'making a fuss' if you rush off to the school without thinking through what you are hoping to achieve, or if you do so without talking to your teenager about it and listening carefully to how he/she sees things. If you've done both of these, and are still worried about something – trust your judgement and go ahead.

Complaining about a teacher

Most teachers take a highly professional attitude to their work. But teachers are only human. Some will be inexperienced, and some less interested than others in their pupils.

If you are concerned, try to identify specifically what you find unacceptable. Don't generalise and say he/she's hopeless or that you can't stand him/her. Try to state exactly what it is you object to and – even more important – what you would like him/her to do instead.

Ideally, it would be best for your teenager to sort the matter out with the teacher concerned. In practice, many teenagers feel too nervous to try this. And many young or inadequate teachers need the support of a more experienced teacher. So you may decide to talk things over with a Year Head, Head of House or Deputy Head. Make it clear that you are not 'telling tales'. Rather, you are concerned that the more experienced senior teacher should be the one to raise the matter discreetly with the teacher concerned.

When talking together is hard . . .

A For some parents, going to their teenager's school revives powerful feelings from their own schooldays. They feel as uneasy or inadequate now, as they remember feeling then. As one parent tester said:
"I can recall being ill at ease and somewhat in awe of my own teachers, and being cramped by the discipline and formality."

If you dislike going to your teenager's school now, it may help to take time to recall your own experiences and emotions at school. Do feelings about teachers at your own secondary school get in the way of your relationship – as an adult equal – with teachers today?

Thinking over the past can help you to disentangle left-over feelings from whatever is of current concern. It may help to share your feelings with your partner, or a friend.

Keeping your teenager in the picture

Home–school communications should not go on behind a teenager's back. The teenager needs to be involved.

○ Discuss with your teenager what should go in any letters you write – and show him/her the letter before you send it. Any letters from school – particularly those about his/her behaviour or work – need to be discussed openly.
○ When you need to talk to the school – discuss with your teenager who you should see, and what you hope to achieve at the interview. Encourage him/her to be present and to speak up for him/herself.
○ During his/her final year(s) at school, shift towards your teenager handling for him/herself any problems at school – or at home – which require the other side to be put in the picture.

Helping with study skills

You don't need to know the subject to help your teenager study.

Parents are aware that, from time to time, their teenagers face study problems. Yet they often feel unsure how to help. The content of the subject may be unfamiliar; or they may feel school failures themselves. This topic deals with practical study skills, where parents have a lot to offer from their own experiences since school. Getting started on a piece of work and planning time, for example, are lifelong useful skills that teenagers need to learn.

The activities in this topic take a practical approach to a range of study problems. They may be similar to the kind of things your teenager does at school. But often, teenagers aren't motivated to learn about study skills at the point they come up on the school timetable. Parents are in a much better position to gauge when, and what kind of help, their individual teenager needs. The desire to improve study skills may only arise when exams loom, or when the teenager wants more time to play football, for example. All our parent testers stressed the need for parents to pick their time to talk about the activities in this topic.

Learning problems

If your teenager has any practical learning problems, he/she 'owns' them in the sense that only he/she can decide whether, and how best, to sort them out.

Parents and teenagers may be at odds over *how important learning is*. Parents – and teachers – tend to have their eyes on the future. Teenagers live more for the present. They may find friends, parents and teachers pulling in opposite directions.

Parents and teenagers may also disagree about *what kind of learning is important*. Parents may value one type of education or training while their teenager is unsure – or would prefer another. The exercises in "Tinker, tailor, soldier, sailor . . ." can be useful in sorting out such differences. Whatever the teenager's subject abilities and interests – the learning life-skills are important.

Looking at skills

In developing any skill – social, academic, practical, sporting, study – the learner needs to know where he/she's going. There are:
Four basic stages
1 assessing your current level of skill
2 setting yourself goals or target
3 actually learning
4 reviewing your progress.
Learning also involves more than just thinking. There are:
Three basic aspects
1 what you think and know
2 what your attitudes and feelings are
3 what your practical abilities are.

When looking at study problems, it can help to review all three aspects at each stage. So, for example, when assessing current level of skill, you might look at what you *think* the problem is, and how you *feel* about it, as well as what you can actually *do*. The 'use of time' and 'reading' activities overleaf illustrate these stages and aspects of learning. You may also find them a useful way of looking at other study problems with your teenager.

Giving support

A This topic looks at four specific areas of study skills in which parents can offer their teenager support: doing homework, planning use of time, reading, and presenting ideas.

Support means helping the teenager to develop his/her own skills and make his/her own decisions about what to do. Your own experiences will stand you in good stead: for example, you can talk about how *you* plan your day, or how *you* feel about reading. Your teenager may not follow your example or your advice – but it can help him/her to share problems and hear how someone else sets about things.

Support needs to take the form of light-handed guidance rather than heavy-footed interference. The youth leader's report extract (right) illustrates the difference well. It also makes the point that some teenagers need a supportive boost to their self-confidence as learners.

You might like to think over the style of support you tend to give – and what changes you might make. For example, after reading this extract, two of our parent testers said:
"I sometimes see my husband turning our two teenagers off in this way. They tend to prefer help from me. I think I'll show him this topic and talk about it."
"My daughter commented that when we discuss things, she gets bored if I go too deeply into things. I said I'd try not to run on so – and she said she'd say when she'd had enough of chewing things over!"

Doing homework

A Homework is often a source of arguments between parents and teenagers. Many of our parent testers saw it as their problem, not just their teenager's. They felt guilty when their teenager didn't do his/her homework – but inadequate to help. They said they didn't understand the subject, or that they couldn't provide the right conditions for the teenager to work in.

As topics in this and the last chapter suggest, there are many ways that parents can help with the learning *process*, even without knowing much about the subjects involved. And, with some planning, teenagers can work in a surprising range of places. What's most important are your, and your teenager's attitudes and feelings about homework.
For yourself: you might like to mull over feelings which make it harder to help.

Your teenager: might like to look at the chart of common homework problems, which was developed for teenagers (right). If he/she's interested, suggest that he/she traces his/her own route through it – ticking (√) the statements which apply to him/her, and following the 'yes' or 'no' arrows as appropriate. Go on to discuss his/her views, and what he/she might do about any difficulties. For example:

○ why does he/she think he/she lacks the motivation to do homework (items 1–6 in the top row)?
○ what would make it worth his/her while to see his/her teachers about problems? What would he/she say to them?
○ can he/she think of other sources of help – things you could do, or ways he/she and friends could help each other?

A Youth Leader's Report

There is such antagonism towards having to go to school, and be with teachers, that it often spills over onto learning itself. Kids at St. Micks will suddenly stop doing something they have begun to do with a worker saying "Ner, I don't want to do this." It makes no difference who initially suggested the activity. Asked why they no longer want to do it, the kid will say something like "I don't feel like it anymore" or "it's boring, this is."

...these school-hating kids have lost confidence in their ability to learn. They give up before they have had a chance to give anything more than a brief try. Sometimes, the arrival of a respected mate who has enjoyed the activity previously, can overcome this low esteem.

The kids are, in the right circumstances, as anxious to learn as anyone else. To avoid having the shutter come down on enthusiasm the worker must not allow his own enthusiasm to get out of hand. When a kid takes an interest in something, the interest can disappear in direct relation to the enthusiasm someone the kid sees as a 'teacher' shows in the same thing. Where the craving for learning is felt by the kid and not sabotaged (often unwittingly) by a 'teacher', the 'kids' interest in practically anything

seemingly limitless. For example...

Simon was saying that he found West Africa the most interesting thing they had done in geography, which was his favourite subject. Dick (the worker) full of enthusiasm and help said "Oh I studied West Africa at College". He proceeded to add information to the discussion, about mineral deposits in the area and its developing industry. Simon turned right off "You sound like a bloody teacher, Dick" he said and left...

In the coffee bar another day Sammy asked Dick whether some city had any slums. "Sure to, Sammy, a big city like that, it's bound to have a slum area, probably on the east side of town. That's where they normally are." Sammy at once became interested in why slums should be on the east side of town. Dick said, casually, "Oh they usually are - it's connected with the wind." That was the end of the conversation. But every time Sammy saw Dick for the next few weeks he asked him about the location of slums in various cities. Gradually his knowledge built up - he kept coming to Dick with exceptions - until it reached the point where Sammy borrowed and read a book of Dick's about location analysis

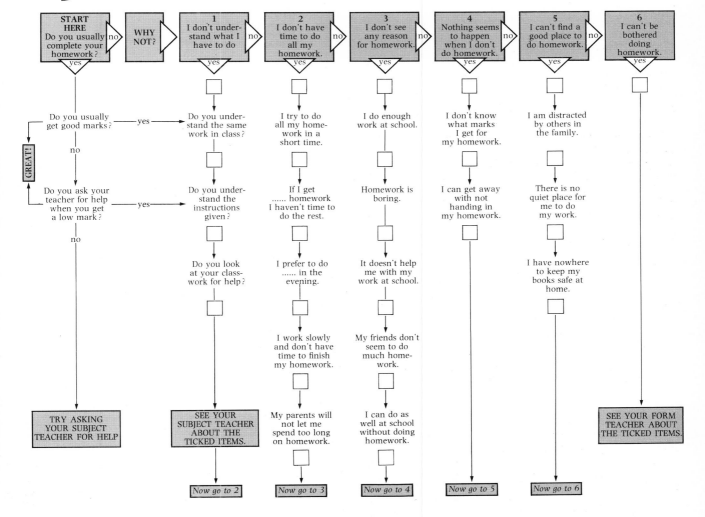

Tick the boxes if your answers are 'Yes'.

(Active Tutorial Work Bk 4. p. 81)

Planning use of time

Planning the use of time should leave more free time to choose what to do . . . or simply take life as it comes. The activities below are based on the four styles of learning – looking at the three aspects of learning in each. They may help your teenager to organise his/her time more effectively.

You might like to suggest and discuss any or all of these with your teenager. But in the end, it is his/her time to use as he/she chooses. Studying is just one of the many practical things teenagers need time to do. They also need time to think and to dream.

Assessment
1 Identify activities you don't think you have enough time for.
2 Describe how you feel about planning and saving time.
3 Over a long weekend, record what you spend your time on. How many hours are really satisfying?

Setting goals
4 List all the major things you could, or have, to do next week. Then mark your 'Top Ten' priorities.
5 Roughly calculate the percentage of time you spend on different activities. Adjust your figures to a pattern you'd prefer. Can your 'Top Ten' help you do more of what you want?
6 Make a 'contract' to help you get your Top Ten done. This means you agree with someone when you'll do things – and they check that you've done them. You can build in bonuses and penalties if you feel you need them.

Learning
7 Keep a diary and/or a 'reminders' notebook, of things to do.
8 Encourage yourself by listing things you like to do – and finding the time to do more of them.
9 Find ways to save small amounts of time – like keeping possessions organised, using waiting time to think about other things.

Review
At the end of a week for which you have a Top Ten:
10 Review what you did. Did you do everything? Put off or forget anything?
11 Review your feelings. Did you enjoy this organised lifestyle more – or less?
12 Make a record, if it helps, of everything you did on, in and about time.

Reading well

Reading can be a source of pleasure or problems for your teenager. It can also be a sore spot for you, as a parent. When your child first started primary school, you were probably keen to help him/her learn to read. Yet, as one of our parent testers put it: "Talking this over with friends, we found we still bore the scars of rejection from those far-off days. We wanted to help them read, but it felt as if the school practically forbade this".

Times have changed – but those feelings can surface again now, when your teenager seems to need help. You may find you need to talk your feelings over with someone in your own 'support network' first.

The section below looks at some common problem areas in reading for teenagers. It draws on the three aspects of learning – thinking, feeling, doing – discussed overleaf. You may find it helpful material to look at with your teenager. "What next?" lists books on reading and study skills which your teenager may find useful.

Thinking about reading
Most books contain only a few basic ideas. The rest of the book is taken up in arguing the case, presenting examples and generally developing the ideas. (This book is no exception.) The reader's job is to work out what the central messages are. It is speed in doing this, rather than just reading, that determines progress.

Thinking about the following list of questions can help the teenager to keep track of an author's ideas:

○ what's this section all about – who/what/when/where/why?
○ where does it lead to – and how does it relate to previous sections?
○ how does it relate to assignment questions?
○ do I already know this – or do I need to know it?

The teenager can also pick out the sections he/she really needs to study by looking at contents lists, summaries, indexes. Size of heading, layout, language used, can all tell him/her something about the style and sequence of the argument in the book.

Information can change so fast these days that knowing where to find out can be more useful than knowing the facts. Encourage your teenager to make use of all sorts of information sources – books, computers, people.

Feelings about reading

Reading needs to be an enjoyable activity. When your teenager feels bored or disinterested, he/she needs to act on those feelings. It doesn't help to think that he/she 'ought' to go on.

You might suggest that he/she gives him/herself small rewards to pace his/her reading. Thoughts ("wow! two chapters before lunch") can be as rewarding as actions (a short break every hour). Describing what you have read, to yourself, or to someone else, is the best way to check you have understood the main points.

Actually reading

High speed reading isn't essential. But a reasonable speed is, otherwise the reader loses the thread of the argument. There are two basic skills which your teenager may still need to practise:

○ being able to read silently, without moving the lips or throat (try reading with a finger on the lips to check this)
○ being able to read words/in small groups/which make sense/rather than/one/ at/ a/ time,/ which/ makes/ your/ reading/jerky.

Presenting ideas

Presenting ideas clearly in speech or writing is a lifelong useful skill. The four steps below outline some of the key things involved. Your teenager might like to look back over a piece of recent school work, to see which steps he/she does well, and which he/she needs to work on. Or you might find it helps to discuss these steps with him/her, the next time he/she is concerned about a speech, essay or report.

Step 1: know the style and approach required. To plan properly you need, for example, to know what the exam question means, what the point of the report is, or who the speech is intended to persuade. Different verbs mean different things: for example describe = give detailed evidence, outline = main points only, criticise = opinion based on a summary of evidence.

Step 2: research the presentation. You may need to make notes on useful sources. Try out ideas in rough. What you want to say needs organising in groups of notes and thoughts.

Step 3: plan the presentation. Any written or spoken presentation needs a clear beginning, middle and end. If you don't know where it's heading, the listener or reader certainly won't.

○ *Introductions* – should set the tone, show how the topic will be handled.
○ *Middle sections* – should set out the arguments or descriptions in a logical order. Each section can usefully start with a sentence which sums up the ideas to be discussed next.
○ *Conclusions* – should wrap up the story, summarise the description, or present an opinion in the light of what's gone before.

Step 4: make the presentation. Any good plan can still fail unless the material is clear, interesting and straightforward. This means clear layout, handwriting, and style; speaking well and possibly using some visual aids. You need to be accurate, to the point – and have an interesting 'angle' on what you have to say. Presentation improves with practice. It helps to leave time for a draft you can think about, or for a run-through with a friendly listener.

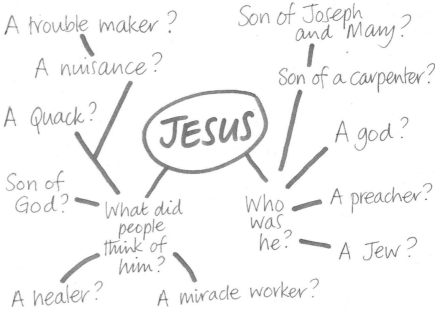

Your teenager might try making pattern notes or lists of notes with blobbed, numbered, or lettered points. Notes need clear layout, with space for additions. Colour, underlining, and headings can highlight points.

Lifelong learning

Informal learning helps parents and teenagers to go on developing.

Your learning experiences

For better – or sometimes worse – school provides a foundation in learning. But at least half our parent testers felt that the learning they'd done since their schooldays was more useful and enjoyable.

For some teenagers, school can damage their self-esteem to the point where they want little more to do with formal education. Informal learning projects which people mostly plan and carry out for themselves, can be a great help.

Informal learning projects are often very practical, with a specific end product in mind – a better job, a new bathroom, a more independent child. The panel (right) gives some examples of the range of activities, knowledge and skills which parents and teenagers may get involved with. Our parent testers were pleasantly surprised to find that, as one of them put it: "what we enjoy and think of as leisure actually counts as learning".

School – and after

🅰 🅓 Think over, or discuss these questions:

○ did school turn you on or off learning?
○ what have you learned about since leaving school?
○ what was the best learning experience you ever had?
○ which is more useful to you now – the learning you did at school or the learning you've done since?
○ do you tend to think that, if something is 'learning' it can't be enjoyable?

It may help your teenager to hear from you that school learning is not all of what you need to learn for life.

Learning projects

A learning project can be defined as a time when: *your major intention is to learn certain definite knowledge or skills which you will retain and use.* In other words, your learning has a clear purpose. You're not just incidentally learning while doing something else, or looking up something you'll soon forget. Your learning is also likely to be fairly sustained. One researcher talks in terms of a minimum of seven hours within six months. But of course needs, time and interests vary. It is *not* failure to think you currently learn nothing. Some years you need to learn more than others.

In terms of your teenager, a small survey of energetic, busy 16-year-olds suggests that teenagers, too, may informally learn more than you – or they – might think. The teenagers studied spent on average ten hours at each of nine different projects in a year. Much of their learning was about sport, music and topics of general interest about which they were curious. Their learning related to new responsibilities, problems and decisions which they were facing at school, at work, with their family and friends.

The survey also suggested that, the younger the teenager, the more likely he/she is to:

○ have a broad range of interests
○ keep learning episodes fairly brief
○ not sustain his/her learning over the year
○ gain knowledge and skill as by-products of activities chosen mainly for interest or fun.

Learning for work: Many jobs now require technical updating. A new job or promotion may depend on taking specific courses. Problems at work may require specific learning to solve them.

Learning for general interest: Sometimes people learn skills they hope they will find useful in a range of situations: for example, relaxation, problem solving. Or they pursue a general interest or curiosity about a subject.

Your family's projects

🅰 🅓 People most often learn when they have a need to know – something to do, a problem to solve, a decision to make. You might like to think back over the last year and see what each member of the family has learned about. For teenagers, exclude school/college work, but include any clubs, projects or extra classes which apply. Draw up a chart like this one (right) from a parent tester family.

Next look forward to next year. What are you planning to do, individually or together? Your family life map (pages 28–29) may suggest some projects coming up. Some times you'll want to learn more than others.

Learning for home life: Learning about childcare, car maintainance, decorating, cooking, sex, are just a few of the wide range of things people learn about in relation to home life.

Learning for leisure: Leisure time is growing as people spend less of their lives in paid or unpaid work. Sports, hobbies and creative interests – are an increasingly important aspect of informal learning.

	Sharon (14)	Alan (17)	Mum	Dad
Work	Flute	Applying for jobs	—	Interview techniques
Home life	Using sewing machine	—	Making clothes	Laying carpet
General interest	Reading 'TA for teens'	Driving, CND	'Action for Peace'	Reading 'Which'
Leisure	Piano	Drumming	Greenhouse gardening	Magic

How parents can help

A D When teenagers want to learn, they're more ready to seek or accept, help. You can help your teenager for life by encouraging him/her to develop skills in planning his/her own learning. There are at least ten things the successful learner needs to decide for him/herself. These are listed below, with ways parents can help. As you read through, you may like to jot down examples of ways you have helped so far.

Our parent testers pointed out that – however much they wanted to help – they couldn't always provide what their teenager wanted. A computer or technical drawing equipment for example. Part of helping is recognising the limits to the help you can give. In discussion with your teenager, you may be able to suggest other people he/she could turn to, or other ways of gaining access to the equipment he/she needs. And you can certainly help your teenager to be more specific about the help he/she wants, whom he/she will accept it from – and how to approach them to get the help he/she wants.

Ten decisions

1 Deciding what to learn: The teenager needs to be clear about what he/she already knows, and what knowledge and skills he/she wants to learn. You can suggest how he/she might find books, or people who know, about the subject.
2 Weighing gains and losses: The teenager needs to be clear about what he/she hopes to gain from learning. He/she also needs to feel happy that this outweighs the costs to him/her in terms of time, money, effort, risk. People who know about the subject, the teenager, or about learning, – you, teachers, librarians, youth leaders, neighbours – may be able to help him/her do this.
3 Beginning: The teenager needs to find out when, where and from whom he/she can learn locally. Often there may be little choice. You can help him/her to review his/her options.
4 Setting deadlines and goals: The teenager may know where he/she's aiming for, but not have set any part-way goals. Small steps are more likely to give him/her a feeling of success. Just pointing this out may be enough.
5 Setting the pace: The teenager may need help with time-tabling or other study skills. If he/she is learning in a group he/she may want to talk about how other people learn.
6 Judging progress: The teenager may not be the best judge of his/her own efforts. In discussion, you may be able to prevent him/her being wildly over – or under – optimistic. Objective measures of the skill he/she is learning may be helpful.
7 Coping with problems: The best solutions to learning problems are usually the ones the learner finds for him/herself. Simply talking through difficulty with you, or another sympathetic listener, helps the teenager to help him/herself.
8 Finding resources to learn: .The teenager may need money, space, or equipment to learn. You may be prepared to help out, if you can, in the cause of learning.
9 Finding time and a place: You may be able to help your teenager arrange study or working space. You may also be prepared to negotiate with the teenager over other responsibilities (such as washing up) which take time from learning.
10 Keeping going: Sympathetic listening can help to stop a teenager from quitting. Knowledge of motivation helps.

143

Careers

Your attitudes to your own work experience and how you see the pattern of employment changing today will affect your hopes – and fears – for your own teenager's career.

A D In "Why work?" you are asked to examine your attitudes in more detail, but stop for a while now and check your own pattern of work. Make a note of:

A Your age now
B The age you started paid work
C Your maximum possible number of working years to date
D The actual number of years you've worked
E The number of years you have been out of paid work
F The age at which you propose to retire
G The number of years you have to go.

Looking back at your own experience, do you think:

○ that you've been lucky enough to have had an interesting and fulfilling career doing work that really suited you?

○ that you have made a living at one or more jobs, without any particularly strong feelings of enthusiasm or dislike about your work?

○ that the sort of jobs you've been doing are not really what interested you at all, and you might have been a lot better off doing something else?

Do you rate job security and staying in the same kind of job very highly? Or perhaps you have been, or suspect you may be made redundant? Can you see changes ahead which mean that you are going to have to make a move whether you like it or not?

The focus of this chapter is on helping your teenager. But you, too, may decide to change your job – or through unemployment have to look for new work. It can seem hard if two generations in the same family are looking for work at the same time. You may find that you feel resentful about younger people coming along and taking older people's jobs away. You may even see your teenager as a representative of this generation and really dislike the idea of his/her having a job while you're out of work.

"Why work?" looks at attitudes to work and how important a part of life a job is seen to be. "Dreams and expectations" explores what your teenager's hopes are and what he/she would really enjoy doing as a job.

The very real changes in pattern of employment are examined in "Which jobs?". It does, however, identify where new types of jobs are developing.

School-leavers may seem inexperienced and to have little hope on the job market today. However teenagers may have acquired in part-time jobs and voluntary work a wide range of work-related skills. "What's it like to work?" will make them more aware of this and of the opportunities for work experience placements while still at school.

If your teenager is coming up to school-leaving age what does he/she plan to do? "Staying or leaving?" will help you both check that he/she has considered the whole range of possibilities open to him/her.

You may be worried that he/she won't find a job. Unemployment today is increasing more rapidly for teenagers than for any other age group; particularly so for teenage girls. "No jobs" helps you consider what you might do about youth unemployment in general and your teenager's situation in particular. There are no easy answers to this problem, but we've spelt out some of the reasons and suggested a few ideas.

Why work?

What has your working life been like? Why is work important?

In this topic we shall take a look at the sort of paid work parents have done and how their feelings about work may affect the way their own children think about work after they leave school.

A D Make a list of different jobs you've done during your working life, with approximate lengths of time. Make a brief note of what you particularly liked or disliked about each job. You may be surprised to look back and see the range of jobs you've done. Your teenager may be interested to hear about your experiences.

What is important about work?

A Tick the answer in each group of statements which is closest to your own opinion:

1 A I would never take a job which wasn't secure. __
 B I would prefer a job which was secure, but would consider something less secure if it was really interesting. __
 C Whether a job is interesting rates far higher for me than security. __

2 A Women shouldn't go out to work – their place is at home looking after their families. __
 B I don't see why women with families shouldn't go out to work if they can cope. __
 C Women, even if they've got families, should have equal opportunities with men to go out to work. __

3 A I hope to do the same sort of job for the rest of my working life. __
 B I would be prepared to retrain for a different sort of job at least once during my working life. __
 C I'm very flexible – I'm prepared to change direction several times. __

4 A The greatest reward I get from work is the money together with knowing I've done my duty. __
 B I think monetary reward, and the job stimulation and enjoyment I get from work, should be evenly balanced as far as possible. __
 C The money I get is always less important for me than the interest I have in my work. __

5 A Work is the most important thing in my life – everything else revolves around it. __
 B Work is pretty important to me, but I think it's important to have a social life as well. __
 C I would never let work take up too important a place in my life – most of my energy goes on my hobbies and my social life. __

6 A If I were made redundant I would be absolutely shattered – it would be the end of the world for me. __
 B I wouldn't want to be made redundant – but if I were I hope I could either get another job or re-train. __
 C The idea of redundancy doesn't bother me – whether I'd get another job or draw unemployment pay; I'd make a go of it. __

7 A I wouldn't think much of myself without a job. __
 B I'd prefer to work, but I wouldn't regard myself as a failure if I hadn't a job. __
 C How I feel about myself is not affected by whether or not I have a job. __

Your answers. How many did you answer as **A** ____, **B** ____, and **C** ____? In general, **A** answers reflect traditional beliefs in the way people feel about work. It is something we do as a duty, an essential part of life which is unavoidable whether you enjoy it or not. Parents who give this sort of answer are bound to feel that their child has failed in some way if he or she hasn't got a job to go to. If their own jobs cease for some reason (redundancy, ill health) they're likely to find it difficult to adapt to being jobless themselves. **C** answers show a more flexible approach where the sexes have more equal responsibilities, and work may not be the most important thing in life. **B** answers strike a balance between the two and will soon probably reflect the opinions of many parents who have themselves experienced unemployment or job insecurity. Would your answers be different if you didn't have children or weren't the sole breadwinner?

Influencing your teenager. How are your opinions about work going to affect the advice you give your teenager? Tick the answer in each group of statements which is closest to your opinion about the sort of job you would like your teenager to think about:

1 A I'd like him/her to do the same job as me.
 B Although I'd tell him/her about my job, I wouldn't necessarily expect him/her to want to do it.
 C It doesn't bother me whether he/she does the same kind of work as me or not.

2 A I want to see him/her in a job with a safe future.
 B I wouldn't worry about him/her being in a safe job.
 C I think secure, fixed jobs are a bad thing and wouldn't recommend one to my child.

Patterns of work

In the introduction to this chapter you were asked to review your own pattern of work.

Here is the chart for Bob and Eileen, a married couple, and Brian.

	Bob and Eileen		Brian
A Age now	42	41	36
B Age started paid work	18	16	21
C Maximum possible number of working years to date	24	25	15
D Actual number of years worked	24	11	9
E Number of years out of work	0	14	6
F Proposed age of retirement	65	60	60
G Number of years to go	23	19	24

Bob has been in work ever since he left school at 18 and became a draughtsman, studying part-time at his local tech. He has worked for two employers since then and has been with the local council for the last eight years.

Eileen worked as a florist after she left school, but gave this work up when their eldest child was born. She has a son of 20 and two teenage daughters. She went back to work six years ago, as a receptionist at the local health centre. She has a shock when she sees that she could be working for another 19 years and wonders whether she would actually want to go on with the same job that long.

Brian is a single parent who has looked after Zak on his own, since Zak was a year old – 12 years ago. Brian has worked at a number of jobs over the last 15 years, mainly with fringe magazines. The only job he has held for any length of time was as a studio manager with the BBC. He has spent quite a lot of time off work, especially when Zak was under five. Brian found it hard to find anyone to look after his child.

What is important about work? Bob's answers for the questions (opposite) were mostly A's. He's reasonably contented at work and certainly doesn't want to change. It took some time for him to decide on his answer about money, but eventually he decided to be honest and admit that the *money* is the most important thing he gets from work. Eileen is rather worried about her future work – her answers are mostly B's, and she realises that she isn't very satisfied with her job and certainly doesn't want to be doing it until she retires. She decides to make enquiries about re-training – perhaps as a physiotherapist. Brian has a mixture of B and C answers. He reckons that if he were on his own all his answers would be C, but having the responsibility of looking after Zak makes him more inclined to give B answers.

Influencing your teenager. Bob and Eileen's son is training to be a medical technician. Both parents have leant on him to train for a career. Bob's not worried about the girls, but Eileen *is* more concerned.

Brian finds it hard to imagine what job Zak might do and says he will leave any decisions to Zak himself.

3 A I'd like him/her to have a traditional type of job – we will always need carpenters and plumbers.
B He/she should look at all types of jobs.
C Old-fashioned jobs are a thing of the past – the microchip is here and there is a technical revolution.

Are you giving the same kind of answers as in the previous section, or do you want something different for your teenager? Why do you think this is? Are you giving these answers on his/her behalf or are they a reflection of your own experiences? If you are basing your answers on your own work experience, consider whether this will be of use to him/her in the working world he/she is going to have to face today. Your opinions are going to count a lot since they are the fruits of your experience, and you want to do the best for your teenager but are you up-to-date enough to be right for him/her?

The 'messages' you give. The earlier questions have been about what you think about work. But what about your feelings – and the messages you pass on about what it's like to go out to work? You may tell your teenager one thing but show by your actions and casual remarks that you have a different attitude to your job.

What do you think are the messages behind:
○ "Oh God – another Monday: I just can't face it"
○ "Nothing but old Jenkins interfering all day"
○ "I've been run off my feet all day"
○ "Hard work never did me any harm"
○ "Only ten more years to go!"

What kind of messages have you given to your teenager? Perhaps your teenager can recall some of them?

Dreams and expectations

Is there a gap between your teenager's dreams and expectations?

Selena: Aged 13
I would like to be a Materials Engineer. If not, I would like to get a degree. I'll learn to spell better. If I cannot do that I would work in a garage. I would expect I'll most likely be a nurse or be in an office doing filing. I'm a girl but I don't like girls' jobs.

Debby: Aged 13
*My hopes and expectations
My hope when I leave school is to become a social worker and help people through their difficulties. If the recession carries on I will probably, like most people, end up doing a stupid job behind a supermarket counter.*

What job does your teenager dream of doing? What job does he/she really think he/she will get? Have you ever asked your teenager these questions? 13-year-olds may have a lot of dreams about jobs, but little practical idea of what they might do. 18-year-olds are more likely to have a much clearer idea about real jobs. Read what four 13-year-olds wrote when asked these questions.

Gary: Aged 13
*When I leave school I want to be a footballer and play for a league team. I want to have a contract with my home town Watford. My cousin was spotted by a scout. When I do get in the football business I want to play my favourite team Liverpool and play for England.
If I don't get spotted I want to be a long-distance lorry driver like my Dad, Grandad and three uncles. I would like my lorry to be an F10 Volvo. I would like to go over to Italy and places like that on a ferry with my lorry.*

Claire: Aged 13
*My ambition for the future is to become a lawyer and a great athlete for Britain and win a gold in the Olympics. Out of the two I would want to become an athlete, but then I'd want another job anyway.
I think that my ambition of becoming an athlete is just a dream. I think it's very unlikely I will ever succeed in doing it. I think there's a great future in becoming a lawyer, being something to do with the law has always appealed to me. I feel I could have a chance in making it work as a career if I really put my mind to it.*

What are they saying?

Debby seems worried about the future. Perhaps she wrote her answer when she was having a bad day, but she seems pessimistic about her prospects. While Debby seems resigned to getting the same sort of job as other girls, Selena resents being typecast. Selena probably realises she faces a struggle if she wants to get away from filing or nursing. Gary and Claire seem to have reality and fantasy sorted out pretty well – and they appear to be really happy about their career choice.

Dreams

A Can you remember, as a young teenager, what you wanted to be when you were grown-up? Did your dream come true? You may even be glad, now, that it didn't. But however satisfied we are with the job we do have, many of us do still have secret dreams of what we might have been.

Sometimes teenagers think their dreams are so unlike reality that they become resigned to a mundane job, or else they won't consider any alternatives to their dreams.

Ask your teenager to share his/her dreams and expectations with you. Go through the following questions twice. The first time thinking about a dream job – that he/she would like above all others. The second time think about the reality job – that he/she might actually get.

1 What type of job?

2 Where would it be?

3 What will he/she be doing in the job?

4 What is it about the job that makes it so attractive?

Is he/she likely to end up doing his/her dream job? If so, fine – help him/her plan how to get it. If not, ask him/her to pick out one or more reasons from this list:

○ I'm not clever enough
○ I wouldn't *really* like it because . . .
○ My parents would never let me take a job like that because . . .

○ There's too much competition
○ I'm not physically capable of it
○ I wouldn't be allowed to stay on at school long enough to do the training for this job
○ I don't want to work away from home
○ The training takes too long/is too expensive
○ Some other reason –

Look carefully at the reasons your teenager gives as to why he/she can't get the fantasy job. What would make it difficult to leave home? Or for you to let him/her stay on at school? Sort out any misunderstandings now and find out more about possible jobs of the kind he/she is interested in.

It's important to sort out what makes the dream job so attractive and satisfying. These satisfactions could be found in jobs that *are* available. For example: You want to be a film star? Is it so that people will look at you? – admire you? – think how well you act? Do you think that becoming a beauty product demonstrator or a school teacher might satisfy some of these hopes? Of course, they probably won't bring you lots of money and lovers if that was what you were hoping for.

You – and your teenager – may be limited by the range of types of jobs you know about. "What next?" lists books and organisations you could consult, which are particularly good at suggesting alternatives; for example, you know you would find working with animals satisfying or you would like to do something connected with medicine but realise you couldn't get into medical school.

Dreams vs. reality

If your teenager reckons he/she has a good chance of getting the job of his/her dreams, then all you need to do is support him/her – so long as you agree that the job is a reasonable one and that it is worth encouraging his/her hopes. If you don't agree that it's reasonable you will need to think hard about why you object to it. Do you have good reasons? For example, it may go against your cherished values if you are a pacifist and he/she wants to go in the army. But it may just go against family traditions: "What does he want to be a hairdresser for? All the men in our family have always been plumbers." Or perhaps you are embarrassed: "She *wants* to be a stripper!" or "He *wants* to be an undertaker!"

What was your first reaction to your teenager's dream job? It may have ranged from indiscriminate admiration – "What a fantastic idea" – to a put-down like – "That's impossible – astronauts have to get up in the morning. And what makes you think they'd want someone as stupid as you?"

It would be worthwhile taking a minute to consider what kind of feedback you usually give your teenager.

Helpful feedback is:
○ **sensitive and given at the right time.** It doesn't tread on his/her dreams. It's OK to have dreams and you shouldn't throw cold water on them unnecessarily. Most teenagers will, after a while, acknowledge that their dream may not come true. Then *you* can move on to helpful feedback.

○ **concrete and specific.** "I don't think your asthma would allow you to work as a deep-sea diver" rather than "What a rotten idea".

○ **dealing with actions rather than general descriptions.** "You could look at careers in social work" rather than "You ought to work with people because you get on with everyone". However, this second statement would certainly be good to hear as a morale booster because it enhances your self-esteem.

○ **an honest admission of your own feelings.** "I must say that I would be upset if you became a dancer in a night club" rather than "You make me furious with your stupid ideas about being a night club dancer".

Unhelpful feedback is:
○ **vague or abstract.** "Well, I suppose we could think about that." "Do you think that's really your thing?"

○ **labelling people.** "Trust a stupid girl like you to think of that."

○ **straight praise or blame.** "What a wonderful idea!" or "You haven't a chance."

○ **delayed** so that the person has forgotten or lost interest in the idea.

Which jobs?

Old jobs are disappearing; but some new jobs are available.

How might today's changing employment pattern affect your teenager's future? In general manual work is decreasing because of automation. One machine can do the work of many hands. Increasing use of computers is gradually doing away with routine jobs such as assembly line and clerical work. In the catering and food industries much of the unskilled work – traditionally done by women – can now be done by machines. Complex machines need only the attendance of a few skilled maintenance people – a job usually done by men.

So there are far fewer jobs for semi- or unskilled workers. To some extent this is affecting women more than men. There has also been a severe cut-back all round in the manufacturing industries. Managers and skilled, as well as unskilled, workers have been made redundant as industries cut back or close down.

New jobs

The employment picture isn't all gloom and cut-backs. The future lies with teenagers who take advantage of today's educational opportunities. That doesn't necessarily mean just staying on at school after 16. Taking further education – part-time while in employment, or full-time in further and higher education – is well worthwhile. So is being prepared to retrain for a different job.

Expanding job opportunities are mainly in managerial, professional and related occupations. But not only at the top. The new jobs don't all require 'A' levels by any means. There is a large 'second tier' group of job opportunities that is expanding. Broadly, this is called 'technical level' work and covers 'support staff' in all kinds of professions.

These 'assistants' need specialised knowledge and therefore training, though possibly not in such breadth and depth as the 'expert' they are helping. Technicians often start with three or four 'O' levels or sometimes lower qualifications. In many professional areas these technicians have their own title and career structure. They may also have their own professional body such as the Association of Accounting Technicians and the Institute of Legal Executives.

Today there are also many types of jobs which didn't exist 20 years ago. Above all, there are the many jobs connected with computers. There are jobs for people of virtually all levels of educational achievement. Computers are the tool which computing people use to help others to do their job more efficiently. So computing isn't one particular career. There is work in virtually any job area a person is interested in. Incidentally, it's a myth that you need to understand maths to go into computing. The ability to think logically and to express what you want to say clearly are far more important.

Besides computer jobs, have you heard of Catering Systems Manager, Recreation and Leisure Manager?

Keeping up-to-date with new opportunities is difficult for parents. But since surveys have shown again and again that parents' views and values still exert the greatest influence on their children's career choice, it's important for you to know how to help your teenager find out more about them.

Information and advice

You should have the chance to discuss your teenager's future at school with the careers teacher, school counsellor, head of year or form teacher.

Careers teachers are school-based and usually also teach another subject. The time they're allowed by the Head to devote to careers work varies enormously. They should have some idea of the teenagers' strengths and weaknesses and run a planned careers education programme. The careers teacher should be able to help pupils make realistic career plans and choose appropriate 'O' and CSE level examinations to take. Career teachers usually run a careers library – though this may be only a pile of leaflets and a row of books. He or she should also know *how to find out the answers* to any questions teenagers or parents may ask.

Careers officers are likely to go into your teenager's school. They work from a Careers Office and divide much of their time between interviewing young people and placing them in work experience or training schemes within Youth Opportunities Programme (YOP) or the new Youth Training Scheme. Careers officers should also keep up with education and training developments as well as national and local employment opportunities.

Finding out more

A If you want to know more about new jobs in general you could ask the Head or the Parents' Association to arrange an evening at which people familiar with these jobs could answer questions. Other parents at the school may work in these fields and be willing to talk.

Schools either on their own or with others in the area may put on careers evenings, displays or even a convention, with representatives from local industries etc. Encourage these but press, too, for information and representatives from a much wider range, including the new job areas, to be there. Too often it's just the local bank manager, the police, a chain store representative and the three armed services who are there.

If you and your teenager have new ideas you want to pursue you can go to the local careers office. You may want detailed information and addresses to write to or just a chance to look at their careers library. You should be able to find the same kind of information at your local reference library.

Try looking at job advertisements in the papers. They will not only give you some idea of what jobs are available, but also show you what qualifications and experience employers are looking for. Friends, relatives and workmates may also be able to help your teenager – after all they are the traditional network by which many young people find jobs.

Men and women's work

The chart shows you the overall employment pattern for men and women in 1980. The most important differences between men's and women's work are:

Men do – far more of the manual work and skilled jobs. They are more likely to work in the manufacturing industries – processing, making and repairing. Most managerial jobs are held by men.

Women do – far more of the unskilled jobs. They are more likely to work in what are called 'service' industries such as catering, shops, hairdressing and cleaning. Most clerical jobs are held by women.

Equal opportunities?

In theory, girls have equal career opportunities with boys. There should be nothing to stop girls becoming electricians or barristers, carpenters or surgeons. But in practice, sex discrimination legislation has so far had a fairly limited effect. That isn't really surprising since legislation alone can't change traditional attitudes to what is and what isn't seen as a 'Good Job' for a girl. These attitudes are slowly changing – employers, parents, advisers *and* teenage girls have to alter their attitudes.

A If you have a teenage daughter are there any jobs you would not like to see her take up because of her sex? What does she think? Are there jobs she sees as not open to women? Or – that she would like to do, but thinks others would disapprove?

If you have a son you may feel equally strongly that there are some jobs you wouldn't like to see him doing. What is it about some kinds of work that makes you see it as 'woman's work'?

Discrimination

It is now unlawful to treat anyone, on the grounds of sex, less favourably than a person of the opposite sex is or would be treated in the same circumstances.

Direct sex discrimination involves treating a woman less favourably than a man *because* she is a woman. Or vice versa – a man less favourably *because* he is a man. Indirect discrimination means that conditions are applied which favour one sex more than the other and which cannot be justified.

Employers may not discriminate against you because of your sex – or your race, colour, religion or whether or not you are married – in their recruitment or treatment of you. This also applies to promotion and training.

Employers may not usually label jobs 'for men' or 'for women'. There are a few exceptions such as for employment in a private household or where there are no more than five people on the staff; or if a person's sex is a 'genuine occupational qualification' (e.g. acting).

If you feel that you have been treated unfairly you have the right to take your complaint to a county court in England or Wales, or sheriff court in Scotland. If your grievance is to do with employment, you go to an industrial tribunal.

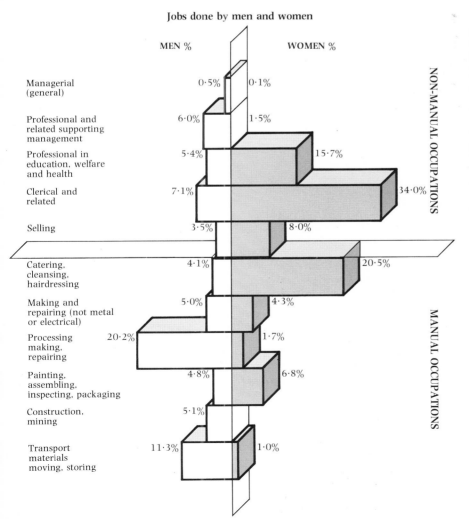

Jobs done by men and women

MEN %   WOMEN %

NON-MANUAL OCCUPATIONS

	MEN %	WOMEN %
Managerial (general)	0·5%	0·1%
Professional and related supporting management	6·0%	1·5%
Professional in education, welfare and health	5·4%	15·7%
Clerical and related	7·1%	34·0%
Selling	3·5%	8·0%

MANUAL OCCUPATIONS

	MEN %	WOMEN %
Catering, cleansing, hairdressing	4·1%	20·5%
Making and repairing (not metal or electrical)	5·0%	4·3%
Processing making, repairing	20·2%	1·7%
Painting, assembling, inspecting, packaging	4·8%	6·8%
Construction, mining	5·1%	
Transport materials moving, storing	11·3%	1·0%

What's it like to work?

What can be learned before leaving school?

Nowadays many teenagers work part-time before they leave school – maybe baby-sitting, working in a shop on Saturdays, or doing a paper round.

Sometimes these jobs lead on to a permanent job of the same kind – nurse or shop assistant. Sometimes teenagers take up entirely different jobs. But whatever may happen, skills they have learnt beforehand can stand them in good stead during their working lives. How can parents help their teenagers to gain such skills?

What has your teenager learnt about work?

If he/she has done jobs, regular or irregular, paid or unpaid he/she should have learnt:

○ Obviously work-related skills – how to clock in, how to take orders, specific skills to do with the job (hairdressing, car maintenance, shelf filling).
○ Less obvious skills – not giving up too easily, being sociable, being reliable – even if there is something else you'd much rather do, having a good memory (for prices, layout of shelves etc.)

Both kinds of skill are going to be useful to your teenager – though the second kind are obviously not quite so easy to list on an application form. If there is a space on the form for 'other relevant information' make a note of them there.

Your teenager's skills

A Make a list, with your teenager if possible, of activities, paid and unpaid, from which he/she will have learned work-related skills. Here is a list from our parent testers' teenagers to help you recall what your teenager has done.

Activities

Member of Red Cross cadets	Weekly egg delivery
Helping with OAPs	Karate club
Helping with harvest	Baby-sitting
Running stall at school sale	Helping at a playgroup
Delivering daily papers	Car cleaning
Filling shelves on Saturdays	Gardening
Drawing fashions in spare time	Helping at jumble sale
Playing for sports team	Singing in a choir
Making wooden toys for mentally-handicapped children	Helping put together a monthly magazine
Talking to relatives and friends about their work	Helping in a club for the disabled

B For each activity check through the skills list, below, and tick or make a note of those skills he/she will have learned. We have given an example for 'Filling shelves in a supermarket'.

Skills	Activities eg	1	2
1 Getting on with work/team mates	✓		
2 Practising mental arithmetic			
3 Being a good time-keeper	✓		
4 Finding out about other kinds of jobs	✓		
5 Having a good memory for prices, where things are	✓		
6 Being sociable			
7 Catering on large scale			
8 Learning to finish a job properly	✓		
9 Being reliable	✓		
10 Following instructions			
11 Being adaptable			
12 Being honest			
13 Handling own wages	✓		
14 Insight into people's problems eg elderly or disabled			
Others . . .			

Most of our parent testers and their teenagers found making these lists very satisfying and made comments such as:
"My teenager didn't realise his Saturday job was teaching him so much."
"It's surprising how much can be learned in an apparently simple 'non-learning' situation. A bright youngster acquires knowledge almost unconsciously, so that all experiences in any contact with work can provide useful experience at a later date."
"This made me think we should change our minds and encourage our teenagers to do part-time work."
"My teenager had previously seen it as just a way to earn money: an attitude to work I don't want to encourage!"

What did Rohan learn?

Rohan took a part-time job on Saturdays at his local supermarket filling shelves and helping out on the tills. When he came to look for a full-time job, he hesitated about mentioning the supermarket on his application forms as it was nothing like the jobs he was applying for (he wanted to be a management trainee in a hotel chain). However, his father persuaded him to go through the check list of his work-related skills he had learned (opposite). They decided that the supermarket job had given experience in:

○ getting on with people (shop customers and other staff)
○ handling money and working the till
○ remembering the layout of the goods on the shelves
○ clocking in and out
○ being reliable and a good time-keeper
○ finding out about a wide range of jobs (warehouseman, shop assistant, parking attendant, shop manager and so on)
○ learning about wine and food.

So Rohan put down his supermarket experience on his application form and added a short note at the end about the skills he had learned.

If your teenager has made a list of his/her activities and work-related skills (see opposite) encourage him/her to keep it for when he/she starts to apply for jobs. Remember you can always add an extra sheet of notes to application forms. When applying for a particular job decide which skills are needed for it and emphasise any past activities which will have helped build up those skills.

Part-time jobs

If your teenager is looking for a part-time job locally, check whether he has considered these:

Job	When available
Paper round	Everyday
Shelf filling	Saturday
Baby-sitting	Evenings
Child-minding (must be done in child's home)	Week-ends or school holiday
Helping with harvest, packing fruit and veg.	Summer holidays
Shop assistant	Saturdays
Dog walking	Every day
Waiter/waitress/washer up (18+)	Weekends, summer holidays
Christmas post (16+)	Christmas holidays
Market stall (17+)	Saturdays
Cleaning/washing/ironing/window cleaning	Weekends, holidays
Stable work	Most days

What sort of jobs can teenagers take?

The law on what age you can do various jobs is complicated, and its effect varies from area to area. If you are under 13, it is illegal for you to work unless you have an entertainment licence – that is, you are a child actor.

If you are aged 13, 14 or 15 the rules are, broadly speaking, as follows:

Hours of work You can take a part-time job for not more than two hours on any school day. You can't work during school hours (9am to 4.30pm) including the lunch hour. You can't start work before 7am or work after 7pm. You can work for eight hours on Saturdays, but only for two hours on Sundays. However, your local authority can make regulations which apply locally and which may be stricter than these general rules. You can get a copy from the town hall.

Types of job In general, you are not allowed to work on a market stall or become a street trader until you are 17, but some local authorities let you work on your parents' stall once you reach the age of 14. Ask at the town hall for details.

Whilst you are under 16, you are banned from working in manufacturing, demolition, mining, building, transport industries. You can't work on a sea-going ship or fishing boat unless the boat is one in which only your family is employed.

Most local authorities have local rules banning you from working in kitchens, cake shops, restaurants, slaughter-houses, billiard saloons, gaming or betting shops or any business requiring door-to-door selling or touting. No-one under 18 is allowed to be employed in a bar.

Work experience

Some of the regulations about what work teenagers may do are relaxed if they are taking part in work experience schemes. Work experience programmes help teenagers to spend part of their last year at school working in a commercial firm for a while – usually about three weeks. The advantages of taking part in a scheme like this are that teenagers are able to find out what they like and dislike about going out to work, and this kind of job in particular, so that they have a much more realistic idea of what they want to do.

Depending on what is available locally work experience within a wide range of career interests may be offered. Some jobs are so popular that demand outstrips supply. There is a lot of competition for opportunities in garage work, building trades, photography, beauty therapy and jobs requiring the use of foreign languages.

Work experience is not job training. More important than the job done will be the experience of working with adults, other than parents and teachers, and the experience of success in accomplishing the tasks they were set in the 'real' world of work.

When this experience of work is shared in discussions back in school, teenagers have the chance of surveying realistically the careers and occupational opportunities in the area where they live and where they are likely to be seeking employment. A disadvantage of work experience might be that a bad experi-

Andrea helping at Simpson Day Nursery.

ence of one particular job could put a teenager off that whole range of jobs for life, when it was just that office, or that factory, that didn't suit. On the other hand a particular job might seem very glamorous or easy, unlike most jobs of that kind.

Trident project

In some schools the career staff set up arrangements with local firms themselves. Other schools may participate with nearby schools within the local authority in the Trident Project.

This project brings together the resources of industry, local education authorities and voluntary organisations to provide young people in schools with experience of work in local firms, voluntary service in the local community, and grant-aid for challenging pursuits.

If approached by a Local Education Authority the National Office of the Trident Trust will attempt to persuade an industry to second a person to be a local project co-ordinator to work with the Local Education Authority. This co-ordinator arranges suitable opportunities for experience of work in local firms and helps teachers match pupils to those jobs. When they are in the fifth form (15–16) teenagers who are about to leave school or decide on further education, can go out to work in a local firm for three weeks in a job of their choice as part of their careers' education. Work experience can also sometimes be arranged for fourth and sixth formers.

Nick preparing canteen dinners at Coles Plastics.

On a smaller scale Trident also links schools with local and national voluntary organisations. A number of teenagers become volunteers in community service projects. A Trident certificate is awarded in the form of a Record of Achievements for creditable performance in work experience and voluntary service. This provides many teenagers with a record that is an alternative, or supplement, to CSE or 'O' level Certificates when they apply for jobs.

Alternatives to work experience

In some work places although they may not allow a teenager to do the actual work, they will allow the teenager to 'shadow' an experienced worker. The teenager goes everywhere with the worker who explains the job as they go along. This can be particularly helpful where the job is too skilled for the teenager to do – but one in which he/she might be interested if he/she had further training. Examples might include 'shadowing' a vet, farmer, solicitor, reporter, TV cameraman or probation officer.

Schools may also build up projects which require teenagers to interview and photograph a wide range of workers.

What was it like to try? Here's what three teenagers felt:

"It felt strange and a bit scary to ride home on a bus in the dark. I live only a few minutes walk away from school and I almost always get home while it's still light."

"Travelling! It took up to one and a half hours a day. I fell asleep on the bus."

"I had to look after the petty cash account and balance the ledgers. It was frightening. Someone else's money seems much more valuable."

"The job is much more physical than I expected. I would not be strong enough to do it full-time, but there were other jobs I did not even know existed that I am now interested in."

"I will never work in this type of office. Thank goodness I found out how boring it is now. I really want to do something with people and will work at my exams so I can qualify as an occupational therapist."

How can parents help?

A You've probably been helping in many ways already. Most parents help their children from an early age to understand the responsibilities work involves by giving them certain jobs for which they alone are responsible, such as – cleaning out the rabbit, fetching in the coal, laying the table. These jobs help them to grow up accepting the idea that certain things have to be done regularly. They learn to become reliable and accept that life is not just about pleasing themselves. Looking ahead to when they go out to work teenagers will realise that all tasks are not equally enjoyable all the time, and that most people have to accept a compromise. In most jobs some of the work is enjoyable, other parts are not.

You can encourage your teenager to take on work, giving him/her practical support if necessary though not running the whole thing for him/her.

Emma's father, for instance, was so nervous about her being a baby-sitter that he walked round to the house with her and insisted on her being ready to come home at a certain time, when he would call for her. He also rang a couple of times during the evening to make sure everything was alright.

Samantha's mother, on the other hand, let her keep her own record of when she had been booked and for her to go and come back as required (though she preferred someone to walk back with her). Samantha knew she could phone her mother in an emergency, but in general her mother left Samantha to her own way.

Practical ways in which you could help your child with a part-time job or a work experience course could be:
○ getting him/her a separate meal at a different time from the rest of the family.
○ make sure he/she gets up in time, or goes to the job on time.
○ give lifts if public transport is really not available.
○ help with bus fares and other incidental costs until your teenager can earn enough to pay for him/herself.
○ if the job is physically demanding, make sure he/she gets extra rest.
○ encourage him/her to continue if he/she dislikes the job at an early stage.

Encouraging the school If your teenager would like to know more about several different kinds of work and the school hasn't managed to arrange work experience, you could perhaps ask friends, relatives or other parents at the school, perhaps in the P.T.A., to help you arrange this. One school's Parents' Association keeps a list of all parents who could provide work experience or 'shadowing' at their own workplace.

Staying or leaving?

What will happen when your teenager reaches 16?

When you were a teenager, and for many years after that, the number of pupils leaving school at 15 (the old school-leaving age) remained more or less the same. Nine out of every ten left school. Only one in ten stayed on – usually to take more exams.

Today more and more 16-year-olds – the present minimum school-leaving age – are staying on at school. They do so partly to get better qualifications and partly because there are far fewer jobs available than there used to be. Sixth forms and colleges of further education all over the country are bursting at the seams.

Why do they want to leave?

Teenagers have many different reasons for wanting to leave school. Those given in a recent study were:

○ 47 per cent wanted to earn a wage and be independent
○ 12 per cent said the family needed the money
○ 19 per cent didn't like school
○ 4 per cent were getting married shortly
○ 22 per cent felt they were not good enough to stay on. What a sad message about yourself to take away from 11 years of schooling. This attitude is often the outcome of schooling focussed on a narrow academic curriculum, which may be suitable for only the top ten per cent of the pupils. The needs of these pupils, for whom high 'O' level and 'A' level grades are essential if they are to go on to higher education, are given priority. In such a system the vast majority of pupils are likely to see themselves as educational failures.

It's interesting that in the above study no-one seems to have admitted that they couldn't face staying on at school because they disliked the curriculum and the teachers. Yet this is a common reaction of teenagers asked in a more informal way for their opinions.

Not all 16-year-olds who decide that they would prefer working to being at school are going to find jobs, at least straight away. What other things could they do which might be useful to them, and that they would enjoy doing? After all, if they are really unhappy at school there is no point in their staying on, just because they believe that the choice is only school or unemployment.

What can they do?

A We have summarised different things that teenagers can do in the chart below. It's shown in the form of a 'brainstorming' chart and you might find it useful to make a similar chart but with personal, individual statements, with your teenager. When trying to think of alternatives it's easy to think of just one or two and feel 'that's all' or 'they will do'. This way you can end up making a decision before you've *really* explored all the alternatives. Also writing ideas in straight lists often makes the first things you put down seem to be the most important. First thoughts aren't always best. With a brainstorming chart the idea is to put down as many ideas as possible without stopping to criticise any of them. Afterwards you can think them through and decide which you consider are the best possibilities.

Some of the options shown below could be done at the same time as others. Voluntary work, for instance. 'Year betweens' – in which the teenager takes a year out before continuing with his/her studies – are available through such schemes as the Trident Project or Community Service Volunteers. It's worth thinking about these matters before your teenager is 16. Voluntary work in a summer play scheme could provide useful experience for training as a primary school teacher. Or with old people for someone interested in taking up social work.

There are obviously more possibilities available as you get older, but there are quite a few things 13-year-olds can do to further an interest which might lead to a job later. Suppose your 13-year-old was interested in computers, for example, he/she could use facilities at his/her own or some nearby school, or maybe attend an evening class in the subject.

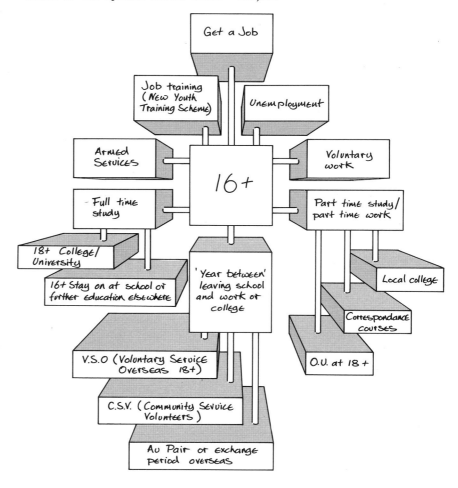

Get a Job

Job training (New Youth Training Scheme)

Unemployment

Armed Services

16+

Voluntary work

Full time study

Part time study/ part time work

18+ College/ University

16+ Stay on at school or further education elsewhere

'Year between' leaving school and work or college

Local college

Correspondance courses

V.S.O (Voluntary Service Overseas 18+)

O.U. at 18+

C.S.V. (Community Service Volunteers)

Au Pair or exchange period overseas

Diana thinks about getting a job

Diana is 15; she attends quite a large comprehensive school where she works fairly hard. She is planning to take four 'O' levels and a CSE in Child Development. She has several younger brothers and sisters and has always had a vague idea that she would like a job looking after children. She has never planned to stay on at school after she was 16, since she wants to earn her own living and perhaps see a bit of the world.

After a discussion with the careers teacher about her future she comes home rather shaken. The careers teacher has said that there aren't a lot of places available for Nursery Nurse training, certainly not near home, and good jobs in this field are getting hard to find. Is Diana sure that this is what she wants? Diana realises that the rather rosy picture she had of herself training and walking into some pleasant job of her choice at the end is optimistic, to say the least.

Over the next few weeks Diana talks things over with her Mum and Dad and her Aunt and Uncle when they come round. Her Mum reckons that someone has to get what places there are available in Nursery Nurse training schemes, so Diana should fight rather than give up. She might perhaps improve her chances by seeing if she could observe or help at the local Pre-School Playgroup in the holidays. Her Aunt says that if she can get a place at the college near them, she could stay with them during the week instead of making the 40-mile journey by train each day. Her Dad says he's not sure you have to have special certificates or anything if you work in an informal way as a Nanny. After all, working as an Au Pair or Mother's Help needs commonsense and a love of children really.

Diana feels a bit more hopeful and even sees herself working as an Au Pair abroad for a while, though she reckons it wouldn't give her much money to enjoy herself. She goes back to see her careers teacher. The careers teacher suggests she asks the teacher in charge of the CSE Child Development Course to help her get a place as an 'observer' in a Play Group as her special project work for the CSE: and she does. The careers teacher also suggests that Diana considers going into Nursing, when she is 18, because it is possible to specialise in Children's Nursing, which might be a better qualification for her.

Diana passed most of her exams – but failed Biology. She decided to stay on for one year to resit Biology and do the general sixth form course. During this time she worked on Saturdays and during the holidays for a single-parent working mum who had two small children. She plans to take a year off and is hoping to get a full-time live-in Mother's Help/Nanny job either here or abroad. After that . . . ? She is keeping her options open but now thinks that a nursing qualification would enable her to get a good job abroad or do voluntary service overseas.

Helping your teenager

A Your teenager may well face setbacks and difficult decisions. Here we consider five possible strategies and see what happened in Diana's case.

1 Don't foreclose on your decisions. Keep brainstorming the ideas. (Diana nearly gave up the whole idea after talking to her careers teacher the first time. She had set her sights narrowly on Nursery Nurse or nothing.)

2 Fight – someone has to get the places at colleges or the jobs that are available. (Diana needed encouragement from her Mum to do this.)

3 Ask plenty of people's advice (Diana did to some extent but she could have found people who work or had worked with children in a variety of ways and talked to them about their experiences.)

4 Consider what you can do before leaving school – to give you more skills. Does your application form show you have more to offer than the average applicant (see pages 152–153)? (Diana did well at this. Doing the CSE Child Development course – although her father opposed it because it wasn't an O-level – helped, particularly the project work she did based in a Pre-School Playgroup. Helping the single-parent mum was a good idea and earned her some money too.)

5 Use 'time between' – to build up work-related skills. 'Time between' leaving school and getting a job or going to college is well worth exploiting. (Diana found out that V.S.O. don't want unskilled school leavers, but would welcome her once she was qualified. So she couldn't combine work abroad with 'time between'. She did think of a temporary job which gave her a chance to live away from home and would count as 'further experience' on her application forms.)

Presenting yourself

How do you show people what you're really like?

The skills of 'presenting yourself' should be taught in schools. Their job is to educate their pupils *for life* – not just cram them for examinations. Life skills – not facts remembered – make for a competent person who has the right approach, rather than the ready answer, to life's challenges.

Examination skills – how to present what you know – can be taught. So can how to present both 'the facts' and what kind of a person you are in an interview for a job or a place at college.

Interviewers want to know what skills you possess, what interests and opinions you have, and why getting a place *with them* is important to you. They are taking on a person – not a certificate of education – and want to know how you will fit in with the other people there.

A What happens at your teenager's school? Ask your teenager – or the headmaster – or bring it up at a Parent-Teacher meeting. Ask how they help teenagers 'present themselves' via:

○ Examinations
○ Letters of application
○ Filling in application forms
○ Interviews

Where there is a special careers teacher he or she may do most of it. Or it may be done as part of the form tutorial work by the form teacher or Year Head.

If it isn't being done then, there are many points *you* can discuss with your teenager and this topic will help you do this. The emphasis of course must be on your teenager being 'in charge of' what he/she does. Choosing how and when to study, and what jobs or further training or education to pursue. But you can help him/her build up his/her skills so that he/she can do what he/she chooses to do as well as possible.

Taking exams

How to study is not the same as *what* to learn. And taking examinations does not always involve telling the examiner all you know. "Helping with study skills", (pages 138–141) gives an introduction to study skills and "What next?" suggests further reading. Many of these books look at examination-taking skills as well as study skills. They give general advice and sometimes 'hard and fast' rules to be obeyed. To some extent your teenager will have to work out what suits him/her best.

The school should provide him/her with plenty of practice in taking examinations, and also have taught him/her how to distinguish between different *types* of questions. It's so easy to answer the 'wrong' question when you are under stress.

You need to work out for your particular teenager how much pressure and support he/she needs from you. It's difficult to work out the right balance. Most teenagers are full of doubts and worries *however calm they seem*: so err on the side of support rather than pressure.

On the day probably the only advice worth repeating is:
○ Read *all* the instructions before starting any answers
○ Answer the right number of questions, and the right parts of the question. Many candidates are confused under stress by such instructions as "Answer as many questions as you can from part A and then any four from two of the sections B, C and D." (Perhaps examiners need to develop their question-setting skills)
○ Decide what approach is required. List, compare, contrast, argue for or against, account for – etc.
○ Make an outline of what steps you will go through before beginning to write out the answers
○ Allocate the time properly. Don't spend most of the time on the question you know most about
○ Read the answers through at the end.

All of this should be second nature before he/she reaches the examination room. It's worth reminding him/her. Some teachers do so – just before the examinations start.

Presenting a true picture

A This requires the teenager to know himself quite well. What follows in this topic is partly based on material from *Life Skills Teaching Programmes* (see "What next?"). The programmes were developed for group work with teenagers in schools and colleges. We've already suggested you check out what is done in your teenager's school. In good discussion groups most teenagers can work out what are the important points themselves. Here we can only provide suggestions and lists of tips. *To be of real use to your teenager you and he/she should discuss together what use he/she can make of them.*

A personal report

D Your teenager will have had many school reports written about him or her. But what would he/she say if he/she had to write one on him/herself and cover both school and outside interests?

Making such a personal report should help your teenager have a clearer picture about him/herself. He/she might include a copy of it with a letter of application, use it to fill in an application form or as the basis of what to say about him/herself in an interview.

Encourage your teenager to think about the following.

A What kind of person am I? What ten things would he/she write down about him/herself that would tell another person *what it is like to be him/her*?

You could try brainstorming together as long a list as possible and then choosing the ten best. Or you and he/she could make separate lists and then compare them. He/she might like to ask someone else who knows him/her well what he or she would say.

Here's what one boy listed:
1 I'm 16
2 I'm the oldest of four children and used to doing a lot of work around the house
3 I'm about average at school
4 I play football
5 I can get on with work on my own
6 I find it easy to get on with people
7 I'm good at mending things
8 I'm quite patient
9 I'm practical and get things done on time
10 I'm willing to work hard

When working with your teenager the emphasis should be on getting him/her to acknowledge his/her good points. It's not encouraging boasting but rather self-awareness. If a person can feel "I'm good at these things" it is easier to *go on him/herself* to consider "what would I like to improve?"

B What public recognition do I have of my qualities?
1 Examinations taken and grades achieved. (At this stage your teenager may only be able to list examinations to be taken and grades it's realistic to hope he/she will achieve.)
2 Awards – sports medals, effort prizes, Duke of Edinburgh awards, St. John's Ambulance Certificates, etc – and what was involved in gaining them.
3 Positions held – at school and in outside organisations – and what skills were learned from them.

C What are my work experiences and skills? Here your teenager needs to sum up the results of the "Your teenager's skills" activities we suggested on page 152 of this chapter.
  Make a list with two columns. In the first column he/she should write down:
1 part-time jobs he/she has had
2 voluntary work he/she has done
3 organisations he/she has belonged to
  In the second column list the work-related skills he/she learned.

Letters of application

Here are six suggestions about how to write a good one. Talk them over with your teenager. Does he/she feel he/she needs help with improving his/her letter-writing skills? Will someone at school help? Can you help?
1 **Observe the basic rules of letter writing.** Addresses and dates, formal openings and closings.
2 **Write it attractively.** How does it 'sound'? What does it look like?
3 **Make it clear what you are writing for.** The reader may have many other letters.
4 **Give enough detail** – to make you sound as though you will match what they are looking for.
5 **Make it clear when you are available for interview –** – or to start if that is relevant.
6 **Decide if there is some way to make your letter stand out from all the others** – special note paper, stylish presentation, appropriate personal detail?

Application form

It's well worth practising filling in application forms. Many people find them tricky to do.
1 **Read it carefully and think about your answer** – what exactly do they want to know?
2 **Have a spare copy if possible** – so that you can practice and produce a final version neatly correct.
3 **Take your time** – don't treat it casually. Your future is at stake.
4 **Watch for particular words** – be sure you know what to fill in for Nationality, DOB, Referee etc.
5 **Print or write?** *Check first* – some forms ask for block capitals. If not, if your handwriting is good it will be a point in your favour.

6 **Keep the form in a good condition** – keep it somewhere safe and flat.
7 **Watch for closing date** – early replies can bring an advantage. Watch out for final dates of application.
8 **Use a checker.** – you can't always spot your own mistakes. Get someone else to check.

Interviews

A The lists below, from *Life Skills Teaching Programmes* are about applying for a job. They can easily be adapted for applying to a college.
  Share your experiences of being interviewed with your teenager. Does your teenager feel he/she gets enough help at school? Perhaps you or the Parents' Association could suggest that other parents, experienced in interviewing people, might offer to do mock interviews or the local Rotary Club might be willing to do this.
  Discuss with your teenager the suggestions, below, as to what he/she might do *before* and *during* an interview. Ask how you can help. Can you help him/her role play interviews or practise certain skills? Find out more for him/her? Or provide practical help on the day – such as offer a lift, lend a tie or talk it over with him/her afterwards.

Before
○ Prepare answers to typical questions: such as what have you done before, how did you get on at school?
○ Work out what are your best 'selling points' – strengths and skills. Make sure these are recognised.
○ Work out what the interviewer is likely to be looking for in the interview and work out how to show him or her that you have the requirements.
○ Work out *what you want to know*: pay, hours, holidays, conditions of work, etc.
○ Find out about the firm so that you can display an interest.
○ Prepare your most appropriate clothes.
○ Rehearse your answers and questions with someone.
○ Leave early enough to arrive without rush or hassle.
○ Take any relevant documents with you.

During
○ Introduce yourself – if need be.
○ Shake hands firmly, if a hand is offered.
○ Keep eye contact; smile appropriately; sit in a position which conveys interest and listening; speak clearly.
○ Answer questions fully, giving details; look for opportunities to indicate why you might be suitable for the job.
○ Show you have found out information about the firm, thereby demonstrating initiative and enthusiasm.
○ When given the opportunity, ask questions about what you want to know – to have no questions is likely to suggest low energy or disinterest.
○ Listen for clues as to what the interviewer is really looking for and be ready to demonstrate how you might have the qualities to match the requirements.
○ Thank the person at the end for the opportunity you were given, and if he or she has been helpful, for that also.

Afterwards
Even if you didn't get the job, talk over what you learnt about presenting yourself, in preparation for the next time.

No jobs?

Times have changed. There aren't now enough jobs to go round.

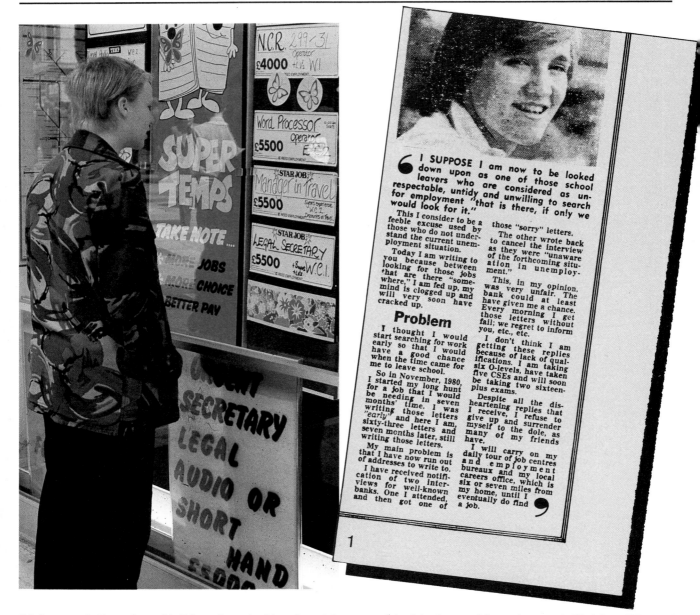

I SUPPOSE I am now to be looked down upon as one of those school leavers who are considered as unrespectable, untidy and unwilling to search for employment "that is there, if only we would look for it."

This I consider to be a feeble excuse used by those who do not understand the current unemployment situation.

Today I am writing to you because between looking for those jobs that are there "somewhere," I am fed up, my mind is clogged up and will very soon have cracked up.

Problem

I thought I would start searching for work early so that I would have a good chance when the time came for me to leave school.

So in November, 1980, I started my long hunt for a job that I would be needing in seven months' time. I was writing those letters "early" and here I am, sixty-three letters and seven months later, still writing those letters.

My main problem is that I have now run out of addresses to write to.

I have received notification of two interviews for well-known banks. One I attended, and then got one of those "sorry" letters.

The other wrote back to cancel the interview as they were "unaware of the forthcoming situation in unemployment."

This, in my opinion, was very unfair. The bank could at least have given me a chance. Every morning I get those letters without fail; we regret to inform you, etc., etc.

I don't think I am getting these replies because of lack of qualifications. I am taking six O-levels, have taken five CSEs and will soon be taking two sixteen-plus exams.

Despite all the disheartening replies that I receive, I refuse to give up and surrender myself to the dole, as many of my friends have.

I will carry on my daily tour of job centres and employment bureaux and my local careers office, which is six or seven miles from my home, until I eventually do find a job.

1

---

2 My name is Pam, I am 16. I have been looking for a job for three months now and I have no luck.

My parents say I haven't bothered, but I have just given up I'm determined that I am not going to stay on the dole for the rest of my life.

My sister wasn't very brainy and she went straight on to the dole, now she says she wished she had a job, she can't afford to pay her keep, she smokes, and she needs new clothes now she comes with me to try and find something.

3 I have been out of work for three months. I am only 16 years old, I left school six months ago. I started working and then I was obliged to move from the area and I had to leave my job. I also got a job where I moved to, that was only temporary then I moved back again. Unfortunately I couldn't get a job. I had several interviews and filled in millions of application forms. The worst thing is there isn't any jobs going anywhere for young people.

The money on the dole is terrible I only get £25 for two weeks. With that I am expected to buy clothes, fags, pay my mum housekeeping, etc.

My parents are always nagging me to get a job but they don't realise there aren't any, they always say it's my fault for not working, but it's not. The thing is it's bloody pathetic, the Careers Office are here to help youngsters but they haven't done a single bleeding thing.

Being on the dole can get bloody depressing. I have been depressed for months now – the doctor says its nothing but it is, it's having nothing to do, sitting at home doing nowt but sulk and lay about.

Reactions to unemployment

Have you ever been out of work for a long time? How did you feel about it?

What three teenagers have said about not having a job is shown left. What feelings can you pick out from what they have written, besides the general one of depression?

Teenagers' feelings

Here is what we picked out from these examples:
○ frustration ("endless searching")
○ lack of a feeling of personal identity ("just one in a queue")
○ indignation, incredulity and anger ("still writing those letters")
○ determination ("I'm determined that I'm not going to stay on the dole for the rest of my life")

Parents' feelings

A What about the parents of these teenagers? They are quoted as being very unhelpful: "My parents say I haven't bothered...", "My parents are always nagging me...". But that may not be how those parents saw themselves.

How do you think you would behave towards your teenager if he/she had been out of work for six months? How would you *feel*? How *do* you feel if he/she already is out of work?
○ frustrated because it's not really his/her fault?
○ glad because he/she can take the opportunity to develop other skills?
○ furious and angry – with him/her for not really trying?
○ furious and angry – with the government and society for mistaken economic policies which have led to high unemployment?
○ worried about his/her whole future?
○ anxious because you see yourself supporting him/her for the rest of his/her life?
○ helpless because you feel there is nothing you can do about it?
○ pleased that he/she won't be caught in the rat-race that you are trapped in?
○ hopeless because you don't believe the unemployment situation will improve? What *can* be done about teenage employment is examined on the next two pages.
○ something different?
D Parents whose teenagers have been out of work say they often feel a mixture of many of these feelings. They sometimes swing between feeling angry with their teenager and angry with the government. Try to describe your own feelings.

Being open about how you feel will help your teenager, in turn, to admit to his/her feelings. Teenagers often keep up a face of 'not caring' or 'keeping cheerful' which leads adults to assume they don't want a job.

This is highly unlikely to be true. After all, in our society a job is still the adult status symbol. ("Whose values" on pages 88–89 describes how unemployment often leads to the prolonged involvement of teenagers in peer groups which do provide status and boost self-esteem.)

Because 'having a job' and 'being grown up' are so often equated it is of extra importance to show unemployed teenagers that they are young *adults*. They have the rights and responsibilities of adults – and should be treated as such.

However hard he/she is trying to get a job there are not enough jobs to go round. This is especially true for teenagers who are almost twice as likely to be unemployed as someone over 20. At the time of writing (1982) there seems little likelihood of improvement.

Why are so many teenagers unemployed?

In January 1981, 19 per cent of under 18-year-olds in the labour market were jobless. Compare this with just 7.4 per cent of school leavers out of work in October 1979. In 1981–82 one in two teenagers leaving school at 16 went into YOP (Youth Opportunities Programme) because they could not find work.

It is true that unemployment figures in general are increasing, but for school-leavers they are increasing much more quickly. The teenage unemployment rate is now roughly double the national average. Teenage girls are even more likely to be unemployed than teenage boys.

Shirley Williams, a former Minister in the Labour Government, spent much of her time, after she lost her seat in May 1979, researching and writing on the problem of youth unemployment at the Policy Studies Institute. She explains that the baby boom generation, born in the 1960's, have been caught in a pincer movement of increasing supply and slackening demand. More teenagers are coming on to the labour market at a time when fewer jobs are available. There has been a savage cut back in the manufacturing industries, especially in the more labour intensive ones. Apprenticeships have been axed as economy measures. Also many of the more traditional openings for young people – messenger boys, tea boys, filing clerks – have been closed.

The least educated and the unskilled are hardest hit. They tend to drift from job to job, becoming more and more apathetic and depressed. The problem has been made worse, she says, by job protection laws, which inhibit employers from taking on young people. Young people, she points out, tend to cost more to employ these days. They are also more likely to be in competition with married women, who are seen as more stable and more reliable workers.

Social policies also affect teenagers. Low cash benefits for the young unemployed (see the teenagers' writings again), reduction in higher education and low investment in areas of high unemployment will all add to their troubles.

It's interesting to look at what happens in some other European countries. Britain is different from France and Germany in that 44 per cent of its 16-year-old school-leavers go on to the labour market as opposed to 19 per cent in France and only 7 per cent in Germany. In France 40 per cent of the school-leavers go into full-time preparation for a job or into apprenticeships. The equivalent figure for Great Britain is 24 per cent. The New Youth Training Scheme (see next page) should take more of our 16-year-old school-leavers off the labour market and into full-time training schemes or apprenticeships.

Ways of helping

Many parents feel helpless when they think about how difficult it is for teenagers today to find jobs. Explaining what has led to such high unemployment doesn't necessarily make it obvious what can be done about the problem. Here we look at what the government is planning to do, what you might do about the general issue and ways in which you can help your own teenager help him/herself.

The new Youth Training Scheme

Many teenagers have taken part in YOP (the Youth Opportunities Programme). YOP is now being phased out and is being replaced by a new Youth Training Scheme and a number of other new ventures. At the time of writing (1982) it's too early to tell yet how this new scheme is going to work, though it is hoped that it will offer a better basic training than YOP.

A training allowance will be paid to young people on the scheme. The precise levels of the allowances will be decided nearer the time of the scheme's starting in 1983, but are likely to be around £750 a year for 16-year-old school leavers and around £1,250 a year for the older group.

The main points in the new programme are:

1 For young unemployed people. The provision of a billion-pound Youth Training Scheme which, from September 1983, will guarantee all 16-year-old unemployed school-leavers a full year's foundation training.

2 For young people in employment. An increased emphasis on developing the Youth Training Scheme to cover employed as well as unemployed young people, including more money for schemes designed to create more jobs with proper training.

More grants will be made to employers providing integrated training programmes to cover 50,000 young people.

3 Apprenticeships and similar skills training. A target date of 1985 has been set by which *recognised standards* will be set for all the main draft, technical and professional skills. This approach will replace the old system of serving an apprenticeship for a certain number of years or until you reached a certain age, which was no guarantee of what you would actually learn.

Financial support will also be continued for apprenticeship places.

The unemployed . . .

In the writings from unemployed teenagers quoted on the previous page you will see that they don't have a very high opinion of the agencies available to them. And until now nobody has found it necessary to help unemployed young people – just to channel them into jobs which are available.

But many careers officers are now beginning to prepare young people for the fact that they may not get jobs and offer them other possibilities. Centres for the unemployed are being set up in different parts of the country with the help of the TUC. Check whether there is one in your area. A typical centre would:

○ provide a place to go where unemployed people can meet regularly and discuss their problems.
○ give advice on legal rights to do with unemployment, dismissal, redundancy, etc.
○ organise activities and become a campaigning body on behalf of its members.

What can you do about teenage unemployment?

A **D** What was your reaction when you read about the reasons for teenage unemployment? Did you want to:

○ join the political party you consider will do most to solve such problems and start campaigning?
○ let someone in power know exactly what you thought?
○ set up a Centre for the Unemployed?
○ find out ways of setting up a firm which would employ school leavers?
○ shrug your shoulders and say "That's life"?
○ say "There's nothing I can do about it: I wish I could."

Some people feel better able than others to take practical action. Consider what you might do.

1 Look around you. Talk about unemployment to
○ your family
○ your friends
○ your workmates
○ other people in your community – your teenager's teachers, youth group leaders, other people you know in your community.

While this may not make any real difference to your own teenager's work prospects, it may make you feel better about the problem. Some of these people might make helpful suggestions and also offer you their views on unemployment, which may be quite different from yours and help you to get a new slant on things. Sharing your own concern will also make some other people more aware of the problems.

2 Look a little further. Do you know anyone who might know of job opportunities (for *all* teenagers, not necessarily yours)? Or is there someone among your friends or at your firm who would be willing to offer YOP places, or informal 'hands-on' work experience? Many employers have never seriously considered this. Or do you have contacts with a leisure centre or sports facility who might be prepared to let unemployed young people in at cut price at quiet times?

3 Take action You may prefer to do this on your own, or you might consider that you could achieve more as part of a group.

You could:

○ write letters to the local and national press about particular aspects of unemployment that you are concerned about

○ lobby local councillors to find out what practical measures – job creation schemes, centre for unemployment – they are working to achieve locally

○ look at the policies of the different political parties and change to the one most in line with your ideas on teenage unemployment

○ seek funding (from charities, local bodies) to set up employment and leisure schemes locally.

Teenagers could . . .

A Here we summarise different courses of action your teenager might take if unemployed and how you could help.

1 Undertake further education.
○ Could you go back to your old school or another school? Check with schools.
○ What courses are available at your local college of further education? Check at college.
○ What other courses are you qualified for and are available to you? Check with careers officer, your school, write to colleges etc.
As a parent:
Ask yourself whether you could afford this; help teenager to investigate different courses.

2 Undertake training.
○ Is there a Youth Training Scheme available for you? Check with careers officer.
○ What other job training schemes are available in your area? Check with careers officer, Job Centre, firms which interest you.
As a parent:
Discuss pros and cons of different types of work with teenager. Look into different training schemes. If job training schemes pays less than social security, can you afford to keep him/her?

3 Look at different jobs from those previously considered.
○ Ask friends and relatives about the jobs they do.
○ Check with careers officer, Job Centre, and public library to find out more about new jobs.
As a parent:
Talk to your friends and relatives about jobs not previously considered. Look back at jobs which interested you in the past which you didn't take.

4 Step up job-hunting activities in your own area.
○ Could you ask friends and relatives about possible vacancies? Go or write to firms you would like to work for.
○ Are you presenting yourself to your best advantage (letter of application etc.)? See pages 158–159.
○ Could you get together with friends in the same position and pool information?

○ Look at more job advertisements – get papers as soon as they come out.
As a parent:
Provide general support for job-hunting. Also help with lifts to interviews, writing paper, stamps and envelopes.

5 Look for jobs further afield.
○ Would it be possible for you to either travel some distance to work or move to another place where jobs are more easily available?
○ Could you find out actual costs of living away from home?
As a parent:
Help consider responsibilities of your teenager working away from home. Could he/she afford it? Would you be prepared to let him/her go? Should he/she go? Should the whole family move?

6 Do informal voluntary community service.
○ Could you help a voluntary organisation to help *you* to fill up your time and maybe gain useful experience, as well as being of use to other people?
○ Could you draw up a list of possible groups and find out whether they want you?
As a parent:
Suggest different possibilities from your own experience. Offer practical help in getting to places – volunteers don't usually get expenses.

7 Consider becoming self-employed.
○ Have you any skills which you could use to go into business on your own?
○ Look into all the questions you need to consider if you are setting up on your own. Can you cope?
As a parent:
Point out skills your teenager possesses which could be used to help him/her make a living. Provide practical support – answering the phone, taking messages, doing book-keeping, sending accounts.

8 Make the most of having a lot of time available.
○ Can you improve yourself (do more sport, learn more skills) or your home (redecorate, dig the garden, make repairs)?
As a parent:
Encourage your teenager to use his/her time profitably – learning sports and skills etc.

New directions

Freely choosing the values and moral standards by which you will live is an essential part of developing your own identity. While teenagers are endlessly questioning values, and choosing 'new directions' for the first time, parents are often reviewing the choices they themselves have made. Conflict may arise because parents and teenagers think in different ways – or because they want to make different choices.

Open to question

A D You might like to identify the 'new directions' which currently concern you and your teenager. In particular:
1 Values you yourself have been reviewing recently. Many of our parent testers had been rethinking decisions about work – whether to go back full-time, aim higher, retire early. Relationships were often under review too.
2 Values where your teenager is making a different choice to you, which you accept. Religious belief – and in particular, church attendance – was frequently mentioned by parent testers. Many also felt that the final choice of work/study was up to the teenager.
3 Values on which you and your teenager conflict. Our parent testers mentioned music, abortion, the pill, women's lib, standards of schoolwork . . . to name but a few. What do you and your teenager disagree about?

Your choices

This chapter looks at some key choices parents and teenagers make – about moral behaviour, about the roles of men and women, and about politics and religion (pages 166–175). Throughout, it stresses some of the different processes involved: stages of development, influences of belief, logic – and prejudice (pages 176–177). And it offers a practical guide to choosing and changing beliefs (pages 178–183).

Most of the activities in the chapter are about gaining insights through talking with your teenager and observing the effects of your own, and his or her, behaviour. What you do is at least as important as what you say, if not more so. If your views do not allow other people to hold different values, then this will be a tough chapter for you.

Parents are most likely to get an angry or sullen response from their teenager if they mock, or are shocked by, their teenager's choice of values. Or if they remain indifferent, or try to impose their own views. Listening to, and accepting the teenager's point of view is vital – especially if you are also challenging it. It's important, too, to acknowledge how your own values may affect your teenager; and, as far as possible, to ensure that they do not hinder them.

Parents are often concerned about the influence of other people, and the media, on their teenager. They may also worry about the effects of the teenager's choices on other people. The most useful course of action is to try and help the teenager make decisions which take into account the needs of others, and in which he/she has enough confidence not to be swayed. Easier said than done, of course, but a sign of succeeding is when your teenager feels able to discuss and explain his/her choices with you – and to accept your choices. Choices are rarely final – so Chapter 9 continues to look at the identity development of both parents and teenagers – and at areas where parents feel they need to be firm.

Moral development

Teenagers are deeply engaged in developing their own morals.

Teenage point of view

This topic looks at moral development from the point of view of teenagers: what they think, and the different stages of behaviour that they go through. But this is not to say that moral development is confined to teenagers. Younger children have their own moral concerns. And adults continue to develop and change their views.

Moral development is essentially about right and wrong, about truth, justice, honesty, and so on. Often, moral, legal, social and personal issues overlap. Situations where people judge each other's ideas and actions are rarely clearcut. So much of this topic simply raises questions and emphasises the importance of discussion.

The examples in the panel (right) illustrate three broad stages in the development of thinking about right and wrong. The stages differ in terms of whose interests the person considers, and the kinds of rules and principles they draw on. They do not necessarily get increasingly better – although later stages do seem to depend on the teenager being able to think more in the abstract.

Discussing situations

A To get a fair idea of a person's moral views, you need to talk over several problems. You might like to discuss the two example situations with your teenager.

Some teenagers won't want to imagine incurable illness, or being an ex-criminal. So you might like to talk instead – or as well – about situations closer to home. Suppose a friend shoplifts, for instance, or gets bullied at school? Or you might talk about issues which arise on TV; for example, the question of killing severely handicapped babies at birth. The more personally gripping the subject for the teenager, the harder it may be for him or her to decide what they would do.

Often, moral problems pose unpleasant decisions, or create painful discussions. Can you face these yourself? Being seen to rethink your own views, alongside your teenager, helps to show him/her that it's always possible to change your mind. The spread overleaf looks at other ways parents can help – and the conflicts they may face.

Doctor's dilemma

A A man's wife is dying, slowly and painfully, from cancer. She asks the doctor to give her an injection, so that she can die in her sleep.
Question: *What do you think the doctor should do?*

Some typical replies from teenagers at the different stages are as follows:

Stage 1A: "Probably he won't, because the police will catch him and put him in gaol." *(Mark)*
"Well, nobody would know if the doctor did, so it would be OK I suppose. I mean everyone'd think the disease got worse." *(Andrew)*

For Mark and Andrew, the only thing that makes an action wrong is the chance of getting caught. Right is what you can get away with.

Stage 1B: "The husband couldn't get a new wife just like that, it's wrong." *(Jane)*

Jane seems to be looking at right and wrong in terms of the value of the person's life, but her reasoning isn't entirely clear.

Stage 2A: "Well it might be better for her, but he shouldn't, because her husband will miss her so much. It's not like putting an animal to sleep, because you love a person different from how you love a pet." *(Tommy)*

Tommy realises that personal relationships are important, and argues that the doctor should not destroy them. Other teenagers might have said OK if the husband agreed, or the wife had no friends and relatives who cared. Trying to define what is important is a first step towards a system of guiding principles.

Stage 2B: "It's murder, God put life into us and we can't decide who should live and who should die. There's something of God in everyone." *(Paula)*

Paula differs from Tommy in that she looks to a set body of rules to make her decision. Legally, it is murder, so it must be wrong. Religious instruction stresses that there are guiding principles for life, such as "thou shalt not kill".

Stage 3: "People should have the right to demand to be killed in a situation like that. A person's body is theirs, and if they have thought it out carefully, they should be allowed to die." *(Bob)*
"It's always wrong to kill a person. Every life is valuable – even if she doesn't want it." *(Judith)*

Bob and Judith have reasoned out for themselves that the laws of society and religion can sometimes be wrong. So a person could be morally right to disobey them. At this stage, people talk in general terms: "every life is valuable" and so on. And because they have worked out their own set of guiding principles, they may – like Bob and Judith – draw different conclusions from similar arguments.

Your teenager Working out the stage a person is at always depends on the *reasons* they give in their answers. Some replies will cut across several stages. It doesn't matter if, even after discussing several situations, you can't pinpoint your teenager's exact stage. What's more important is whether you each find the discussion interesting and helpful. Where does it lead?

Some parents may find this type of discussion challenges them. "To be honest, when I discussed this with Kathleen, I found she was reasoning at a more advanced stage than I was. I'd just accepted my parents' thinking."

In this example, it's not just the doctor's decision, and he doesn't have to say just yes or no. So you might also talk with your teenager about who else the doctor could involve, and what other courses of action he might take.

The story of Jim Smith

A Jim Smith had spent most of his life getting into trouble. At the age of 23 he was sent to prison for causing grievous bodily harm in a fight. After a year he escaped and decided to try to go straight. He changed his name and went to the other end of the country, where he gradually built up a small business and settled down with a wife and baby. His wife knew of his past but no-one else did.

One day Jim saw a serious motor accident in which a small child was hurt. No-one else was around. Jim was afraid that if he stopped to help, or reported the accident, he would have to appear as a witness in court. His past might be revealed.

Question: *What should Jim do?*

Some typical replies from teenagers at the different stages are as follows:

Stage 1A: "He should report the accident, or else the police might blame him if the child died." Here, the teenager's concern is mostly for Jim. The worst thing is to be caught out.

Stage 1B: "He should make sure the child is OK, but then clear off and keep quiet. Reporting the accident is too risky, he won't want to lose his wife and baby." Here there's a little more thought being shown for other people. But the teenager's concern is still mostly for Jim.

Stage 2A: "Jim ought to see the child is comfortable and then report the accident. He could make an anonymous phone call. He wouldn't like it if some-one left his child hurt in the road." Here the teenager can see things from the point of view of both families.

Stage 2B: "Jim should report the accident and stay until help comes. Law and order would fall to pieces if people didn't do the right thing like reporting accidents. Hit and run drivers should be punished. If Jim wants to prove he's a reformed character, he should face the consequences of being honest." Here the teenager is looking to the established rules of law and justice to sort things out.

Stage 3: "Well, obviously Jim ought to look after the child. He could report the accident anonymously, so that the child can get compensation for being run over. If Jim is recognised, the authorities should take his responsible actions into account when sentencing him. If he didn't report the accident he wouldn't be 'going straight'. I don't think he'd be able to live with his conscience." Here the teenager notes the established rules to guide him. The teenager may be keen for everyone to get their rights, as in his answer.

Stages and behaviour

Discussions can be one thing, and your teenager's behaviour another. Moral actions aren't always at the same level as moral thought. And teenagers may be readier to apply moral thinking to other people's behaviour than to their own. Having said that, here are some general patterns of behaviour which match the stages of thought:

Stage 1A: "Anything goes . . ." A teenager who thinks anything is OK, as long as he/she can get away with it, may behave selfishly or dishonestly at times. However, it soon becomes clear that other people will not co-operate with him/her if he/she is totally selfish.

Stage 1B: "I'll scratch your back . . ." The next stage is characterised by bargaining, in which trust and interest in other people begins to be more apparent. Teenagers dislike people who break their word, so they often single out 'trustworthiness' as an important value.

Stage 2A: "Do as you would be done by . . ." Treating others as you would like to be treated is the golden rule here. It requires being able to see things from another person's point of view. It can be difficult to decide what to do when faced with conflicting points of view – parents' and friends' for example.

Stage 2B: "It says here . . ." Teenagers at this stage have reasoned out for themselves that some of society's rules are right; and they adopt them. They are no longer guided only by their feelings for other people. The rules may be difficult to keep, but at least they know what they ought to do. Teenagers have to cope with so many changes that they may find a fixed set of rules helps. But they may also become very self-righteous and intolerant.

Stage 3: "In all conscience . . ." People at this stage modify in their own minds the fixed rules they have learned. They abide by their own conscience. Conscience first develops in stages 2A ("I ought to do that because then they'll like me") and 2B ("I ought to do that because it's right"). A person at stage 3 also says "I ought to do that because it's right" – but they have worked out their own ideas of right and wrong, and accept that other people wouldn't necessarily agree.

Helping development

This spread looks at some of the ways parents can help their teenager develop his/her own view on moral behaviour. At times, parents themselves will face dilemmas over what to do.

Parents with teenagers at Stages 1 or 2A may sometimes find they clash, simply because the teenager's thinking is less mature than their own. The teenager needs the support of discussion and positive personal relationships.

What do we talk about? It is easy to find more stories like the ones we've given, in the pages of teenage magazines as well as in films and on the news. Discussions – not lectures – about the reasons for moral actions will help your teenager to pick out the key issues and the guiding principles being used. Some basic questions to ask are: How would you feel if this happened to you? Why did they behave that way? What would happen if everyone behaved like that?

What kind of relationships? It helps the teenager to experience a variety of relationships in which trust and honesty are valued for their own sake, not simply for what they bring in exchange. Good examples, from parents, teachers and peers alike, are better than any amount of advice. Friendships with other teenagers are essential in learning to see and accept another person's point of view.

Later stages

Teenagers at Stages 2B and 3 are more likely to provide an uncomfortable challenge to their parents. In a way these stages are alternatives. Each fits a different set of circumstances and experiences, as the extract (right) suggests.

'Stage 3' teenagers can be particularly awkward company. They may insist on reform and personal morality at all times. They may ignore what parents have learned from experience.

Equally 'Stage 2B' parents may be a hindrance to teenagers when they say there's no time or need in life to work out rules for yourself. Giving teenagers fixed packages of ideas may help them to cope at first. But later on they may well want, and need, to sort out their own values.

As society changes, a rigid set of guiding rules about what's right and proper behaviour may be less useful than a personally reasoned-out morality. For example, current changes in employment are challenging the conventional 'work ethic'. Some people are thrown by what's happening. Others see it as a chance to encourage more diverse attitudes to work.

Conflicts over behaviour

People can do the 'right' and 'wrong' thing for many different reasons. Discussion is essential for you to understand the choices your teenager makes. Moral ideas and actions will vary according to the situation involved, and no-one can be pigeon-holed as being at one stage on all issues.

Next time you disagree, ask yourself:

○ Is this because we are at different stages?
○ Do I need to review my own feelings and actions?
○ What helped me in such situations when I was a teenager – and will this help my teenager now?
○ Should I challenge my teenager to live up to his/her ideals?
○ How can I best influence his/her decision?

Different views

A The following extract quotes two 20-year-olds. One is a police recruit, the other an educational 'drop out' who runs a record shop. They grew up in apparently similar domestic and educational environments. But they now hold completely different views. As you read the article, consider:

○ what stage does each young man seem to be at?
○ which one do you have more sympathy with?
○ what kind of relationship do you think each had with his parents? (And which is more like you and your teenager?)
○ how would you, and your teenager, each define responsibility?

The copper

'My parents have been the major influence on my life. They taught me respect. It was my parents gave me a guiding kick up the backside every now and then; I'd say in the right direction. If I came in late, or if I was knocking around with what they'd term the wrong sort of kids they'd point it out to me in no uncertain terms...

The policeman in my head is a sense of responsibility and respect for law and order, rules and regulations. The old Ten Commandments, that's where I started off from. Thou shalt not do this, that and the other. We've had rules and regulations for the last 2,000 years. Without them there'd be a lot of dead people about.

If Maggie Thatcher suddenly said, right, no more rules and regulations, that'd be it. Everybody would go loopy. Well, for the first few weeks they would. Then with what was left of them they'd come to realise they have to have something to control their baser instincts. It would all be back to morals, what was morally wrong as opposed to legally wrong, and morality is a question of opinion.

If you're going in for what is morally right and morally wrong you're going to have a lot of people going around thinking different things.'

The dropout

'Once I dropped out I became very restful. I refused a lot of things for a while. Then I sort of branched out and I thought, I'm going out there and I'm going to take in as much as I can. I'll be a sort of diverse person. I went out and saw a lot of films, listened to a lot of bands and that led to books so I got into sort of saturation reading... I've flirted with political ideas, the Socialist Workers' Party for one, and I've checked out Marxism and at the moment I'm hanging in with the Ecology Party.

I don't want to have a career. Embarking on a career implies that you intend to work your way up, as though life is lived only on the vertical level. I think having a career today is quite irrelevant to the sort of comings and goings of Western civilisation as it is...

If there was no law, it implies there would be no crime. I think we would open up a lot more and realise where our morality really lies...

I know it's a hard, painful and long-winded process, just trying to begin to find out who you are. It's not easy. Sometimes you feel very uncomfortable. But I'd very much like to state that you can find yourself out. It is possible. An I don't know what else responsibility means.'

e Pages

Law v. love

Parents can sometimes feel torn over how far to protect their teenager. Parents are not agents of the law, but they are in a position to help develop their teenager's sense of right and wrong – even if at times they feel they need better support.

What would you do?

A D Suppose you found that:
A your teenager had been shoplifting for the first time
B your teenage daughter had been raped
C your teenage son would be gaoled if he (or you) didn't pay an outstanding fine he owed.

What would you do? Or what have you done when faced with similar dilemmas in your own life? Almost certainly your answers will vary according to the situation involved.

In the case of an occasional incident, like the shoplifting, helping the teenager decide for him/herself what to do is more helpful than turning a blind eye – or turning him/her in.

Much harder are situations where your teenager is a victim of something such as rape or the more common case of bullying, where parents fear that revealing information may damage the teenager further. Yet witholding it may let others get hurt as well. Parents can only decide in the light of knowing, and talking to their individual teenager.

The third example (C) was reported in the press because the father of the boy concerned refused to pay, saying his son needed to be taught a lesson. But punishment is rarely as helpful as finding the teenager more positive support. "What next?" suggests sources of counselling and help.

Different kinds of rules

Some conflicts occur between parents and teenagers because they don't distinguish between different levels of rules.

Moral rules involve issues of honesty, truth, justice, not hurting others. Teenagers think like most adults on serious moral rules. In a recent study, a large majority of teenagers said that killing people, torture, rape, drug-pushing and blackmail were definitely wrong and that lying and stealing were nearly always wrong.

Social rules are everyday rules about clothes, manners, behaviour in public. Sometimes these may even be laws, like those for litter or parking offences. Teenagers sometimes break these to shock adults. More often they have different ideas about what these rules ought to be.

Personal rules are rules where the person says "it's my business, it's not harming anyone else." But parents might say "it is my business if you harm yourself or get into trouble. And what you do reflects on me."

Conflicts over rules

A You might like to discuss these different types of rules with your teenager. In particular:

○ do you disagree on any major moral rules?
○ what social rules have you each broken recently?
○ do you agree that you can have different personal rules?
○ are there any issues – like sexual behaviour perhaps – where you disagree about the kinds of rules involved?

Men and women

Do sex roles affect what your teenager wants to do and be?

Talking to your teenager

A The article (right) recounts part of a discussion with a class of fifth formers in a comprehensive school. The interviewer asked three main questions:
1 What do you expect to do when you leave school?
2 What will you be doing in ten years' time – where will you be living, what will your life be like?
3 What's the life you'd most like to be leading in ten years' time?
The interviewer also clearly added her own opinions.

You might like to show your teenager the article and ask what he/she thinks of the values expressed in it. What are his/her own answers to the three questions? It's worth noting that ideas about life in ten years' time – yours or your teenager's – are fantasies. Fantasies are an important source of values and goals. They let you try out images in your head of what life could be like. But they are fragile and changeable, so they need treating with caution in discussion.

Sex roles – what men and women do – are part of everyday life. So you can pick your own time to discuss them with your teenager. The article may be a starting point. Or you may find this topic helpful when you are talking about particular events or comments with your teenager. Many of our parent testers said it didn't so much tell them new things, as prompt them to have more, and fuller, discussions with family and friends.

In talking to your teenager, it will help to have looked afresh at your own views and choices (see right and overleaf). At first glance it might seem a topic most suited to girls – but there's just as much to discuss with boys (below).

What is a man?

When people make statements about the characteristics of men – or women – they often have two things in mind:

○ the 'natural' characteristics, good and bad, they suppose each sex to have
○ the virtues they would like men, or women, to have.

These can sidetrack people into arguments about what is natural and what is ideal. Such discussions are often based on bias and belief rather than on sound evidence. They tend to focus on differences between the sexes, rather than similarities. And they ignore the basic question – *why do men and women come under different pressure to develop certain characteristics?*

Take, for example, the issue of beauty. There are clearly different pressures on men and on women to put effort into looking good. Some feminists would say beauty is worth little, if any, effort. But logically, if you do not care for beauty in people, you do not care about beauty at all. And if you *do* care about it, then why not have more of it, in men as well as women? Why not have broader definitions of beauty?

The same kind of argument applies to all the other positive values which are usually assigned to one sex only: grace, strength, tenderness, and so on. It is not these that need to be attacked, but rather the unequal pressures on men or women to be the sole providers of them. With different kinds of pressures, more pleasures in life could be created.

An interview with fifth-formers

Intentions. In answer to the first question about their immediate intentions on leaving school, every single one of the boys hoped for some kind of further education, training or apprenticeship. They all talked of jobs with prospects for promotion and advancement. They thought in terms of a career that would last them a lifetime . . .

But of the ten girls, only one had selected a job with any career prospects at all. She was an Asian girl who wanted to be a bank cashier. The other girls listed their jobs as follows: two receptionists, two copy typists, two office juniors, one boutique shop assistant, one helper in an old people's home, and one religious enthusiast who would be saving souls . . .

Ambitions. The girls' ambitions were considerably lower than the boys'.

All the girls thought they would be married in ten years' time. Some wanted to be married by the time they were 20, all by the time they were 24. Seven of them thought they would stop work when they married and let their husbands support them. One girl thought she would work part-time in a supermarket after marriage. The bank cashier thought she would still be at work in her bank . . .

Most of the boys expected to be married in ten years' time, and most expected their wives to be at home minding the children . . .

Ideals. Answering the fantasy question, most of the girls wrote of grander houses, better dressed children and more expensive cars. Oddly enough, husbands got scarcely a mention. It was as if the point of marriage was a house and children, and the man was only a distant adjunct . . .

The boys' answers were a little different. Five of them imagined exceedingly powerful and successful jobs for themselves, though the rest, like the girls, only dreamt of money and possessions . . .

The boys' attitudes towards working wives was purely economic. If a man earned enough, then his wife would not work. It did not seem to occur to them that a woman might have a job from which she

A D You might like to reflect, with your teenager, partner or a friend, on the kind of messages you give to sons and daughters. What unequal pressures do you apply? For example:

○ what do you say to boys and girls about the need to be sensitive? independent? beautiful? mechanically minded?
○ what behaviour do you think is OK for boys but not for girls? And the reverse . . .?
○ how do the messages you give differ from the ones your parents gave you as a teenager?
○ what do your teenagers make of your messages?

Look at ways to help your teenager cross existing social conventions. How can you help your son to talk more about his feelings? Or your daughter to assert herself more often?

got much satisfaction. Yet the boys themselves expected, by and large, to enjoy their work . . .

Influences. I asked how many of their mothers worked. It turned out that most of them did, and most mothers had jobs less skilled and less well-paid than the fathers. Did any of the children in that room think their mothers might have used their talents better if they had had better opportunities? They shook their heads. I asked who they thought was most dominant in their households. All the girls said their mother was, and all the boys said their father was . . .

Although the teachers agonised about it, and some of them kept badgering their girls about it, they could not think of any way in which they could change the pattern . . .

Comment. Some people ask indignantly why it matters at all. These girls are clearly happy to become filing clerks and shop assistants. So who are we to say they do something else? But by the time they are thirty or so, it's a fair bet that they won't be all that happy. The chances are that they will join that great legion of intelligent, slightly embittered, self-mocking women, who are too clever for the chimpanzee jobs they find themselves doing . . .

Lack of fulfilment drives women mad. Nearly twice as many women end up in mental hospital. Women consume vastly more Valium and other tranquilisers than men. Recent research suggests that women at home with small children suffer far greater depression and dissatisfaction than even those husbands doing routine factory work.

Why do so many women need to be tranquilised? Because in those few crucial adolescent years they have made the wrong decisions about their lives, decisions that are often irrevocable. They have bought a cheap, tatty, glamourised image of what makes a woman happy and fulfilled, and they have tried hard to conform. Teenage years are usually the most conformist. These girls are trying desperately to fit themselves into what they see as the pattern for "normal" women. How do we break that deadly mould? (Polly Toynbee, Guardian Women, 8.6.81).

What is women's work?

There are many widely-held beliefs about what is 'natural' or 'proper' work for men and for women. These beliefs help to shape the expectations, and limit the ambitions, of boys as well as girls. And they cloud the basic questions: *Why should teenagers come under different pressures about work choices, and find that men's and women's work are not equally valued?*

Women's job opportunities, and childcare provision, tend to expand (as in war) or contract (as in recessions) according to what men are doing in and with the economy. Equally, work in the home is often valued less than work outside, because it is private, commonplace, and in the end, limited.

Certainly it is true that many women like children, and choose families as a way of life. But it is also true that many

Looking at yourself

A D Mid-life is a time for reviewing commitments. Parents may well be asking themselves questions about their own work . . . "Am I too old to (re)train?" "Shall I look for a full time job now?" "Did I work too hard when the children were small?"

As the article suggests, some people get to mid-life feeling vaguely dissatisfied. They wonder why they made the choices they did, and whether there are any alternatives left now. Some parents script their teenagers lives and values – tell them what to do – so strongly that they never really make their own choices.

You might like to think over your own choices about work:

○ did your own family give you a script message about what to do – and did you follow it?
○ with a partner and/or children, how free have you felt to make choices?
○ have you encountered discrimination of any kind at work?
○ what would be the gains and losses in changing your job?
○ how do you think the choices you have made may affect the work your teenager chooses?

Such questions can be painful to answer fully and honestly. You may find you want to review your feelings (pages 40–43) or your values about work (pages 178–181). It can hinder a teenager to tell him/her your thoughts in a way that blames or ties the teenager: "I'd be at the top now if it wasn't for you", "men with families need steady jobs". But it can help to show that rethinking is possible, and that it's OK to make different decisions at different ages.

men – in the form of governments, employers, fathers – benefit from having children, families and households mainly cared for by women.

So – what would make things more equal for women? Arguably, wages for female housework (like women's disability benefits) would reinforce the unequal treatment of the sexes. So too would straightforward role reversal, even though this seems a more major change. Maternity leave and creches just leave things as they are, with a few adjustments for childbearing women. The most radical solutions lie in social arrangements that provide fully for the care of families and households *and* make full use of both sexes' abilities.

A D You might like to reflect with your teenager, partner, or a friend the kinds of messages you give to sons and daughters about men's and women's work. For example:

○ do you say grudgingly, "that's good . . . for a girl?"
○ do you mind more about boys' career prospects?
○ do you encourage both boys and girls to be able to look after themselves in the home?
○ do you press for both boys and girls to get the support they need to develop their individual talents at school?

You may find that you apply – or encounter – unequal pressures which prevent both sexes from becoming fulfilled.

As women's lives and work change, so will men's. So you might also like to discuss the changes you would each like to see. What would be the advantages, and disadvantages, for each sex? And as individuals, what kind of working future would you each really like?

171

Against sexism

Sexism is uncalled-for discrimination on the grounds of sex alone. It can apply to both boys and girls. The teenage years are a crucial time to look at sexist issues because:

○ the teenager's developing self-image will benefit from the teenager being able to like him/herself as a person, not just as a member of one sex or the other
○ the teenager's new mind means he/she can, and may want, to debate the rights and wrongs of a sexist society
○ teenagers are making choices about values which will shape the whole direction of their lives as men and women
○ adolescence is a time of insecurity, when social pressures can push teenagers towards the certainty of traditional roles, rather than free them to make their own choices.

Parents can be influential in each of these respects. They can treat their teenagers first and foremost as individuals; or they can put different pressures on sons and daughters. They can scoff at ideas, try to script their teenager's new directions, and generally provide little support. Or they can encourage their teenager to make his/her own choices, through informed discussion, and being open to new ideas and change themselves. For this last reason, you may find it most useful to review your own views on feminism and sexism before discussing this spread with your teenager.

Your discussions will benefit from being logical. That means thinking straight about relevant ideas, and taking into account even evidence which doesn't fit your opinions. It also means being clear about your feelings – and the attitudes and beliefs which give rise to them. Many men, and some women, feel upset or under threat, for example, because new developments in 'women's liberation' do not accord with the opinions they hold about the roles of men and women.

Feminism

The basic feminist argument is that *women suffer from systematic social injustice*. In other words, because of their sex, women are picked on and pressured in ways that men are not.

Most people would agree that some injustices exist. The disagreements and debates come mainly over what to do about righting those wrongs. Some feminists make their solutions so unattractive that they fail to get support for their basic cause.

Other feminists do not help themselves by being illogical. For example, to say that everything male is bad ignores all other criteria of 'goodness' and 'badness'. To fight only for what is good for women would merely create another unjust society. And to argue aggressively or emotionally obscures the facts and the reasoning behind the arguments.

This spread suggests that less discrimination against women could result in more choices for both sexes. It looks at how this might be so, concentrating on what is natural, free and fair.

What is natural?

"Women are naturally weaker than men."
"Natural breastfeeding is best."
The word 'natural' can mean several things. Sometimes it is used to mean what is done without interference. But for some people, what is natural in this sense will not be best. At other times it is used to mean what is good for our society. But that is an idea which changes with the times. Often, it is used to mean what we see and know now. But to know the nature of something, you need to see it in a great number of situations. Studies of men and women in other times and places are important because they show much more of the varied nature both sexes can develop.

Only when both men and women have tried out many more roles will their nature truly begin to be known. Currently, circumstances often make it harder for a woman to try something new, than for a man with the same abilities. For example, political selection tends to operate against women being chosen as party candidates. But both sexes might be freer if more roles were available for everyone.

What is freedom?

"Women are tied by the demands of childcare."
"Women need to be freed from oppression by men."
A person's freedom is restricted to the extent that different social arrangements might make it possible for them to do what they wanted – without reducing the freedom of others.

Today the sexes have equal opportunity under the law. But in practice, rules are bent. And some rules still go against women; for example, some tax and social security rules. Nor do women have an 'old boy network', or much of a place in ruling bodies, such as Parliament or managing boards. Of course men face restrictions on their freedom too, but by and large a woman in an equal position to a man has had to make sacrifices to get there, eg. giving up marriage or a family.

Genuine liberation would mean increasing the options available to everyone. It would mean giving individual men and women the chance, and the support, to make their own choices, to do what they do well and are interested in. It would not mean imposing restrictive solutions on either sex. For example, simply freeing women from childcare would leave a lot of unsatisfied women who wanted that choice; and a lot who wouldn't at first know what to do instead.

What is fair?

"When jobs are short, married women should not take them."
"Men would like to take more part in raising children."
Justice is about how the good and bad things in life are shared out. It is, of course, true that some women are better off than men. And that men miss out on some things. But overall, being female usually makes you worse off than a man would be in the same circumstances.

Many women still face discrimination in applying for jobs. Positive discrimination has been introduced in some quarters as a way of trying to improve the position of women relative to men; for example, setting quotas of men and women for entry to medical schools.

Different treatment is a source of injustice. In trying to right injustice, it is important not merely to swap one injustice for another. Justice for all would mean allowing each individual to choose their lifestyle, without undue or unequal pressures. If there were fewer differential expectations of the sexes, then status and responsibility, dependence and caring, could be chosen by the individual rather than imposed according to their sex.

Talking points

🅐 🅓 Discussion at home, at school and with friends will help your teenager to develop his/her own views on sexism. You might like to talk over some of these questions in your family:

○ What are your thoughts, and your feelings, about the content of this topic? How do you react to the picture below?
○ Is there anything now you might discuss or do differently?

○ Could more choice for you mean more choice for your teenager and/or partner?
○ What range of roles have you seen men and women successfully take?
○ If women were equally represented in Parliament, what changes might take place? What would happen if more men were encouraged to be housewives, typists, nurses?
○ In what ways do you think society is unfair to men and to women? What changes would you like to see?

Politics and religion

Your teenager needs to choose his or her own beliefs and values.

Causes for concern

Religion and politics each involve whole networks of ideas, which provide an outlook on life and rules for behaving. Each also includes an element of doctrine or dogma. You may be expected to accept and believe what is taught. Thinking for yourself is not always encouraged by Church or Party, and there may be group pressures on members to conform.

Yet thinking through your own beliefs is an essential part of development, as a teenager and as an adult. If, as a teenager, you simply accept the 'packages' of religious or political beliefs given to you – then you will almost certainly find yourself questioning these at some later point in your life.

In saying that teenagers need to make their own choices, it's worth remembering that often – if let go – they eventually come back to choose values close to those of their own parents. In the meantime, though, teenager's beliefs can often give their parents cause for concern. Taking a closer look at your own worries can prepare you to talk more constructively with your teenager about uncomfortable issues in religion and politics.

What worries you?

A D Imagine for a moment that your teenager became, or associated with, each of the following: anti-Nazi league member, pro-abortionist, fascist group member, pacifist, IRA hunger striker, Social Democrat, moonie or lapsed believer.

○ *Which one of these would worry you most?* If your own greatest fear isn't listed – add it.

○ *Can you say why you'd be so concerned?* Would you feel:
fear for your teenager's safety . . .
hurt that your values are being rejected..
powerless to intervene . . .
. . . or add your own greatest emotion, and the reason for it.

Our parent testers were concerned about extreme influences of any kind – particularly those which seem likely to override home values. Of the list here, the moonies worried them most because, as one parent put it, "They take over at a susceptible age and alienate the teenager from his family." Another

A classic mix of politics and religion, in Northern Ireland.

commented on fascist groups, "If only they remembered the war, they'd never get tangled with people like that."

Thinking over your concerns can help you to hold back from pressing your own views on your teenager. Or from hitting him/her with your worries when he/she's in need of your understanding. Some differences of opinion stem from differences in stage of thinking. A working knowledge of political and religious thinking (right) can help you to appreciate your teenager's view.

If you are very concerned about a group your teenager joins, you may need to seek support from people who know more about the group concerned, and who have relevant experience.

Talking things over

Some of our parent testers said that they didn't discuss politics or religion very much with their teenagers. Or, if they did, the discussions didn't amount to much. Others described their talks as ranging from "frank" to "fiery".

You can't force opinions to develop, but discussions can help. For some families, this topic brought out differences of opinion. Newspaper stories, and local events such as religious crusades, can also be good starting points for discussion. Even if you agree now – or if your teenager isn't interested – things may change in a year or so, as his/her own ideas begin to develop.

Political thinking

A The teenage years often show a dramatic shift from total lack of political thought to intense discussions of – and perhaps involvement in – politics. One research method used to look at political thinking is to ask teenagers to discuss the following problem:

Suppose that a thousand men and women, dissatisfied with the way things are going in their own country, decide to buy and move to an island. Once there they must make up their own laws and forms of government. What do you think they should do?

If your teenager is interested you might like to discuss this problem together. In particular you might look at issues such as:

○ what would the purpose of government be?
○ how would a government be formed?
○ would there be a need for laws and policing?
○ would there be political parties, and what would they be like?
○ how would minorities be protected?
○ what would be done about providing education, welfare etc?

Comments

Politics isn't everyone's cup of tea. Our parent testers commented that younger teenagers often found this activity quite hard, while older ones were bursting with ideas. Two common trends in teenager's replies as they get older are:
A shift from concrete to more abstract thinking. For example, when talking about the needs for laws, a 12-year-old said: "If we had no laws, people would go around killing people". According to his 16-year-old brother: "Laws are to ensure safety and to enforce government . . . they are guidelines to help people understand what's right and wrong".
A decrease in authoritarian solutions. For example, younger teenagers typically respond to the idea of law-breaking by saying that punishment is needed. Older teenagers tend to be much more aware of different sides to the argument, whose interests are served and whose damaged. They might discuss whether the ends justify the means or whether reform is possible.

Religious thinking

In a recent survey of 14–15 year olds, only 12 per cent said that they definitely did not believe in a god. The rest ranged from unsure to definite believers. So teenagers are clearly open to religious thinking, and are often fascinated to talk about it and to find out about a variety of religions. However, 65–75 per cent said that they thought religious education and church services were boring. And in recent years, teenage attitudes to religion have become slightly more negative.

Teenagers need beliefs they can accept, and observances which are meaningful for them. This does not necessarily mean strict dogma, which they may well see as a threat to their independence. They need a religion which will help, rather than awe or mystify them. In particular, religious beliefs can provide teenagers with emotional support in terms of:

○ reducing feelings of tension or guilt
○ increasing feelings of security
○ providing a sense of belonging
○ giving a basis for a philosophy of life

During adolescence, religious beliefs and behaviour change – as do most ideas and values – from the simpler views of childhood. Five broad stages in the development of religious thinking may be seen in those who are interested.

Five stages

1 Religious awakening. This is often gradual, the start of slow changes in interest and beliefs during the teenage years. It may coincide with the shift to more logical, abstract thinking. Occasionally it may be an abrupt and vivid experience, haunting and absorbing for the teenager.
2 Religious doubt. Again, this may be a more or less intense phase. The teenager may have doubts about doctrine in general: "I don't believe there's any kind of afterlife". Or he/she may doubt the doctrines of a particular church: "I don't see why we can't drink alcohol". Or he/she may doubt written sources: "I think Adam and Eve are a load of old rubbish". Doubt is a necessary stage in choosing any belief or value. Faith means coming to terms with uncertainty, and holding beliefs which cannot be proved.

3 Changing beliefs. Beliefs are based on ideas which change with increased knowledge and experience. This stage often coincides with a general challenging of authority by the teenager. If he/she is not allowed to think through his/her own beliefs, he/she can find that, as an adult, he/she is left with a set of childish beliefs which are no longer helpful. For example, a child may believe in a God who is the Creator and a powerful ruler, whereas a teenager might see God as a friendly intelligence working in accordance with nature. The Sabbath may be seen as a day of religious observance by a child and as a day of refreshment by a teenager. Heaven and Hell may signify eternal happiness and misery to a child, but a teenager may doubt their existence. A child's prayers may focus on obtaining desires, but teenagers see it as having a wider purpose.
4 Changes in observance. All religious observances – church attendance, prayer, church-related activities – decline in adolescence. This does not necessarily imply a decline in belief. Rather, it is a sign of the teenager working out for himself what is important.
5 Increase in religious tolerance. Older teenagers often show a growing acceptance of other religious beliefs. They are less concerned about how important differences are. Interfaith dating and marriages are becoming more common.

You and your teenager

A Even if you or your teenager wouldn't particularly call yourself religious, you might like to reflect on these questions:

○ do any of these stages strike a chord in terms of your own, or your teenager's experiences?
○ do you know what your teenager's beliefs currently are?
○ how do you feel about any changes in your teenager's religious beliefs or behaviour?
○ how may your feelings help or hinder your teenager in working things out for himself?

Many of our parent testers described differences of opinion within the family. By and large they were happy to accept their teenager's changing views. Are you?

175

Prejudice

Prejudice involves pre-judging people or issues.

Adults and teenagers

Prejudice is a lot to do with attributing undesirable motives and values to other people. There's some prejudice against the young. But adults in general hold quite positive attitudes towards teenagers – even if a few do link all teenagers with drugs, demos and violence. At the same time, though, adults can be prejudiced about other groups to which teenagers belong: peace groups, women's groups, racial minorities, for example.

With their new interest in self-image, teenagers are acutely sensitive to prejudice that occurs at school, on the street, at interviews – and at home. Research suggests that, on the whole, teenagers are well-disposed towards adults. They are less likely to express disapproval of adults than adults are of them. Yet teenagers in their turn may hold prejudiced views about other groups. And they may find it harder to see their own prejudices than to see those of others.

What's your poison

A 1 You might like to talk to your teenager about some of the things he/she is told about being a teenager by parents, teachers, youth workers, interviewers. In particular, can he/she recall statements which begin:

○ Teenagers always_____
○ Teenagers never _____
○ Teenagers are just _____

2 You might also like to think over how each of you describe different groups of people. For example:

○ Catholics are _____
○ Working mothers are _____
○ Conservatives are_____
○ Working class people are _____

The kind of phrases in **1** above are a good clue to prejudice. When people are lumped together as a group, in one sweeping statement, this will be an underestimate of their varied individual abilities and personalities. Such statements tend to reveal more about the speaker's feelings about the group in question. What feelings do you and your teenager's replies to **2** above suggest?

Stereotypes

Prejudice is often based on treating people as 'types'. Assumptions are made about them in terms of just a few of their characteristics. Some stereotyping happens because the person has never met members of the group about whom they are prejudiced. More often it happens when a person is treated as an example of some group they belong to, rather than an individual.

Putting prejudice into words

A Some stereotypes and prejudices are engrained in well-known words and phrases: "emotional women" or "mean as a Scot" for example. Descriptions can be positive, or at least neutral. Or they can be negative and prejudiced. The chart gives some examples. You and your teenager might like to see how many words you can think of, that you've heard each other or other people use. Is it hard to think of positive words for some of the people listed? If so, what does that suggest about their position in society? How are they likely to be treated?

	Positive or neutral	Negative
old woman	senior citizen	
homosexual man		
mental patient		nutcase
working class person		
teenager		yob
black person		
policeman		
young girl		

Acting on prejudice

Prejudice shows itself in acts of discrimination – when people are treated unfairly because of the way they are misperceived. Discrimination is always offensive. It can seriously affect a person's job prospects. And it can harm their prospects of a safe, happy life. Violence towards minority groups, and the growth of groups committed to spreading their prejudice, pose serious questions for society. How do people come to hold beliefs that will let them attack a person who doesn't belong to their group? What should society do about this?

There are a growing number of social movements which aim to counter prejudice through education and law. There are organisations which work for the rights of women, gay people, handicapped people, for example, at a political rather than simply a personal level. But legal changes alone are not enough. There can be ways round the law. And changes in the law do not necessarily change attitudes – as you may know from personal experience.

Personal prejudice

A Have you or your teenager had personal experience of any kind of prejudice? Stop for a few moments and describe it.

Parents are in a unique position to show teenagers, through both words and actions, they can review and change how they feel and behave towards other people. In discussion you can challenge your teenager to look again at his/her own ideas.

At one level it helps to check the logic of what you think or hear. What evidence is there for it? What exceptions do you know of? But, in the end, prejudice isn't simply about logic. It grows out of fear, envy, anger and other emotions. And it ignores the feelings and attitudes of others. So any discussion of prejudice needs also to include emotions.

Spot the stereotype

A This school 'thinkstrip' was designed to get teenagers thinking about talking about mixed dating and about racial prejudice. You might like to discuss it with your teenager – including also some of the stereotypes shown. For example:

○ What are the mothers shown doing – and the fathers?
○ Which characters are shown to hold prejudiced views?
○ What kind of looks and clothes are the young girls given – and how do they compare with their mothers?

Choosing values

Values are decisions which guide how you behave.

Values and behaviour

A Ⓓ "I'm a person who values . . ."
○ If you were asked to complete this sentence five times – what would you say? Hard work? Fun? Honesty? Hugs and kisses? Try it now.

Holding a particular value implies that you will act on it in everyday life. Of course, no-one lives up to their ideals all the time. And not all values fit all circumstances. But it can help to review the values you say you hold and ask yourself: *Do* I act on these as a rule? (Real values). Or do I hold them, but seldom or never act on them?
○ Check your list of five values above. Are all of them real? For example, you may say you value honesty . . . but do you take time off (= money) or stationery from work without a qualm?

Priorities, conflicts and pressures

Different values have different levels of importance. Sometimes you will put one value above another – or abandon one for the sake of another. For example, suppose you value life and are anti-abortion – but your daughter is desperately unhappy about being pregnant.

There are many times when, for one reason or another, people do not act on their values. But if you never do – it's time to ask why you continue to hold them. It may be because of pressures from other people – or from yourself.

Occasionally, pressure from other people takes the form of adopting something in them that you admire. More often, pressure means choosing a value because someone in authority says you must. Or threatens you with rejection, guilt, or punishment if you don't. People who feel confused, scared, or negative about themselves are particularly open to such pressures.

People also put pressures on themselves to adopt certain values. These are usually tied up with fantasies about ideals. Two kinds of fantasy seem important: how you would like other people to see you – and how you would like to see yourself, your qualities and your lifestyle.
○ Can you put the five values you listed in order of priority? Were there pressures on you to choose them? Or did you put pressures on yourself?

Choosing freely

On the whole, young children accept without challenge the values they receive from adults. As teenagers, they will need to rethink these values, and freely choose their own.

Very often, teenagers end up choosing to commit themselves to many of their original received values. But in-between they may well go through a stage of adopting, with little questioning, the values of their peer group.

Like any convert, the teenager may see the 'new' values he/she chooses as the only ones to hold. He/she may condemn anyone who disagrees, and try to persuade everyone else to hold his/her values. In time, most teenagers go on to value other people's values, even when these differ from their own.

Teenagers – and adults – can sort out if they have a freely chosen, independent set of values, by asking themselves:
○ do I *only* hold this value because someone else wants me to? Or because all my friends do?
○ what made me realise this was an important value I want to hold?
○ how would I explain to someone else why I hold this value?
○ what do I think of people who hold an opposing value?
○ if you apply these questions to your five values – which ones would you say are freely chosen?

Getting stuck

Sometimes people get stuck with values in adolescence in a way that hampers them in later life. For example:
○ **accepting many received values** without thinking them through and freely choosing them, can leave a person rigid, unable to cope with change.
○ **retaining peer group values** can leave a person behaving inappropriately later on. For example: the father who wants to remain 'one of the lads in the pub'. Or the woman who thinks being young and slim is the only way to be sexy.
○ **not accepting other people's values** can leave a person permanently angry, alone or depressed.

Everyone needs to change values with experience. In each of these cases, it becomes particularly important for adults to review and sort out their values.

Sorting out values

A Ⓓ Choosing values is a process which starts in adolescence – and goes on for life. This topic offers a 4-step guide to making choices. It's not a cure-all, simply one way of looking at what you do. There are no right and wrong answers. But there are more or less helpful ways of expressing yourself. *Make your own notes as you go along.*

For each step we give the running example of *Fiona*. She's 40, with two teenagers aged 14 and 12, a full-time job and a husband who plays little part in family life. She's finding that everything is getting her down. She nags and cries easily. Basically, two of her values conflict. She wants to be a super mum – efficient, organised, spotless house, lovely kids. And she wants a relaxed family life where everyone gets on.

Fiona's example concerns her whole lifestyle. You may well prefer to start with something smaller. Here are some of the experiences our parent testers looked at with this topic, which led them to clarify their values:

○ a neighbour's dog is being maltreated
○ girls misbehaving at a guide meeting
○ daughter's handbag being stolen
○ an invitation for the parents which meant dragging the family away again
○ being told that concerns as a parent conflicted with being a school governor

Your teenager

When you work through this topic, look at a value of your own first. Then you'll have personal experience to draw on when you discuss the process with your teenager. The process is the same for both of you. But it may help to bear in mind some developmental differences:
○ Teenagers' interest in themselves often means they have a greater drive than adults to review their values. At the same time they may need more support to do so. Adolescence, especially, is a time of self-doubt and vulnerability to outside pressures. They may also need help to develop skill in sorting out ideas and values.
○ Teenagers' need to experiment may mean they try out a whole range of values, often reviewing their entire set of values at once. In contrast, adults tend to look at only one or two values at a time, with a clearer idea of changes.

Step 1: Expressing values

○ examine personal, concrete examples from your own life
○ describe them in detail

It's all too easy to make general statements about values: "Stealing is wrong", "People should . . ." and so on. It's more difficult, and sometimes quite painful, to consider values in simple everyday terms of what you feel, think and do. But this is the only way to be clear about the values you hold. Try answering these questions:

A Describe the details of the *experiences* you've had. Who was involved? What happened? When? Where?
B What were your *reactions*? What did you feel? Think? Do?
C What would you like, or do you plan to do about it? In other words, what are your *intentions*?
D Are there *pressures* on you to feel or behave in certain ways about it?
E What *values* – what's important to you – can be deduced from the way you've felt, thought and acted?

Fiona's example illustrates the kind of things you might say.

Step 1: Fiona

My experience: Things came to a head last Saturday. We were all in the kitchen when I spilt my cup of tea.

My feelings: I felt upset and angry – and silly for behaving like that.

My thoughts: I thought it's only people who are cracking up that do that . . . perhaps *I'm* cracking up?

My actions: I often screech in the evenings about quite unimportant things, then everyone snaps back.

My intentions: I'll have to do something about this soon – or else everything may become too much.

My pressures: I think of myself as a superwoman and drive myself on. The family is getting fed up with my nagging and crying.

My values: From all this, it looks like I value nagging, being tense and having a tidy house. In fact I value the opposite for the first two – but I find it hard to be nice and relaxed at the moment. And tidyness isn't so important.

Step 2: Values into practice

○ specify your intentions – and how you'll achieve them. Before you go on, complete the sentence: if . . . then . . .
○ find out more *working knowledge*
○ seek *support* from others who share the value
○ develop *skill* in your value through practising and reviewing your progress

Working through Step 1 can help you to decide what it is you need to change in your life. You may want to choose a new value, or give different priorities to the ones you hold. Or you may want to bring your behaviour more in line with the values you hold.

General decisions like "I'll be a nicer person" are too vague. You need to be able to describe your intentions more specifically – and how you'll achieve them. An "if . . . then . . ." kind of statement, as in Fiona's example, can help you be specific. Then you can plan in detail what you'll do, when, where, and with whom.

When you actually put a value into practice, you may find it works for you. Or you may find, with experience or changing circumstances, that it doesn't fit. Doubt is a very useful step on the road to deciding whether you want to give this value top priority – or even hold it at all. Whatever you finally decide to do, you need to accept yourself. (See Steps 3 and 4 overleaf.)

Step 2: Fiona

If . . . then: If I can cope better with the stress I'm under then I won't nag the family so much.

Finding out more: This course is helping me understand me and my teenagers more. Perhaps the 'Health Choices' course will help me manage the stress in my life.

Seeking support: If I join a yoga class, then I'll do it at least one night a week – and learn to do it properly. I'll be able to get right away from the house – which will give me a break. And I might make some new friends there.

Practising: I need everyday practise as well. If I can, I'll make half an hour each evening when I sit down alone and have a cup of tea. I'll tell myself it's OK to take a break – it'll stop me nagging and help me relax. I can also use the time to plan something positive I can say to each member of the family before bedtime.

"I like children to be obedient – but I want my teenager to think for herself."

Unhelpful doubts

Unhelpful doubts are the ones that make reaching decisions difficult. They tend to have their roots in underlying general problems, and simply surface when there is an important decision to be made. There are three main sorts:
(a) Doubts of self-worth – feelings and thoughts which say "Who do you think you are? You're not pretty/clever/wealthy. You're not good enough."
(b) Doubts about the worth of living – depressive feelings and thoughts which say "It's not worth it. Why bother".
(c) Anxious doubts – feelings of nervousness or fear which say "You couldn't do it. You couldn't cope".
Everyone experiences these kinds of doubt from time to time. If these feelings swamp you you need to seek help from your support system (see pages 16–19, and "What next?").

Step 3 : Doubt – and deciding

○ Review your motivation
○ Weigh up gains and losses
○ Balance your – and others' – values
○ Examine unhelpful doubts

Doubt is a hesitating feeling, mostly negative. It is not based purely on evidence. If it were, it would be easy to prove or disprove doubts. You need to find out what 'doesn't feel right'.

Normal doubt

A certain amount of doubt is useful because it can stop you from plunging into something that is unsuitable for you. It also helps commit you to whatever it is you finally choose. Normal doubt involves three processes which help you end your doubt and come to a decision:

(a) Review your motivation. "Why do I want to do this?" and "Do I really want to do this?" are vital questions. There's no harm in saying, after reflection, that something is not for you. There is more likely to be harm in pretending you value something that you don't.

(b) Weigh up gains and losses. For you to feel comfortable with a value, the gains in the long term have to outweigh the losses you incur by adopting that value. Some values – like deciding what to study – can affect the whole of your life. Others will be less far-reaching. You may find that it helps to look at the gains and losses in different areas of life: family, social life, health, self esteem, career, relationships. You can just list the pro's and con's, as you did in Chapter 1 (page 31). Or you can rate them on a 4-point scale, as Fiona did. You'll also need to plan how to keep the losses to a minimum.

(c) Balance conflicting values.
Sometimes a value you choose may conflict with other values you hold. Or putting it into practice will have an unacceptable effect on other people, given the values they hold. People have different ideas about what is right and wrong, and deciding which value has priority can be difficult. Here are some situations involving conflicting values. Can you add more, from your own experience in choosing values?
"Do I put honesty first – or loyalty to family members?"
"I think children suffer if parents divorce – yet parents suffer if they don't."

Step 3 : Fiona

Reviewing motivation: I'm scared of cracking up. I want to be calmer, and spend more time with the family.
Weighing gains and losses: My plan of action (yoga, Health Choices and my evening half hour) looks as if it'll affect most of my life positively.

Area	+★	−★	Comments
Family	4	2	Beware losing family time
Social life	2	1	Study at night
Health	2	–	I hope I'll feel better
Self esteem	2	–	in myself . . .
Career	2	–	and get on better with
Relationships			other people.

★(1 = almost none, 2 = a little, 3 = some, 4 = a lot)

Balancing values: Being a supermum isn't as important as being a relaxed and happy one. The family agrees.
Examining the unhelpful doubts: I think feeling depressed and worried is part of the stress – and will go with it.

Step 4: Self-acceptance

○ come to terms with your limitations
○ work on a compromise between the real and ideal
○ commit yourself to new ways of behaving
○ encourage yourself by talking, and with other rewards

Self-acceptance is the ability to look at yourself, your values and behaviour and think – taking all things into consideration – "I'm OK".

Many people tend to remain dependent on others for acceptance. They constantly ask themselves – Do 'They' (figures who they feel judge them) – agree with my decisions? Share my values? Approve of what I do? Such people are not sure of themselves unless someone else reassures them.

Taking charge of yourself

It can save much time, energy and heartache if you can take charge of your own values. Setting aside doubts about yourself, and putting your plans into action, require you to do three things:

(a) Come to terms with your limitations. There are all kinds of limitations on the things people can choose to value. Your:

○ motivation may not be great enough (see Step 3)
○ ability – skill, intelligence, appearance – may limit what you want to do.
○ material resources may limit your ability to practise your values for lack of money, facilities, and so on.

(b) Work on a compromise between the real and ideal. You have to compromise the value in your actual life with your ideal as you picture it in your mind. One of the most important things about self-acceptance is realising that real life rarely lives up to your ideal.

You don't need to be able to achieve perfection, only come as close as you are able. "If it's worth doing at all, it's worth the risk of doing badly". One parent tester recalled her father saying. As a teenager, this advice encouraged her to try many different things.

(c) Commit yourself to new ways of behaving. This means showing by what you do that, for the time being at

least, you've made the value part of your life. For example, if you accept a job, you go to work every day and do not actively look for another job.

Encouraging yourself

It's one thing to talk about compromises and commitments, another to make them. You can show self-acceptance practically, by giving yourself rewards as you put your values into practice. There are two approaches you can take:
(a) Talk to yourself – about doubts, limits, ideals. This involves having a conversation with yourself in which you ask questions, put another point of view, argue and make demands.

Talking to yourself is a surprisingly effective source of punishment and reward. More hopes and plans have been undermined by defeatist self-talk than by anyone else's arguments. Try to avoid putting yourself down when you talk to yourself.

One of the best rewards that encourages you to keep on with new ways of behaviour is instant self-praise. How often do you say to yourself something like – "That was great", "I really tried hard there", "I did that well" or "I'm proud of myself"? It's not conceited to say things like that to yourself. Far

from it – it helps maintain your emotional health.

(b) Build up rewards to help change your behaviour. Rewards can be quite small – like a cup of tea or five minutes sitting down with a magazine. You should give them to yourself as soon as they have been 'deserved'. Don't wait. And don't set yourself impossible standards. Rewarding yourself can be just as effective as being rewarded by others. Thoughts and words – self-talk as well as praise from other people – are as useful as more practical rewards.

Step 4: Fiona

It was through talking to myself that I realised I'd been aiming too high. I have my limitations – and I think now I can accept the reality and keep the ideal for what it is. The real question is 'Am I good enough with the family?' – and the answer to that is 'yes!'

Doing the Health Choices course helped me learn a lot about changing habits and using rewards on myself as well as for other people.

And – yes – the stress is beginning to get less. Life at home's a lot better now, and that in itself is a reward. And I do enjoy a night out once a week.

Changing values

You don't have to accept whole 'packages' of values.

Unpackaging values

Political parties offer 'packages' of policies and values. Religions offer 'packages' of beliefs. And parents show and discuss with their teenagers packages of values about marriage and family relationships. Even if teenagers accept these at the time, they are likely to make changes later – as these quotes from parent testers show:

"My mother brought us up almost singlehanded. My husband takes far more of a part with the family, so that I can follow my own individual interests too."

"My parents still believed in the sanctity of marriage. While I think it's a good idea, I disagree with them now that marriages should never be ended."

"I value close mother-child relationships, as my own mother did. But I worked for six years to have them in relative comfort. My mother disapproved of this 'materialism'."

Teenagers often want to be different from older generations. Revolutionary solutions for their own and world problems often seem more attractive than reform. But a total reaction against the past denies the chance of keeping any of the good things from it. And the very process of sweeping away all that's gone before can itself cause problems.

More radical changes tend to come from splitting up old packages of values, and creating your own: keeping what you want from the past, and blending in the new. Marriage (right) is just one example of where teenagers – and parents – from a variety of backgrounds may be making such changes.

Making changes

○ Think back to your own adolescence for a moment. When you were a teenager, who tried to sell you packages of values? Parents . . . friends . . . teachers . . . employers . . . politicians . . . ministers . . . newspapers . . . ? Who did you accept them from?

○ Think about the topics in this chapter for a moment. Have you changed your packages of values, or split them up in some way, when it comes to:

A Religion – are you more or less of a believer now? Do you behave in a different way?

B Politics – do you support a different party now? Are you more or less politically active?

C Sex roles – do you do different kinds of work in and outside the home now? What about your partner?

It will help your teenager to hear from you that you haven't kept the same packages of values all your life. Certainty is useful for a while, but being able to make your own choice of values – and to change them – are the skills you need to find your own identity. (See also Chapter 9.)

The best of both worlds?

For some teenagers, these skills are particularly crucial. Second generation immigrant teenagers, for example, may be faced with the choice between an old culture they cannot fully experience, and a new culture which often – if subtly – discriminates against them. An increasingly common response is for such teenagers to seek their self-esteem in their ethnic background; to maintain and modify their cultural traditions, rather than completely move away from them. But often they lack models to learn such skills from. So they must be pioneers when, developmentally, it is easier to follow.

Often, too, they lack support. Parents may still be under stress from the transition to life in a new country. Or culturally, they may expect high levels of obedience in the family. Also, members of the 'helping professions' are often from other cultures. They may insist on seeing issues in terms of conflict. And they may assume that the teenager should follow white norms rather than make their own compromises. So the advice and help offered can be inappropriate. For example, an Asian girl describes her response to the help she was offered after rows at home over her boyfriend: "I had three sleepless nights at a hostel and then I went back home. I couldn't stand being alone. I missed my family terribly in spite of it all. I knew that by sleeping away from home I might be getting into real trouble for the future".

A recent research study suggests that most Asian teenagers value the supportiveness, the economic co-operation, and the clear morality which their families provide. At the same time, many are making their own successful blend of values from different cultures. As one girl student comments:

"I have to behave differently at home than I do at college, like I can't dress in really fashionable clothes and of course I can't smoke. But I don't want to because I'm proud of my family and being Indian. I don't mind taking orders from my brother, in fact it's right that I should. He's paying for my education and he trusts me to do well."

All teenagers need the flexibility to play different roles in different situations. And making their own choice of values helps them to answer the fundamental question: "Who am I?"

Changes in marriage: an example

Well over 90 per cent of women in Britain still get married. The radical change comes in the increasing number of couples who are trying each other out first. In the late-1950's, only one per cent of all women lived with their husband before marriage. By the mid-1970's this figure had risen to nine per cent. And of couples who married in the late-1970's, one in five had lived together before marriage. Among re-married couples, the proportion is even higher.

Splitting up the package

Separating virginity and cohabitation from marriage can have the advantage of helping a person to find out what kind of relationship he/she values. Separating adult sexual relationships from childbearing can make it easier to choose whether, and when, to have children. And separating the relationship from the traditional symbols of marriage may help each individual to retain and develop his/her identity.

At the same time, splitting up values can create new social and personal problems. For example:

○ how do you describe your partner?
○ whose name do you give the children?
○ should there be 'palimony' when the affair is over?
○ what can you do about discrimination in tax/housing/ social security, against couples who don't marry?
○ who owns what when the relationship ends?

Creating your own package of values is a challenge. You need to be prepared to sort out difficulties which arise, to weigh the gains and losses, and make your own decisions.

For example, as more couples try each other out first, so the average age of first marriage – which has been going down all this century – has started to go up again. And since the divorce rate for teenage marriages is twice the national average, this could be seen as a good thing. But even if a legal disaster is avoided, there are still the practical and emotional costs of 'premarital divorce' as couples who find themselves unsuited, part. However, the illegitimacy rate has not changed much, despite the rise in living together.

Cultural variations

Conforming to the 'norm' in marriage is, in a way, a test of cultural belonging – whatever the culture. When white teenagers, after a period of rebellion and perhaps living together, marry and take up many of their parents' values, this is generally welcomed. Yet the same *process* in Asian teenagers – a consideration of the alternatives and then a chosen return to arranged marriages – may be seen by critics as undue restriction of freedom.

In all cultures today, young people are making their own changes to marriage values. Asian teenagers, for example, are asking for, and getting, a longer time to get to know each other – and the chance to veto a match. They may also decide of their own accord to delay a family for a while, to create time after marriage to get to know each other better.

Thinking things over

A D Parent testers who had experienced separation, single parenthood, remarriage, all commented that their values about marriage have been affected by these changes in their lives. Whatever your own personal experience, it will help to shape and change the values you hold. And it will affect your hopes and expectations for your teenager. You might like to think over the following questions, alone, or with your partner or a friend:

You and a partner: reflections on experience
○ if you (re)married now, what value would you place on the ceremony?
○ have you ever found that you held values about marriage which were difficult or damaging to put into practice?
○ what values about marriage did you split up in the past?
○ what kind of things do you say to your teenager about marriage and men . . . and women . . . and society?

You and your teenager: hopes and expectations
○ what would you feel if your son/daughter did not get married?
○ what kind of ceremony – but more important, what kind of relationship – would you want for them?
○ how would you feel if your son/daughter lived with someone before marriage?
○ do you know your teenager's views on marriage now – and would you mind if they changed?

It's important that your feelings and values about marriage do not hamper your teenager in his/her search for his/her own 'new direction' in personal relationships. Is there anything you might say, or do, differently now, regarding marriage and your teenager?

New lives

This final chapter looks at two important points concerned with coming to an end . . . of being a teenager . . . of raising children . . . of working through this book.

Getting it together

Thinking about what has been achieved involves drawing things together and looking at the overall picture.

For teenagers – all the life tasks they have tackled should equip them to lead a self-managed life. By now, they should have the beginnings of a sure sense of a mature identity.

"Towards independence" and "Setting limits" consider how parents can do their best to ensure that their teenagers will be able to live independent lives, in which they set their own limits and decide for themselves what risks to take.

"Who am I?" follows the normal path towards developing a clear sense of identity. However, many people encounter difficulties in achieving this, so "Escape and despair", "Drugs" and "Depression" focus on what parents should watch out for, and how they can help.

For parents – at times this book may have seemed to have over-emphasised the problems. Its aim was to help you cope better with – *and enjoy more* – this life task which you are now completing. It should have helped you:

○ Have a better working knowledge of the process of adolescence and the many changes which occur during the teenage years.
○ Build up a range of communication skills so that you can talk *and listen* to your teenager more easily. Doing the 'activities' in the topics should have helped with this.
○ Be more aware of your and your teenager's need for a good support system, and of how to find skilled help or additional information if you need it.

A As part of looking at the overall picture, stop for a while and consider:
A What have been the good things about being the parent of a teenager?
B What have you learned from your teenager? It hasn't been only a one-way relationship!

Moving on

For teenagers "The teenager moves on" outlines the new life tasks of a young adult, but also counsels against moving on too soon.
For parents Throughout the book we've emphasised that all transitions – times of change – however much desired, are stressful and involve 'losing the old way of life'. It helps to look at both the losses and gains at these times. You are asked to do this in "A turning point". "Your new life" helps you realise what you have learned from being the parent of a teenager. It also guides you to decide for yourself what changes, if any, you want to make in your life as you, too, face new life tasks.
Coming to the end of this book. The team who, together, wrote this book have also come to a turning point. They too have to consider: what has been achieved? and – what happens next? If you have any comments on this book or suggestions for future courses we would be happy to hear from you.

Towards independence

What has been achieved? What happens next?

Your teenager is rapidly becoming more able to make decisions for him/herself. In many ways he/she *can* run his/her own life. Leaving home is sometimes seen as the final point at which independence is achieved. He/she may be leaving home . . . for a job in another town, . . . a flat with friends, . . . to go off to college, . . . because he/she is getting married. The age at which this happens varies a good deal, but is often between 18 and 25. He/she may already have been living a largely independent life whilst still at home.

A Like other life tasks, becoming independent is a process that most people have to work at throughout their lives. Stop a moment and think back over the last year. What have you learned to do that makes you better able to cope with life? . . . Drive a car? . . . Cook a casserole? . . . Get on better with your teenager? . . . Accept help from neighbours when things were going badly for you?

Is this last suggestion a part of becoming more independent? Yes! Being independent does not mean being fiercely determined to do everything yourself, on your own. It involves choosing, at times, to ask other people for help when that is the most sensible action to take. *Interdependence* is a better word for mature independence.

Four stages

In becoming maturely independent most people go through four stages. Dependence, counterdependence, independence and interdependence. Some people get stuck in one of the first three stages.

1 "I can't do it without you" (Dependence). It's perfectly OK for a young child to feel like this most of the time. And for everyone to feel like it some of the time. But for a teenager to

be excessively dependent would indicate that something is wrong. Either with him/herself or his/her support systems: particularly family or school. In earlier childhood, parents may be too restrictive or demand too much independence too soon. In either case the child is likely to feel that self-management is too great a challenge. He/she may become full of doubts about his/her ability to manage his/her own life. Schools as well as family can offer too little or too much challenge. Teenagers who are full of self-doubt need long-term encouragement to take small steps forwards. They also need their successes to be acknowledged and praised.

At certain times of crisis everyone feels dependent. Like a child, we want our 'Mummy or Daddy' – or at least someone to nurture us. This is a perfectly normal way of coping with high levels of anxiety. Teenagers often feel that independence means 'going it alone

– always'. They need to see other people in the family asking for or offering support at times of crisis. It is worth explaining this normal need to them. In fact many teenagers – and younger children – can sometimes, providing it's not for too long, be 'good parents' to their own parents.

A D Think of some recent examples of:
A things *your teenager* has said – and
B things *you* have said –
which showed feelings of dependence.

Most of our parent testers quoted examples of their teenagers asking "Where's my . . . clean shirt, jeans, PE kit, etc". They also give examples of mature acknowledgement by their teenager of the need to be dependent at times: "I need a cuddle, I had a horrible day today".

Their own examples of feeling dependent were often along the lines of "The car's broken down can you sort it out?"

2 "I don't need you at all" (Counterdependence). This is the normal first step away from dependence. Do you still remember the first time your child screamed in anger "Me do it!"? During adolescence most teenagers alternate between feeling "I don't need direction or support from anyone!" and feeling "I need you desperately." "I can run my own life" may be almost immediately followed by "Did you iron my shirt?".

Counterdependence can help a teenager to test limits and see how far he/she can go. This is a valuable part of understanding him/herself and moving towards self-imposed limit setting. However, counterdependent people are not easy to live with. Fortunately most teenagers soon grow out of it. Counterdependency occurs when a person is just moving away from dependency and is not feeling too confident about it. Permanently counterdependent people need help to look at their underlying feelings of dependency and self-doubt, which they are probably trying to hide. Unfortunately they are usually so prickly that it is difficult to get close enough to suggest it.

Most adults have moments of counterdependency. These moments are often interpreted as bloody-mindedness by others. They normally occur when help is offered at a time when we are not too sure of our ability to cope. Help will be refused because we see it as someone else judging us to be incompetent. If our self-esteem was higher we would be able to see the offer as being genuine, from someone who wants to help.

A D Think of some recent examples of:
A things *your teenager* has said – and
B things *you* have said –
which showed feelings of counterdependence.

"You don't have to tell me – I know!" is a typical example of the prickly statements from our parent testers' teenagers. A common one from the parents was "I can do without your help!" – which sounds very similar.

3 "I can do it myself" (Independence). Independent people don't say this in a sarcastic way. They *can* do it themselves. They do not need help with everyday life. However, if they are too proud of their independence, they *can* become lonely. Never needing to ask for help as an adult can make it painful in old age to accept that in some ways they do become dependent again. They may also despise themselves as weak, when at times of crisis they are desperately in need of nurturing. They are too proud to let others know of their needs.

You should help your teenager to realise that it is OK to ask for help.

A D Think of some recent examples of:
A things *your teenager* has said – and
B things *you* have said –
which showed feelings of independence.

Our parent testers more often quoted examples of what their teenagers had done rather than said. Such as – doing homework without being reminded and cleaning out their room. Open acknowledgement of independence, however, serves to encourage the teenager to become even more independent: "I prefer to buy my shoes on my own now" (teenager). "That's OK" (mother).

Some parents found it difficult to think of examples of their own independence. Perhaps they see themselves too much in terms of their relationships with their partner and their teenager? "I've got a job – Deputy Crossing Patrol Officer" – was one example of sturdy independence.

4 "I could do it without you – but I'd prefer we did it together" (Interdependence). This is mature dependence – where, although competent to manage on their own, people chose to allow themselves to need and be needed by other people. Life seems fuller when it is shared with other people. It's important to see the difference between "I can't manage without you" (dependence) and "I don't want to manage without you" (interdependence).

For many teenagers this is difficult to do because they put such a high value on their newly achieved independence. They may need a model, from their parents' behaviour, that it is a mature thing to do.

A D Think of some recent examples of:
A things *your teenager* has said – and
B things *you* have said –
which showed feelings of interdependence.

Typical examples from our parent testers were: "Will you listen to my French verbs? It's more fun to learn that way" (teenager) *and* "Come shopping with me and help me spend my birthday money" (parent).

Parents' feelings

Teenagers sometimes want to be fiercely independent and at other times want to be quite babyish. Parents, too, have mixed feelings about their teenager becoming independent. They sometimes long for – and demand – that their teenager acts like a grown-up. At other times they don't like to think they are losing 'their baby' yet. There is often a mis-match between the teenager's and parent's feelings, so that progress is not always smooth.

Parents often hold their teenagers back out of habit. They are used to looking after their children – and they probably find it easier to go on doing things the old way. It needs more effort to help a teenager learn to do it for him/herself *and* provide the encouragement so that he/she does do it. Your teenager may set different standards for him/herself than you would for him/her. So for example, what he/she sees as tidy might not measure up to your idea of tidiness. But then part of allowing someone to be independent is to 'allow' them to have different standards and values!

A self-managed life

In becoming autonomous – able to lead an independent, self-managed life – teenagers show changes in four major areas. They become:

1 less dependent on others for approval
2 more able to cope independently
3 more able to initiate planning and problem solving
4 more able to keep a balance between their own needs and the needs of others.

1 Less need for approval. No-one really stops needing approval. We may learn not to keep asking for it and to be satisfied with more subtle signs of approval. We also learn to tell ourselves that what we are doing is OK – that we *are* managing well. While an inner sense of self-approval is building up your teenager will still need plenty of approval from you. Not, of course, in terms of 'you are a good boy/girl' – but approval which defines what he/she did and how you feel about it. It also helps to show you understand that he/she feels proud of him/herself or more confident or more satisfied when he/she knows he/she is managing well. Hearing you acknowledge how he/she feels will reassure him/her that it *is* OK to feel good about yourself. It's crippling to think you shouldn't feel proud of yourself because it is labelled as conceit or boasting.

A D Over the next two days make a point of showing approval of at least four things that your teenager has managed well. In at least one case acknowledge that he/she, too, feels good about it. Don't just make a vague promise to yourself to do this. Make a written note of each occasion and of what you said. After you have done this task you should feel good that you *did* carry out your decision to practise giving approval to your teenager. You may find that doing this activity is difficult because it feels awkward and artificial, but 'giving approval' is a skill that's well worth improving. You could build up your skill by keeping a diary for a while and making a note of every time you give approval to someone.

Most of our parent testers enjoyed doing this activity even if they did find it difficult. One parent got her teenager to do the same thing back for her. Here are some examples of what they said:
"*I guess you feel really proud of the way you organised your revision – it certainly paid off. You deserved an A.*"

"Instead of telling my teenager he needed to wash his hair (he is blond and it really shows when it's dirty), I praised him when he washed it without being told – and watched him blossom with praise."

Not all teenagers accept approval gracefully. They may resent it because they know you don't really mean it. But more likely they enjoy hearing it without liking to admit it. "We were busy in the garden over the weekend, but without asking, Jane kept the younger children happy for a while. 'Thanks for giving up some of your time' I said. She replied 'Oh, it's nothing, I enjoyed playing with them'. Sunday evening, Jane was particularly tired, and took herself off to bed. 'That was sensible' I told her when I went to say goodnight. 'Getting better aren't I' was her reply."

2 Coping better. As well as needing approval, teenagers also need to be challenged to become more competent. These demands may be placed on them by parents and teachers or by changes in their way of life. For example, many teenagers find that their first paid job – perhaps babysitting, a paper round or a Saturday job – is a great challenge, but one which helps them become more competent in many ways. Organising themselves and their time for studying for examinations is another major challenge. You could challenge your teenager to identify areas in which he/she would like to become more autonomous by suggesting he/she does the "Monitoring progress" activity (right) and that he/she works through the course related booklet for teenagers which will help him/her check out how competent he/she is.

3 Planning and problem solving. Competency involves doing things efficiently. Autonomy goes beyond this and also involves deciding on plans of action. It's important to help your teenager realise that making decisions will sometimes involve choosing solutions which, when tested out, prove not to work. It's OK to make mistakes – they are an important part of learning to be autonomous.

4 Other peoples' needs. The extent to which you and your teenager take into account other peoples' needs when considering what's best for you will depend on the values you hold about other peoples' rights. "I'm alright, Jack" implies that you don't care too much about other peoples' rights; so does "do your own thing" and "charity begins at home". Many of the values which people hold can be summed up by phrases like this. As Chapter 6, "New Directions", explains, it is up to you what values you hold.

It can help to rehearse with your teenager situations in which he/she needs to reconcile his/her needs with the needs of others. For example, what would he/she do if: he/she has promised to babysit next Saturday night and then gets an invitation to an exciting party? Remember you have to help him/her decide what to do – not solve it yourself.

Your job is to help him/her feel he/she *is* able to sort it out. He/she should be able to think of a few alternative solutions which will enable him/her to balance his/her need to have fun and his/her commitment to babysit.

Different settings

Progress towards autonomy is not steady and it may vary from one setting to another. For example, a 'mother's boy' at home, waited on hand and foot, may be highly independent at school, where his teacher may see him as making good progress towards autonomy. Or a girl, seen by parents to be independent, may in fact be highly dependent upon the others in her peer group.

Monitoring progress

A D It's worth encouraging your teenager to monitor his/her progress towards autonomy. He/she can feel good about what he/she is managing well *and* challenge him/herself to work out ways to become less dependent in other areas. In this next activity, it would be better if your teenager fills it in and then either plans for him/herself or discusses it with you. However, if your teenager does not want to do this activity, it would still be useful if you filled it in on the basis of what you know about him or her.

Make a chart like the one right. For each setting think of three examples of autonomy and write them against the independence–dependence scale.

Sue: 13 years old **Settings**

Scale	Family	School	Peer group
6 Highly Independent		Which school clubs I belong to.	
5 Moderately Independent	Spending money: I can spend my pocket money how I like.		I like classical music: they don't: I don't go on about it.
4 Slightly Independent		Usually do homework without too much nagging from Mum.	
3 Slightly Dependent	I usually have to be told to go to bed.		
2 Moderately Dependent		What exams to take: have to depend on teachers and parents.	I usually go where the group decides on Saturdays
1 Highly Dependent	Earning money: I only get pocket money.		I like to wear exactly the same fashions.

Think about the statements which come nearest the bottom of the scale in each setting. Does your teenager want to do anything about these situations? If so – what *might* he/she do? – what *will* he/she do? For example, here is what Sue decided.

Home Sue decided to brainstorm how she might earn some money. She decided to investigate her best ideas: offer to clean the car; ask an elderly neighbour if he would like his dog taken out for walks; find out about the possibility of doing a paper round; discuss with her parents which household tasks she might do for payment.

School Most of the advice Sue received was about doing the subjects she was good at. She thought she should think about the subjects she would need to study in order to do certain jobs she was interested in. She decided to talk to people doing these jobs too to find out what was involved.

Peer group Sue decided that half the fun of being in the group was that they all wore the same fashions. She wanted it to be like that, though she didn't always think the fashions suited her.

Your teenager Using this monitoring activity will only result in looking at three things, at any one time, that might be changed. This way, a teenager doesn't get demoralised by too many examples of how badly he/she is managing. *And* he/she will have the reward of acknowledging areas in which he/she is doing well.

189

Setting limits

Setting limits for yourself is part of managing your life.

As a parent you need to help your teenager learn how to set his or her own limits. This is a gradual process, best achieved by your teenager learning through joining in family decision-making sessions. In these he/she will have been able to explain how he/she feels and what he/she wants to do, even though you, as the parent, have the right to make the final decision. In most cases, a decision acceptable to everyone involved can be reached. He/she will have learned to speak up for him/herself and explain his/her point of view, so that when you do disagree you will all be clearer about what *exactly* you are disagreeing over.

Teenagers need limits

Teenagers need limits to be set. Though they should be decided by negotiation and mutually agreed, *they are needed*. A survey of teenagers showed that they dislike lax parents who don't set them any limits. They also disliked authoritarian parents who set rigid limits without explaining the reasons for them.

Teenagers need set limits to:

A **Support them.** It helps them to know what is acceptable and to feel more sure of themselves. They can see themselves in clearly defined roles; for example – "I'm not the kind of person who accepts lifts from strangers" – "I'm a responsible person – I tell my parents where I am going and if I change my plans". If no limits are set they are likely to feel that their parents don't care what they get up to.

It's helpful to see 'limits' more as a supportive framework to help a plant grow rather than as a cage to keep a wild animal confined!

B **Invoke when they need to protect themselves.** Being able to exaggerate and say "My mother would kill me if she found out" has often been used by a teenage girl to avoid being pressured into sexual activity when she's not really ready for it. These kinds of limits do not – if they have been explained fully – lead to inhibitions later on. A more mature girl can easily work out for herself her reasons for abandoning earlier parental limits, when she is sure she wants to become sexually involved.

Limits can be invoked, too, against peer-group pressure. It's easier to say "If I don't get back now I'll lose my pocket money or not be able to come out on Saturday" than to admit that you are a bit scared or don't feel it's OK to do what the group is suggesting. This kind of excuse does seem more

acceptable in peer groups and is helpful in the early days when a teenager finds it difficult to stand up for what he/she thinks is right.

Perhaps you have sometimes thought that your teenager would like you to set a limit which he/she can invoke if need be? What does your teenager think? Maybe it could be a secret between the two of you that you sometimes set this limit. "My father says I've got to go and see Gran on Sunday" is a useful excuse to have sometimes.

C Kick against. It does seem as though teenagers need to test out limits as a part of learning how to negotiate. They also need to discover how far they can go before the limit-setter reaches breaking point. This might best be done over minor issues. One school Head said that one of the reasons she wanted to keep a school uniform was that it was a 'limit' about which girls could complain and negotiate. It used up their energies which might have been diverted to more aggravating issues. This kind of reasoning lies beyond the idea that by keeping marijuana illegal it gives a relatively safe area for teenagers to get a kick out of breaking the law without them having to experiment with a more dangerous drug.

D Internalise or reject. Examining limits leads them to ask – 'Do I want to set this limit for myself?'. If yes – then it becomes part of their own value system. If no – then they will be aware of their own reasons for not accepting their parents' opinions.

Sorting it out . . .

What follows may sound like a long list of pitfalls. Most parents have many moments when they feel they will never sort out this limit-setting business. They are likely – on one or more occasion – to recognise that they are affected by all of the feelings listed below. Being aware of this makes it easier for them to be the kind of parent their teenager needs, rather than the kind of parent their feelings urge them to be.

If, as a parent, you *almost always* behave in one of the ways which make limit-setting difficult you can get help by talking it over with another understanding, experienced parent or teacher or counsellor. (See "What next?").

1 "I don't want him/her to be hurt". Almost all parents would like to protect their teenager from having to learn the hard way. They want to pass on their own accumulated wisdom, but this can't be handed over like a parcel. In many areas, particularly in personal relationships, people have to learn by trying for themselves. This is bound to be painful sometimes. However, learning from our mistakes is much better than being too timid ever to risk making a mistake.

A You can help your teenager understand how to 'learn from mistakes' within your own family.

Think back to a time when someone in the family – not necessarily your teenager – has made a mistake. What happened? What was the outcome?

A *Was the mistake denied?* ("I never meant to go swimming anyway" – when swimming costumes were left behind)

B *Was the mistake excused?* ("It's my fault for not reminding

you about the bill: I know you've been busy")

C *Was a lot of energy spent on deciding who was to blame?* ("It's not my fault; if you hadn't . . .")

D *Did you despair and make hopeless resolutions for the future?* ("I'll never let you go to Anne's again" – "You must always be back by 9.30 pm in future")

It's best to think carefully about how it came to happen and see what you have learned from this that will be of help in the future. If this is done openly in the family the teenager (and younger children) can join in. They may have good ideas for avoiding the same problem in the future. Joining in this kind of problem-solving is very different from having someone pass on to you their own solutions.

Can you recall an example of your teenager having learned from his/her mistakes? Most of our parent testers could:

"My son borrowed a friend's push bike. Unfortunately an accident occurred, the bike was a write-off. This is involving a court case, and an insurance claim taking many months. This has ended in us buying a new bike for the friend and my son paying us back until the insurance company settles. I hope he has learnt a lesson!"

"Nicola was given wrong change in a shop, and came home very angry because she felt it had been done on purpose. After we both went back to the shop the manager said if he had too much when he checked the till he would return it to her. This he did. Nicola is now quicker to check her change but also not too quick to condemn."

"He agreed to play rugby for a school team – but then later decided to play football (which he prefers) for another team – thus letting the school team down. Was surprised at the furore it created – learnt that he must stick by his original choice – or else make adequate provision for changing his mind – so they are not left in the lurch."

It's difficult to help teenagers learn from their mistakes without damaging their, often fragile, self-confidence. They need to feel – "It's OK to experiment. Sure, I'm bound to make mistakes sometimes, but I can learn from them".

2 "My father set the rules for me – and they have stood me in good stead". In a stable society with limited opportunities and strictly-defined roles, parents often do know best about the guidelines which will ensure their teenager fits into society when he/she is an adult. In this kind of society – where people know and accept their place, authoritarian, *but loving*, parents produce compliant, polite teenagers willing to fit in to such a society. However this type of compliant, polite teenager has been shown to be less creative, and more hostile towards others in their inner thoughts and fantasies.

In a rapidly changing society people need to be flexible, non-conforming and independent. They need to be more free-thinking. Warm parents who encourage the step-by-step development of autonomy by appropriate limit-setting, will bring up teenagers who can cope. This way of parenting produces adults who have been shown to be more outgoing, active, socially assertive, independent, friendly and creative. These people feel sufficiently sure of themselves to be rebellious and disobedient when they feel the circumstances demand it.

. . . Your problem or theirs?

1 "Young people today have too much freedom (I never had it so good)". If you feel like this ask yourself – "If the truth was known, am I jealous of my teenager?" or "Am I full of anger left over from my teenage years?". These can be very difficult to answer truthfully if you *are* full of jealousy and anger. (You should find it helpful to go back to "Parents' feelings" on page 40 and think through your past and present experiences in the way suggested there.) These strong feelings can make a parent cold (hostile) and restrictive towards his/her teenager. This is likely to cause the teenager to turn the anger he/she feels towards his/her parent in on him/herself, in which case he/she is likely to develop various neurotic problems.

Talking about your feelings to someone who can help (see "What next?") can free you to show more warmth towards your teenager and encourage him/her to become autonomous. You'll probably still feel jealous of his/her freedom but you will realise that coming to terms with your feelings is a problem that belongs to you. It should not be allowed to interfere with helping your teenager to grow up.

2 "I never had it so good – I want him/her to have all the opportunities I never had". This *can* be OK, but can be linked to an unwillingness to set limits. Teenagers often interpret unwillingness in setting limits as "my parents don't care about me". They feel uncontrolled and unsure of themselves. Parents may even encourage their teenagers to go beyond reasonable limits – to live the life *they* wanted to live as a teenager. They may buy a powerful motorbike for a son who feels he has to use it. Or encourage their son or daughter to play the field sexually: their teenager may then experience the painful loss of self-respect that empty promiscuity can cause.

If you feel you may do this then "Parents feelings" (page 40) should help you sort out where your feelings are getting in the way of your being the kind of parent your teenager needs.

Conflict over limits

"You *must* be home by 11pm."

"You *can't* go there"

"You *mustn't* go around with him"

"*Never* do that!"

Must, can't, never, don't are key words that suggest you and your teenager are going to get into an argument over some limit that you are trying to impose. They may also result in your teenager deciding to lie to you.
"I'll . . . never sleep a wink . . . die if anything happens to you! . . . never forgive myself! . . . kill you!"
These are all statements that show your feelings are desperately getting in the way of sensible negotiation. You'll find yourself rapidly reaching deadlock with your teenager if you start negotiations whilst swamped by your worries. Try to think through your anxieties before talking to your teenager about your reasons for worrying.

What worries you?

A The worries which lie behind the limits parents set seem to fall into three groups. What worries you? Tick those which apply to you in each category. Add any other worries you have, too.

A "I'm worried about the risks"
I'm afraid he/she will:
○ have an accident   —
○ get killed   —
○ harm him/herself   —
○ harm someone else   —
○ get into a fight   —
○ get into trouble with the police   —
○ get pregnant/get some girl pregnant   —
○ get on to drugs   —
○ be assaulted/raped   —

B "I'm worried about how worried I'll be"
I'll:
○ be sick with worry   —
○ never sleep a wink   —
○ never forgive myself   —

C "I'm worried about what other people will think of me (as a parent)"
What if:
○ the police were called in?   —
○ the neighbours knew?   —
○ your father/mother found out?   —
○ they told the school?   —
Usually if we're worried about what other people think it's because a part of us is being critical in the same way; but we are trying to ignore it. Do you often say:
○ "your grandfather would turn in his grave if he knew"   —

Taking risks

Most of our parent testers were worried about their teenagers taking risks.

"Self-managed health" (pages 58–63) discusses health-related risks and the issue of 'informed risk-taking'. "Taking risks" (pages 80–83) looks at risk-taking in personal relationships and sexual activities.

The other major worry of our parent testers was concerned with "Where are you going?" They wanted to know where – who with, and what time and how would their teenager get back.

This is a perfectly reasonable worry and one for which it's well worth negotiating limits so as to reduce both worry to the parent and risk for the teenager. Make sure that your teenager realises that you believe, very strongly, that – "*A responsible person makes sure that someone knows where they have gone and lets others know if they change their plans*".

You might want to add – "They also carry something that identifies them".

It's fairly easy to get your teenager to realise that you think this is important. The trouble is that if it is only seen as a rule you set for him/her then it can be very tempting to break the rule. Particularly if he/she is angry with you or wants to get his/her own back in some way. *Show that you – as a responsible adult – do it too.*

This is a sound limit to set, but you may make it difficult for your teenager to abide by it if you set other limits too rigidly. If he/she decides to break these other limits he/she may have to lie about where he/she is going or how he/she will get home.

Suppose you set a limit *which you cannot physically enforce* such as – "You must not go to . . . Anne's house, . . . the disco, . . . a pub." If he/she decides he/she will go, despite your wishes, then he/she is quite likely to lie and say he/she is going somewhere else of which you do approve. He/she may excuse this lie on the grounds that he/she will be saving you a lot of worry.

Would you rather be lied to? Or would you prefer to handle your worries by at least agreeing to hear each other out and trying to reach a negotiated agreement acceptable to you both? (A course related booklet and tape deals with negotiation skills. See also "What next?")

If your teenager won't agree to the limit you would like to set, try at least to end up with your teenager saying something like this:

"I *am* going to X. I know you don't want me to. Your reasons for this are . . . (states clearly the reasons you have given). I disagree with them for these reasons . . . If it will make you less worried I will . . . (Whatever is the best agreement you both can reach such as . . . phone you . . . go with Bill . . . leave by 11 pm . . . be sure not to smoke, take drugs, sleep with him/her etc.)."

This way at least he/she is not lying, you know where he/she is and you have done your best to minimise your worries. It will also help you reduce your worries about what others will think of you as a parent. You will know you have done your best to explain what you think the limit should be, have been open with your teenager about it and kept your lines of communication open instead of driving your teenager away from you.

Who am I?

"Who am I?" is a question that recurs throughout life.

During the teenage years "Who am I?" is *the* question. Though forming a secure sense of identity is one of the most important tasks of adolescence, the question can never be answered once and for all. It recurs as a part of the natural process of growth that goes on throughout life. Major life changes may make a person acutely aware of the need to rethink the answer.

Identity

Identity is knowing who you are without having to ask the question. It is the feeling that deep down you remain the same person – whatever your feelings or behaviour in a particular situation. It is being able to respond with certainty to questions about your views or feelings. It is not feeling threatened or insecure when others disagree with you. During adolescence everything is in flux.

A There are three stages in forming a secure sense of identity. Make a note of what comes to your mind about yourself, or someone else you know well, as you read through this section. We have included the comments of one of our parent testers.

Childhood identity. Children usually adopt the views of others without much question. Most often they simply hold the views they see their parents put forward. They identify themselves with them. With adolescence these views start to be questioned, first in one area of life and then in another. A new identity has begun to be shaped.

Time to decide. The psychologists' word for this phase is "moratorium". It is a time of struggle and change. Different views and beliefs are thought about. Some are rejected at one time, and later returned to and accepted. It is a difficult time for the teenager who may at times feel quite unsure about who he/she is. It can also be a difficult time for those around him/her who have to cope with his/her unpredictable changes of view. *"I wanted to be a nurse very much, but could not seem to resist pressure into another field, now, years later I find I have ended up in a field of nursing after all."*

Sure of who you are. Psychologists call this "identity achievement". The result of teenage flux and change is the gradual emergence of a stable sense of "Who I am". The way the person be-

haves is now the result of the choices made. It no longer depends on rules set down by others. Safe in his/her own identity, the person can allow others to be who they are and accept and value the differences between them. *"It took me some time to become sure of myself and to say, amidst criticism, I am black, Catholic and proud of it."*

There are two other identity states often found in adolescence – and indeed, later in life as well.

It's all too much. Psychologists call this state "identity diffusion". They mean that the person hasn't yet started the search for their own beliefs. Neither has he accepted or rejected the beliefs of others. Such people don't seem concerned about life choices. They often seem aimless. They may drift through life afraid of making deep friendships. They are often depressed, living a life of "quiet desperation". *"I have seen this in a friend, she wanted very much to be the model daughter and now the model wife and mother, but unable to succeed perfectly in those states, she became severely depressed."*

Choosing too soon. Psychologists call this "identity foreclosure". They mean that the person has carried forwards parts of his/her childhood identity without questioning them. In adult life it often means that the person is defensive about his/her own views and finds it hard to accept those of others. It can sometimes be hard to distinguish this state from identity achievement, since a person may freely choose, in the end, to adopt views similar to those of his parents. The difference is whether or not a period of questioning has been gone through. *"I found that certain attitudes, primarily from my mother, dominated and when in doubt as whether to have a drink in a pub with colleagues the knowledge 'she wouldn't like it' stopped me."*

Areas of life

There is not a smooth movement from one identity state to the next. A person can be in a different state for each area of his life. Someone may take a sideways step into "identity foreclosure" or "identity confusion". However, most people who do this eventually become more sure of their identity. Throughout life most people will also have minor

periods of "moratorium" in which they rethink certain areas of their life.

In the chart (opposite) we have given examples of statements teenagers or older people make about four major areas of life which are typical of the different identity states.

You and your teenager

A **D** Make three blank charts like the one opposite. Please note – childhood identity and identity foreclosure have been put together in one line of the chart. They both involve *adopting without questioning* the views of your parents. For a child this is quite appropriate and normal. For a teenager or adult this can cause problems – they should be choosing for themselves their views on life.

Chart 1. What sort of views does your teenager hold about the four areas of life? Which of the four states do you think he/she is in for each of the four areas? Think of a statement he/she might make about each of the four areas and write it in the appropriate square of your first chart.

Chart 2. Think back three years ago. What sort of views did your teenager hold then? Think of a statement he/she might have made and write it in the appropriate square of your second chart. Now compare your two charts. What changes, if any, do you see? Statements of children made at 10 or 11 probably all fall into the 'Childhood identity' squares. Three years ago (age 11), Robert had hardly begun to think about what lay behind his opinions. Today he is beginning to think quite deeply about what he wants to do when he's grown up and is clearly unsure of, but reconsidering his religious beliefs. Both politics and sexual morality are areas which he appears to discount. This is probably because he realises that complicated issues are involved, which either he doesn't understand or is not personally involved with. In a year or so his views on religion may have stabilised and moved into the "achievement" box. Work may take longer to settle. It will probably not be resolved until he has left school and is settled in a job he likes. As these two areas stabilise he may be better able to cope with the questions of politics and sex.

Area of life/ Identity State	Occupation	Religion	Politics	Sexual Morality
Sure of who you are (Achievement)	"This is something I feel fairly sure about now. I know what I'd like to do at college, and the sort of job I'd like after."	"I've decided I don't need to believe in a god. That doesn't mean I don't respect others' need for religion."	"I more or less agree with one political party – but I make it known if I disagree with party policy!"	"As long as it doesn't harm anyone else – and they both want to do it – then it's OK."
Time to decide (Moratorium)	"I change my mind so often about what I want to do: one week I want to stay on at school, the next I want to get a job."	"I think probably there is a god, but I've stopped going to Church – though sometimes I think I ought to."	"I do try to get involved with the Peace Campaign – but I think if you look at history it's the strong countries that win."	"I think I've thought out what I think are the rights and wrongs. It's OK in theory; but I don't always practise what I preach!"
It's all too much (Diffusion)	"I don't think I've really thought about it yet, but something will turn up I suppose – if not I'll live on the 'dole'."	"God? What god?"	"Politicians are all a load of shit."	"If I get the chance I take it – girls are all slags anyway."
Choosing too soon (Foreclosure)	"I'm going to secretarial college, all my friends are going too, and we'll have a great time."	"The Catholic faith was good enough for my parents – it's good enough for me, too."	"Well – I've always been a member of The Young Conservatives – everyone around here is."	"Well, I don't believe in sex before marriage, I mean it's not a good idea is it. You're not supposed to."

Robert's chart — This chart combines notes on Robert aged 11 and *Robert aged 14*

Sure of who you are (Identity achievement)				
Time to decide (Moratorium)	*"I'd still like to be a carpenter but I'd also like to have a job that took me to other countries."*	*"I don't think there is a God like religions say but sometimes I think there must be somebody greater than us."*		
It's all too much (Identity diffusion)			*"Politics is silly."*	*"Sex is boring: girls are silly anyway."*
Choosing too soon (Identity foreclosure) and – Childhood Identity	"I'd like to be a carpenter – like my Dad."	"None of our family go to Church."	"All the best people are socialists."	"Sex is how grown ups have babies."

Most teenagers cope well with forming their identity. Remember that it is a time of stress and upheaval. Don't expect it to go smoothly. Most of your worries will be groundless. In the next topic we look at those times when there may be cause for concern.

Chart 3. Now try to fill in one for yourself. You may be feeling very sure of yourself at the moment and put all your statements in the identity achieved boxes. Absolute certainty about this may be a sign that you have actually foreclosed on your identity. You will need to think back to decide did you really go through a period of questioning this viewpoint before choosing it as your own.

Many people will find they are in a state of moratorium in some areas. This is particularly likely if a major life-change, such as divorce or redundancy, has made them rethink their life.

Parents' identity states may affect how they get on with their teenagers. Parents who foreclose are usually more legalistic with their own children. These parents set rules which are based on "because I say so", and feel particularly threatened when their teenagers challenge them.

It can be difficult too for a parent in a moratorium state, to know what advice to give a teenager. Perhaps he used to teach that sex outside marriage is wrong but is now himself rethinking whether he believes this to be 'true'.

It's quite common, too, for parents to realise that their teenager has thought through his/her views far more than they ever have done. This may jolt them into a new viewpoint themselves.

Escape and despair

It isn't always easy to weather the problems of identity formation.

In this topic we look in more detail at some of the problem routes an adolescent may follow in his/her search for his/her own adult identity. Choosing these routes may cause problems but they should not be seen as dead ends. It's possible to get through these problems and find a way to a more secure identity. It's important too to remember that a person is unlikely to encounter problems in all areas of his/her life. Identity may be worked towards in one area despite problems in another.

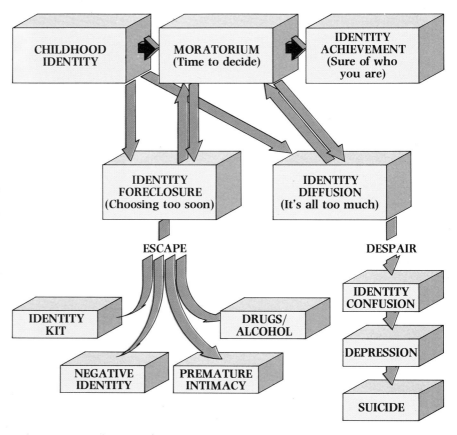

Escape

Choosing too soon – identity foreclosure – can be seen as a way of escaping from having to face the difficulties of discovering who you are and who you want to be.

There are several ways of avoiding the painful moratorium phase during which it's difficult to make your mind up about life. But this questioning phase is an essential part of becoming mature. Avoiding or escaping from it can lead to a way of life which in the long run is unsatisfactory. There are basically four ways of escaping:

Pre-packaged identity kit. Here the teenager is looking for a leader who can tell him/her 'who he/she is'. These are often religious or political leaders who demand complete obedience. The follower has to accept, without query, the whole values' package.

Negative identity. A teenager may come to feel so at odds with his/her parents or society that he/she comes to despise any role of which they approve. For someone who doesn't want to be 'good' any name is better than none. He/she will often opt to be bad. 'Junkie', 'drop-out', 'mad', 'thief', can be important labels for him/her. They make him/her feel that he/she is someone. It is of course important *not* to label a confused teenager in this way. An official label makes him/her feel confirmed in his/her negative identity. He/she will then live up to his/her label.

Premature intimacy. Here the teenager seeks frantic reassurance of "who he/she is" in close relationships. Close friendships and close sexual relationships require partners who can share themselves with another (see Chapter 3 – "Intimacy"). If you're not sure of "who you are", it is hard to do this. Such teenagers have desperate needs, but can't give in return. Their attempts at intimacy often fail. They may then go from partner to partner in a desperate search, or withdraw and become socially isolated. Sometimes teenagers like this adopt a false mask of maturity. They tackle adult life tasks before they are ready. Many teenage marriages have this quality and are consequently unstable.

Drugs and alcohol. This escape route is often the most disturbing to parents. It is discussed in the next topic.

Despair

"It's all too much" – identity diffusion – is a state in which a person has given up his/her childhood identity, but has now abandoned the search for an adult self. The problems of identity formation seem unsolvable. He/she is all mixed up and full of despair.

Despair may deepen from the common identity confusion state into depression and, for a few, end tragically in suicide.

Identity confusion. A teenager in this state may give the impression of not caring about who he/she is. However "couldn't care less" is usually a cover up for anger and hurt which is too painful to admit to. Almost all teenagers occasionally feel like this about some area of their life.

A Ask your teenager which of the following statements describe how he/she has felt at some time during the last six months.

1 He/she may be unable to concentrate on study or work. But he/she may also spend hours on one or two activities to which he/she seems addicted. ___
2 He/she doesn't want to take any exercise. ___
3 He/she may feel desperately bored and long for excitement. ___
4 He/she may find it impossible to plan for the future. He/she may not even feel that he/she has a personal future. ___
5 He/she may find it difficult to get up

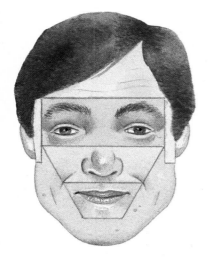
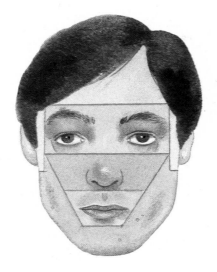
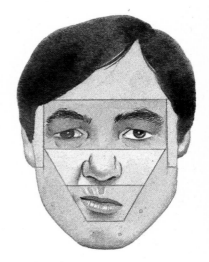

and face another day. It will be equally difficult to go to bed. ___
6 He/she has little sense of time. It may hang heavily on his/her hands or pass without him/her noticing it. ___
7 He/she may feel unable to derive a sense of accomplishment from any kind of activity. ___
8 He/she may reach a point at which he/she doesn't want to go out and so becomes socially isolated. ___

Severe identity confusion may affect a teenager in nearly all of these ways and his/her confusion may become more despairing so that he/she sinks into depression.

Depression Most of these feelings in the list above *may* be seen as signs of depression. Depression, is generally considered to be linked to a loss of some sort. (See "Transitions" in Chapter 1.) In the case of a teenager with identity confusion, this would be seen as the loss of his childhood identity, made worse by the failure to develop a sense of adult identity. Not knowing who you are anymore is a hopeless, lost state to be in. Teenage depression and its possible outcome – suicide – are examined in greater detail in the next topic.

Ways of helping

A D Most parents want to know what they can do to help a teenager who is having these problems. One way of looking at this is to try to recall what helped *you* as a teenager.

Your problems. Go through the list of problem states (below) thinking about the four areas of life: occupation, religion, politics and sexual morality. Make a brief note about each problem.

1 Identity kit
2 Negative identity
3 Premature intimacy
4 Drugs/alcohol
5 Identity confusion
6 Depression

What helped you? Now try to remember what helped you with these problems. Who helped you? What did they say? What did they do? It may have been your parents who provided this support. It may equally have been friends, a teacher, youth club leader, relative, or any other adult you happened to know. Listed below are some of the things they may have done which helped: tick any which happened to you.
1 Listened, without patronising or criticising you, when you talked about your views and confusions ___
2 Listened when you talked about your feelings, distress or unhappiness ___
3 Provided practical help and supported your experiment ___
4 Allowed you to make decisions – without abandoning all responsibility to you ___
5 Praised you for the things you did for yourself ___
6 Encouraged and supported you in taking responsibility for your own life ___

All the things on our list are things which would help a teenager who has problems in the period of identity formation. Indeed, provided with such support your teenager may avoid most of the problems. Does your teenager have sources of this type of support? Try to provide this support if you can. Also, try to see that your teenager gets it from other people too. Encourage contact with other adults and with a wide circle of friends.

Why is it all so difficult?

So far we have only talked about problems of identity formation from the inside – from the way the person feels them. However there may also be outside causes – social and political reasons – for teenagers finding this particular life task so hard. For many teenagers society provides little support and much disillusionment.
○ Teenagers are rarely allowed to participate as responsible people in the running of the community. They are seen as a sub-culture that doesn't mix with adults and has no role in society.
○ Too many schools seem only to value academic achievement and to reward docility and conformity.
○ Recreational opportunities are often poor. Community action groups in which teenagers can become involved are few.
○ Even the sure thing that makes teenagers feel grown-up – getting a job – is no longer guaranteed.

Drugs

A teenager may use drugs to escape from problems.

Parents usually fear the worst if they think about teenagers taking illegal drugs. What really happens is rather different. This topic looks at why teenagers might take drugs and what can be done to help.

Setting an example?

As adults we take a whole variety of drugs. Tobacco, alcohol, coffee, sleeping pills, aspirins, tranquillisers pass many of our lips daily. They are all drugs – but because they are legal and socially acceptable we may not think of ourselves as drug users. Yet often we take these drugs to escape from the pain and frustration of modern life. They help us cope without asking ourselves awkward questions about our underlying feelings. Is it surprising that teenagers adopt the same solutions? The drugs they take may be different. They may be illegal or illegally obtained. But some of their reasons for drug use are reasons they have learnt from us and the culture they grew up in.

Why do teenagers take drugs?

A Escape is only one of the many reasons teenagers take drugs. Listed right are 16 reasons why teenagers take drugs.
○ In the first column, tick the six which you think are the most common reasons for teenagers to take drugs.
○ Then go through the list again and, in the second column, tick the most likely reasons you think why your teenager, if he/she were to, might take drugs.

Experimenting

Reasons 1,2,5,8,11 and 14 are the most common reasons for teenage drug use. Teenagers feel a great urge to experiment and see how far they can go with taking risks.

Health-related risk-taking and experimenting are examined in "Self-managed health" (pages 58–63). Through this experimental phase teenagers learn to set their own limits. Most teenagers who take drugs do so as part of this process of growing up. Temporarily the drug may fulfill a need. It may give relief from anxiety. It may calm an angry mood. It may make the teenager feel acceptable to his peers. It may remove his shyness. It may just be fun. As he/she grows up and becomes more confident about who he/she is, he/she will find the drug an unsatisfactory solution. He/she will get more amusement from friendships. He/she will find other ways to deal with anger.

If your child falls into this category there is little cause for real alarm. However much you disapprove, try to remain tolerant and supportive.

Depressed

Reasons 3,6,9,12 and 15 indicate that drugs are being used as a solution to depression. *Not many teenagers will fall into this category*. All teenagers are depressed sometimes. Extreme mood swings and patches of feeling lonely, empty or hopeless are normal. It is only when this condition seems permanent that there is cause for alarm. Only when depression is deep-rooted will drugs become an attractive escape from the pain.

Reasons why teenagers take drugs:	Most teenagers	Your teenager
1 Drugs are available		
2 To please a friend		
3 They feel empty inside		
4 They've no-one to rely on		
5 Because they want to be accepted by a peer group that uses drugs		
6 They feel angry/violent		
7 Because they have very poor or non-existent relationships with their parents		
8 For fun		
9 Because they feel miserable and confused		
10 Because they are confused sexually		
11 Out of curiosity		
12 Because they feel cut off from family and friends		
13 Because they can tolerate no frustration		
14 To rebel against parents		
15 Because they feel worthless and out of place		
16 They cannot relate to other people		

If your teenager falls into this category it may be hard for you to help. (It may also be hard for you to face the fact that it's hard for you to help.) Skilled counselling may be necessary for your teenager to develop self-esteem and work through the feelings that lie behind the depression and the drug use. Parents may be the last to know that their teenager is depressed. At home he or she keeps up a veneer of agressive, rude, or irritating behaviour. The underlying feelings of emptiness, fear and hopelessness are kept well-hidden. It may well be someone else – a teacher, youth worker or friend – who first suggests your teenager needs help. If this happens to you, try not to be offended or feel inadequate. You may not have been in a position to know. See "What next?" for organisations that specialise in youth counselling.

Seriously disturbed

Reasons 4,7,10,13, and 16 indicate that a teenager is seriously disturbed and is using drugs as a solution and an escape. *Only a tiny minority of teenagers will fall into this category.* They usually have a history of deprivation of some kind. There may have been family conflict, violence or rejection when they were small that has left them unable to cope with the demands of growing up. Professional help is necessary. If someone does suggest to you that your teenager is in this state and needs help, it can be hard to face. Feelings of denial or self-blame at having failed your teenager are bound to surface. You too may need help in facing up to whatever happened and the feelings it has left you with. See "What next?" for details of the kind of help that may be available for both you and your teenager.

Dealing with drug use

Read through the following two accounts. How serious do you think the drug use they describe is? What would you do if you were the adults in these situations?

Lisa. Stephen had some friends round one afternoon. After they had left his mother, Stella, discovered that some pills were missing from the bathroom cabinet. A bottle of tranquillisers, half a bottle of migraine tablets and some aspirins were gone. When questioned, Stephen said he thought it might have been Lisa who'd "pop any pill she can lay hands on". Stella remembered Lisa as a rather aggressive, provocative girl who could be alternately cheerful or sulky.

David. David came home from a party in a strange and giggly mood. He admitted to drinking a bit and then announced that drink had nothing on dope (marijuana). "Everyone should try it," he said. "You too can be like me!" This shocked his parents. They were more shocked when he produced from his pocket two small blue pills. He wasn't sure what they were, but had been told they would give him a good time. He was about to swallow them, when his father stopped him. **What would you do in these two situations?**

Lisa. Stephen's mother asked him to bring Lisa round. She came the next day, sulky and taciturn. When confronted she admitted to taking the drugs. Stella pointed out that it was dangerous to take drugs when they hadn't been prescribed for you and you didn't know what they were. At this Lisa became angry and left. Later she came back, saying she'd left her scarf behind. She was tearful and pleaded with Stella not to tell her mother. "She'll kill me if she finds out." Stella assured her that she wouldn't tell her mother and explained that she was worried. She thought Lisa was unhappy and that if she couldn't talk to her mother she might find it helpful to talk to some other adult. Lisa left without accepting or rejecting this suggestion. Stella found the address of the local Youth Advisory Service and gave this to Stephen, suggesting he might give it to Lisa. Some weeks later Stephen told his mother that Lisa had been to see a counsellor there.

David. After their initial shock his parents calmed down. Although they disapproved of his drug use, they were pleased that he hadn't tried to hide it from them. When they talked about it, David admitted that he had at times been frightened of the way the drugs made him feel. However it had also been exciting. He continued to experiment for a short while and continued to talk to his parents about it.

Two different cases

On the surface, David and Lisa's cases are similar. Both take drugs. Both 'pop pills' without knowing what they are. Underneath, David's case is clearly quite different from Lisa's. He is into what we have called 'experimental use'. His good relationships with his parents means that he can talk freely about it. Provided they keep the communication lines open, he will pass through this phase without damage. Lisa's drug use, on the other hand, goes further than experimentation. She is afraid of her mother. She clearly wants to talk to adults but finds it difficult. Her theft of Stella's pills – a theft bound to be discovered – can be seen as a plea for help. Whether Lisa is depressed or more seriously disturbed is difficult to tell. In the circumstances – dealing with a girl she hardly knows – Stella does well to offer the life-line of the youth counselling service and for it to be accepted.

Drug use is often difficult for parents to deal with because of the frightening images it conjures up. It can also be hard if it brings up issues about your relationship to your child.

Remember that most drug use *is* experimental and will be grown out of. If the problems run deeper do seek outside help.

Some guidelines

If you discover your child is taking drugs
don't panic:
○ keep communication open
○ find out how serious the matter is
○ find out what lies behind it
○ be open about your own beliefs and values
○ don't let disagreement be seen as rejection
○ respect your teenagers right to make his/her own decisions
○ seek help, but do so with your child's agreement if possible.
Don't let it be seen as a punishment.

Depression

Identity confusion can *turn to despair and depression.*

Levels of depression

It is useful to distinguish different levels of depression,

Mild depression. One study of teenagers found that almost half of them "sometimes felt miserable or unhappy to the extent that they were tearful or wanted to get away from it all." This degree of depression is so common as to be considered normal. It is usually short-lived. It may happen in response to outside events. A disappointment, a loss or an argument can bring it on. This kind of depression is usually helped by a sympathetic ear and supportive approach.

Severe depression. A smaller group of teenagers will become severely depressed. They may complain of feeling empty and having no feelings. They may seem withdrawn and lonely. They may produce bodily complaints such as fatigue or headaches. They may find it hard to talk about how they feel. This kind of depression is closely linked to identity confusion. It can be seen as a response to a loss. The 'loss' is the childhood part of the self which has been left behind. This loss is felt so acutely because the teenager is finding it difficult to move on to adult identity.

This kind of depression can be overcome with care and support. Some teenagers will be helped by supportive parents and friends. Others may find it easier to resolve their problems with counselling from a skilled helper.

Total despair. This is an acute state of depression which needs to be taken very seriously. Not many teenagers will be affected in this way but those who are usually need professional help. Teenagers like this often have long-standing experiences of defeat. Everything they try seems to end in failure. Often there is a history of family problems. The teenager has few emotional resources and no-one close to him/her he/she can rely on. Problems in childhood may have left him/her ill-equipped to cope with the tasks of adolescence. This, combined with a series of day to day disappointments or losses can lead him/her to give up on him/herself. He/she feels worthless and that life is pointless. Suicidal feelings are common amongst this group and must be taken seriously.

Recognising depression

A Depression in teenagers isn't always obvious. It can take many forms.

Which of these statements (below) would suggest to you that a teenager was depressed? (✓)
○ A big change in eating or sleeping patterns   —
○ Friends being dropped or ignored   —
○ A feeling of hopelessness or self-hatred   —
○ Irritating or aggressive behaviour
○ A sudden change in school work   —
○ Inability to concentrate or apply him/herself to anything   —
○ Constant search for new activities
○ Dangerous risk-taking (eg. with drugs or reckless driving)   —
○ Boredom and restlessness   —

If you have never had to cope with a depressed teenager you may have wondered which to tick. If you have known a lot of depressed young people you may have ticked most of the statements. In fact all the statements *can* be warning signs. The problem is that many of them can also occur without the young person being depressed. It can be hard to know when you *should* worry.

When should you worry?

Three questions to ask yourself are:

1 How many signs of depression does the teenager complain of or show?

2 How often do they occur?

3 How long have they gone on for?

The more signs there are, the more frequently they occur and the longer they go on, the more likely it is that a teenager is depressed. However you should also ask yourself:

○ To what extent do the problems cause suffering to the teenager?
○ How far do they restrict him/her in relationships with others?
○ How far do they interfere with his/her normal development?
○ How far do they upset others?

If the answer to these questions is "greatly" or "a lot" it may be time to seek help.

Seeking help

You and your teenager should consider whether you might discuss his/her problems with your doctor and/or with someone at his/her school. Alternatively your teenager could go directly to a Youth Counselling Service, if one is available locally. The important step is to encourage your teenager to realise that it is OK to ask for help for such problems. It is the skills the person possesses, rather than their status, which should determine the choice.

A *Which would you choose to go to? How would your teenager feel about going for help? Do you know of a Youth Counselling Service in your area?*

Think over these questions with your teenager, in case you ever need to seek help. Our parent testers and their teenagers were about equally divided as to whether they would approach their doctor or the school.

"Our G.P. is very understanding and I'm sure my teenagers would prefer to discuss their problems with her, rather than the school. I presume the school would record the discussion on the teenager's school record."

"G.P. 'feels' too busy for me to talk. School is very responsible in attitudes to children and deputy Head is especially good."

Some parents thought the Youth Counselling Service might be better in some ways because it would be confidential and no-one at school need know. However, facing a stranger seemed more difficult to some teenagers.

All three – G.P., school, Youth Counselling Service – should know who to send your teenager to if he/she needs more expert help.

Suicide

Severe depression can sometimes involve suicidal feelings, suicide attempts and successful suicide.

Facts and myths

A It's important to understand the facts (and the myths) about suicide. Read through the following statements. Some are true and some are false. Tick for true and cross for false.

A People who talk about suicide rarely try it —
B More girls than boys try to kill themselves —
C More boys than girls succeed —
D Teenagers who try suicide are trying to get back at parents —
E Someone who has the strength of mind to kill him/herself also has the strength of mind to seek help —
F A person who talks about suicide is likely to try it —
G A person who has tried suicide once is likely to try again —
H Teenagers who try suicide are often copying friends to get attention —

Myths many people believe these, but they are false.
A Talking about suicide is often one of the signs that someone is thinking about it. It may be a plea for help.
D There may be an element of "They'll be sorry when I'm dead" in some suicide fantasies, but it is never the real reason for a suicide attempt.
E A suicidal person feels worthless and hates him/herself. He/she cannot imagine overcoming these feelings. What strength he/she has is turned towards ending them.
H Some of the behaviour leading up to suicide may be an attempt to get attention in the sense that it is a plea for help. The attempt itself happens because the teenager has given up on getting help and given up on him/herself. Suicide is much too serious to be copied lightly.

Facts these are all true and it's particularly important to accept **F**.
B It isn't known why more girls than boys try suicide, but it is a fact.
C Boys tend to use methods that are more likely to succeed such as guns and hanging. Girls are more likely to cut their wrists or take overdoses of drugs.

F Almost everyone who attempts suicide, talks to someone about it beforehand.
G 40 per cent of teenagers who attempt suicide have already tried it before.

Indications of suicide

The signs of severe depression can indicate that someone feels suicidal. The following can also be warning signs:
○ Prolonged, deep depression after the break-up of a relationship.
○ Giving away prized, personal possessions.
○ A previous suicide attempt.
○ Talking about suicide.

The build-up to a suicide attempt often follows a common, recognisable pattern. This is always easier to see after the event, but knowing the pattern may make it easier to spot.
○ There is a long standing history of problems.
○ There is a period when these problems get worse.
○ The teenager's way of coping with problems start to fail him/her. He/she becomes more and more isolated.
○ In the days and weeks leading up to an attempt, all relationships break down, contact breaks down with parents, other family members and friends.

What should you do?

A If a teenager tells you that he/she feels suicidal:
○ Find a quiet, secure place to talk and *listen* receptively to what he/she tells you. Stay calm. If you can't stay calm, find someone else who can as soon as possible. Don't argue or offer advice. *Listen.*
○ Tune into your own feelings. They are often the best clue to how someone else is feeling.
○ Don't leave him/her alone. If you have to go, get someone else to come and talk to him/her or take him/her along with you.
○ Make it absolutely clear. He/she deserves to live, however he/she may feel at the moment.

After an attempt:
○ Deal with the immediate situation (brush up on your First Aid).
○ Call an ambulance.
○ Take any bottles or weapons with you to the hospital.

Moving on

Your teenager will soon move on to face new life tasks as an adult.

As we explained in Chapter 1, many life tasks are important throughout life, but are of peak significance at a certain stage. Many of the life tasks of adolescence will not be completed during the teenage years. Indeed many adults are still at an adolescent stage of development as far as certain life tasks are concerned. Some adults, for example, may find the task of making a close, intimate relationship with another particularly difficult.

The major part of some of the tasks are unlikely to be completed during the teenage years. These include: setting own limits, choosing own values, making an intimate relationship and early work experience or career decisions. These are also the tasks whose final outcomes are less influenced by parents.

Individuals vary a lot as to how long they need to spend on these tasks. Rushing on to the new tasks of adult life *may* be a way of escaping the problems of adolescent life tasks. A young person may feel that 'All will be well – if only I can leave home and lead a life of my own" or ". . . once I find someone to settle down with". Parents may feel the same way. But in general, it pays to take your time and sort out one part of your life (your current life tasks) before rushing on. Moving on too soon may lead to a commitment to a lifestyle which, although attractive at the time, may prove to be disappointing and unsatisfactory in the long run.

New tasks

The major concern of young adults is with new life tasks in which their parents no longer play a directive role. Most young adults:

○ **Develop new patterns of living** – perhaps away from home on their own and then with a chosen partner.

○ **Begin to be a parent** – perhaps by 'accident' since the arrival of a child is not always fully planned; or when the couple have considered when and how many children to have.

○ **Actively chose their lifestyle** – where they will live, how they will live, and their own circle of friends.

○ **Develop work plans** – though unfortunately for many, what jobs – if any – are available will restrict their choice.

○ **Give to their local community** – by becoming involved in community activities.

They have to manage their lives for themselves. Premature offers of help from parents are often a handicap at this stage. Of course, hopefully, they will reach a stage of mature interdependence in which they are happy to offer and to ask for help *when needed*. They will then choose to ask for your advice and support. But parents cannot (and should not) force their opinions and offers of help on these new adults. It can be difficult not to interfere because at the time you do it you can usually justify it, to yourself, in some way. "I'm only doing it . . . to save her getting hurt, . . . to prevent them making the same mistakes as we did, . . . because I love her."

However, while encouraging independence and freedom parents must be careful not to make their adult children feel cut off and unwanted. A welcoming home where they feel they belong and can return to, is much appreciated.

Your adult children

A **D** Do you have strong opinions as to how your adult son or daughter should tackle these new life tasks? Try completing the following two sentences for each of the tasks. You could make a chart like the one below in which we show what one parent answered.
1 *"What I would really like would be for him/her to . . ."*
2 *"What would upset me would be if . . ."*
Here is what Mary said about her daughter Joanne

	1 Would like –	2 Would be upset –
A Job/career	"A job that would really satisfy her: not one just done for the money."	"If she just wasted away, had no interests to develop. Was in a dead-end situation."
B Partner	"A well-adjusted man – easy to get on with and with a sense of caring for and about others."	"If she married someone less intelligent than she is!"
C Having children	"A baby as soon as possible: I'm longing to be a grandma."	"If they didn't want children because of the responsibility."
D Lifestyle	"Her to settle down, get married and then to buy their own house."	"If she just lived with a man – and didn't get properly married."
E Involvement in the community	"That she had been given encouragement at school to do community work."	"If she led a uniquely self-centred, money-pursuing life."

Look through your own comments. In some cases they will express hopes and fears that your son or daughter would share with you. (Mary and Joanne agreed about A1 and 2, and E1 and 2.) For others you may realise that they are not in line with what he or she wants. (Joanne disagreed with her mother over B2, C1 and D1 and 2.)

Young adults must be free to make their own decisions. Of course, as with your teenager, you are fully entitled to explain the values you hold. But this is not the same as trying to put unfair pressure on the other person to adopt your values. (Mary and Joanne disagreed over D2. Mary explained that she believed that it was important for a couple to show their commitment to each other by exchanging marriage vows "in the sight of God and the community". Joanne believes that personal, private vows are what is important.)

Does your comment reflect a freely-chosen value, which you have thought through carefully? (Mary decided her comment in C1 made it clear that it wasn't a value she held. She did not believe that young couples should have a child as soon as possible. It was her feelings and needs – "how nice to be a grandparent; I'll have a new baby to love, now that my own child is grown up" – that lay behind her comment.) If *your* own feelings and needs may lie behind your comments you should find it helpful to go back to "Parents' feelings".

Settling down too soon?

Ideally, young people should be encouraged to take their time to sort out who they are and what they want to be. They can then gradually build up a sense of their own identity as a unique individual. Unfortunately the older generation often finds the questioning of their rules and values so threatening that they put all sorts of constraints on young people to make them conform.

Throughout this book the emphasis has been on helping your teenager become what he/she wants to be rather than on what you would like him/her to become. Good schools, too, keep their rules to a minimum and their curriculum options as wide as possible to encourage teenagers to experiment and reach their full potential.

Many parent testers emphasised this approach in how they filled in the chart in the previous section:
"I would like him or her to really have the chance to experiment and find themselves, and come up with challenging ideas. I would be upset if he or she were to conform."
"*I would like her to live* as she pleased *and hope I would have the courage to support her.*"
"Just to be happy in whatever he does. The variety of life-styles of other members of family adds to my life."

Certainly once teenagers leave school there are often strong pressures on them from society to settle down and conform. They may settle down into the first job that comes along. Many marry quickly and may soon start a family. They settle down, too, into the same life and 'identity' as those around them. They foreclose their identity – without experimenting or considering all the options – to conform to the expectations of their workmates and marriage partners.

It is difficult not to be seen to be passing judgement on people who settle down like this. Of course, it is not for others to suggest to people, who are *happy* in their chosen lifestyle, that they might have experimented more. But it *is* often the case that people who close early on their identity, find the challenges of later life tasks disturbing and difficult. They may also reconsider their chosen lifestyle later on and decide they are unhappy with it. Many marriages break up because one or both partners did some more 'growing-up' after the marriage and the partners no longer suit each other. Fortunately in some marriages both partners support each other's attempts to continue to experiment and explore their continually developing sense of identity. Here the partners grow together. More often, with easy divorce, the couple split up. One partner claims that the other is not "the person they married any more" (*You have changed*), or – "not the kind of person I need any more" (*I have changed*).

As a parent, you will increase these pressures on your adult child to conform if you feel your task of being a parent is not complete until he or she is settled down in a 'good' job with a 'good' partner and raising a new family. You can reduce these pressures if you see your task as accomplished by launching a competent adult on a self-managed life, free to take his/her time to choose his/her own way of life. Free, too, as he/she grows older to become more genuinely a unique individual and more confident of his/her place in the world. We hope this book will help you to do this.

A turning point

One of your *major life tasks* will soon be accomplished.

Raising your children until they can lead independent, self-managed lives can occupy many years of your life. On the whole it's a rewarding life task – but you have had your own life to lead as well. This isn't always easy to do, when looking after teenagers uses up so much of your time.

Losing a role

If you have several children the role of 'being the parent of a teenager' may go on for many years. As each teenager leaves, part of your job is done. You gradually accept that this role is coming to an end. If you have only one child then his/her departure abruptly leaves you having to face the same loss. The loss is of a time-consuming, aggravating and rewarding role in life. However much you have looked forward to having your children off your hands the loss of this role can be upsetting.

A D All transitions – times when a life change is being made – even welcome ones, can be upsetting. The old way of life is over – and a part of you will be sorry to be losing it. Coming to terms with this loss can be made easier by looking at the losses and gains of the transition. Make a list of your 'losses' and 'gains' as in this chart (below). Our parent testers could give endless examples of both gains and losses. Some of their points are shown in the chart.

What I'll lose –
when my role of 'being
the parent of a teenager'
is over:
○ The satisfaction of being needed in a practical way
○ The challenge of new ideas and attitudes which make me re-examine mine
○ Someone who tells me truthfully if I look alright
○ Keeping in touch with fashion and new ideas
○ Social contacts via the school (PTA events)
○ The contented feeling of being all together as a family

What I'll gain –
when my role of 'being
the parent of a teenager'
is over:
○ No more having to nag about homework
○ A tidier house and fewer dirty clothes to wash
○ More money now I don't have to keep him/her
○ More time alone with my partner
○ A new adult friend (my ex-teenager!)
○ Time to pursue some of my dreams
○ Peace and quiet

Empty nest?

The effect of the 'empty nest' – when the last child has left home – is supposed to be a profoundly depressing one, particularly for women. The term was originally invented by doctors who had to treat severely depressed middle-aged women. If a woman became depressed after her children left home then the depression *must have been caused* by the children leaving. But this need not be cause and effect. Other experts claim that the depression is due to society placing little value on women once they had raised their children. Society was seen as equating being a woman with being a mother.

"A new life" in the next topic looks at how both mothers and fathers can build up their other roles once they have raised their children. This *can* be more difficult for women,

particularly if it involves seeking new jobs at a time of rising unemployment.

But does actually finishing being the parent of a teenager cause depression? What do you think? How do your friends who have already reached this stage feel about it?

As none of our parent testers had reached the stage of their last child having left home the quotations we use here are from a study of middle-aged women. This study found that "almost all the women responded to the departure of their children – whether actual or impending – with a decided sense of relief". Women may miss having their children around – and have to come to terms with this loss – but they are not plunged into depression.

"I can't tell you what a relief it was to find myself with an empty nest. Oh sure, when the last child went away, for the first day or so there was a kind of a throb, but believe me, it was only a day or two."

"I've had as much as I ever need or want of being tied down with children."

Because many of them were expecting to feel upset some felt guilty when they didn't:

"To tell the truth, most of the time it's a big relief to be free of them, finally. I suppose that's awful to say. But you know what, most of the women I know feel the same way. It's just that they're uncomfortable saying it, because there's all this

1 How much time do fathers spend with their children?
Generally mothers spend more time with their children than fathers do. In a way, this increased contact leads a mother to realise, almost everyday, that a child is slowly growing up. At first a child needs everything to be done for it. But very soon it can feed itself, then use the toilet, dress itself, go off to school alone and so on. Each step forward reminds the mother that she is no longer needed. Leaving home is the final step in a natural sequence of development in which she has played a full part. However a father may only see his children for relatively brief periods. He often misses the small steps actually happening. So for him their departure seems a more abrupt step.

2 How easy is it for fathers to show their feelings? Men are often trained from their early years not to show emotions – "Boys don't cry", "Men aren't . . . afraid of the dark, – upset when people die, – soft, – tender or affectionate". Well, of course they *have* all these feelings, but they are trained not to show them. Unfortunately some men get to pretend they don't even have the feelings. Fortunately today more and more parents realise that this is not the way to raise their sons. However there are still many fathers who do feel unable to show their children how they feel. Their children may not realise the affection their fathers have for them. By mid-life many of these fathers *do* want to be more emotionally involved with their children. The sad thing may be that, by the time these fathers want to show their love, their teenagers are at a stage of rejecting their parents and their values. Where this is the case, when they leave home their fathers may feel: "I never really knew him" or "I was just beginning to get close when she left".

Feelings of failure

It *is* distressing to realise that you haven't been as good a parent as you would like to have been. Some parent testers feel they made a lot of mistakes with their first-born. Their later children fared better. Many parents felt that their attitudes to children changed over the years. One said that having read an earlier OU course – The Pre-School Child – *after her child was five* had made her wish she could have a second go at bringing him up.

The truth is that all parents are as good as they can be at the time. They do their best. With extra knowledge and insight, everyone can see how they might have been better. But then this is true of most of life. It is important, too, to remember that as a parent you only have to be 'good enough' – not perfect.

Whatever their age it is always worth trying to improve relationships with children. We hope this course will have helped you do this. If you have only read the book and not joined the Open University course you may like to know that the TV programmes look more closely at family relationships and the course pack includes booklets and cassette tapes on communication, negotiation and decision-making skills.

It is also worth trying to improve relationships with adult children. Explaining what you learned as you helped them grow up will show them that you did your best at the time, and that you are prepared to go on learning and trying. It will encourage them, too, to learn all they can about being a 'good enough' parent when their turn comes.

talk about how sad mothers are supposed to be when the kids leave home."

Where the parent had been looking ahead for some time to when their children would leave home – and had a definite date for this, for example when they went off to college, the separation was particularly easy.

"By the time my daughter left for college, I had already dealt with the issues. From time to time in her senior year in high school, I'd get a pang thinking about what was coming. I must admit, though, that by the time it actually happened, even I was surprised at how easy it was. I guess I had just grown accustomed to the idea by then."

If the son or daughter was seen as staying at home until marriage the parting, when it did come, was more painful – but only for a short time.

What about fathers?

If anything the parting for fathers may be more difficult. "For me, it's enough! They've been here long enough – maybe too long. It's a funny thing, though. All these years, Fred was too busy to have much time for the kids, and now he's the one who's depressed because they're leaving. He's really having trouble letting go. He wants to gather them around and keep them right here in this house."
There may be two explanations behind this:

Your new life

What next? What about your life after your teenagers leave?

Of course you're not losing your children in that, hopefully, they will share their adult life with you. But you will have more time for other areas of your life and new life tasks to tackle. Even though it may be several years before they do leave home, it's worth thinking about this now. Some things, including training for a different job, may be able to be started now. Others you can spend longer thinking about instead of rushing into changes or being at a loss to know what to do when the time comes.

A growth experience?

You could look on your years of being the parent of a teenager as a 'growth experience'. Like all 'growth experiences' although you have learnt a lot about yourself it certainly had its painful moments. Consider the advantages of having had this experience.

You've learnt a lot about:
○ **human development** – this will help you understand other people
○ **communication skills** – how to listen, argue, negotiate and assert yourself. All skills which will help you get on with other people
○ **how your past and present experiences hinder or help your relationship with your teenager** – and other people too. You know more about yourself and these insights will help you in all your relationships
○ **your own teenage life tasks** – living with teenagers, seeing the mistakes they make, envying their youth and energy and the future they have before them, revives memories of your own teenage years. You may find you have 'unfinished business' left over from these years – life tasks that you didn't tackle too well at the time.

You may have done quite a lot of catching up whilst being the parent of a teenager yourself. This in turn may have led you to want to make a lot of other changes in your life. However, accepting that things didn't always go well for you and that some opportunities are lost for ever for you involves mourning their loss. You need to grieve for the person you didn't become. Most people find that it helps to talk about this to someone who will listen and support them. Their partner or their everyday friends, who know them well, will probably be best. They often find that they, too, can listen and provide support for the other person who would also like to talk about their own experiences.

If you don't have anyone to talk to like this do consider going to someone who is a professionally trained counsellor.

Realising what you missed out on also challenges you to examine: "what can you do to make up for it?" – and "what can you do to become the person you would like to be?" One parent tester decided that – "Though I was unaware at the time, I think this is one of the reasons I undertook OU (study). My daughter introduces me to friends as a 'late developer'!"

A new life ahead

A **D** You have new life tasks to tackle yourself. We have already looked at coping with children leaving home. Here we look at three more:

Evaluate commitments. One of the gains from children leaving home is that you have more time for yourself. For many men, life will go on very much as before. They have major commitments to their work that mean a large part of their life will remain unchanged – unless they become redundant. Today the majority of mothers work at least part-time. When the children leave home, a woman can look at whether she wants to spend more time developing her career and the extent to which it is possible for her to do this. Single parents – in the absence of a partner – will often seek more rewards from their work to give them a sense of involvement and self-esteem.

This is a time, too, to review your lifestyle. Do you still want to go on living in the same way? Are there other things in life you've always wanted to do – and might try now?

Many of our parent testers had started thinking about this several years before their teenagers were due to leave home. Here are some of their ideas:

"Planning and saving now for the time away with partner alone."

"Give more time to strengthen relationship with own parents, caring and nurturing as they get older and explore the possibilities in that relationship. An issue not touched on often is that once your children have left home your widowed parent may move in."

"Try to make myself a more complete person – develop areas which I have neglected."

"I will definitely travel more; I may even leave my present job and either retrain or try something completely different."

"Make use of experience, eg. divorce counselling or man phone for groups like those you can phone if you feel you might batter a child."

Develop relationship with partner. Research has shown that, in general, satisfaction with marriage reaches an all-time low around 35 to 40. This time coincides for most parents with having teenage children. Certainly once the children have left home marriage satisfaction usually increases again. A divorced parent is more likely, too, to remarry when the teenagers leave home.

With the children gone, partners turn to each other to seek again the deep commitment they had in the early days. If the relationship has just been neglected a bit it often rapidly improves. Many men do want to show more tenderness and be more emotionally open at this age.

There will, of course, also be couples who find they have grown apart – although they may not have realised how serious the gap was while their children were at home. With help, perhaps from a marriage counsellor, they may get things together again. For others, the best solution will be to separate.

Ironically, as men reach a stage at which they wish to be more loving and expressive of their emotions, many women tend to become more assertive and want to become a more separate person, pursuing their own aims now that they have more time to 'be themselves'.

A *Have you changed?* Many couples will look forward to their relationship being like the old days again, before they had their children. It won't be the same but it might be as good – or even better. In a way, both parents have probably done a good deal of growing up, themselves, while their children were also growing up.

Someone who looked for security and reliability when young and unsure of himself – or herself – may now want excitement and the chance to experiment. Others, who did more experimenting in their youth may now seek commitment.

There cannot be a set of standard questions by which you can review such a personal matter as your relationship with your partner. However, you should find considering how you would complete the following sentences a helpful starting point.

1 Since we've been together I think I've changed . . .
2 Since we've been together I think you've changed . . .
3 Over the last few years it seems to me that we have . . .
4 What I'd like us to consider changing:
A about our love-making . . .
B about the way we get on together . . .

Involvement in the community. Taking care of, teaching and serving others are ways in which our desire to nurture and take care of others may be made use of in the community. It gives us a satisfying sense of being needed, which is particularly good if we have no permanent partner. Parents who have raised their own children are usually highly skilled at nurturing others. Some, like the parent tester we quote here, start all over again with other children:

"As our teenagers grew up, my husband and I became aware that we had still plenty to offer. When our youngest was 14 years, we fostered four young brothers and at the same time became involved with a youth club for physically-handicapped children. We both went on to become part-time Youth Leaders. My husband finally decided that he would like to totally commit himself and is now at a Polytechnic doing a full-time course in Youth and Community studies."

Other people, perhaps mothers in particular, may feel they have had enough of nurturing with their *own* children. They want to branch out in other creative directions, pursue other ambitions which were closed to them when they were busy raising their children. Or take part in community action groups which seek to improve the community or change the nature of society itself.

Whatever changes you hope to make it's worth considering – as we did at the beginning of this book – what working knowledge do you need to acquire? What skills do you need to build up? What support is available to you?

These three life tasks may sound daunting to you particularly if you are almost exhausted by the stress of being the parent of a teenager. You may be longing for a rest. But ask yourself – when you go on a holiday, how much total relaxation can you stand before you become bored and restless for new stimulation? When the time comes, you will be keen to tackle the rest of your life.

What next?

Contents

Introduction

This is a guide to sources of information and help that's available from people, places and books.

Help is available to you in many forms – through individuals or organisations (which can be statutory or voluntary) or through books or magazines. Access to much of this help is available to you locally, not only through local branches of statutory and voluntary bodies but also through the many locally-organised help/information/advice schemes which are constantly coming into being. You may care to make a list of the addresses of the local organisations which might prove helpful in your particular circumstances.

This introductory section lists some general organisations with details of the kind of people who staff them and the sort of information they provide. You can get a list from your nearest library or information centre or you can look them up in your local telephone directory.

Using a telephone directory

Using a telephone directory isn't always easy. Directories do not always follow the same pattern, nor do they always put names under headings you would think of first. For example health centres may come under the general heading of your health authority (such as Bedfordshire Area Health Authority). As a start, look under the name of what you want first. If you can't find it then try headings such as your local health authority, local council or social services department. If you have no success using the ordinary white pages directory, try the Yellow Pages entry 'Social service and welfare organisations' which usually yields a mine of information. If you still have problems, Directory Enquiries may be able to help you.

Citizen's Advice Bureau

Your local Citizen's Advice Bureau is a good place to go if you are uncertain as to which organisation you should be contacting for help relevant to your particular case. There is a country-wide network, so you will find a branch somewhere in your area. The staff are trained. Some are paid, but many are volunteers, and they keep themselves up to date on changes in the law and the kind of information people require. The advice they give is free, confidential and impartial; they will know what you are entitled to and who will be able to help among the official bodies and voluntary organisations. They will also help with filling in complicated forms like applications for benefits.

Public libraries

Part of the job of a public library is to supply information (whether you are a member or not). If it is a small library the staff at the counter may help you, but if it is a larger library you may be directed to the reference section, where you will find a variety of reference books and directories. You can either consult these with the help of a librarian or you may wish to explore them yourself. Above all, don't be afraid to ask the staff for help. The library should also have a list of local organisations or people to contact.

Careers Offices

As these are run by local education authorities, their main task is to help and advise school children and college students. However, their services are also available to those returning to work after a gap. A Careers Officer can advise you on training opportunities, need for formal qualifications, etc.

Community Health Council

The Council is staffed by representatives of the community, some elected by local organisations, and it represents consumer interests in health. Contact the Council if you have problems or complaints about health facilities in your area. The staff will also know about organisations in the area which may be of help.

Council of Social Service Council for Voluntary Service Community Council

You will find the address of your local council (which may have any one of the above titles) in the telephone directory. These councils find needs and opportunities for development within the community and initiate action to meet these needs.

Department of Health and Social Security

This department deals with allowances and benefits, such as Supplementary Benefit. It is staffed by civil servants who can tell you what you can claim and who will handle it.

However, if you have any problems concerning benefit which cannot be settled at the DHSS you can contact *The Claimants Union*, 296 Bethnal Green Road, London E2 0AG whose aim is to establish the rights of claimants in the Welfare State.

Education Department

The local Education Department may be listed in your telephone directory under the name of the local authority. It will be able to tell you about local secondary schools and will have a Youth and Community Officer who should be able to advise you about facilities in your area.

Jobcentres and Employment Offices

These are run by the government and can be found in most towns. Jobcentres are self-service, so you can go in and have a look at the jobs on display. A receptionist will telephone the employer for more details and to make an appointment if you see something which appeals to you. If you need advice you can speak to an Employment Advisor or a Training Opportunities Advisor.

National Council of Voluntary Organisations

The National Council of Voluntary Organisations (NCVO), 26 Bedford Square, London WC1B 3HU is an independent voluntary organisation which aims to:

○ extend the involvement of voluntary organisations in responding to social issues
○ be a resource centre for voluntary organisations
○ protect the interests and independence of voluntary organisations.

It also produces *Citizen's Advice Notes* which is a digest of current legislation relating to social and industrial policy.

Social Services Department

The Social Services Department, which may be listed under the local authority in your telephone book, employs social workers who look after families and individuals and this can include visiting them at home. They may be able to provide help where needed with accommodation, maintenance and the bringing up of children, and they will advise on any benefits or allowances which can be claimed through the Department of Health and Social Security. They will also know of any local organisations or groups which may provide support, information or facilities.

Voluntary Organisation Centres

These centres exist in many towns and are a useful source of information on voluntary organisations in their particular areas.

Organisations and books

A list of organisations and books which you might find useful is given in this section.

Voluntary organisations can provide you with a wide variety of services, e.g. information, advice, counselling, booklists, magazines, newsletters. Due to lack of funds many of these organisations have to charge a fee either for joining or for using their services, so you should check beforehand. Also if you write to a voluntary organisation for information, you should enclose a stamped addressed envelope for the reply.

The following list of organisations is arranged under specific subject headings which are arranged in alphabetical order, with *see* references from headings which are not used to headings which are.

Abortion *see* Birth control

Accommodation *see* Youth counselling/advice/welfare

Addiction *see* Drugs

Adolescent development

Adolescence: generation under pressure
John Conger
Harper and Row, 1979
Part of the 'Life-Cycle' series, this book covers a wide range of adolescent issues in a popular style.

Adolescence and youth: psychological development in a changing world
John Conger
Harper and Row, 1977
This book interprets current research findings to provide a comprehensive and contemporary view of adolescence. Written to

appeal to parents and adolescents as well as to students and professionals.

Cognitive development
Johanna Turner
Methuen, 1975
Part of the Methuen 'Essential Psychology', this book discusses theories of cognitive development.

Contrary imaginations: a psychological study of the English schoolboy
Liam Hudson
Penguin, 1967
The author argues that personality is as important as ability in deciding what subjects children choose at school. A distinction is made between scientific 'convergent' thinking and artistic 'divergent' thinking.

The moral judgement of the child
Jean Piaget
Routledge and Kegan Paul, 1950
A classic book on moral development.

Moving into adulthood: themes and variations in self-directed development for effective living
Gerard Egan and Michael Cowan
Brooks-Cole Publishing Co, 1980
Looks at the developmental tasks encountered during the transition into adulthood. An American based handbook for teenagers which uses a life tasks approach.

Nature of adolescence
John Coleman
Methuen, 1980
Interprets research findings and discusses different theoretical approaches to understanding adolescence. Comprehensive and interesting, but rather academic.

People in systems: a model for development in the human-service professions and education
Gerard Egan and Michael Cowan
Brooks-Cole Publishing Co, 1979
Provides a model for understanding human psychology in the context of social systems. A fairly difficult book, but useful for those involved with adolescents.

Studies in adolescence: a book of readings in adolescent development
Robert Grinder (ed)
Macmillan, 1975
A collection of theoretical papers and articles which present and interpret research on a wide range of adolescent issues, including schooling, drug-taking, suicide, intellectual and physical development.

Tom Crabtree on teenagers
Tom Crabtree
Elm Tree Books, 1980

An interesting look at the issues of adolescence, but from a rather anecdotal approach.

Adult's own life

Middle age: the prime of life?
Marjorie Fiske
Harper and Row, 1979
Discusses coping with and understanding what has been termed the 'mid-life crisis'.

Passages: predictable crises of adult life
Gail Sheehy
Corgi, 1977
On the basis of American interview data, discusses the pattern of adult life stages and emphasises identity development as a life-long process. A lively and positive book.

Women of a certain age: the midlife search for self
Lilian Rubin
Harper Colophon Books, 1981
A detailed and interesting presentation of interview-based research on women whose families are leaving home. Considers the issue of whether there is an 'empty nest syndrome'.

Alcohol *see* Drinking

Anorexia Nervosa *see* Diet

Bereavement *see* One-parent families

Birth control and abortion

British Pregnancy Advisory Services
Head Office
Austy Manor
Wootton Wawen
Solihull
West Midlands B95 6DA
A non-profit making trust which offers information and help on matters relating to sex and birth control, specialising in the provision of an abortion counselling and referral service. BPAS carries out vasectomies and artificial insemination and has established a sperm bank. It produces a wide range of leaflets.

Brook Advisory Centres
153a East Street
London SE17 2SD
There are Brook Advisory Centres in several cities. They offer advice to young unmarried people of any age on sex and birth control, and offer a counselling service. A pregnancy testing service is also available. Many publications are available from the Centre including: *Safe sex for teenagers; Teenage birth control; A look at safe sex.*

Family Planning Association
Margaret Pyke House

27–35 Mortimer Street
London W1N 7RJ
Offers a professional service of medical help and advice. It aims to educate people in methods of contraception and to promote sexual health. It publishes numerous leaflets on matters relating to sex including one on sexually-transmitted diseases.

Marie Stopes House
The Well Woman Centre
108 Whitfield Street
London W1P 6BE
Supplies information and advice on abortion and birth control (including morning-after methods, vasectomy and sterilisation) and provides well-woman care (i.e. cancer screening, etc) and psycho-sexual counselling.

New Grapevine
416 St. John Street
London EC1 4NJ
A sex education, information and counselling service for young people.

Pregnancy Advisory Service
40 Margaret Street
London W1
PAS offers counselling and medical help to women with problems of unwanted pregnancy.

Careers *see* Employment and unemployment

Counselling *see* Crisis counselling; Family counselling; Youth counselling

Crisis counselling

OPUS (National Co-ordinating Committee of Organisations for Parents under Stress)
35 Mill Hill Road
Eaton Ford
St. Neots
Huntingdon
Cambridgeshire PE19 3AG
There are some fifty self-help groups registered with OPUS. You can be put in touch with your local group through the National Co-ordinating Committee. The groups aim to help parents under stress who might physically or emotionally abuse their children. The NCCOPUS assists and supports self-help groups, keeps them informed through a quarterly newsletter *Parent News-link* and produces information sheets.

Parents Anonymous (London)
8 Manor Gardens
Holloway Road
London N7 6LA
PAL runs a Lifeline telephone service manned by volunteers on 01-263-8918 which is designed to offer help to parents who are likely to abuse their children. Although help

is given initially over the telephone, a be-friender scheme does exist to provide further help. PAL also hopes to educate sixth-formers and parents-to-be about the negative side of parenthood as well as the positive.

Release
1 Elgin Avenue
London W9 3PR
Release is a national twenty-four hour welfare and advice agency which can be contacted at anytime on 01-603-8654. It aims to provide counselling, advice, education and information on a multitude of problems including drug use and abuse, criminal law, immigration and abortion.

The Samaritans
17 Uxbridge Road
Slough SL1 1SN
A national organisation with local branches all over the country which provide a twenty-four hour telephone help service. Samaritans are ready to help people who are in despair over anything or who just need someone to talk to. If required, they can put you in touch with appropriate counselling services or professional help. The number of your local Samaritans is in the telephone directory, or ask the operator to put you through.

Diet

Anorexic Aid
The Priory Centre
11 Priory Road
High Wycombe
Bucks
Offers support and information to anorexia nervosa sufferers and their families. Self-help groups are organised regionally and co-ordinated by a newsletter. You may contact them direct.

British Dietetic Association
305 Daimler House
Paradise Street
Birmingham B1 2BJ
A professional association which produces leaflets on aspects of diet.

British Nutrition Foundation
15 Belgrave Square
London SW1X 8PS
The Foundation promotes education and research in the field of nutrition. It publishes leaflets on healthy eating and provides a booklist on nutrition.

Vegetarian Society
53 Marloes Road
London W8 6LA
The Society promotes education and research in the field of nutrition. It produces numerous leaflets and books on vegetarianism, nutrition, cookery and other such subjects.

Weight Watchers
635-7 Ajax Avenue
Slough SL1 4DB
A national organisation which runs classes all over the country to help people lose weight and maintain the loss. Teenagers, of both sexes, are welcome to attend the classes.

Act thin, stay thin: new ways to manage your urge to eat
Richard Stuart
Hart-Davis MacGibbon Ltd, 1978
A very practical book that helps you look at why, when and how you eat, and then helps you plan to lose weight.

Fat is a feminist issue: the anti-diet guide to permanent weight loss
Susie Orbach
Hamlyn, 1979
An original and sensible discussion of why women become compulsive eaters, why they get fat and often regain lost weight, as well as a look at anorexia nervosa. Interesting case-histories and useful self-help exercises.

Disability *see* Handicap

Disturbance and breakdown

Adolescent disturbance and breakdown
Moses Laufer
Penguin Books (in association with MIND), 1975
Written by a psychoanalyst very experienced in working with teenagers, this book describes normal psychological development and discusses the causes and symptoms which characterise mental disturbance and vulnerability to breakdown.

Growing pains: a study of teenage distress
Edna Irwin
Macdonald and Evans, 1977
Designed not only for those who are professionally involved in caring for the disturbed adolescent but also for the parent who may be completely unprepared to cope with the problems that will be encountered within the family.

Drinking

Al-Anon Family Groups UK and Eire
61 Great Dover Street
London SE1 4YF
An organisation which enables the relatives and friends of alcoholics to meet and learn from each other about ways of facing their common problems. Members have demonstrated that changed family attitudes can bring about recovery. A list of publications and details of group meetings are available from the above address.

Alateen
61 Great Dover Street
London SE1 4YF
Alateen is an organisation under the wing of Al-Anon, but was formed especially for twelve to twenty year olds to enable them to discuss the problems and experiences of living in a family where a member has a drinking problem.

Alcoholics Anonymous
11 Redcliffe Gardens
London SW10 9BG
A nation-wide society made up of several hundred groups. The only qualification for membership is a sincere desire to stop drinking. AA publishes several leaflets including one entitled *Young people and AA*.

National Council on Alcoholism
3 Grosvenor Crescent
London SW1X 7EE
The Council has a network of regional centres which provide information and advice to alcoholics, their families or employers. Its main purpose is to create greater public awareness of the problems associated with alcoholism and its prevention.

Scottish Council on Alcoholism
147 Blythswood Street
Glasgow G2 4EN
Provides a service for Scotland similar to that of the National Council on Alcoholism. Give information, advice and provides educational materials.

Teachers' Advisory Council on Alcohol and Drug Education (TACADE)
2 Mount Street
Manchester M2 5NG
TACADE is a resources and information centre concerned with health education. It publishes basic facts leaflets on alcohol, drugs and smoking and guidelines for parents on alcohol and drugs.

Turning Point (Helping Hand Organisation Ltd)
8 Strutton Ground
London SW1P 2HP
A voluntary organisation working to rehabilitate recovering drug addicts and alcoholics. Its aim is to help and counsel such people in its residential or day-care centres.

Drugs

City Roads (Crisis Intervention)
William Hart House
358 City Road
London EC1V 2PY
City Roads provides sheltered accommodation with ready access to nursing, psychiatric, medical and social work support for young multiple drug users. The maximum stay is three weeks.

Drugline
28 Ballina Street
London SE23 1DR
Addicts or their parents can dial 01-291-2341 after 6p.m. if they want to discuss their problems concerning drugs, or be given advice on which agencies can best deal with their particular problem.

Drugs Information and Advisory Service Ltd (Formerly Association for the Prevention of Addiction Ltd)
111 Cowbridge Road East
Cardiff CF1 9AG
DIAS aims to prevent drug abuse through education and to provide help through counselling. A twenty-four hour telephone answering service is provided on Cardiff (0222) 26113. Many booklets are available.

Institute for the Study of Drug Dependence (ISSD)
Kingsbury House
3 Blackburn Road
London NW6 1XA
ISSD exists to provide a centre for the study of drug dependence and to advance public understanding of the subject by disseminating information.

Standing Conference on Drug Abuse (SCODA)
3 Blackburn Road
London NW6 1XA
SCODA meets several times per year. It provides support and consultation to both established and new projects, collects together information and advises those wishing to make referrals to drug treatment and rehabilitation services.

TACADE *for details see* Drinking

Teaching about a volatile situation: suggested health education strategies for minimising casualties associated with solvent sniffing
Institute for the Study of Drug Dependence, 1980
A sane paper about a topic which worries many parents unnecessarily because of its extensive media coverage.

Youth who use drugs
Stephen Proskauer and Ruick Rolland
in **Studies in adolescence: a book of readings in adolescent development**
Robert Grinder (ed)
Collier-Macmillan, 1975
A key paper by highly experienced case workers which examines the categories of young drug abusers.

Education

Advisory Centre for Education (ACE)
18 Victoria Park Square
London E2 9PB

ACE encourages co-operation between home and school. It is an independent source of information for parents and other individuals concerned with education. It publishes *Where to find out more about Education* in which topics of current educational concern are discussed. ACE aims to bring the consumer's viewpoint to the notice of government, LEAs and teachers. In addition ACE publishes numerous books and information leaflets.

Campaign for the Advancement of State Education (CASE)
Elizabeth Wallis
Information Officer
25 Layborne Park
Kew Gardens
Richmond
Surrey TW9 3HA
CASE is concerned that parents should know their rights with regard to education. It also wants to encourage debate about all sectors of education and to stimulate public interest in the subject. There are many local branches. A quarterly newsletter *Parents and Schools* is published.

Home and School Council
Hon. Sec. Mrs B. Bullivant
81 Rustlings Road
Sheffield S11 7AB
The Council was formed to co-ordinate the work of ACE, CASE and NCPTA (see below). The general objects of the Council are the advancement of education both locally and nationally and the achievement of closer relations between homes and schools in the interests of children. The Council has published numerous booklets including *A school-leaver's handbook*.

National Bureau for Handicapped Students
40 Brunswick Square
London WC1N 1AZ
The Bureau aims to act as an information centre, to offer or arrange specialist advice, to promote the extension of careers guidance and placement, and to initiate study and research in education and employment. The Bureau publishes a newsletter *Educare* which covers news and information on many aspects of a student's experience.

National Confederation of Parent Teacher Associations (NCPTA)
Gen. Sec. John Hale, MBE JP
43 Stonebridge Road
Northfleet Gravesend
Kent DA11 9DS
NCPTA aims to develop good relations between home and school, and acts as a channel for the expression of parent opinion. Publications include a variety of leaflets on educational topics and the Association's official journal *Home and School* which is sent to every member school.

National Union of Students
3 Endsleigh Street
London WC1H 0DU
NUS aims to promote and maintain the educational, social and general interests of students. It disseminates information on matters of educational and social concern and deals with individual cases.

Scottish Parent-Teacher Council
4 Queensferry Street
Edinburgh EH2 4PA
Provides a service for Scotland similar to that provided by NCPTA (*see* above)

Deschooling society
Ivan Illich
Penguin, 1971
A celebrated book which discusses the possibility of abandoning the present school system and looks at the alternatives.

Effective study skills
Philip Hills and Howard Barlow
Pan, 1980
Aimed mainly at 'O' level students, this book covers a range of skills involved in studying effectively, including help with punctuation, spelling and handwriting.

Fifteen thousand hours: secondary schools and their effects on children
Michael Rutter
Open Books, 1979
Presents the findings of a detailed investigation of the progress of children in twelve secondary schools. Vital reading for anyone seriously interested in educational issues.

Governing schools
Open University, 1981
An Open University short course which discusses the issues involved in governing schools.

How to study effectively
Chris Parsons
Arrow Books, 1976
A help to students at all levels. Gives exercises and examples for all stages of studying: particularly helpful on planning your study time.

Parent-teacher communication: one school and its practice
Rex Gibson
Cambridge Institute of Education, 1980
An interesting look at what one school tells its parents. The issues of what teachers and schools should tell parents, and why, are discussed.

Pastoral care in schools and colleges: with specific reference to health education and drugs, alcohol and smoking
Kenneth David and James Cowley
Edward Arnold, 1980

A practical and supportive book, written primarily for teachers and counsellors which emphasises the importance of a 'social' education. Of interest to parents as well.

School reports and other information for parents
Laurie Green
Home and School Council, 1975
Discusses communication between home and school.

Where to find out more about education
ACE, 10 issues per year
Frequently contains articles on options and job education choice.

Employment and unemployment

Careers and Occupational Information Centre
c/o Manpower Services Commission
Moorfoot
Sheffield S1 4PQ
COIC produces leaflets and books intended to help individual members of the public to make informed decisions about jobs and careers.

Careers Research and Advisory Centre (CRAC)
Bateman Street
Cambridge CB2 1LZ
CRAC aims to assist and improve careers education by means of courses and conferences, publications and programmes of education and training and of research and development work. Its publications include guides for students and parents to educational and employment opportunities at home and abroad, such as *Time between* and *The job book*; and also guidance on how to choose specific subjects at school in such publications as *Your choice at 13+*, *15+* and *17+*, also *Your choice of A-levels*.

CASCAID
CASCAID is a computerised vocational guidance system operated by Leicestershire Careers Department. It provides guidance and counselling on career and training choice. It is intended for pupils with three or more O-levels and has a bank of nearly 400 careers. It is accessible through your local education authority, if they are subscribers.

Centres for the Unemployed
TUC
Congress House
Great Russell Street
London WC1B 3LS
There are many of these centres throughout the country providing advice to the unemployed. It is hoped that the centres will involve the unemployed in a wide range of educational and social activities.

National Advisory Centre on Careers for Women (formerly Women's Employment Federation)
Drayton House
30 Gordon Street
London WC1H 0AX
NACCW is a non-profit making educational charity. The information centre will answer specific queries by post, but will also arrange individual consultations. In cases of real need fees can be reduced. Paperbacks on special aspects of careers are published.

National Council of Young Men's Christian Associations
640 Forest Road
London E17 3DZ
Besides providing hostel accommodation and recreational facilities, the YMCA is also active in the areas of youth unemployment and youth at work. Its *Training for Life Scheme* provides the young unemployed with a variety of work experience and training in social skills.

Trident Trust
11 York Terrace East
London NW1
Project Trident aims to help schools to provide for pupils of all abilities an appropriate amount of work experience, community service and recreational education, enabling young people to discover the world of work, the community in which they live and themselves and their own power to do things in that world and community. Project Trident is set up at the request of LEAs.

Youth Opportunities Programme
YOP is a scheme administered by the Manpower Services Commission which offers a range of work experience and work preparation courses. The Programme is open to all young people who are under the age of nineteen and who have been unemployed for at least six weeks. The aim of the scheme is to improve young people's prospects of finding employment. Access to this scheme is through your local MSC office, or your jobcentre or employment office.

Career choice
Audrey Segal
Pan, 1981
A very exhaustive introduction which is intended to help parents. It contains chapters headed: tomorrow's world of work; where the family fits in; careers diary year by year; choosing and deciding.

Career information: a job information index
Michael Kirton (ed)
Heinemann Educational, 1979
A series of quizzes designed to test your understanding and knowledge of the jobs you are considering.

Equal opportunities: a careers guide for women and men
Ruth Miller
Penguin, 1981
A comprehensive guide to a wide range of jobs, with special emphasis on opportunities for women.

Which career for you
Catherine Avent
Robert Hale, 1978
Though aimed at career choosers, it gives a good introduction to what determines choice. It looks at the different values children might attach to different aspects of career choice. Written in a chatty, yet informative, way.

Equality *see* Rights

Family counselling/advice/welfare

Child Poverty Action Group
1 Macklin Street
London WC2B 5NH
CPAG aims to promote action for the relief of poverty among children and families with children. It researches into family poverty in Britain and publishes facts about it. It also investigates methods of preventing poverty, and provides information on existing benefits, including appeal machinery. It publishes a periodical called *Poverty*.

Church of England Children's Society
Old Town Hall
Kennington Road
London SE11 4QD
The Society works to keep families together by providing counselling and practical support for families at home and in the community. It provides residential care, fostering, adoption and day-care for under 5's. It also runs some Family Centres which offer self-help play-groups, mother-and-toddler groups, recreation for teenagers from difficult or disturbed backgrounds and counselling for parents.

Family Network
National Children's Home
85 Highbury Park
London N5 1UD
Family Network is a phone-in service for families with problems. The phone is manned twenty-four hours a day by volunteers who will give help and advice if they can, or put you in touch with an agency which can help if they can't. Look for the phone number in the local press or ring the organiser on 01-226-2033.

Family Service Units
National Office
207 Old Marylebone Road
London NW1 5QP

FSU provides an intensive service for families in severe personal, social or financial difficulty. There are several units around the country.

Family Welfare Association
501–505 Kingsland Road
Dalston
London E8 4AU
Although the FWA primarily exists to help families in need, it does also work with isolated and lonely individuals, the elderly, adolescents and the recently bereaved. The Association has centres in London and Milton Keynes.

National Children's Bureau
8 Wakley Street
London EC1V 7QE
This is an organisation which brings together people from all areas of concern with children. The Bureau maintains a library and provides an information service. It has a considerable research and publishing programme which includes its journal *Concern*. It runs a network of local groups.

National Children's Centre
Longroyd Bridge
Huddersfield
West Yorkshire
The NCC is an advice and information centre. It maintains a register of parent self-help groups up and down the country to which parents can turn if they are feeling overwhelmed by the pressures of coping with children. The Centre will also provide information on how to set up a self-help group.

National Children's Home
85 Highbury Park
London N5 1UD
NCH runs homes for children and adolescents, and has Family Centres in large cities providing day-care for children. It runs Family Network (see above) all over the country. Through its Family Aid service it works to strengthen families in such a way as to avoid the necessity of children having to be received into care. One of its many publications is a book entitled *It's a great life*, which attempts to guide young people through their sexual development.

Soldiers', Sailors' and Airmen's Families Association (SSAFA)
27 Queen Anne's Gate
London SW1H 9BZ
SSAFA provides a comprehensive service for the families of Service and ex-Service men and women. There are hundreds of branches throughout the country and at Service stations overseas.

Westminster Pastoral Foundation
23 Kensington Square
London W8 5HN

Offers a counselling service to people in need of help with emotional problems of any sort.

Gambling

Gam-Anon
17–23 Blantyre Street
Cheyne Walk
London SW10
Gam-Anon was formed to work in conjunction with Gamblers' Anonymous (see below) to try and help families to cope with the difficulties of living with (or maybe without) a compulsive gambler.

Gamblers' Anonymous
17–23 Blantyre Street
Cheyne Walk
London SW10
A fellowship of men and women who have joined together to try to overcome their own gambling problems and to help other gamblers to do the same.

Gay *see* Sexual and personal relationship counselling

Glue sniffing *see* Drugs

Handicap

The following are a few of the umbrella organisations dealing with handicap. To trace the numerous organisations dealing with specific disabilities you should check in *Directory for the disabled* (*see* Finding more organisations and books).

Disabled Living Foundation
346 Kensington High Street
London W14 8NS
The Foundation is concerned with all disabilities (mental, physical and sensory) together with multiple handicaps and the infirmities of old age. It provides an information service for the disabled, undertakes enquiries and maintains a library. It also maintains an Aids Centre.

MIND (National Association for Mental Health)
22 Harley Street
London W1N 2ED
MIND offers information, advice and counselling to people with all types of problems connected with mental disorder. It also runs several residential establishments for mentally ill or handicapped people.

National Society for Mentally Handicapped Children and Adults (MENCAP)
123 Golden Lane
London EC1Y 0RT
Mencap provides a wide range of services for mentally handicapped people and their families including its Pathway scheme which provides work training for teenagers.

Sexual and Personal Relationships of the Disabled (formerly Sexual Problems of the Disabled)
The Diorama
14 Peto Place
London NW1 4DT
SPOD provides information, advice and access to counselling on the sexual and personal relationships of the disabled. It is particularly aware of the problems of teenagers and one of its advisory leaflets is entitled *Your handicapped child and sex*. It produces a quarterly *Information Bulletin*.

Health

Health Education Council
78 New Oxford Street
London WC1 1AH
The Council is concerned with health education in England, Wales and Northern Ireland. It produces posters and leaflets for the public on a wide variety of health subjects and interests including fitness and health, nutrition, smoking, alcohol, sexually-transmitted diseases and drugs. It organises campaigns to increase awareness of health. It also runs a library and funds research.

Scottish Health Education Group
Woodburn House
Canaan Lane
Edinburgh EH10 4SG
SHEG serves Scotland and has similar aims and functions to the Health Education Council.

The art of sensual massage
Gordon Inkeles and Todris Murray
Unwin Paperbacks, 1979
A good relaxed book on massaging techniques which is profusely illustrated with photos that you'll either love or dislike.

The good health guide
The Open University in association with the Health Education Council and the Scottish Health Education Unit
Harper and Row, 1980
This book forms part of the Open University short course 'Health Choices'. The emphasis is on health rather than on illness and that health is to do with feelings, relationships and lifestyles, and the choices we can make.

Know your body
Dorothy Baldwin
Penguin, 1981
An A–Z guide which provides simple, straightforward information and advice about health for young teenagers.

Living well
Health Education Council Project 12–18
Cambridge University Press, 1977
Widely used in schools, these health education materials look at both emotional and physical health.

The massage book
George Downing
Penguin, 1972
Excellent, straightforward instructions on how to massage your partner or yourself.

Our bodies ourselves: a health book by and for women
Boston Women's Health Book Collective. British edition edited by A. Phillips and J. Rakusen
Penguin, 1980
A refreshingly different approach to women's health which concentrates on finding out about yourself, your body and feelings. Includes women's personal experiences as well as research finding.

Homosexuality *see* Sexual and personal relationship counselling

Identity

Identity
Myra Barrs (ed)
Penguin Education, 1973
A thought-provoking collection of poetry, prose and illustration on the subject of the development of and feelings about identity. An excellent source book.

Identity: youth and crisis
Erik H. Erikson
Faber & Faber, 1968
A classic collection of essays which examine the concept of identity and discuss identity development and crisis.

Identity and the life cycle
Erik H. Erikson
W.W. Norton, 1980
A classic book on the development of personality.

Juvenile delinquents *see* Offenders

Leisure-time activities

British Red Cross Society
9 Grosvenor Crescent
London SW1X 7EJ
The Red Cross offers a wide variety of courses on health and safety. Young members can be involved in first aid duties, blood donor sessions and welfare activities, particularly with the elderly or handicapped children.

British Sports Association for the Disabled
Stoke Mandeville Stadium
Harvey Road
Aylesbury
Bucks
The Association caters for a wide variety of sport for the disabled. Its work is organised in regions.

Community Projects Foundation
60 Highbury Grove
London N5 2AG
Exists to help all kinds of local community groups and produces free factsheet *Getting involved*.

Community Service Volunteers
237 Pentonville Road
London N1 9NJ
CSV is a national volunteer agency which aims to involve young people in community service and to encourage social change. It runs an advisory service which disseminates literature, information and ideas to help schools and colleges to develop their own programmes. Its youth employment programme deploys around one thousand young people in full-time work in the social services, with Government funding.

Duke of Edinburgh's Award Scheme
5 Prince of Wales Terrace
London W8 5PG
The scheme aims to provide a programme of leisure activities offering a wide range of choice for those aged fourteen to twenty-five, with the prospect of attaining three awards: bronze, silver, gold. It is operated in schools, youth organisations, firms and through award scheme centres and committees who make provision for individual participants. To gain an award participants, including the handicapped, must successfully attempt four sections: service, interests, expeditions and either design for living or physical activity.

Girl Guides Association
17–19 Buckingham Palace Road
London SW1W 0PT
The Association runs a nationwide network of groups for girls of eleven and over. The activities of the groups are designed to help develop character, skills and initiative in accordance with the principles of the movement.

Holidays without Parents
It is possible for youngsters to take supervised holidays without their parents being present. To find out the wide range of holidays which are available you should consult the following books:

Activity and special interest holidays in Wales, annual, Welsh Tourist Board

Adventure and special interest holidays in Scotland, annual, Scottish Tourist Board

Education yearbook, annual, Councils and Education Press

England: holidays, annual, English Tourist Board

Or see your travel agent.

National Association of Boys' Clubs
24 Highbury Grove
London N5 2EA
The Association aims to promote the mental, physical and spiritual well-being of boys and young men and to provide opportunities to widen their interests, sharpen their initiative and use their leisure time more profitably.

National Association of Youth Clubs
Keswick House
30 Peacock Lane
Leicester LE1 5NY
This is a national body to which many local youth associations are affiliated. It gives support to local initiatives and publishes books and a magazine entitled *Youth Clubs*.

National Council for Voluntary Youth Services
Wellington House
29 Albion Street
Leicester LE1 6GD
The council operates as the national intermediary body for National Voluntary Youth Organisations and Local Councils for Voluntary Youth Service in England.

National Council of Young Men's Christian Associations *for details see* Employment and unemployment

National Federation of Eighteen Plus Groups
Nicholson House
Old Court Road
Newent
Gloucestershire GL18 1AG
18+ groups are open to young adults between the ages of eighteen and thirty and are organised by the members themselves. The groups are financially self-supporting and have no allegiance to any political, religious or other body. The essential part of group life is meeting new friends and widening personal interests and knowledge.

National Federation of Gateway Clubs
117 Golden Lane
London EC1Y 0RT
Gateway Clubs provide leisure activities for the mentally handicapped and occasionally for the physically handicapped. Both handicapped and able-bodied teenagers are encouraged to take part in the activities.

PHAB (Physically Handicapped and Able-Bodied)
42 Devonshire Street
London W1N 1LN
PHAB exists to further the integration of the physically handicapped into the community by providing opportunities for the physically handicapped and the able-bodied to come together on equal terms. Although the clubs are basically run for those aged sixteen to twenty-five, some groups run clubs for juniors and/or those over twenty-five.

St John Ambulance Brigade
1 Grosvenor Crescent
London SW1X 7EF
The Brigade teaches first aid, nursing, hygiene, etc. to children of eight and up-wards to enable them to provide assistance at anytime. It publishes books on first aid and health.

Scout Association
Baden Powell House
Queen's Gate
London SW7 5JS
The Association organises groups for boys on a country-wide basis. Besides the scouts there are specialist groups such as Sea Scouts, Air Scouts, Venture Scouts and Extension Scouts (for the physically handi-capped aged eight to twenty). The aim of the Association is to provide adult leadership for activities which contribute to a healthy environment for young people.

Sports Council
16 Upper Woburn Place
London WC1H 0QP
The Council was established in 1972, and its aims are to encourage more people to engage in sport and to improve facilities. The Council should be able to give you the address of an organisation concerned with any particular sport which interests you. A considerable range of publications is avail-able to people visiting the Information Centre. The Sports Council provides tech-nical and advisory services to local author-ities, voluntary sports bodies and other organisations. The separate Councils for Scotland, Wales and Northern Ireland share the same aims and perform the same functions.

The Volunteer Centre
29 Lower King's Road
Berkhamsted
Hertfordshire HP4 2AB
A national advisory agency on volunteer activities. It maintains an information department and a Volunteer Bureau which will advise on voluntary schemes which exist in particular areas.

Woodcraft Folk
13 Ritherdon Road
London SW17 8QE
The Folk run groups for girls and boys all over the country. The emphasis is on out-door activities and contact with children from other countries, usually at camps.

Young Women's Christian Association of Great Britain
Hampden House
2 Weymouth Street
London W1N 4AX
Provides hostel accommodation and leisure activities.

Youth Environmental Action
173 Archway Road
London N6 5BL
YEA is a national federation of concerned youth groups and individuals aiming to assist, promote and co-ordinate environ-mental action and education amongst the youth of today. The society publishes infor-mation sheets, guides and a newsletter.

Youth Hostels Association (YHA)
Trevelyan House
St. Albans
Herts
In spite of its name, the Association has no upper age limit and its aim is to provide simple, but adequate, overnight accommo-dation for individuals, families or groups.

Lifeskills and values

Active tutorial work. Books 1 to 5
Jill Baldwin and Harry Wells
Basil Blackwell in association with Lancashire County Council, 1980
A five year programme of project work for use in schools on lifeskills and helping teen-agers sort out their values.

Choices and decisions
Michael Bargo
University Associates, 1980
This book discusses what values are, and how they relate to beliefs and attitudes.

The farther reaches of human nature
Abraham Maslow
Viking Press, 1971
A classic book which suggests that there is a hierarchy of human needs, and discusses how they are fulfilled.

Lifeskills teaching
Barrie Hopson
McGraw-Hill, 1981
An interesting theoretical discussion of why lifeskills need to be taught.

Lifeskills teaching programmes
Barrie Hopson and Mike Scally
Lifeskills Associates, 1980
Designed for use in schools and colleges, this handbook provides information and activities which parents may find useful in their own lives.

Meeting yourself halfway
Sidney Simon
Argus Communications, 1974
A very American book full of activities to help sort out your values.

Values clarification: a handbook of practical strategies for teachers and students
Sidney Simon et al.
Hart Publishing, 1972

A basic American textbook which explains the theory and practice of sorting out of values. Lots of useful activities but the American jargon may need adaptation for use in a British setting.

Mental health

MIND (National Association for Mental health) *for details see* Handicap

Offenders

Family Rights Group
6–9 Manor Gardens
Holloway Road
London N7 6LA
FRG works to improve the law and practice relating to children in care. The Group believes that more support should be given to parents so that children would only need to be taken into care as a final resort.

Justice for Children
35 Wellington Street
London WC2E 7BN
This is a pressure group which aims to achieve reforms in the juvenile justice sys-tem. It runs study and research groups; provides an information and advice service for parents, children, social workers and lawyers; publishes a newsletter and papers on different topics relevant to the cause.

National Association for the Care and Resettlement of Offenders (NACRO)
169 Clapham Road
London SW9
Brings together voluntary organisations, statutory services and individual members with an interest in the care and resettlement of offenders and in the prevention of crime. Provides an information service and pub-lishes material on a wide range of criminal justice subjects.

National Association of Young People in Care (NAYPIC)
c/o Coventry Resource and Information Service
Cox Street
Coventry

One-parent families

CRUSE
Cruse House
126 Sheen Road
Richmond
Surrey TW9 1UR
Cruse is a national organisation with over sixty branches providing counselling, prac-tical advice and social activities for widows, widowers and their families. Cruse pub-lishes booklists, books and leaflets, one of which *My father died* helps older children and teenagers to cope with bereavement.

Gingerbread
35 Wellington Street
London WC2
A nationally organised self-help association for one-parent families with a large number of local groups. Gingerbread offers practical help, information and advice on all kinds of problems faced by people bringing up children on their own, and on coping with divorce.

National Association of Widows
c/o Stafford District Voluntary Services Centre
Chell Road
Stafford ST16 2QA
Although the Association was founded to combat the financial problems of widows, its aims have expanded to cover all aspects of widowhood. Through the Widows Advisory Service widows can seek help with both practical and emotional problems. Its publication *A handbook for widows* covers the problems of widowhood including those of being a lone parent. The Association has ninety-one branches.

National Council for One-Parent Families (formerly National Council for the Unmarried Mother and her Child)
255 Kentish Town Road
London NW5 2LX
The Council watches over legislation and administration on behalf of one-parent families and offers a service to parents and the social workers who are advising and helping them. It aims to inform the general public in order to make people more sympathetic to their needs. Scotland has its own organisation the *Scottish Council for Single Parents*, 44 Albany Street, Edinburgh EH1 3QR.

One-parent families: a practical guide to coping
Diana Davenport
Pan, 1979
One of the best books on one-parent families. This is a really practical book with a good appendix on sources of help for single parents.

Parenting

Between parent and teenager
Haim Ginott
Avon Books, 1969
Uses a common-sense approach to suggest ways of dealing with the problems of adolescence. Its American style makes it either particularly useful – or annoying.

P.E.T. parent-effectiveness training: the tested new way to raise responsible children
Thomas Gordon
Plume Books, 1977
A readable American book which gives practical help for parents and emphasises that children are people too.

Parents vs children: making the relationship work
Marvin Fine
Prentice-Hall, 1979
Reassuring and constructive. Using a chatty style and plenty of examples, the author suggests activities which will enhance parenting skills.

Self-esteem: a family affair
Jean Ulstey Clarke
Winston Press, 1978
Using theory and techniques based on Transactional Analysis, talks about how self-esteem can develop within the family. Fun to read and rewarding, if its being obviously American doesn't bother you.

T.A. for teens (and other important people)
Alvyn Freed
Jalmar Press Inc, 1976
Using Transactional Analysis as an aid to understanding people, this wittily illustrated book provides a lively and practical guide for parents and teenagers.

You and me: the skills of communicating and relating to others
Gerard Egan
Brooks-Cole, 1977
This book aims to develop our awareness of others, and assertiveness, through the use of activities and discussion of examples. Especially good if used as a group activity.

Pregnant

If you think you are pregnant, you should go to your family doctor immediately. If you do not want to see him and are unhappy or unsure about being pregnant, you should go to your nearest Brook Advisory Centre or British Pregnancy Advisory Service (*see* Birth control and abortion). If you want to keep your baby and need more help than your family or doctor can offer, contact Life (*see* Sexual and personal relationship counselling).

Rape

Rape Crisis Centre
PO Box 42
London N6 5BU
The Centre provides a twenty-four hour phone-in service on 01-340-6145. Emergency and on-going support is given to any woman or girl who has been raped or sexually assaulted (including victims of incest). Information is given about pregnancy prevention after rape, pregnancy testing, sexually-transmitted diseases and abortion.

Rights

British Council of Organisations of Disabled People
5 Crowndale Road
London NW1 1TU
This is a co-ordinating body whose concern is to bring together national organisations for the disabled in order to reach a consensus of opinion and thereby present a united front on matters concerning the rights of the disabled.

Campaign for Homosexual Equality
BM CHE
London W1N 3XX
An organisation which is concerned to fight for the rights of homosexuals by campaigning and increasing public awareness.

Commission for Racial Equality
Elliott House
10-12 Allington Street
London SW1E 5EH
The Commission was set up under the Race Relations Act 1976 to help enforce the legislation and to promote equality of opportunity and good relations between people of different racial groups. It acts as a principal source of information and advice and has discretion to assist individuals who consider themselves victims of discrimination.

Equal Opportunities Commission
Overseas House
Quay Street
Manchester M3 3HN
EOC exists to fight sex discrimination – e.g. in your pay packet, prospects of promotion, chances of getting a mortgage – and generally to encourage equal opportunities for men and women. The Commission publishes leaflets and booklets with advice on returning to work, sex discrimination, equal pay and your rights under the law.

Family Rights Group *for details see* Offenders

Justice for Children *for details see* Offenders

National Council for Civil Liberties
21 Tabard Street
London SE1 4LA
NCCL is an independent, voluntary organisation which defends basic freedoms – in particular freedom of speech, expression and association – and the rights of individuals. It publishes a number of pamphlets and factsheets on the rights of individuals.

ROW (Rights of Women)
374 Gray's Inn Road
London WC1
ROW is concerned to promote the rights of women.

Scottish Homosexual Rights Group
(formerly Scottish Minorities Group)
60 Broughton Street
Edinburgh EH1 3SA
SHRG exists to promote the rights of homo-sexuals. It publishes leaflets on various aspects of life and a monthly newsletter.

Connexions: the language of prejudice
Fred Hooper
Penguin, 1969
One of a series of topic books for schools, this is a thought-provoking source book about the power of language and prejudice.

Women's rights: a series of information sheets and discussion notes
Marion Lowe
Rights for Women Unit, National Council for Civil Liberties, 1980
Information on abortion, education, equal opportunities, equal pay, rape and domestic violence, social security, taxation, work and childcare. Available separately, or as a set.

Self-help

Grapevine
c/o BBC TV
London W12 8QT
The BBC runs a programme called Grape-vine: The Self-Help Show which is designed to encourage people to start self-help schemes and to distribute information about schemes which are already in existence. Grapevine puts out a wide range of leaflets containing useful addresses and advice on topics such as gay information centres, youth counselling and advice services, STD, anorexia nervosa, one-parent families and stopping smoking.

National Children's Centre *for details see* Family counselling/advice/welfare

Sex roles

Connexions: his and hers: an examination of masculinity and femininity
Joy Groombridge
Penguin, 1971
A schools topic book which looks at what society encourages and expects men and women to be like, and asks why.

The gender trap: a closer look at sex roles. Books 1–3
Carol Adams and Rae Laurikietis
Virago, 1976
A three-part series of books which analyse the expected behaviour and accepted sex-roles of men and women in our society. *Education and work, Messages and images* and *Sex and marriage* are thought-provoking and suggest interesting further reading.

Just like a girl: how girls learn to be women
Sue Sharpe
Penguin, 1976
Based on a survey carried out in schools, this book analyses some of the pressures girls face from society.

Little girls: social conditioning and its effects on the stereotyped role of women during infancy
Elena Gianini Belotti
Writers and Readers Publishing Cooperative, 1975
A thought-provoking discussion of sex roles and conditioning.

Sex, gender and society
Ann Oakley
Temple Smith, 1972
This book tries to untangle fact and value judgements in the sex differences debate.

Sexual and personal relationship counselling

Albany Trust
24 Chester Square
London SW1
The Trust is concerned to help people with psycho-sexual problems, especially those in medical service.

British Association for Counselling
1a Little Church Street
Rugby
Warwickshire CV21 3AP
The Association's aims are to promote the education and training of counsellors and to increase the awareness of the public to the part that counselling can play in society. It gives up-to-date information on how to get help and publishes a directory of psycho-sexual counselling agencies.

Catholic Marriage Advisory Council
15 Lansdown Road
London W11 3AJ
Offers a counselling service similar to that of the National Marriage Guidance Council (see below) with, in addition, a legal and medical service.

Gay Liberation Front Information Service
5 Caledonian Road
London N1
GLFIS acts as an information service for the Gay Movement in the U.K. and abroad. Initial contact is usually made through Gay Switchboard (01-837-7324) – a twenty-four hour advice and information service.

Jewish Marriage Council
529b Finchley Road
London NW3 7BG

The Council provides confidential marriage and family counselling. It also offers marriage education courses for young people, engaged couples and newlyweds aimed at preventing marital difficulties.

Joint Council for Gay Teenagers
BM JCGT
London WC1N 3XX
JCGT is a group of organisations, both local and national, which work to improve the situation of young gay teenagers. The Council provides an advice and information service and a certain amount of counselling, although enquirers are more likely to be referred to other agencies. It publishes a magazine *Gay Youth*.

Life
7 Parade
Leamington Spa
Warwickshire
Life exists to protect the life of the unborn child and in particular to achieve the repeal of the Abortion Act 1967. Local Life groups offer a telephone-based advice and help service. They also 1) offer advice about many problems: financial, housing, social security, medical; 2) offer private accommodation during pregnancy for unmarried mothers; 3) refer mothers to all sources of voluntary and statutory help in the area.

London Friend (Gay Counselling)
274 Upper Street
London N1 2UA
London Friend is a group of men and women who offer help to members of sexual minority groups by letter, telephone (01-359-7371 7.30p.m. to 10p.m.) or in person. The group can also put enquirers in touch with sympathetic legal advisers, psychologists, doctors, clergy etc. There are local organisations in several cities which can be contacted through London Friend or the magazine *Gay News*.

National Marriage Guidance Council
Herbert Gray College
Little Church Street
Rugby
Warwickshire CV21 3AP
The Council co-ordinates the work of about 150 local marriage guidance councils. It offers a professional counselling service to people needing help in marriage and family relationships including, where necessary, counselling over separation and divorce. NMGC publishes literature on a wide variety of topics relating to marriage and family life and produces book-lists.

Parents' Enquiry
16 Henley Road
Catford
London SE6 2HZ

Organiser Mrs Rose Robertson
Provides an advice, information and counselling service on 01-698-1815 for homosexual children and/or parents and families with a homosexual child. Parents' Enquiry has access to a network of helpers all over the country. The service is not, therefore, restricted to London.

The Responsible Society
Family and Youth Concern
Wicken
Milton Keynes MK19 6BU
The Society's primary aim is to encourage responsible behaviour in sexual relationships. It is an educational and research body and does not take part in demonstrations or public protests. It publishes pamphlets on areas of interests to the Society, one of which is a leaflet written by young people for teenagers entitled *Saying no isn't always easy . . .!*

Scottish Marriage Guidance Council
58 Palmerston Place
Edinburgh EH12 5AZ
The Council serves Scotland in the same way as the NMGC (see above) serves England and Wales.

Sexual and Personal Relationships of the Disabled (formerly Sexual Problems of the Disabled) *for details see* Handicap

Boys and sex
Wardell Pomeroy
Penguin, 1970
The companion book to *Girls and sex.* Frank and authoritative.

Children's sexual thinking
Ronald Goldman and Juliette Goldman
Routledge and Kegan Paul, 1982
On the basis of one thousand interviews, this book looks at British, Swedish, American and Australian children's attitudes, knowledge and beliefs about love, sex, contraception and marriage.

Divorce and your children
Anne Hooper
George Allen and Unwin, 1981
A practical and supportive book which includes advice on handling children's questions, case studies and information on law and useful organisations.

The facts of love: living, loving and growing up
Alex Comfort and Jane Comfort
Mitchell Beazley, 1979
Focusses on caring relationships and responsibility. While open and frank, it emphasises the importance of parents explaining their own values about sex to their teenagers.

Girls and sex
Wardell Pomeroy
Penguin, 1971
A good basic book for young teenagers, although some find it unrelaxed in style.

The joy of sex: a gourmet guide to lovemaking
Alex Comfort
Quartet Books, 1978
The common-sense approach and clear illustrations of this book are not just about sexual technique, but about happy relaxed love making. Aimed at adults, there is little emphasis on the importance of the relationship.

Learning to live with sex: a handbook of sex education for teenagers
Family Planning Association, 1980
Directed at teenagers, this book covers a wide range of topics using medical terms with a glossary of slang words.

Make it happy: what sex is all about
Jane Cousins
Penguin, 1980
Winner of a T.L.S. award, this sex education book is open and frank, and well-written for teenagers. However, some people have strong opinions about it. As with other sex education books, you should read it before passing it on to your teenager.

Making sense of sex: the new facts about sex and love for young people
Helen Kaplan
Quartet Books, 1979
A detailed and comprehensive book about the physiology and psychology of sexual development and sexual response. A clear and sensible 'sex is O.K.' approach.

Mia
Gunnel Beckman
Longman, 1976
A novel about a seventeen year old who fears she is pregnant.

My mother said . . .: the way young people learned about sex and birth control
Christine Farrell
Routledge and Kegan Paul, 1978
A well-written book which presents the results of research into how and where young people acquired knowledge about sex and birth control.

Older teenagers' sex questions answered
Robert Chartham
Corgi, 1973
Gives information and reassurance by means of a 'problem page' question and answer format. A good basic book.

Red Shift
Alan Garner
Armada Lions, 1975
A novel about how lack of communication enters a teenage relationship after the boy forces a super, intimate but non-sexual friendship to become sexual out of jealousy of a previous boyfriend.

Sex and the handicapped child
Wendy Greengross
National Marriage Guidance Council, 1980
This is more than a book about sex. It also discusses the particular problems of parents of handicapped children who must accept the sexuality and transition into adulthood of their children. Good for suggesting other sources of help.

The sexual behaviour of young adults: a follow-up study to 'The sexual behaviour of young people'
Michael Schofield
Allen Lane, 1973
This and the next book are almost essential reading for parents. These books contain hard data on what teenagers *do* as opposed to other people's opinions about teenage behaviour.

The sexual behaviour of young people
Michael Schofield
Penguin, 1968
Presents the results of interviews with nearly two thousand teenagers. Rather technical language in places, but contains a lot of reliable information.

Treat yourself to sex: a guide for good loving
Paul Brown and Carolyn Faulder
Penguin, 1979
A self-help sex therapy guide by authors who believe firmly that good sex is based on the skills of relating together, and that these skills can be learnt. A book for parents rather than teenagers.

Toward intimacy: family planning and sexuality concerns of physically disabled women
Task Force on Concerns of Physically Disabled Women
Human Sciences Press, 1978
A sensitive and understanding book which emphasises intimacy rather than sexual performance. Many quotes from individual disabled women.

Very long way from anywhere else
Ursula Le Guin
Penguin, 1978
A novel dealing with a friendship between two teenagers which is nearly ruined by peers' and parents' expectations of a sexual relationship.

Will I like it?
Peter Mayle
W. H. Allen, 1978
Aimed at inexperienced young people, this attractively presented book deals with the emotional, psychological and physiological reactions of adolescents to sex.

Sexually-transmitted diseases (STD)

STD Clinics

If you suspect you have a STD and don't want to go to your family doctor, the easiest place to have a check-up is a special STD clinic. These special clinics are held at most big hospitals. Advice and treatment are completely private and confidential and free. You can go to the clinic without a letter from your GP.

Smoking

Action on Smoking and Health (ASH)
27-35 Mortimer Street
London W1N 7RJ
ASH acts as an information agency, as a pressure group and promotes research. It will refer people to smoking cessation clinics and give advice on other smoking cessation methods. It has produced a *Giving up smoking* pack and a leaflet aimed at teenagers *Smoking: basic facts.*

TACADE *for details see* Drinking

No smoke: psychologically based manual of information and self-applied exercises for use in giving up smoking
Robert East and Bridget Towers
Kingston Polytechnic, 1979
Based on research into behaviour modification and social psychology, this guide gives constructive support to those who intend to give up smoking.

Suicide *see* Crisis counselling

Unemployment *see* Employment and unemployment

VD *see* Sexually-transmitted diseases

Women

A Woman's Place
48 William IV Street
London WC2
Provides a meeting ground for all women's groups. Runs a bookroom which includes liberation news-sheets and magazines from all over the country and from many places abroad. An information and referral service is also available.

The sceptical feminist
Janet Radcliffe Richards
Penguin, 1982
An academic but readable book which analyses the arguments associated with feminist issues.

Shocking pink
A magazine by and for young women with news, photo-stories, discussions of sex and sexuality, and music reviews amongst its contents. Subscription address: 90 Cromer Street, London WC1.

Spare rib
A monthly women's liberation magazine, produced by a collective, which discusses women's issues and gives good information on events, campaigns, and support groups. Subscription address: 27 Clerkenwell Close, London, EC1R 0AT.

Women as winners: transactional analysis for personal growth
Dorothy Jongerrard and Dill Scott
Addison-Wesley, 1977
Activities, case histories and 'techniques for positive change' are provided to help women increase their awareness and fulfil their potential.

Working abroad *see* Employment and unemployment

Youth

British Youth Council
57 Chalton Street
London NW1 1HU
BYC's aim is to represent the views of young people and, more widely, to look at ways of giving young people a voice in society at both local and national level. It publishes books, leaflets and information packages.

National Youth Bureau
17-23 Albion Street
Leicester LE1 6GD
NYB aims to act as a national resource centre for information, publication, training, research and development, and as a forum for association, discussion and joint action in the broad field of the social education of young people. It publishes a monthly journal *Youth in Society* and a monthly newspaper *Scene* plus books and pamphlets.

Youthaid
9 Poland Street
London W1V 3DG
Youthaid acts as an independent pressure group developing policy proposals, undertaking research and disseminating information on youth unemployment, education and training.

Youth counselling/advice/welfare

The majority of the services listed in this section are local to the London area. However, many similar services are available throughout the country. To find out what is available in your area you could make enquiries at any of the following: your library, CAB, Council of Social Services, Social Services Department or Youth and Community Office (*see* introductory section).

Alone in London Service
Advice and Information Centre
West Lodge
190 Euston Road
London NW1 2EF
Offers an advice and information service to new arrivals entering London through mainline termini plus a specialist service for young women who are homeless and at risk in London by providing initial support and emergency accommodation and helping to formulate a long-term plan for achieving a more stable way of life.

Brent Consultation Centre
Johnston House
51 Winchester Avenue
London NW6 7TT
The Centre offers help to people between the ages of fifteen and twenty three. It is not necessary to make an appointment and you can talk about whatever happens to be worrying you.

Centre Point Emergency Services
St. Anne's House
57 Dean Street
London W1
The Centre Point Night Shelter at 65a Shaftesbury Avenue, W1 provides basic accommodation, food and counselling support for up to twenty-five young people who are new to and at risk in central London. Centre Point also runs a hostel at 14 Sinclair Road, W14.

Great Chapel Street Medical Centre
13 Great Chapel Street
London W1
Any young person without a G.P. can attend the Medical Centre on a walk-in basis to acquire help on any medical query.

Intake
3 Frederick Street
London W1X 0NG
Intake is a mixed hostel for up to eight eighteen to twenty-five year olds staying for a maximum of six months. Members of staff provide advice and support when needed, but the emphasis is on sharing household chores and living together peacefully. Referrals are only taken from the other agencies in membership of WECVS (see below).

London YWCA Accommodation and Advisory Service and London Council for the Welfare of Women and Girls
16 Great Russell Street
London WC1B 3LR
The Acc and Ad helps anyone in need to find proper accommodation either in hostels or in approved private bedsits and flats.

London Youth Advisory Centre
26 Prince of Wales Road
London NW5 3LG
LYAC provides information and advice by letter, telephone or to personal callers on careers and employment, accommodation, contraception, drugs, youth clubs, holiday schemes and general services and resources available to young people. The Centre also provides a counselling service and referrals to specialist agencies. Although primarily for young people aged thirteen to twenty-five, the services are also available to parents.

National Association of Young People's Counselling and Advisory Services
c/o Youth Counselling Development Unit
National Youth Bureau
17-23 Albion Street
Leicester LE1 6GD
NAYPCAS is an independent association of individuals and agencies providing counselling, advice and information for young people.

National Cyrenians
13 Wincheap
Canterbury
Kent CT1 3TB
The Cyrenians seek to help homeless single people either through their night shelters or residential homes.

New Horizon
1 Macklin Street
London WC2
New Horizon is a centre for young people aged between sixteen and twenty-five who are homeless and rootless in the West End of London. The centre provides a day-time base where visitors can find advice and help on all sorts of problems, individual counselling, leisure activities and practical facilities for washing and shaving, storing luggage, etc.

Nightline
Nightline is a service provided on University and College campuses for students who have personal problems which they would like to discuss.

Off The Record
5 Woodhouse Road
Tally Ho Corner, Finchley
London N12 9EN
Provides counselling for teenagers.

Open Door
12 Middle Lane
Crouch End
Hornsey
London N8 8PL
Open Door offers help to young people with problems of all kinds – emotional or practical. It also maintains an information service which is available to both teenagers and older people.

Piccadilly Advice Centre
1 Great Windmill Street
London W1
The Centre provides an advice and referral service to newcomers to central London. It provides factual information on all sorts of problems. Its services are not restricted to any particular age group.

Portobello Project
49-51 Porchester Road
London W2
This is an ILEA Youth Project. The centre provides an advice and counselling service to young people under the age of twenty-one. It runs day-time courses on such subjects as typing, book-keeping, working with children, etc. It has produced many helpful leaflets listing sources of information on such subjects as sexual problems, getting a job, finding accommodation, family planning and your legal rights.

SHELTER (National Campaign for the Homeless)
157 Waterloo Road
London SE1 8UU
A pressure group which acts on behalf of the homeless and inadequately housed and provides direct assistance to the homeless through housing aid centres.

The Soho Project
142 Charing Cross Road
London WC2
Offers advice and help on a wide range of problems both on those who are new to London, and to those who already have some regular involvement in the West End scene.

West End Co-ordinated Voluntary Services for Homeless Single People
5 Dryden Street
London WC2E 9NW
WECVS comprises nine agencies working with single homeless people in central London, all of which are listed above except for the two agencies dealing solely with those who are over twenty-five years of age. The member agencies are: Alone in London Service; Centre Point Emergency Services; Great Chapel Street Medical Centre; Intake; New Horizon; Piccadilly Advice Centre; Single Homeless Project (25+); Soho Project; West London Day Centre (25+).

Finding more organisations and books

It may be that you have not found an organisation or book in the preceding pages which deals with your specific area of concern. If this is so, to try and find out whether there is an organisation dealing with this particular concern you could:

Consult some of the following directories in your local library (or any other relevant directories which you find there):

Charities digest, annual, Family Welfare Association.

Social services yearbook, annual, Councils and Education Press.

Education yearbook, annual, Councils and Education Press.

Education authorities directory and annual, annual, School Government Publishing Co. Ltd.

Directory for the disabled: a handbook of information and opportunities for disabled and handicapped people, compiled by Ann Darnbrough and Derek Kinrade, 1982, *Woodhead–Faulkner for Royal Association for Disability and Rehabilitation.*

If it still seems that there is no specific organisation, you could write to an organisation which deals with concerns akin to yours to see if they might be able to broaden their scope to encompass your concern.

If it proves that there is no relevant organisation for you, perhaps someone should start something – you maybe, through your Community Council or Council for Voluntary Service.

To find books relevant to your interests you could go to your library and ask the staff to help you; or you could contact a relevant voluntary organisation to see whether they could suggest suitable literature or provide a book-list.

Illustrators

Gerard Browne	pages 100, 118–119, 126–127
Paul Chappell	pages 36–37, 48–49, 111, 113, 114, 120
Ken Cox	pages 26, 52, 80–81, 166–167, 177, 192–193
Sally Davies	pages 12–13, 44–45, 52, 64–65, 84–85, 104–105, 124–125, 144–145, 164–165, 184–185
Barry Glynn	page 55
Rosemary Harrison	pages 28–29, 66, 75, 173, 179, 180–181
Sally Launder	pages 17, 27, 34–35, 54, 68–69, 73, 132–133
Tony McSweeny	pages 31, 51, 189, 197
Michael Munday	pages 130, 142–143
John Pead	pages 50, 59, 107, 137
Ingram Pinn	pages 16, 19, 91
Joe Wright	pages 88, 169, 190
Kathy Wyatt	pages 56–57, 77, 186, 199
All Artworks by Clive Frampton, Millions Design, London	pages 15, 28–29, 46–47, 62, 73, 108, 110, 135, 139, 141, 151, 156, 168, 196

Photographic Library Shots

Robert Haas	pages 103, 182–813
Popperphoto	pages 40, 174
Rex Features	pages 160, 162
J. S. Sainsbury Plc	page 156
Spectrum	pages 58, 86 (right)
The Photographer's Library	page 40 (right)
Topham	pages 42–43, 86 (left), 96–97
Vision International	pages 61, 87 (left), 109, 112, 203

Photographers

Gary Compton	page 60
John Melville	pages 21, 25, 34–35, 53, 63, 108
Chris Schwarz	pages 70–71, 94–95, 200
David Sheppard	pages 92–93, 129, 148, 154–155, 157
Brian Shuel	pages 32–33, 140–141, 146–147, 151, 204–205, 206–207

Acknowledgements

p. 15. Lifeskills chart taken from *Life-skills Teaching Programmes* by B. Hopson and M. Scully (Lifeskills Associates).

p. 20. Life tasks chart based on *People in Systems* by Gerard Egan (Addison-Wesley).

p. 78–79. Sex education case studies based on an article in *Woman* magazine.

p. 79. *Make it Happy* (Virago Press) cover design by Mike Jarvis.

p. 100. Four system diagram based on a diagram in *People in Systems* (as above).

p. 108–115. Topics developed on the basis of materials and sources referred to in *Cognitive Development*, E362, Book 3 (Oxford University Press) and *Cognitive Development in the School Years* by Anne Floyd (Croom-Helm in association with the Oxford University Press).

p. 113. "Waving Not Drowning" from *Collected Poems of Stevie Smith* (Allen Lane).

p. 114. Food chain from *Adolescent Thinking and Levels of Judgement in Biology* by A. W. H. Pitt (M.Ed. thesis, University of Birmingham).

p. 116–123. Taken from or closely based on CRAC materials *Decide for Yourself*.

p. 134. Checklists A and B are taken from *Teacher-Parent Communication* by R. Gibson (Cambridge Institute of Education).

p. 135. School rules and reports are taken from Vandyke Upper School, Bedfordshire, as quoted in *Teacher-Parent Communication* (see above).

p. 139. Youth leaders report taken from *Kids in a New Town* by M. Cowan (National Association of Youth Clubs).

Homework chart is derived from *Active Tutorial Work Book 2* (Blackwells).

p. 141. Jesus notes derived from *Active Tutorial Work* (see above).

Presenting ideas text derived from *How to Study Effectively* by C. Parsons (Arrow).

p. 160. Out of work extract from a National Youth Bureau poster.

p. 160. Doctor's dilemma and Jim Smith based on materials and sources referred to in *Cognitive Development* (as above).

p. 170-1. Interview with fifth formers taken from the *Guardian*, 8/6/81.

p. 177. *The Cartoon strip* is taken from a Longman Thinkstrip entitled *"It's not easy"* by Gillian Crampton Smith and Sarah Curtis.

p. 204–5. Empty nest quotations from *Women of a Certain Age* by Lillian Rubin (Harper Colophon Books).